D1636937

The New York Times
AT THE SUPER BOWL

The New York Times
AT THE SUPER BOWL

Edited by Leonard Koppett

NYT

Quadrangle/The New York Times Book Co.

Library of Congress Catalog Card Number: 73–79918
International Standard Book Number: 0–8129–0386–2

Design by A. J. Pollicino, Inc.

All pieces included in this book were written by
The New York Times writers unless otherwise indicated.

CONTENTS

Introduction

"Nothing," an old saying goes, "is deader than yesterday's newspaper."

"History," a wise man once noted, "is the version of events told by winners."

Today's sport event, I say, owes much of its appeal to the spectator's awareness of yesterday's related sport event.

Assuming that all three statements have at least a bit of truth, mixing them together may provide certain advantages.

Certainly the idea of continuity is a basic feature of mass spectator sports interest. Championships are decided annually, and the cyclic pattern makes last year's result and next year's prospects highly relevant to most sports fans. Records automatically relate the present to the past, and records are the life-blood of much fan interest; but myth and personality are even more important, and both depend on familiarity with what happened in the past.

In sports, then, history is not something for scholars; it's the very substance of the entertainment. Seeing a 6-foot 2-inch man with a slight limp throwing a football 50 yards in an open field in the middle of a public park thrills nobody, no matter how artistically the ball spirals through the air; seeing the same action with the knowledge that it is Joe Namath, in the context of a National Football League game, is another matter; and it is the spectator's consciousness of sports history that makes this possible.

And there is no shortage of literature in the field. Chances are more people—and certainly more people under the age of 20—read "history" about sports than about any other subject. Any event of note—a baseball World Series, a heavyweight championship fight, a famous horse race—is promptly recorded for posterity in all sorts of books and articles. The participants (with some help, of course) produce first-person accounts. Any number of observers give their own analyses. Statistical records proliferate.

Yet all this material has one quality in common: it is written after the event, when the result is known. This is not necessarily a disadvantage, but it is not necessarily an advantage, either. For analysis, overview, interpretation, illumination of every corner and careful weighing of values, after-the-fact history is best. But for immediacy of flavor, it may not be best.

Here, then, is something the old clippings can provide: immediacy. Especially in the pregame material, the atmosphere *as it was then* is accurately reflected, as is the *immediate* postgame reaction, within minutes and hours of the denouement, what we actually experienced at the time.

In this way, *The New York Times at the Super Bowl* touches upon two current interests, nostalgia and television technology.

Nostalgia deals with recalling the way things felt, not merely learning about what they were.

Television technology has given us the instant replay, a chance to see again what used to be an unrecapturable moment and to see it exactly as it was the first time, unedited and unaltered. Our whole sports experience has been enriched by this possibility.

So here is the story of Super Bowl football in a series of snapshots "as it happened"—not as it seems looking back, not as it is judged in perspective, not with the wisdom of hindsight, but as it unfolded. It won't tell you all you could, would, or might know about the subject, but it will re-create these games and their time in a unique way.

And the events they re-create, eight Super Bowl football games, were unique in themselves, as what follows I hope makes clear.

—L. K.

Chapter 1

Super Bowl I—1967

It was the biggest build-up a sport event ever had.

And it didn't sell out.

Super Bowl I was seven years in the making, in one sense, but closer to 20 years in another. Before World War I, the basic pattern of super-sports in America had been set by baseball's World Series, the bringing together of the two champions of "independent" (but really partners) major leagues. Right after World War II, a comparable structure seemed possible for football, with a new league, the All-America Conference, challenging the more established National Football League. But these were truly rival leagues, and a championship confrontation between their respective champions never took place, although many fans yearned for it. (That it would have been a worthy confrontation was soon proved: after the A.A.C. folded up in 1949, its champion, the Cleveland Browns, joined the N.F.L. and became just as victorious there.)

For a decade, the N.F.L. was alone, as the popularity of pro football mushroomed (thanks largely to television). In 1960, a new rival appeared, called the American League, and its goal was explicit: to attain acceptance as a major league and work towards the equivalence of the baseball World Series, the point the A.A.C. never reached.

So from the very beginning of the American League, the possibility of a championship game was in the air. Promotion of such talk by the new league was obviously self-serving; resistance by the N.F.L. and its adherents was equally self-serving. But the subject was gaining currency.

The key to A.F.L. survival was television, just as it had been the key to N.F.L. growth. The older league had long ago given an exclusive package to the Columbia Broadcasting System. As ratings for Sunday afternoon football games soared, the chief rival of C.B.S., the National Broadcasting Company, had to do something. It did. It bought the A.F.L. games, providing the new league with millions of dollars to spend on development. But, even more significantly, it gave one of the two largest information media in the country a vested interest in building the new league up to equality with the old.

Once N.B.C. entered the picture as a backer of the A.F.L., in 1964, it seemed inevitable that a championship game would eventually come about—and a championship game would only constitute the beginning of some sort of full-scale merger of the two leagues.

There were still obstacles: agreements had to be negotiated, anti-

5

trust exemption had to be obtained from Congress, personal emotions among club owners had to be defused. But the process was on, and the public, on the whole, began having its appetite whetted from that point on.

Finally, in 1966, Congress came through (in a back-door maneuver, it's true), and the way was clear for the climax. Since the full resources of two television networks were devoted to promoting the inpending championship event, and since this in turn stimulated more and more newspaper and magazine coverage, and since football—as a once-a-week game—is peculiarly suited for anticipatory drum-beating, the intensity of interest surpassed that of previous sports promotions.

And as soon as the two individual league championships had been settled, there was nothing else to think about. Was the A.F.L. really capable of fielding a team that could compete with the older, self-confessed excellence of the N.F.L.? It was not a question for the ages, but it was most decidedly the question of the day.

Chiefs Seen as Powerful Enough and Fast Enough to Score Upset

By FRANK LITSKY

Jan. 8, 1967—The young advertising executive seemed completely normal, down to the last neurosis, but why the gleam in his eye? "In October," he said proudly, "I took the National League champion in the Super Bowl and gave 22 points. I wished I had bet more." The East Side restaurateur, a man of action, collared a friend who supposedly knew much about professional football.

"I'm going to do you a favor," he told the friend. "I'm going to give you Kansas City and 13½ points. You're going to take it because you think I'm nuts, but it's like stealing money from you."

It's like stealing something, all right, but what? Common sense? Reason? Logic?

It's All UNREAL

To listen to members of the Union for Negative Reaction, especially to the American Football League (known informally as UNREAL), the Green Bay Packers will mop up the Los Angeles Coliseum with the Kansas City Chiefs next Sunday in the Super Bowl.

The Chiefs, they say, might have a chance against the Pittsburgh Steelers. They could beat the New York Giants (but who couldn't, or didn't?). But the Chiefs beating the Packers? The UNREALS shake their heads sadly and smile the smile of charity.

But will the Packers overrun, trample, decimate, and humiliate the Chiefs? Or will the Chiefs perhaps make the game respectable? Or will the American League champions have a chance—even a remote chance—to beat the great Packers?

The odds—8 points, or 13 points, or whatever they may be—indicate that the game should not be a runaway. Neutral observers—if there are such animals—agree that the Chiefs should be in the game all the way, and these people would be surprised, but not astonished, if the Chiefs won.

A.F.L. Develops Talent

The UNREALS say the American League is a haven for National League castoffs, rejects, the ill and infirm. When the American League started playing seven years ago this was largely true. But, as the years have gone by, the American League has developed most of its talents.

The Chiefs, for example, have only two regulars who came from the National League. Len Dawson, the Chiefs' all-league quarterback, was an understudy to Bobby Layne of the Pittsburgh Steelers (1957–59) and to Milt Plum of the Cleveland Browns (1960–61). Mike Mercer, the Chiefs' pacekicker, played for the Minnesota Vikings (1961–62).

All other Kansas City regulars began their professional careers in the American League and not always because the National League didn't care. National League teams swallowed hard when the Chiefs signed Mike Garrett and Aaron Brown a year ago.

They were stunned two years ago when Otis Taylor slipped away from their baby-sitters.

All these players could have made it big in the National League. For the truth is that the good players in one league would be good players in the other.

The Chiefs have had good players for years, but they went from 1963 to 1966 without a championship. One reason was that they were overloaded with no-cut contracts. Another, as Coach Hank Stram points out, was a lack of speed.

The no-cuts have run their course, and the inferior ones have been cut. The speed has been supplied by Garrett, a sawed-off halfback who has become the league's most exciting runner, and Taylor, who may already have outstripped Lance Alworth (also an American Leaguer) as the best flanker in the sport.

With this speed goes size and power. The Chiefs' offensive line, averaging 6 feet 4½ inches and 266 pounds from tackle to tackle, will face a Packer defensive line averaging 6-3½ and 250. The Chiefs' defensive line (6-5 and 260) will have a size advantage over the Packer offensive line (6-2½ and 245).

The height and weight differences are not huge, and in the end they will become secondary to quickness, mobility, desire, and skill. But the Chiefs are solid up front and they have played together for years. No one has pushed them around yet.

Chiefs Pack Power

Football, as Coach Vince Lombardi is fond of saying, is a game of blocking and tackling, and no National League team blocks or tackles better than the Packers. But football is also a game of explosiveness, and the Chiefs have the potential to explode.

The Packers are so sound on defense that they seldom blitz the passer. The Buffalo Bills, a team in the mold of the Packers, turned blitzers in the American League championship playoff last Sunday and threw Dawson seven times. But Dawson would take a 9-yard loss on one play and pass for 25 yards on the next.

The UNREALS aren't interested in such an argument. They contend that the two leagues play a different kind of football.

They say the American Leaguers bump bodies, while the National Leaguers rack up one another (that used to be true). They say American League quarterbacks don't have the completion record of National Leaguers (true, but maybe because American League pass defenses are more varied).

Equal Battle Anticipated

They say American League stars couldn't make it in the National League (well, Homer Jones couldn't make it in the American).

Obviously, there are no hard answers to these arguments, which is of no importance because the arguments are beside the point. The point is whether the Chiefs can beat the Packers.

Forget the desire for glory, or for the $15,000 that goes to each winning player. Forget that the Chiefs carry the aspirations of an entire league. They have a good chance simply because they are a good enough football team to play the Packers on equal or near-equal terms.

A Defeat in Next Sunday's Game is Inconceivable to Packer Fans

By WILLIAM N. WALLACE

Jan. 8, 1967—Jerry Kramer said it best. Speaking of the Green Bay Packers' long history of success, Kramer commented, "We've made winning a habit. It's a matter of pride. We never consider the possibility of losing."

Kramer, a big handsome blond now 30 years old, embellished his thought last Sunday after the Packers had won their fourth National League championship. "The thrill of winning the championship," he said, "intensifies each time it happens. I don't know why, but it does."

That would sound like a platitude coming from someone other than Kramer, a man of vast sincerity.

So, winning is an absolute habit with the disciplined, seasoned Packers. And the thrill of winning is still there.

Since the Super Bowl game in Los Angeles next Sunday between the Packers and the Kansas City Chiefs, the champions of the American League, represents a new mountain to climb, the Packers seem amply motivated without taking into account the $15,000 prize that will accrue to each player.

Lombardi's Winning Ways

To those who have been students of the reign of Vince Lombardi at Green Bay, "the friendliest little city in the world," it is inconceivable that the Packers will fail to take the big prize.

Football games, especially the ones the Packers play in, are often won and lost on account of errors, meaning fumbles, fewer interceptions, poor kicks, inappropriate penalties, missed blocks and tackles.

The Packers make fewer errors than other teams, and they are drilled that way by Lombardi. They are not perfect. In last Sunday's championship game a fumble by Elijah Pitts cost them an almost certain touchdown.

A missed block that resulted in a blocked conversion kick, followed by Don Chandler's weak punt, gave the Dallas Cowboys a chance to tie. But when the pressure was at its heaviest, it was the other team that made the errors—two dropped passes and an offside penalty—which assured Green Bay's victory. It usually works out that way.

The Packers are no super team. Their offensive line is on the small side. It will be outweighed by Kansas City's on an average of 16 pounds a man, 244 to 260.

Although Green Bay prefers to run rather than pass, the rushing game has not been especially productive. But it must be honored, and that gives the passer, Bart Starr, his openings. He exploits them.

On defense, the Packers are superior. The suspicion here is that Willie Wood, an all-pro safety, will help Herb Adderley and Bob Jeter to curb Otis Taylor, the big Kansas City receiver threat, and little else will be difficult for the N.F.L. champions.

Mike Garrett? He is evasive rather than fast. He might get away on a broken play, but the interminable Packer pursuit will not let them steal the game.

The Packers are obvious, even repetitious. "We have no secrets," says Lombardi. It is easy to take frequencies on their offense—to determine beforehand how they operate—and, in addition, the Chiefs have a former Packer of recent vintage, Tom Bettis, on their staff as an assistant.

The Kansas City players should know all about the Packers before the kickoff. But after that, it will be a matter of outexecuting Green Bay, which is something else again.

The size factor seems unimportant. A citation would be Fred Thurston, the Green Bay left guard. Against Bob Lilly, the Dallas defensive right tackle, Thurston gave away 10 pounds and four inches to a man considered to be the outstanding defensive player in the league.

Fuzzy, who is 31, accepted the challenge. He belted Lilly all day and did things to Bob that the younger Cowboy had never seen before. Thurston neutralized Lilly's force. That's the way the Packers are.

If size is unimportant, perhaps age and experience will be important. The Packer regulars average 28.4 years of age and 7 seasons of professional play. The Kansas City figures are respectively, 26.2 and 4.9. Expect the Packers to have the wiseness, the composure that comes with greater experience.

Freddy Williamson, the Kansas City defensive back, wears white leather shoes to attract attention. He is a showboat, a hot dog. None of the Green Bays has white shoes. That would be unthinkable on a Lombardi team.

This squad does have its individualists, even its characters, but Packer football is a deadly serious business. Says Bart Starr, the quarterback, "We always think and act as a team." He means a winning team.

Sports of The Times

By ARTHUR DALEY

From Across the Tracks

LONG BEACH, CALIF., *Jan. 11*—"Five years ago, when my son was only 5 years old," said Lamar Hunt, the multimillionaire owner of the Kansas City Chiefs, "I brought him with me to watch the Green Bay Packers practice in Dallas. 'Daddy,' he said, 'why don't we play the Packers?' I had to explain to him that the teams were in different leagues and could never play each other."

A trace of a smile creased Lamar's face, tipping off the obvious denouement.

"But now that my son is 10," he added, "we finally will have that meeting in the Super Bowl. Frankly, he's worried to death."

If the heir to the Hunt fortunes is overly concerned about Sunday's collision between the Packers and Kansas City Chiefs, no signs of worry furrow the brow of the cheerful Hank Stram, coach of the Chiefs. He was totally at ease after today's secret workout behind carefully guarded gates in the Long Beach stadium.

"Here's the way I look at it," he said, bright and chipper. "The Packers have pride and tradition to spur them on. But we're the kids from the wrong side of the tracks and we're out to prove that we're better than they are. I think that's stronger motivation." He sounded awfully convincing.

Film Critique

For night after night Stram and his staff—and his players, too—have been studying game movies of the Packers, watching for flaws that can be exploited and strong points that can be counterbalanced. Hard realism dictates every moment of such study, never any wishful thinking.

"I've been impressed," said Hank, the merry-eyed pragmatist, "by Green Bay's overall ability and execution. It's the quality of the people in the films that gets you. The name of the game is react, pursue, and tackle. They do it all so well. Their techniques are so good that it's easy to see why they have been such consistent winners over the years."

But the Chiefs are bigger physically than the Packers. In some respects they resemble the Dallas Cowboys, who gave Vince Lombardi's champions such a rough outing in the NFL playoff. Like the Cowboys, they have a wide variety of offensive formations, perhaps 8 to 10.

"These many alignments," said Hank, "represent our personality. But everything in this game comes down to execution. Regarding all those formations, we like to create as many problems for the opposition as we can, not only in the game itself but in preparing for it. The Packers must get ready to defend not against one or two formations, but against 10. Any time we can create momentary indecision on their part, the percentages are in our favor."

Stram's deep respect for the Packers was obvious, but just as obvious was his unshakable belief that he had the size, youth, and speed to bring about the downfall of the mighty.

A strangely different kind of movie critique was offered by Len Dawson, the Kansas City quarterback. The oldest of the Chiefs at the tender age of 31, Dawson lolled in the stands after practice, luxuriating in some blazing California sunshine, and warming himself in the 77-degree heat. He is a handsome man with the finely etched profile of Frank Gifford.

Point of Concentration

"I've been concentrating on Packer defenses," he said softly, "because it's my job to attack it. Their secondary is similar to Oakland's, with quick reactions. The front four is big, strong, and fast, with the same great second effort that Boston has. They present problems in getting by them, just as they did to many teams over the years. We must overcome it.

"Their linebackers hit and jam the tight end well. Ray Nitschke is a horse and Lee Roy Caffey and Dave Robinson are both big and agile. They remind me of Buffalo or San Diego linebackers. It's a solid defensive unit and a fundamentally sound team all the way."

Dawson might not have been aware of it, but he was taking the best features of the top defensive teams in his league and endowing those qualities on the Packers, making them emerge in composite form. That's why Green Bay exerts tremendous pressure on a quarterback without blitzing.

"If there is anything I prefer," he said with a smile, "it's protection. One thing we have going for us, though, is a multifaceted offense. We'll show them many looks.

"I know that Green Bay reads plays well, but if we can create doubt in their minds and cut down on their reaction time, that will be a plus for us. We won't fool them all the time, but we may fool them some of the time. As Hank says—and I think he borrowed the word from Casey Stengel—execution will be the big thing. If we can execute better—and I think we can—we'll win.

"Yessir, we can run on Green Bay. We're counting on it."

Sports of The Times

By ARTHUR DALEY

Listening to the Packers

SANTA BARBARA, CALIF., *Jan. 12*—"It's a relative thing," Vince Lombardi was saying. "If the Kansas City Chiefs had played even one team from our league, I could make a better judgment. Studying the films still doesn't give me an accurate appraisal of abilities because I don't know the personnel of that league. Offhand, I'd have to say that this is a club with many strengths."

"Lack of familiarity with them," said Bart Starr, the quarterback, "is our main problem because there is no basis for true comparison. As a defensive unit they seem to do a fine job but we really won't know until we start testing it."

"Films are deceiving," said Herb Adderley, the all-league cornerback. "I still can't tell how fast Otis Taylor is because I don't know how fast the men covering him are. Pass patterns? The cornerbacks in that league play so close to the line, 2 yards to my 6, that I can't be sure."

"We've played a lot of pressure games over the years," said Paul Hornung, insouciant as ever despite his relegation to a minor role. "And no one ever panics. We always seem to get better as the season moves along and we'll go at 'em as if they're the best team we ever played."

"That Buck Buchanan is so big," said Fuzzy Thurston, the pass blocker deluxe, "that he might just trip over l'il me." He grinned.

Constant Topic

Naturally enough, they were talking about Sunday's Super Bowl game between the Packers and the Chiefs in the Coliseum, the most shattering event hereabouts since the earthquake of 1932. They have been relaxing— and preparing—in glorious California sunshine at this lovely coastal town up the pike from Los Angeles.

"Sorry," said Don Chandler, the kicker, looking at his watch and breaking off the conversation. "We have a meeting at 3:30 and I can't be late." All the Packers headed upstairs. It was then 3:10. Unlike Pavlov's dogs, they don't even wait for the ringing of a bell or the crackle of Lombardi's whip. They have learned to play it safe with their dandy little martinet.

"Before we met Dallas in the playoff," Lombardi had been saying earlier, "we felt we had to stop Bob Hayes. I was proud when Adderley and the others held him to one catch for a gain of 1 yard. We didn't double-team him but we covered him inside and outside.

"Will we give Otis Taylor the same treatment? I won't say. I'm inclined to compare Taylor with Dave Parks of San Francisco in our league and we have done reasonably well with Parks. They're the same type—speed, hands, and moves, each a tough runner to bring down after he catches the ball.

"But they have no one as fast as Hayes. I doubt if they have anyone as fast as Adderley or Bob Jeter. I'd also say that Mike Garrett is similar to Gale Sayers of the Bears—presuming that anyone can be similar to Sayers.

"Folks have been saying that Fran Tarkenton of Minnesota has given us more trouble than any other quarterback because he scrambles the way Len Dawson of Kansas City does. But Tarkenton has only beaten us twice in seven years—if that answers any questions."

The Lombardi grin was owlish.

The Probe

"Will I probe at the start?" repeated Starr, the most valuable player in the league. "We always go into a game with a plan and we have to start somewhere to see if our thinking is logical. Coach Lombardi has always stressed one thing: If what you're trying to do doesn't work, try something else.

"Because you're an old friend of Hornung's, I'd like to put in a plug for him. No one has helped Elijah Pitts more than Paul. He coaches him constantly and he's given Elijah the confidence to make himself a star. I never met a sharper football player than Paul. Many a time he'd come back in the huddle and say to me:

'Bart, I can beat my man but not from the formation you used on the last play. Call it from the one we used on the previous play and I can take him.'

"He was always right, too. Now he's coaching Pitts to make the same observations. The spirit of the Packers? It has to be Paul Hornung."

Paul's closest buddy is Thurston, the guard who threw up such a protective shield in front of Starr that Bob Lilly of the Cowboys, all-league defensive tackle, never laid a hand on him.

"Buchanan is taller and heavier than Lilly," said the good-natured Fuzzy, "and has all the qualities of a great player. But I'd never met a big man as quick as Lilly. Come to think of it, I've held off a lot of great ones over the years.

"Ernie Stautner was the toughest. Even though I could stop him in his later years, he would beat me to a pulp, making me feel as if a dozen bulldozers had run over me."

These self-assured Packers already have proved themselves the best in their own league. They are just as determined to prove that they also are the best in both leagues.

The Super Bowl: Football's Day of Decision Stirs Nation

60 Million to Watch Packers and Chiefs Play Today on TV

By WILLIAM N. WALLACE

LOS ANGELES, *Jan. 14*—The Super Bowl game, a sports contest that has piqued this nation's curiosity through a set of unusual circumstances, will begin tomorrow at 4:05 P.M. New York time and endure for about 150 minutes.

When that span of time is over many questions will have been resolved, questions of no great significance but ones that will have taken sports-minded Americans out of the routine of their lives for an afternoon. When the game is over, we can all go back to what we were doing before.

The Green Bay Packers, the older and therefore wiser team, will represent the N.F.L. whose adherents like to think theirs is the wiser and better league. The Kansas City Chiefs, a younger, faster and at the same time larger team, is the representative of the A.F.L., which recently merged with the National.

Product of Peace Treaty

The fascinating question is: How good are the Chiefs in relation to the Packers? There are no yardsticks because no American League team has ever before played a National League one. The two leagues had been antagonists since the A.F.L. was formed in 1960, and the pro football war did not terminate until last June 9.

The Super Bowl is the product of that peace treaty, bringing together the two league champions in Memorial Coliseum before a crowd that is expected to number between 70,000 and the Coliseum capacity of 93,000. The ticket prices are stiff, $12, $10 and $6, but 60,000 seats were sold in advance.

The television version of the game will be free except in Los Angeles, which has been blacked-out for the game. Pro football in general and the Super Bowl in particular have generated so much interest that an audience of 60 million is expected to watch the game. It will be televised nationally by the National Broadcasting Company and the Columbia Broadcasting System (Channels 4 and 2, respectively, in New York), and each has paid $1 million for the TV rights. Since the gate receipts may reach $1 million, this may be a $3-million sports event.

In sports history only a handful of heavyweight fights, utilizing closed-circuit television into a chain of theaters, has done better.

The American League at the outset sought to copy the successful formula of the National, founded in 1920. Therefore the differences between the leagues are small.

The footballs used in each league, made by different manufacturers, differ slightly in size, shape and feel. The A.F.L. football, made by Spaulding, is one-quarter-inch longer, has sharper ends and a more tacky feel than the N.F.L. equivalent. Wilson makes the N.F.L. ball.

This issue was easily resolved. When the Chiefs are on offense, the American League football, familiar to their quarterback, Len Dawson, will be in use. When the Packers go on offense, the N.F.L. football will be in play.

The playing rules are the same. The A.F.L. 2-point option conversion rule following the scoring of a touchdown has been dropped. One extra point, made usually by a place kick, will apply following touchdowns.

There will be six officials, three from each league, dressed in black-and-white uniforms designed specifically for this game. The Packers will wear green jerseys, each with a number. The Chiefs will be in white jerseys that will have on them both the player's number and his name, following American League custom. Names are omitted in the N.F.L.

Should the game be tied at the end of the regulation 60 minutes, it will continue with sudden-death overtime periods of 15 minutes. The team scoring first will be the winner.

The Rewards Are Ample

The winning players, and losers, too, will be well-rewarded. Each winning share has been set at $15,000 and each losing one at $7,500. Money left over from the player pool will go into the two league pension funds (40 per cent); to the Green Bay and Kansas City managements (30 per cent) and to the two league offices (30 per cent).

The weather is expected to be seasonal, which means good. Temperatures here in January range usually between 47 and 65 but can go higher.

Much preparation and study of the opponent goes into football games. This one is unusual for pro football in that the players know very little about one another. Each side has merely studied the other through the medium of three exchange game films.

The Packers, who have won six conference and five league championships in the last seven seasons, have an average age of 28.4 years in their starting line-ups compared with 26.2 for the Chiefs. Green Bay's regulars average seven seasons of professional experience, Kansas City's 4.9.

Vincent Lombardi, the Green Bay coach, characterizes his team as small. This shows in the match ups of the two lines, Kansas City outweighing Green Bay in each case. For example, Fuzzy Thurston, the Green Bay left guard who is 6 feet tall and weighs 245 pounds, will be opposite Buck Buchanan, the Chiefs' defensive right tackle who stands 6-7 and weighs 287.

The Harder They Fall

Another large Chief is Jim Tyrer, the offensive left tackle who is 6-6 and weighs 292. Opposite him for Green Bay will be Lionel Aldridge, 6-4 and 245.

No one seems too concerned about the size factors. Of more importance is quickness and poise, especially on defense. One reason almost all authorities like Green Bay to win is its solid defensive platoon with outstanding backs in Willie Wood, Herb Adderley, Tom Brown, and Bob Jeter. The Kansas City receivers, Otis Taylor, Chris Burford, and Fred Arbanas, will be well-covered.

Lombardi has five receivers, Boyd Dowler, Carroll Dale, Marv Fleming, Bob Long, and Max McGee to test the Kansas City secondary in varying combinations and Bart Starr to do the passing. Starr this season was pro football's leading passer.

The Packers are an orthodox team in formations and plays, one depending upon superior execution to win. The Chiefs try to be tricky by using

12 different offensive line-ups and two different basic defenses. Hank Stram, the coach, says that formations do not win football games but he believes variety puts a slight burden on the opponent. Lombardi would disagree.

Records of the Teams

PACKERS (13–2)		CHIEFS (12–2–1)	
24—Baltimore	3	42—Buffalo	20
21—Cleveland	20	32—Oakland	10
24—Los Angeles	13	43—Boston	24
23—Detroit	14	14—Buffalo	29
20—San Francisco	21	37—Denver	10
17—Chicago	0	13—Oakland	34
56—Atlanta	3	56—Denver	10
31—Detroit	7	48—Houston	23
17—Minnesota	20	24—San Diego	14
13—Chicago	6	34—Miami	16
28—Minnesota	16	27—Boston	27
20—San Francisco	7	32—New York	24
14—Baltimore	10	19—Miami	18
27—Los Angeles	10	27—San Diego	17
335	163	448	276

A Big Day for Passes: Screen, Flare and Free

LOS ANGELES, *Jan. 14*—Figures compiled 48 hours before game time showed that 1,049 press credentials had been issued for tomorrow's Super Bowl game.

Of these, 338 were for newspaper, magazine, and news service men, 262 for television and radio, 170 for photographers, 88 for pressbox services, 78 for officials, 73 for communications services, and 40 for sideline services.

The National Football League's championship game between Green Bay and Dallas Jan. 1 at Dallas drew about 200 fewer people. A press corps of 737, a record for a college game, covered the Notre Dame-Michigan State tie Nov. 19 at East Lansing.

Little Action on Game Reported at Las Vegas

LOS ANGELES, *Jan. 14*—Reports from legal bookmaking establishments in Las Vegas, Nev., have revealed that the Super Bowl contest here tomorrow has not been an especially attractive betting proposition.

Professional gamblers who bet heavily with the Las Vegas books apparently have too little information on the Green Bay Packers and Kansas City Chiefs.

The contest is described as an attractive one for head-to-head bets between friends for small sums. This does not interest bookmakers.

The Packers have always been favored and the point line has wavered from 12.5 to 14 points, which is not much. It was 13 yesterday.

The point line makes Green Bay a 4-1 favorite in the customary translation of points to odds. A 3-point line means 7-5 odds; 6 or 7 points is 2-1 and 11 to 14 points 4-1.

Battle Goes Through 'Channels'
C.B.S. Pits Big Four Against Top Three in N.B.C. Line-Up

By FRANK LITSKY

LOS ANGELES, *Jan. 14*—To the average, everyday, run-of-the-mill man in the street the key adversaries in tomorrow's Super Bowl game are the Green Bay Packers and the Kansas City Chiefs.

Nonsense. To insiders, to sophisticates, to people who know professional football and how and why it is blacked out, saturated, and financed, the big battle is between the Columbia Broadcasting System, which televises National Football League games, and the National Broadcasting Company which shows American League Games.

In a milestone as significant as Sammy Baugh's first touchdown pass, Joe Namath's first date, and the New York Football Giants' only victory of 1966, the two networks will televise one game simultaneously—each with its blue-ribbon set of announcers.

Both sides talked today of the impending collision, of the fears, the hopes, the tortures and agonies of the final hours before the battle is joined. The words were uttered by television men, but if you closed your eyes and listened, you would swear they had been listening too long to the cliches uttered all week by the football coaches.

"Sure, it's our biggest game ever," said the C.B.S. man. "The money is great, but we're concerned with pride, not money. We don't take them lightly. But remember this—we didn't come here to lose."

"This is a team effort," said the N.B.C. man, "and we've come a long way working as a team. And don't let anyone tell you this is just another game. We've never faced a more important one. We're representing every man who ever had anything to do with this league. We have great respect for them, but don't underrate us. Our boss is hard to live with when you lose."

"I remember," said the C.B.S. man, "what Edward R. Murrow once said, that all men would be brave if they could leave their stomachs home. Sure, I'm nervous, but don't say that. If they think we're superhuman, let them keep thinking that."

"Normally," said the N.B.C. man, "I get no butterflies in my stomach until the day of the game. But we've felt the tension all week."

"We have experience," said the C.B.S. man, "but we're still young. We're making some changes, but basically we will do the same thing we've done all year. I don't know how to compare them with us because we've never had to contend with them or with anyone in their league."

"Experience?" said the N.B.C. man. "Our top men have worked together for seven years. When one makes a move, the other reacts automatically. What if anything happens to one of our big guys during the game? Well, we're ready for that. But I'm not going to tip our game plan to you or anyone else. But we will have a few surprises."

N.B.C.'s big guys are Curt Gowdy (play by play) and Paul Christman (analysis). Gowdy is 48 years old, 5-feet-10-inches tall (according to official N.B.C. statistics) though that seems exaggerated by a couple of inches and 180 pounds. Christman is 46, 6-0, 193 and a former National League quarterback. Charlie Jones (36, 6-2, 190) will do pregame and postgame work.

C.B.S. will have two play-by-play men in Jack Whitaker (42, 5-11, 158), and Ray Scott (5-9, 180, 47). Frank Gifford (6-1, 190, 35) will do analysis and Pat Summerall (6-3, 215, 35) will be heard before and after the game. Gifford and Summerall played for the Giants.

It is more than coincidence that Summerall and Jones were University of Arkansas classmates. Obviously (at least it is obvious to C.B.S.), Jones was added to the N.B.C. team at the eleventh hour to isolate Summerall and leave the battle to the others.

N.B.C. certainly likes it that way because it has great faith in Gowdy and Christman.

"When I started in this business," said Christman, "Bert Bell was the National League commissioner. He told me to talk to the ladies and the men will understand. I'm still doing it, and I'm not about to change for one game."

The C.B.S. man smiled. Christman is handsome and middle-aged. C.B.S. has Gifford, who is handsome and young.

"Gifford may beat me in looks," said Gody realistically, but football consists of many things. We're very loose, we're the underdogs, and we have everything to gain and nothing to lose."

C.B.S. is aware of that. Whitaker, for example, said he had given up breakfast this week to reach peak form.

"This is serious stuff," said the silver-haired Whitaker. "I weighed 162 at the start of the season. But in most of the TV booths in our league, you can't get anything to eat at half-time, and I've lost weight. I may be down to 155 by game time. I don't care. It's all for a good cause."

"There's tension, all right," said Jones, "but after the first verb, we'll relax."

"We'll be okay," said Whitaker, "right after the first adjective."

Take your pick—verbs or adjectives.

Sports of The Times

By ARTHUR DALEY

A Super-Duper Attraction

LOS ANGELES, *Jan. 14*—Ken Strong, a wondrous halfback for the New York Giants some three decades ago, was soaking in the blazing California sunshine the other day alongside the swimming pool at the swank training base of the Green Bay Packers in Santa Barbara. When mention was made of the physical superiority of the larger Kansas City Chiefs, Ken's gaze settled on Forrest Gregg, five times all-pro tackle for the Packers.

"I'd rather have a man his size who knows what he's doing," said Strong, "than a bigger man who doesn't."

In describing the abilities of one man, the ex-Giant inadvertently described the abilities of the entire Green Bay team. Experience has sharpened Packer skills and the crucible of countless pressure games over the years has hardened them.

These are the main assets they will have on the morrow when they collide with the Chiefs, champions of the younger American Football League, in the Super Bowl at the Los Angeles Coliseum.

Going for them also are some intangibles, a fierce pride in their eminence along with the deep tradition of superiority. They regard this assignment as a sacred trust and treat it with the starry-eyed zeal of Sir Galahad seeking the Holy Grail.

Social Climbers

The Chiefs have a different kind of motivation. They will be the standard bearers of a league that has only been in existence for seven years and was once reviled as a bush league without class.

With this game comes a recognition that the entire A.F.L. has long been yearning to gain. The Chiefs now have an opportunity to prove beyond cavil that they rate on the same high level as the champions of the National Football League, the Packers.

Kansas City has a lot going for it, principally size and speed and an explosive attack, one that can hit the touchdown target from anywhere without warning.

But the wily, knowledgeable Packers are football's strongest defensive team and they make fewer mistakes than any other. Therein lies their strength. The Chiefs, however, are huge with one 292-pounder and one 287-pounder.

"So what?" scoffs Vince Lombardi, the coaching genius of the Bays. "We're also smaller than every other club in our league."

At a quick glance no one would ever suspect malnutrition among the

Packers or think they needed muscle-building exercises. Their 245-pounders merely seem smaller by comparison. But they do superlatively well and know all the tricks that experience alone can teach.

It is that same experience that has led to the development of Bart Starr into a super-quarterback for the Super Bowl. He has become so uncannily accurate that the Packers now attack more through the air than on the ground.

"Bart reads defenses so well now," says Lombardi, "that if the primary receiver is covered, he senses which of the other receivers should be free. Then he throws to that open man without hesitation."

It's a rare gift and it is shared to some extent by Zeke Bratkowski, the best back-up quarterback in either league. It was the Brat who won a key game from Baltimore by hitting Max McGee with a pass that set up the winning touchdown. Jim Taylor, the Packer fullback, was talking about the play just the other day.

"Zeke read their minds when he got to the line of scrimmage," said the fullback terror. "He knew that Alvin Haymond was gonna blitz and that McGee would be open. He changed the play. When Haymond came through I hit him a block that gave me a bigger thrill than scoring a touchdown."

Another Viewpoint

Billy Sullivan is the president of the Boston Patriots of the A.F.L. and there's no mistaking where his allegiance lies.

"I can't help but think back," he said, "to last year when the Colts used Tom Matte, a quarterback for only two weeks, against the Packers and forced them into overtime. Lenny Dawson of the Chiefs has 10 years' experience, not two weeks. That's why I have such hopes."

Dawson also is an artist, one who loves to throw the bomb. And he has extraordinary receivers in Otis Taylor, Chris Burford, and Fred Arbanas. There's also the rookie, Mike Garrett, exceptional both as ball-carrier and receiver.

Yet none has ever confronted such masters of defense as Herb Adderley, Willie Wood, Bob Jeter, and, to a lesser extent, Tom Brown. And their jobs will be made easier if the other Packer defenders can put their usual crushing pressure on Dawson. If Lenny gets time to throw, he can be deadly.

As a matter of fact, this will be a pressure game all the way. Less likely to succumb to such strains are the battle-hardened Packers. No roar of enemy gunfire will unnerve them. But the Chiefs are green troops in an unfamiliar warfare against an implacable foe who makes no mistakes and will pounce on the mistakes of others.

Logic and common sense dictate the choice of the Green Bay Packers to win the first Super Bowl game. They are so picked here.

KANSAS CITY CHIEFS ON OFFENSE

SE
88-Chris Burford
6'3"—220 lbs.

RB
21-Mike Garrett
5'9"—195 lbs.

FB
32-Curtis McClinton
6'3"—227 lbs

QB
16-Len Dawson
6'0"—190 lbs.

LT
77-Jim Tyrer
6'6"—292 lbs.

LG
71-Ed Budde
6'5"—292 lbs.

C
66-Wayne Frazier
6'3"—245 lbs.

RG
64-Curt Merz
6'4"—267 lbs.

RT
73-Dave Hill
6'5"—264 lbs.

TE
84-Fred Arbanas
6'3"—240 lbs.

FL
89-Otis Taylor
6'2"—211 lbs.

GREEN BAY PACKERS ON DEFENSE

RE
82-Lionel Aldridge
6'4"—245 lbs.

RLB
60-Lee Roy Caffey
6'3"—250 lbs.

RCB
26-Herb Adderley
6'0"—210 lbs.

RT
74-Henry Jordan
6'3"—250 lbs.

MLB
66-Ray Nitschke
6'3"—240 lbs.

FS
24-Willie Wood
5'10"—190 lbs.

LT
77-Ron Kostelnik
6'4"—260 lbs.

LE
87-Willie Davis
6'3"—245 lbs.

LLB
89-Dave Robinson
6'3"—245 lbs.

SS
40-Tom Brown
6'1"—190 lbs.

LCB
21-Bob Jeter
6'1"—205 lbs.

GREEN BAY PACKERS ON OFFENSE

FL
86-Boyd Dowler
6'5"—225 lbs.

TE
81-Marv Fleming
6'4"—235 lbs.

RT
75-Forrest Gregg
6'4"—250 lbs.

FB
31-Jim Taylor
6'0"—215 lbs.

QB
15-Bart Starr
6'1"—200 lbs.

RG
64-Jerry Kramer
6'3"—245 lbs.

C
50-Bill Curry
6'2"—235 lbs.

RB
22-Elijah Pitts
6'1"—205 lbs.

LG
63-Fred Thurston
6'1"—245 lbs.

LT
70-Bob Skoronski
6'3"—250 lbs.

SE
84-Carroll Dale
6'2"—200 lbs.

KANSAS CITY CHIEFS ON DEFENSE

LE
75-Jerry Mays
6'4"—252 lbs.

LT
58-Andy Rice
6'2"—260 lbs.

MLB
69-Sherrill Headrick
6'2"—240 lbs.

RT
86-Buck Buchanan
6'7"—287 lbs.

RE
83-Chuck Hurston
6'6"—240 lbs.

RLB
55-E. J. Holub
6'4"—236 lbs.

RCB
22-Willie Mitchell
6'1"—185 lbs.

LLB
78-Bobby Bell
6'4"—228 lbs.

LCB
24-Fred Williamson
6'3"—209 lbs.

SS
20-Bobby Hunt
6'1"—193 lbs.

FS
42-Johnny Robinson
6'1"—205 lbs.

KANSAS CITY SUBSTITUTES

No.	Player	Ht.	Wt.	Pos.
10	Pete Beathard	6-2	210	QB
14	Bobby Ply	6-1	196	S
15	Mike Mercer	6-0	210	K
17	Fletcher Smith. . . .	6-2	188	RCB
18	Emmitt Thomas. . .	6-2	189	LCB
23	Bert Coan	6-4	220	HB
25	Frank Pitts.	6-2	190	SE
35	Smokey Stover . . .	6-0	227	MLB
44	Jerrel Wilson.	6-4	222	FB
45	Gene Thomas	6-1	210	FB
52	Bud Abell	6-3	220	RLB
56	Walt Corey.	6-1	233	LLB
60	Al Reynolds	6-3	250	RG
61	Denny Biodrowski .	6-1	255	LG
65	Jon Gilliam.	6-2	241	C
72	Tony Di Midio. . . .	6-3	250	OT
80	Reg Carolan	6-6	238	TE
87	Aaron Brown	6-5	265	DE

GREEN BAY SUBSTITUTES

No.	Player	Ht.	Wt.	Pos.
5	Paul Hornung. . . .	6-2	215	HB
12	Zeke Bratowski . .	6-3	200	QB
27	Red Mack.	5-10	185	FL
33	Jim Grabowski. . .	6-2	215	FB
34	Don Chandler . . .	6-2	210	K
37	Phil Vandersea . . .	6-3	225	FB
43	Doug Hart	6-0	190	DB
44	Don Anderson . . .	6-2	210	HB
45	Dave Hathcock. . .	6-0	190	DB
56	Tommy Crutcher .	6-3	230	LB
57	Ken Bowman. . . .	6-3	230	C
68	Gale Gillingham . .	6-3	250	G
72	Steve Wright	6-6	250	T
73	Jim Weatherwax . .	6-7	275	DT
78	Bob Brown	6-5	270	DE
80	Bob Long.	6-3	190	FL
85	Max McGee.	6-3	205	E
88	Bill Anderson. . . .	6-3	216	TE

Comparison of Super Bowl Rivals

OFFENSE

	Chiefs	Packers
Total Points	479	369
First Downs	280	250
Rushing.	112	101
Passing	148	129
Penalty	20	20
Net Yds. Gained. . .	5,391	4,642
Rushing.	2,387	1,775
Passing.	3,004	2,867
Passes Attempted . .	401	346
Completed	215	212
Had Intercepted .	15	5
Fumbles Lost	17	20
Yds. Penalized	720	567
Times Tackled Att. to Pass.	38	36
Yds. Lost Att. to Pass.	346	268

DEFENSE

	Chiefs	Packers
Opponents' Points .	283	190
Opponents' First Downs	231	234
Rushing.	77	102
Passing.	132	116
Penalty	22	16
Opponents' Net Yds	4,214	4,021
Rushing.	1,385	1,831
Passing.	2,829	2,190

	Chiefs	Packers
Opponents' Passing Att	521	421
Completed	238	217
Had Intercepted .	35	29
Opponents' Fumbles Recov . .	10	20
Times Opponents' Dropped Passing .	30	21
Yards Opponents' Lost Att. to Pass .	300	269

INDIVIDUAL PASSING

Chiefs	Att.	Com.	Yds.	Int.
Dawson . . .	308	175	2,691	10
Beathard. . .	90	39	578	4
Packers				
Starr	279	175	2,561	3
Bratkowski .	64	36	569	2

INDIVIDUAL RUSHING

Chiefs	Att.	Yds.	Avg.
Garrett	160	840	5.25
McClinton. . . .	151	578	3.82
Coan	98	527	5.36
Packers			
Taylor	214	742	3.46
Pitts.	127	459	3.44
Hornung.	76	200	2.68

INDIVIDUAL RECEIVING

Chiefs	No.	Yds.	TDs
Taylor	63	1,375	9
Burford	62	834	8
Packers			
Arbanas	24	349	5
Taylor	46	354	2
Dale	42	1,004	8
Fleming	34	411	2
Dowler	32	441	1
Pitts	27	477	3

INTERCEPTIONS

Chiefs	No.	Yds.	TDs
Robinson	11	208	1
Hunt	10	113	0
Packers			
Jeter	5	142	2
Robinson	5	60	0
Adderley	4	125	1
T. Brown	5	21	0

SCORING

Chiefs	TDs	EP	FG	Pts.
Mercer	0	37	21	100
Coan	9	0	0	54
McClinton	9	0	0	54
Garrett	10	0	0	60
Taylor	8	0	0	48
Burford	8	0	0	48
Packers				
Arbanas	5	0	0	30
Chandler	0	45	12	81
Pitts	11	0	0	66
Dale	8	0	0	48
Taylor	6	0	0	36
Hornung	5	0	0	30

Super Bowl Match-Ups, 1967

OFFENSE

Split End

Packers—Carroll Dale, from Virginia Tech. Probably is Green Bay's best deep receiver, a cutie in the Del Shofner mold. Caught 37 passes for 876 yards and seven touchdowns.

Chiefs—Chris Burford, from Stanford. A stylish receiver but does not have exceptional speed. Caught 58 passes for 758 yards and eight touchdowns.

Left Tackle

Packers—Bob Skoronski, from Indiana. Strong and a good blocker.

Chiefs—Jim Tyrer, from Ohio State. An exceptional blocker and an all-A.F.L. selection.

Left Guard

Packers—Fuzzy Thurston, from Valparaiso. A solid pass protector equally proficient at pulling to lead running plays.

Chiefs—Ed Budde, from Michigan State. Outstanding on rushing plays and an all-A.F.L. selection.

Center

Packers—Bill Curry, from Georgia Tech. Good blocker, but only in his first year as a starter.

Chiefs—Wayne Frazier, from Auburn. Also in his first full year, but has learned his trade.

Right Guard

Packers—Jerry Kramer, from Idaho. Exceptional on Green Bay's patented power sweep and an all-N.F.L. selection.

Chiefs—Curt Merz, from Iowa. Is as strong as they come, a good pass protector and an all-A.F.L. selection.

Right Tackle

Packers—Forrest Gregg, from Southern Methodist. Potent blocker on power sweep, good pass protector and an all-N.F.L. selection.

Chiefs—Dave Hill, from Auburn. Improving rapidly. Better on pass plays than rushing plays.

Tight End

Packers—Marv Fleming, from Utah. Still developing as a receiver, but caught 31 passes for 361 yards and two touchdowns.

Chiefs—Fred Arbanas, from Michigan State. A fine blocker who has overcome the handicap of loss of sight in one eye. Caught 22 passes for 305 yards and four touchdowns and was an all-A.F.L. selection.

Quarterback

Packers—Bart Starr, from Alabama. Probably had his best year with 156 completions, a .622 completion percentage, 2,257 yards gained. 14 touchdowns, and just 3 interceptions. An all-N.F.L. selection.

Chiefs—Len Dawson, from Purdue. Also had his best year with 159 completions, a .560 percentage, 2,527 yards, 26 touchdowns, and 10 interceptions. An all-A.F.L. selection

Running Back

Packers—Elijah Pitts, from Philander Smith. Replaced Paul Hornung—and played like him. Gained 393 yards on ground for a 3.4 average and 7 touchdowns; caught 26 passes for 460 yards.

Chiefs—Mike Garrett, from Southern California. Size has been no handicap because of his tremendous balance. Gained 801 yards rushing for 5.4 average and 6 touchdowns; caught 12 passes for 175 yards.

Fullback

Packers—Jim Taylor, from Louisiana State. Good short-yardage runner used consistently as a receiver this year. Gained 705 yards rushing for 3.5 average and 4 touchdowns; caught 41 passes for 331 yards.

Chiefs—Curt McClinton, from Kansas. A capable runner also used as key blocking back. Gained 540 yards rushing for 3.8 average and 4 touchdowns.

Flanker

Packers—Boyd Dowler, from Colorado. Not overly fast, but has sure hands and is tough on sideline patterns. Caught 29 passes for 392 yards but didn't score.

Chiefs—Otis Taylor, from Prairie View. Has been described as a Lance Alworth with better size. Caught 58 passes for 1,297 yards and 8 touchdowns and was an all-A.F.L. selection.

DEFENSE

Left End

Packers—Willie Davis, from Grambling. Probably the quickest end in the league, smart, reacts well, and an all-N.F.L. selection.

Chiefs—Jerry Mays, from Southern Methodist. A quick, exceptional pass rusher and an all-A.F.L. selection.

Left Tackle

Packers—Ron Kostelnik, from Cincinnati. A strong boy who bowls people over.

Chiefs—Andy Rice, from Texas Southern. Good, but still learning the trade.

Right Tackle

Packers—Henry Jordan, from Virginia. Strength is his biggest asset. Forms a solid duo with Kostelnik.

Chiefs—Buck Buchanan, from Grambling. Strong pass rusher with good mobility for his size and an all-A.F.L. selection.

Right End

Packers—Lionel Aldridge, from Utah State. Not as quick as Davis, but strong.

Chiefs—Chuck Hurston, from Auburn. Fast, uses speed well. Still learning.

Left Linebacker

Packers—Dave Robinson, from Penn State. Very quick and strong and has long arms that make him an outstanding pass protector.

Chiefs—Bobby Bell, from Minnesota. Outstanding speed, good strength, can stop both pass and rush and was an all-A.F.L. selection.

Middle Linebacker

Packers—Ray Nitschke, from Illinois. Strong, hard tackler who is also quick enough to go back for the pass and was an all-N.F.L. selection.

Chiefs—Sherrill Headrick, from Texas Christian. Tough is the word. Could be the best openfield tackler in league.

Right Linebacker

Packers—Lee Roy Caffey, from Texas A. and M. Rangy, good tackler and pass protector and an all-N.F.L. selection.

Chiefs—E. J. Holub, from Texas Tech. Not exceptionally fast or strong, but has great desire.

Left Cornerback

Packers—Herb Adderley, from Michigan State. Quick, a gambler on defense and an all-N.F.L. selection.

Chiefs—Fred Williamson, from Northwestern. Cantankerous, quick, and a big gambler.

Left Safety

Packers—Tom Brown, from Maryland. Good reactions but only in his second full year and still developing.

Chiefs—Bobby Hunt, from Auburn. Good reactions and mobility and an all-A.F.L. selection.

Right Safety

Packers—Willie Wood, from Southern California. The free safety, roams very well, covers a lot of ground. A defensive leader and an all-N.F.L. selection.

Chiefs—Johnny Robinson, from Louisiana State. Strong, clever at diagnosing plays, and an all-A.F.L. selection.

Right Cornerback

Packers—Bob Jeter, from Iowa. Quick, a gambler who will step inside quite a bit in interception bids.

Chiefs—Willie Mitchell, from Tennessee A. and I. Has speed and quickness, but still is learning.

Kickers

Packers—Don Chandler handles punts, kickoffs, and place-kicking for Green Bay. Had off-year, made only 12 of 28 field goals attempted.

Chiefs—Jerrell Wilson handles punts; Fletcher Smith handles kickoffs, and Mike Mercer handles field goals. Mercer made 20 of 26 attempts.

Green Bay Wins Football Title
National League Champions Beat Kansas City, 35–10, in Super Bowl Game

By WILLIAM N. WALLACE

LOS ANGELES, *Jan. 15*—Bryan Bartlett (Bart) Starr, the quarterback for the Green Bay Packers, led his team to a 35–10 victory over the Kansas City Chiefs today in the first professional football game between the champions of the National and American Leagues.

Doubt about the outcome disappeared in the third quarter when Starr's pretty passes made mere Indians out of the American League Chiefs and Green Bay scored twice.

Those 14 points stretched Green Bay's lead to 28–10 and during the final quarter many of the spectators in the crowd of 63,036 left Memorial Coliseum, which had been only two-thirds filled.

The outcome served to settle the curiosity of the customers, who paid from $6 to $12 for tickets, and a television audience estimated at 60 million, regarding the worth of the Chiefs.

The final score was an honest one, meaning it correctly reflected what went on during the game. The great interest had led to naming the event the Super Bowl, but the contest was more ordinary than super.

McGee Catches 7 Passes

Starr, methodical and unruffled as ever, completed 16 of 23 passes, six producing first downs on key third-down plays. Seven completions went to Max McGee, a 34-year-old substitute end who was in action only because Boyd Dowler, the regular, was hurt on the game's sixth play.

McGee scored two of Green Bay's five touchdowns, the first one after an outstanding onehanded, hip-high catch of a pass thrown slightly behind him.

Veteran Green Bay receiver Max McGee registers the first Super Bowl score as he trots into the end zone after grabbing a Bart Starr pass. The first Super Bowl, obviously, did not sell out.
UNITED PRESS INTERNATIONAL

The Packers, who had been favored by two touchdowns, knew they were in a challenging game for at least half of the 2½-hour contest.

Kansas City played very well in the first two quarters and the half-time score, 14–10, made the teams just about even. Green Bay's offense was sluggish. Kansas City had stopped the Packer rushing game and Starr had not exploited the Chiefs' defensive men—Fred Williamson and Willie Mitchell—who looked vulnerable. Bart was to take care of that matter in the second half.

The Chiefs, with Lenny Dawson running the offense at quarterback, had found they could pass on Green Bay, so three times the team was in scoring range. Out of that came one touchdown, scored by the fullback, Curtis McClinton, on a 7-yard pass from Dawson, and a 31-yard field goal by Mike Mercer.

Packers Close the Doors

But that was all for Kansas City. In the second half the mighty Packer defense shut out the Chiefs, who were in the Green Bay half of the field only once—for one play. And they were only four yards into Packer territory.

The Packers changed their defensive tactics for the second half. They had not blitzed their linebackers during the first two periods and the four rushing linemen were unable to get at Dawson.

But the blitz came in the third period and Dawson found himself harassed.

Three times he was dropped for losses and once, under blitzing pressure, he threw a weak pass that Willie Wood intercepted for Green Bay and ran back 50 yards to the Kansas City 5-yard line.

Elijah Pitts, the halfback, scored on first down from the 5, running off left tackle behind a power block from Bob Skoronski, a tackle. That gave the Packers a 21–10 lead and they were in command for good.

The pass rush that led to Wood's interception was the key play. The Chiefs and Dawson never recovered. The Kansas City quarterback later left the field and Pete Beathard took his place in the fourth quarter.

Richest Sports Event

For their efforts the 40 Packer players won $15,000 each, with $7,500 going to each Chief. Gate receipts were estimated at $750,000 and the two television networks—the Columbia Broadcasting System and the National Broadcasting Company—paid $1-million apiece for the TV rights. So this was a $2,750,000 event, the richest for any American team sports event.

Starr was worth every cent of his $15,000. In the first period he took his team 80 yards in six quick plays for the opening score. The sixth play, on third down, was the 37-yard pass to McGee on which Max made his great catch.

Kansas City tied the score at 7–7 in the second quarter with a six-play, 66-yard drive featuring three passes by Dawson to Mike Garrett, Otis Taylor and McClinton, the one to McClinton for a touchdown.

Starr connected on a 64-yard touchdown pass play to Carroll Dale (on third down), but a Packer lineman was illegally in motion and the play was called back. That failed to bother Starr, who after 11 subsequent plays had the Packers over the Kansas City goal line.

It was a beautiful series of plays. On four third-down situations, Starr passed successfully for the first down. The score was made from 14 yards out by hard-running Jim Taylor on a sweep behind blocking by the guards, Fred Thurston and Jerry Kramer.

Just before the half, Kansas City drove to the Green Bay 31, but a pass to Garrett failed to pick up a first down and Mercer kicked a field goal that cut the N.F.L. team's lead to 14–10.

In the second half Starr concentrated on Mitchell, the cornerback who had so much trouble covering McGee and Dale. Bart had great protection and on two touchdown drives that featured the pass, he probed at Mitchell's position successfully five times.

On these drives, one of 56 yards in the third quarter and one of 80 yards in the fourth, Starr completed seven of eight passes with cool precision. The Chiefs were helpless to stop him.

The first score was made by McGee from 13 yards out. He casually bobbled the ball, then caught it for six points, performing as if he were back in Green Bay during a routine practice on a Wednesday afternoon. McGee had caught only four passes during Green Bay's regular 14-game season.

The second touchdown went to Pitts, who slid off left tackle from a yard out as the Packer line closed down to the inside.

The Green Bay execution was as impeccable as ever. The only mistake was a harmless interception by Mitchell of a pass by Starr. It was the first interception against Starr since last Oct. 16. He had thrown 173 passes without an interception.

The Packer defense held the elusive Garrett to only 17 yards and Kansas City's offense had a net gain of only 239 yards. At the end the Packers were playing substitutes, but Paul Hornung never got in the game.

The Super Bowl games will now go on year after year, but it may be some time before an American League team will be good enough to win one, especially if the National League champion comes from Green Bay.

Green Bay (35)

Ends—Dale, Fleming, Davis, Aldridge, Long, Anderson, B. Brown.
Tackles—Skoronski, Gregg, Kostelnik, Jordan, Wright, Weatherwax.
Guards—Thurston, Kramer, Gillingham.
Centers—Curry, Bowman.
Linebackers—D. Robinson, Nitschke, Caffey, Crutcher.
Quarterbacks—Starr, Bratkowski.
Offensive Backs—E. Pitts, J. Taylor, Dowler, McGee, Anderson, Mack, Vandersea, Grabowski.
Defensive Backs—Jeter, Adderley, T. Brown, Wood, Hart, Hathcock.
Kicker—Chandler.

Kansas City (10)

Ends—Burford, Arbanas, Mays, Hurston, F. Pitts, Carolan, A. Brown.
Tackles—Tyrer, Hill, Rice, Buchanan, DiMidio.
Guards—Budde, Merz, Reynolds, Biodrowski.
Centers—Frazier, Gilliam.
Linebackers—Bell, Headrick, Holub, Corey, Abell, Stover.
Quarterbacks—Dawson, Beathard.
Offensive Backs—Garrett, McClinton, O. Taylor, Coan, Thomas.
Defensive Backs—Williamson, Mitchell, Hunt, J. Robinson, F. Smith, Ply.
Kickers—Mercer, Wilson.

Green Bay Packers 7   7   14   7—35
Kansas City Chiefs 0   10   0   0—10

G.B.—McGee, 37, pass from Starr (Chandler, kick).
K.C.—McClinton, 7, pass from Dawson (Mercer, kick).
G.B.—Taylor, 14, run, (Chandler, kick).
K.C.—FG, Mercer, 31.
G.B.—Pitts, 5, run (Chandler, kick).
G.B.—McGee, 13, pass from Starr (Chandler, kick).
G.B.—Pitts, 1, run (Chandler, kick).
Attendance—63,036.

Individual Statistics

Rushing—G. B.: Taylor, 16 attempts for 53 yards; Pitts, 11 for 45; Anderson, 4 for 30; Grabowski, 2 for 2. K. C.: Dawson 3 for 24; Garrett 6 for 17; McClinton 6 for 16; Coan 3 for 1.

Passing—G. B.: Starr, 16 completions in 23 attempts for 250 yards; Bratkowski, 0 in 1. K. C.: Dawson 16 in 27 for 211; Beathard 1 in 5 for 17.

Receiving—G. B.: McGee, 7 receptions for 138 yards; Dale, 4 for 59; Fleming, 2 for 22; Pitts, 2 for 32. K. C.: Burford, 4 for 67; Taylor, 4 for 57; Garrett, 3 for 28; McClinton, 2 for 34; Arbanas, 2 for 30; Carolan, 1 for 7; Coan, 1 for 5.

Statistics of the Game

	Packers	Chiefs		Packers	Chiefs
First downs	21	17	Interceptions by	1	1
Rushing yardage	130	72	Punts	4-43	7-45
Passing yardage	228	167	Fumbles lost	1	1
Passes	16-24	17-32	Yards penalized	40	26

Man in the News: Maestro of Offense
Bryan Bartlett Starr

Jan. 15, 1967—Unlike some of his swinging teammates, Bryan Bartlett Starr, the quarterback for the Green Bay Packers, goes to bed early. He says, "yes, sir" to almost everyone and most notably his coach, Vince Lombardi. He works with a Boy Scout troop and if he has ever tried a cigarette or swallowed a beer there are no valid witnesses. At the same time, Bart Starr, as he is known to football fans, is a vicious competitor. He will find ways to beat people, as he showed yesterday in the Super Bowl against the Kansas City Chiefs. Starr runs the offense for the Packers, which is not their strongest asset (the defense is that), but a ruthlessly efficient one. Besides, Starr, who is 32 years old and in his 11th professional season, seems to be getting smarter all the time.

"It's not hard to read the Packer offense," a rival coach has said. "It's almost a Rinky-dink attack—not much imagination, simple meat-and-potato plays. But it is hard to read Starr. He takes those simple tools and uses them to the hilt. He has all kinds of guts, especially on third-down."

With yardage needed on third-down, the defense can move in for the kill. The offense is predictable, but not Starr's offense. In the National Football League's championship game in Dallas last New Year's Day, the one that matched the winning Packers and the Cowboys, Starr showed why he was acclaimed as pro football's best quarterback.

During the winning touchdown drive in the fourth period. Starr faced three third-down situations in which he had to gain 12 yards, 19 yards and 12 yards again. In each case this good-looking blond Alabaman coolly dropped back and waited for the pass receiver to break free, and then threw the football. The passes were pretty enough to belong in a museum. Each one was caught and each first down attained.

Following that exhibition there were few Starr doubters left. There have been many in the past largely because Starr came from humble football beginnings and he has never been the flashy athlete.

His first claim to fame was established on New Year's Day of 1953, when as a freshman quarterback he helped Alabama crush Syracuse, 61–6, in the Orange Bowl.

Starr later went into professional football, but nothing happened for a long time. When Lombardi arrived in Green Bay in 1959 to revive a dying franchise, Starr was a fourth-string quarterback behind Lamar McHan, Joe Francis and Paul Hornung. Lombardi made him first-string by 1960 because he was the best of a mediocre lot. Besides, he said, "yes sir," and followed this positive coach's orders to the letter.

In 1960, the Packers won the first of five division or league championships that were to come in the next seven seasons. Starr was good enough then and he has since become a lot better. He completes 55 per cent of his passes, a very high figure, and he is almost never intercepted.

"I don't know where the story began that Bart could not throw the long pass," said Lombardi yesterday. "That's ridiculous. He can throw with anyone. He's a fine quarterback and I'm delighted that he's finally getting the recognition that he has long deserved."

Starr's recognition last season included his third title as the N.F.L.'s best passer and the Jim Thorpe Trophy for being voted the most valuable player in the league.

Starr lives in Green Bay in a house half a mile from and within sight of the stadium and field house where the Packers work. A father of two young boys, this businessman recently stopped selling insurance and now spends his off-season time taking on speaking engagements and doing product endorsements. There is a stock brokerage firm in Milwaukee ready to give him a $100,000-a-year job when he gives up football.

Starr has been named "the man of the year" by numerous Wisconsin civic groups. He is chairman of a committee raising funds for a boys' Green Bay and when it comes to charity requests Starr is an easy mark. He is one of the state's best known personalities, respected from Oshkosh to Oconomowoc and beyond.

His teammates, some of them rowdy extroverts in contrast to Starr's quiet simplicity, have great respect for him. He is one of their leaders and he is the man who more than anyone else puts the points on the scoreboard that make winning a habit at Green Bay.

Wood's Steal Left Chiefs Stunned
Stram Terms Play the Turning Point—Starr Praised

By FRANK LITSKY

LOS ANGELES, *Jan. 15*—The way the Kansas City Chiefs looked when they returned to their dressing room after today's 35–10 Super Bowl loss to the Green Bay Packers, it was difficult to tell whether they had won, lost, tied or even played.

There was no crying, no shoe-throwing, no outbursts of temper. There was disappointment with their performance and, to a lesser degree, there was praise for the Packers as a good—but not perfect—team.

But most of all, the Chiefs seemed stunned. They took the field thinking they could win, and they left at half-time sure they could win. Then, early in the third quarter, came the play that, they agreed to a man, broke their back.

It was Willie Wood's interception and 50-yard return that put the ball on the Chiefs' 5-yard line and set up the touchdown that put the Packers in front, 21–10.

Chiefs Break Down

"That play seemingly changed the personality of the game," said Coach Hank Stram of the Chiefs. "We played well in the first half and we got off to a good start in the second half," Stram said. "We were doing the things we should have been doing. Then came that one play. After that, we just broke down, and then they got to Len Dawson."

Until that interception, Dawson, the Chiefs' quarterback, had been having great success.

"The interception did it," said Dawson. "It gave them the momentum.

Let's face it. Their offense took the ball and drove it down our throats. Do I blame myself? Yes, I generally blame myself when we get beat."

Many Chiefs were impressed by the way Bart Starr, thy Green Bay quarterback, connected so often on third-down passes.

"We kept trying to change our defensive picture on third down," said Stram, "but he still pierced our areas."

"They pick out a weak spot and stay with it much better than any team I've seen," said Mike Garrett. "Which weak spot? Well, they were passing like mad on us and hitting those third-down plays, so there must have been a weakness in there somewhere."

Cornerbacks The Targets

The weaknesses appeared to be at cornerback, where Fred Williamson played the left side and Willie Mitchell the right.

The Packers' wide receivers caught 11 passes for 197 yards, and Max McGee spoiled Mitchell's day by beating him on two touchdown passes and a 37-yard completion that set up a third score.

"Were they picking on Mitchell?" Stram said. "Well, it was very evident that they were working on our right side in critical passing situations."

"Starr was throwing the ball as the receiver made his break," said Mitchell. "They seemed to run more or less a time pattern. I'll tell you—cornerback is the most embarrassing position to play. When you make a mistake, it is there for all to see."

Williamson, wearing only a frown, said he made a gross error in the second quarter. The result was a 64-yard touchdown pass that was called back because of a penalty.

"It was third and one," said Williamson. "It was a running situation. He gambled on a pass, and the way he faked a run was tremendous. It fooled me."

The usually loquacious Williamson was knocked cold making a fourth-quarter tackle.

"A little rest and a little nighty-night will cure me," he said.

Williamson was one of three Chiefs who suffered minor aches. Fred Arbanas, the tight end, missed a few plays because of a leg cramp and a jarring of his slightly separated left shoulder. Sherrill Headrick banged up a knee but was quickly back in action.

Why did the Chiefs lose?

"We didn't play our kind of football long enough," said Stram.

"They make mistakes," said Mitchell, "but they made less than we did."

"We just made too many mistakes," said Buck Buchanan.

"We lost our poise after the interception," said Jerry Mays. "That's no excuse. Great teams don't lose poise."

Then Mays summed up the thousands of words that have been uttered and are yet to be uttered on what happened.

"The Packers," he said, "beat us in the first half. The Packers and the Packer mystique beat us in the second half. The Packers beat us. They beat the hell out of us."

A Typical Coast Show

Super Bowl Is Unable to Measure Up to Advance Billing as TV Attraction

By JACK GOULD

Jan. 15, 1967—The Super Bowl yesterday was a representative example of most television dramas coming out of Los Angeles.

The advance build-up was more impressive than the show, and the script fell apart in the second act. Universal Pictures and Metro-Goldwyn-Mayer can comfort professional football. There is a million-dollar dud in everyone's closet.

The confrontation between the Green Bay Packers and Kansas City Chiefs reflected the usual difficulties of casting a TV special. The starring roles were methodically rendered by the Packers, but the bit parts were forlornly played by the Chiefs.

To the viewer untutored in the expertise of football, one conclusion seemed inescapable: Isn't it early to begin the 1967–68 exhibition-game schedule?

An omen of the anti-climax that might lay ahead came before the game. After all the rivalry, both networks carried the same introductory half-hour. The pooled 30 minutes were a lackluster interval bereft of excitement and seemingly designed only to accommodate additional spot announcements.

As for the championship game, the viewer at home had brief stirrings of hope in the first half when the Chiefs showed a touch of spirit. But thereafter it was downhill viewing all the way.

The best TV sports of the afternoon, in fact, was the basketball game between the Boston Celtics and Philadelphia 76ers.

All the chitchat over the competition between commentators of C.B.S. and N.B.C. similarly proved to be malarkey. The play-by-play accounts of Curt Gowdy of N.B.C. and Jack Whitaker and Ray Scott of C.B.S. were almost the same, word for word. In the analysis it was a toss-up between Paul Christman of N.B.C. and Frank Gifford of C.B.S. Never were two networks more alike.

The iron-clad control that pro football exerts over its commentators was entertainingly illustrated on both networks. Each mentioned as briefly as possible that the attendance in the Coliseum was 63,036, but not a word about how that figure had fallen short of expectations. Sports reporting is not to be found on TV during a game.

In this regard, however, the director of the pooled TV coverage had a problem during the half-time ceremonies. The best shot of Al Hirt, the trumpeter, was from an angle that showed rows on rows of empty seats in the background.

The pictorial coverage was conventional, without any special shots or innovations for a championship.

But the afternoon did carry one immense blessing. With the game finally over, there will be no more of those Super Bowl commercials. The campaign of ballyhoo and promotional material was woefully overdone.

Sports of The Times

By ARTHUR DALEY

One for the Old Pros

LOS ANGELES, *Jan. 15*—The Green Bay Packers regained their cool, their calm and their competence in the second half of the extravagantly produced and advertised Super Bowl in the 70-degree-plus heat at the Coliseum on this delightful afternoon. They knocked all delusions of grandeur out of the Kansas City Chiefs and returned to normalcy a game that looked as though it might have generated an upset.

Maybe the Packers were a wee bit overconfident. Even before the contestants took the field, there was considerable bantering in the Green Bay dressing room. A sepulchral voice boomed out a query to Marv Fleming, the tight end.

"Who we playin', Marvin?" said the voice.

"The Super Chiefs," said Fleming.

For two astonishing quarters Kansas City played like Super Chiefs. The champions of the American Football League behaved as if they were at least the equals of the champions of the National Football League. Despite the fact that the A.F.L. had been generally derided as the much inferior group, they were totally unawed by their assignment of bucking the Establishment.

Too Close for Comfort

The Chiefs tackled with excessive zeal. They crashed in on Bart Starr and dumped that paragon of excellence on his britches. They stopped the Packer running game and almost—but never quite—slowed the Green Bay passing attack. With Lenny Dawson flimflamming Packer defenders with his slick ball handling and puncturing them with his passing, they did well.

The Packers led at half-time by an uncomfortably close margin of 14–10. Buddy Young, once a great star himself and now a trouble-shooter for the N.F.L., looked glum. He turned thumbs down.

"Old age and the heat are gonna get the Packers in the second half," he said. "The Chiefs are a mighty good football team."

He was right and he was wrong. Nothing got the Packers in the second half because they had the savvy to compensate for all else. And the Chiefs are a mighty good football team. They just happened to meet a better one.

If it didn't look that way in the first half, it was proved beyond doubt in the second half. The computer mind of Vince Lombardi, their coaching genius, gave the Packers panaceas for all ills during the intermission. It was a complete recovery.

Hardly had play resumed when the Packers poured in on Dawson to stop the fakery that had been bedeviling them. Under the pressure of the first effective rush against him, he passed hurriedly and the bottom fell out in a close contest. Willie Wood cut in front of Mike Garrett and intercepted the throw, carrying the ball 50 yards to the 5. A moment later Elijah Pitts scurried over the goal line and the Packers were beyond pursuit.

The pressure on Dawson never let up. On two successive plays he was smothered for losses of 25 yards. The statistics tell the story and figures never lie—almost never anyway. He hit on 11 of 15 passes for 152 yards in the first half, on only 5 of 12 for 59 yards in the second.

By then a familiar pattern had begun to assert itself. The Packers took over ball control and the Chiefs were helpless to do much scoring when Green Bay had the ball. They only took it away once. That was near the end when Starr threw a heaven-help-us pass half the field to the 11-yard line. It was intercepted, but was no worse than giving away the ball on a punt. Incidentally, it was the first interception against this remarkable man since mid-October. He had tossed 173 passes without having one plucked by the enemy.

Momentum is Maintained

Before the end Lombardi was using his junior varsity in many positions. Naturally enough, they did just about as well as the varsity because the momentum gained by Wood's interception early in the second half was never lost. The elderly codgers in the Packer line-up merely needed this break to put a stranglehold on the Chiefs with sharper blocking, sharper tackling and sharper everything else.

If Green Bay rooters, overjoyed though they were, grew a little misty-eyed, it was because this game marked the end of the Packer trail for Jim Taylor, again the rampaging second-effort fullback, and Paul Hornung, the once wondrous halfback, who didn't even see action. They carried the Packers for nine years and neither is expected back next season.

The 35–10 victory of the Packers upholds the prestige of the N.F.L., just as it was supposed to do. But there were ominous warnings for the future. The young Chiefs will be around for a long while and they will get better. Some day they will win the Super Bowl Game. But today the Packers were too much for them.

Vince Lombardi looks on with a stern smile as his Packers put the finishing touches to the Kansas City Chiefs in Super Bowl I.

LOMBARDI CALLS CHIEFS GOOD TEAM BUT NOT EQUAL TO TOP ELEVENS IN N.F.L.

Coach Maintains Dallas is Better
Starr Says Chiefs Stacked Defenses— McGee Bows Out in Blaze of Glory

By BILL BECKER

LOS ANGELES, *Jan. 15*—"Kansas City is a good football team," Vince Lombardi, the Green Bay factotum, said generously today after his Packers had mopped up on the Chiefs. Then the gray, gruff coach added the kicker:

"But their team doesn't compare with the top National Football League teams. I think Dallas is a better football team."

Vince made the statement coolly while reporters and televison men were losing their notes and equipment in the steamy Packers' dressing room. He punctuated his remarks by slamming a football from hand to hand.

"The boys gave me the game ball," said Vince proudly. "An N.F.L. ball," he added with eyes twinkling behind his heavy spectacles.

Chiefs' Speed Hailed

Regarding the Chiefs, he continued: "The Chiefs have great speed, but I'd have to say N.F.L. football is tougher."

He declined to specify how much tougher, or how many teams he rated higher than the Chiefs.

The Packers broke the game open in the second half by "getting more aggressive on defense and blitzing at least three or four times," Lombardi said. At half-time he told the defense they weren't tackling well and he expected a better rush in the third period.

"We got the message," said Willie Wood. Willie, the former Southern California Trojan, intercepted Len Dawson's pass and ran 50 yards shortly afterward to set up the Packers' third touchdown. From then on, the momentum was all Green Bay's.

Wood said that this was "the greatest run (if not the longest) I ever made in the Coliseum." Willie played all of his collegiate home games in this stadium. "But this has to be my biggest thrill in Los Angeles," he emphasized.

"I was stung by the pass Otis Taylor caught against me in the first half," said Wood, one of the N.F.L.'s stellar safety men. "So I was sort of waiting for a chance. We were all kind of anticipating a sideline pass on the third-down-and-five situation."

Wood cut in front of Fred Arbanas, the Chiefs' tight end, and nearly went all the way in the game's key play. Ironically, the man who kept him from scoring was another ex-Trojan, Mike Garrett. Garrett tackled Wood from behind on the Chiefs' 5-yard line.

Lauds Foe's Defense

Bart Starr, the Packers' directing genius, lauded the Kansas City defenses—up to a point. "We just didn't execute well in the first half," said Starr. "But we knew that their stacked defenses could not contain our passing all day."

Starr explained that the Chiefs, by stacking their line-backers in tight behind their line, exposed their flanks.

"The offensive end has the advantage in that he only has to worry about the cornerback," Bart said. "We have the ends that can beat anyone in a one-on-one situation."

And the man who did most of the catching in this fortuitous turn of events was Max McGee. This was McGee's final game as a pro, he said, adding: "I can't think of a nicer way to go."

McGee caught touchdown passes of 37 and 13 yards and set up a third score with another fine long reception. "I should have scored," he laughed, "but I darned near tripped over my tongue."

McGee, 34 years old, said Boyd Dowler's shoulder injury forced him to play "a lot more than I figured on and I got a little tired."

McGee said he might like to coach—"If Lombardi wants me."

Lamar Hunt, the Chiefs' owner, congratulated McGee on his great game and added: "Don't retire now. We want to come back and get you next year."

Low-Key Celebration

The Packer dressing room was relatively quiet compared to most championship chambers. Doug Hart, a defensive back, the first to come off the field, let out a tentative whoop or two.

Henry Jordan, the all-everything defensive tackle, came in singing softly, "Money, money, money" in the key of G, probably for greenbacks, $15,000 worth. That was what each Packer will get for the victory; each Chief will receive $7,500—a balm of sorts.

The spirit of the Packers, although perhaps they would be too blasé and professional to call it that, was exemplified by Elijah Pitts and Paul Hornung, the regular left halfback and the former regular left halfback.

Pitts scored two touchdowns, while Hornung didn't get into the game at all.

"Naturally, I would have liked to play," said Hornung, who remained mum on his future plans. "But it is great just to be associated with this team and these fellows."

Here he slapped Elijah on the back and Pitts, duly grateful, responded: "Paul helped me to become the player I was this season. His tips improved my running."

Financial Facts, Figures On Super Bowl Game

LOS ANGELES, *Jan. 16* (AP)—The financial facts and figures on Sunday's Super Bowl football game between the Green Bay Packers and the Kansas City Chiefs, based on figures estimated by Commissioner Pete Rozelle:

Attendance—63,036.

Gate Receipts—estimated, $775,000.

Radio-Television Receipts—$2-million.

Total Receipts—estimated, $2,775,000.

Expenses—estimated, $300,000.

Guaranteed player shares—$1,170,000; $15,000 to each winner,
$7,500 to each loser.

N.F.L. Player Pension Plans—estimated, $261,000.

A.F.L. Player Pension Plans—estimated, $261,000.

Green Bay Club—estimated, $195,750.

Kansas City Club—estimated, $195,750.

N.F.L. Office—estimated, $195,750.

A.F.L. Office—estimated, $195,750.

Chapter 2

Super Bowl II—1968

A year later, the "once in a lifetime" anticipations were being stirred again, with several differences.

There was a new site: Miami, Florida, instead of Los Angeles.

There was a new A.F.L. representative: the Oakland Raiders.

There was only one network (C.B.S.) televising the game instead of two (under an agreement to alternate from now on).

There was a new starting time: 3:05 P.M. local time, two hours later (for the players) than the game in Los Angeles had been.

And there was a sellout.

But a lot of things were the same.

The Green Bay Packers, at the absolute peak of the Vince Lombardi mystique, were there to defend their title.

The Packers were favored, just as universally, as they had been the year before.

The league champions still had independent identities, since the actual merger (which would join regular-season schedules) was still two years off.

And the sense of epic was still being assiduously promoted.

Actually, it was easier to believe that the Raiders would prove tougher for Green Bay than the Chiefs had. Oakland had gone through a 13–1 regular-season, and had won its league championship game (from Houston) by a score of 40–7. The Packers had only a 9–4–1 record, and had barely beaten Dallas, 21–17, in their title game. Allowing for a difference in levels, the degree of superiority in the Oakland record offered hope of a more dramatic contest.

But one ingredient was really missing, or at least diluted. The true curiosity, the fully unknown quality of what to expect, had been present in Super Bowl I; it wasn't there for Super Bowl II, because Super Bowl II was inevitably comparable. Instead of feeling "anything may happen," which non-experts could honestly imagine before the first game, they now felt "will it be like last year, or not?"

In retrospect, Super Bowl II will always be that, a shadow (or perhaps, a deepening shading to give dimension) of Super Bowl I. But that's in retrospect. At the time, it was simply that the unique, unprecedented, never-equalled and never-again-to-be-experienced event was with us again, predictably on schedule.

43

Raiders Use Soft Talk to Lull Packers

By DAVE ANDERSON

OAKLAND, CALIF., *Jan. 1*—For the next two weeks, the Oakland Raiders will be preparing for the Super Bowl—mentally, physically and vocally. And should they somehow upset the Packers in Miami on Jan. 14, their vocal preparation might be the most significant.

What a Raider dignitary described as "the great snow job" has already begun.

Unlike the Kansas City Chiefs, who aroused the Packers with their comments a year ago, the new American Football League champions have adopted a policy of peaceful propaganda. Seldom was heard an encouraging word after their 40–7 rout of the Houston Oilers.

The Raiders profess to be from "lil' ol' Oakland," as their major domo, Al Davis, likes to say.

"Imagine us on the same field with the Green Bay Packers," he says, producing the proper awe.

Moments after his team's coronation yesterday, the quiet Raider coach, John Rauch, set the tone.

"Beating the Packers is always in the realm of possibility," Rauch said, "but we'll go into that game with the same confidence we've had all season and we'd rather play the Packers because they represent the best of their league, the best for three years."

Rauch's phrasing was quite different from that attributed to Hank Stram, the Kansas City coach, on the day the Chiefs qualified for last year's Super Bowl. Regarding the champagne, Stram was quoted that "there'll be plenty more when we beat" the Packers.

One of the Kansas City players, Fred Williamson, a loud cornerback, also threatened to "drop my hammer" on Packer receivers. He never fulfilled that threat.

Must Apply Pressure

In assessing the Packers, perhaps the most significant performer on the Raider offense, the quarterback, Daryle Lamonica, predicted simply that the Super Bowl game "would be a matter of execution," a phrase often employed by the wise old Packers.

One of the Raiders, the huge rookie guard, Gene Upshaw, opposed the Packers last August in the College All-Star game.

"I'm a better player now than I was then," is about all that Upshaw will say. "I've got to be seasoned to oppose them."

Upshaw remembers Henry Jordan, the clever tackle who tricked him constantly. Another critical pass blocking pairing puts Harry Schuh, a mammoth tackle, against Willie Davis. On defense, four Raiders must produce if the A.F.L. champions are to pressure Bart Starr.

In the pass-rush, Ike Lassiter must get by Forrest Gregg and Tom Keating must fool Gale Gillingham. In the secondary, the cornerbacks, Kent McCloughan and Willie Brown, must handle Boyd Dowler and Carroll Dale and perhaps Max McGee, the old pro who wrecked the Chiefs.

Wally Cruice, who scouted the Raiders yesterday for the Packers, phrased his comments in the same manner.

Cruice was "particularly impressed with the Raider running game" and estimated that "on offense, they get off the ball faster than Kansas City and they have a sounder all-round defense." But neither team is fooled by the gentle words for public consumption.

The true feeling, at least among the Raiders, appeared to be summed up in four words by Keating, the 250-pound tackle, after the team physician displayed X-ray plates that showed that his troublesome right ankle was merely sprained, that there was no tendon or ligament damage.

"Get the cortisone, Doc," said Keating.

Sports of The Times

By ARTHUR DALEY

Mutual Respect

Jan. 3, 1968—The Oakland Raiders will advance into the Super Bowl a fortnight hence with an 11-game winning streak. The Green Bay Packers will reach that same Miami destination with a winning streak of two. But what a two!

Many a Grandstand Quarterback developed the unshakable conviction that the sensational climactic victories of the Packers over the Los Angeles Rams and the Dallas Cowboys outweigh the entire Raider string. Until there is proof to the contrary, the National Football League is generally regarded as the superior of the American Football League in over-all strength, balance and depth.

One scornful dissenter is dynamic Al Davis, the front office boss of the Oakland squad and the man who assembled the team. In the San Francisco Bay area he is known as "The Genius." Not being one to let false modesty mislead people, Davis has accepted the nomination. Flamboyant though the description is, it has a reasonable foundation in fact.

During a three-year stretch as Oakland coach, Davis raised the team from innocuousness to respectability. He took a sabbatical to become commissioner of the A.F.L. and sparked so many talent raids on the N.F.L. that he forced the merger of the two leagues. Tough fighter that he is, Davis wanted no part of it and quit to become "managing general partner"— whatever that is—of the Raiders. As a part owner he outranks Scotty Stirling, the general manager, and Johnny Rauch, the coach. This Oakland team is strictly Al's baby.

Soft Soap

The average pro football nut grew up as an N.F.L. fan and he is not too familiar with either the A.F.L. or its champion, the Raiders. He's known the Packers ever since Curly Lambeau brought them out of the Wisconsin woods four decades ago. And he has since developed a vast amount of admiration for the slick machine that Vince Lombardi has turned off his assembly line.

When the Packers manhandled the Kansas City Chiefs in the Super Bowl a year ago, Lombardi didn't even need a pep talk. He merely posted on his bulletin board rash statements from the camp of the Chiefs, careless remarks of what they'd do to the Packers. The discreet Green Bays lied beautifully in saying how scared they were of Kansas City and how much they respected the A.F.L. champions.

The nimble-minded Davis has always been quick to learn from his own and other people's mistakes. The Raiders already have grown muscle-bound from patting the Packers on the back, exalting them as the world's greatest and innocently saying that it will be a privilege to be allowed on the same field with such demi-gods. This approach has the Davis touch.

It is the correct technique. Fresco Thompson is now a vice president of the Los Angeles Dodgers, but many years ago he was the captain of the Philadelphia Phils, baseball's worst team. He has never forgotten a lesson he learned.

"Don't get opponents mad at you unnecessarily," he once said. "In my day the Yankees showed how it should be done. They always inquired after the other guy's health and the welfare of his wife and family. Then they'd beat the guys brains out, but they were so nice about it that it seemed painless.

"But the Chicago Cubs of that era were downright nasty. They snarled at everyone and they insulted us the most, riding us as the worst collection of clowns ever assembled. One September they came to town with the pennant almost won. But they got us so mad that we played over our heads and knocked them out of it. Let sleeping dogs lie. It keeps them harmless."

The Raiders

The Packers can drowse blissfully away for all the Raiders care. Oakland won't disturb them. But where Lombardi built his team over the years, Davis built his in pretty much of a hurry. He drafted shrewdly, traded astutely and made more skillful evaluation of undiscovered talent on other teams for waiver or free-agent grabs. His key move was the acquisition of Daryle Lamonica, the quarterback who put all the pieces into place for him.

Davis went to the draft in search of a quarterback, but he also wanted Gene Upshaw, a man who may soon be the best running guard in pro ball —if he isn't that already. Al solved his dilemma by trading for Lamonica and drafting Upshaw within 10 minutes. His new pass-master was voted the most valuable player in the league.

Five star regulars were discards—Ben Davidson, Ike Lassiter, George

Blanda, Clem Daniels and Howie Williams. Eight came in judicious trades and the rest were homegrown. Billy Cannon, a disappointment elsewhere as a running back, became a sensation as a tight end while Hewritt Dixon, a disappointment elsewhere as a tight end, became a crashing fullback.

No wonder they refer to Davis as "The Genius" in the Bay area. Some experts think that the current Raiders represent the strongest and best balanced team the A.F.L. has yet produced. The Super Bowl will reveal how significant the Oakland 11-game winning streak really is. Does it carry more weight than the Packer winning streak of two?

Odds Maker Picks Packers by 14 And Says They'll Hold the Line

Jan. 4, 1968—Throughout the nation, the betting line for the Super Bowl lists the Green Bay Packers as a heavy favorite over the Oakland Raiders. But the "number," as the gamblers like to say, varies. Here on Broadway, the Packers have been established as a 13½-point choice. Out at Harrah's Tahoe Racebook in Stateline, Nev., the number is 10½. And in Las Vegas, Nev., Jimmy (The Greek) Snyder, who makes the line for much of the country, rates the Packers a "strong 14" over the American Football League champions in the game at Miami Jan. 14.

In a telephone interview yesterday, Snyder, a self-titled "sports analyst," explained how he arrived at a 14-point difference.

"The team speed is about equal, so there's no points involved there," he said, "but I had to give Bart Starr 2 points over Daryle Lamonica at quarterback. You can't call Lamonica a great quarterback off one big year, he's got to do it year after year, like Starr has. And you don't know if Lamonica is going to hold up in a big game like this. Starr will.

"On the defensive front four, it's another 2-point edge for the Packers. They have four fine pass-rushers, the Raiders only have two—Tom Keating and Ike Lassiter.

"A middle linebacker, Ray Nitschke is worth 3 points. The kid the Raiders got, Dan Conners, is good, too. He's a 1-point player, but that's a 2-point difference. On the defensive backs, the Packers have a big edge, 4 points, I'd say. Herb Adderley, Bob Jeter and Willie Wood, they are the best. The Raiders don't have defensive backs in that class. Look what the Jets did to them with George Sauer and Don Maynard.

"The Packers get 2 points for their receivers, too. Boyd Dowler and Carroll Dale, they catch the ball against everybody. That's 12 points so far, and then you've got to give the Packers 3 more on intangibles—the coach [Vince Lombardi] is a big intangible, so is their record in a big game.

"That's 15 points for the Packers, and take one away because of George Blanda. He's a better place-kicker than Don Chandler, you've got to give the Raiders a point for him. That brings it down to 14 points, a strong 14 to me. That number should hold up. I doubt if it would drop much below 13½, if it drops at all. The intangibles are too much in favor of the Packers."

Snyder does not rely on exhibition results, but he recalled that the Raiders lost to the San Francisco 49ers 13–10, prior to the season. The Packers did not play an exhibition game last summer against an A.F.L. team.

"The Packers will probably play a conservative first quarter," said Snyder. "Lombardi will want to find out who's working on who, and his game plan for the second half should be something. That's how they beat Kansas City [35–10] last year, in the second half, and that's when the Raiders will be in real trouble."

•

Even if you have a color TV set, the Super Bowl will be mostly black and white. The Raiders will wear their black jerseys, the Packers white. . . . The Raiders received $6,321.77 each for their 40–7 triumph last Sunday over the Houston Oilers, who were consoled with $4,996.45 each. . . . Sonny Jurgensen, the quarterback of the Washington Redskins, may not perform for the Eastern Conference All-Stars in the Pro Bowl. Jurgensen has complained of a sore passing arm, and his club president, Edward Bennett Williams, reported that Sonny was "very, very tired."

Al Davis Takes Raiders to the Top in Five Years

By DAVE ANDERSON

Jan. 7, 1968—The Oakland Raiders originated in 1960 as an afterthought by the American Football League.

Five years ago at this time, the Raiders had lost 19 consecutive games, a pro record.

Next Sunday in Miami, the Raiders will challenge the Green Bay Packers in the Super Bowl.

Strangely, the saga of the Raiders is somewhat similar to that of the Packers, starting with the franchises themselves. Green Bay, Wis., is the last outpost of the old town teams in the National Football League. Oakland, Calif., possesses the last of the original franchises awarded by the A.F.L.

The Packers were desperate when Vince Lombardi reorganized them in 1959, the Raiders were equally desperate when Al Davis reorganized them in 1963.

In addition, Green Bay was in danger of losing its franchise before Lombardi arrived. So was Oakland before Wayne Valley, the tough-talking owner, hired Davis and demanded that local politicians provide a modern stadium.

Ironically, when the A.F.L. was organized, Oakland was not among the charter franchises.

Instead, the A.F.L. had granted a franchise to the Minneapolis-St. Paul area of Minnesota. But when the N.F.L. accepted the Minneapolis-St. Paul group, too, it chose to join the established league.

Several months later, Oakland was selected as the A.F.L. replacement for Minnesota.

By that time, virtually all of the college players who had been selected in the A.F.L. draft by the phantom Minnesota franchise had signed with N.F.L. clubs. Oakland had a franchise, but no players. In addition, it had no stadium in Oakland, and no nickname.

First Nickname Vetoed

While the club owners were negotiating to share Kezar Stadium with the San Francisco 49ers, residents were invited to suggest nicknames. The local Chamber of Commerce selected "Señors" as the winner, an allusion to the old Spanish settlers of northern California.

"That's no good," complained Scotty Stirling, now the team's general manager but then a sports writer on the Oakland Tribune, "we don't have the accent mark for the n in our headline type."

Despite their late start, the Raiders put together a respectable 6–8 won-lost record under their coach, the late Eddie Erdelatz. But when the Raiders lost their first two games in 1961, Erdelatz was dismissed. His successor was Marty Feldman, who guided the team to 10 more defeats while winning twice.

The next season, five consecutive losses resulted in Feldman's dismissal. Under his successor, Bill Conkright, the Raiders lost eight more games that year and won their finale, ending the 19-game losing streak.

The lone victory did not fool Wayne Valley, who had made his millions in the construction business. In searching for a new coach, he did not have to look too far. At the time, Al Davis was an assistant coach with the San Diego Chargers. But other candidates were available. Why did Valley pick Davis?

"Because everybody hated his guts," Valley said last week prior to his team's coronation as the A.F.L. champions. "Al Davis wants to win, and he'll do anything to win. And after losing all those games, I wanted to win, any way I could."

Multiple-Sports Stadium

Davis assumed command, while Valley battled the local politicians for a new stadium. After their first year in Kezar, the Raiders had moved to Candlestick Park, also in San Francisco. In their third season, 1962, they shifted again, this time to Youell Field, a bleacher-type ballpark with 12,000 seats.

"At least it was in Oakland," Valley recalled, "but I knew we had to have a new stadium."

He threatened to shift the franchise elsewhere unless a new stadium was provided. His threat was successful. Construction was started soon after that on the Oakland-Alameda complex, an outdoor football-baseball-soccer stadium and an indoor basketball-hockey arena.

Davis, meanwhile, had turned the Raiders from a loser into a winner. After a 1–13 record in 1962, his first squad won 10 games and lost four to challenge San Diego for the Western Division title.

In altering the team, Davis retained only four players from the early years—Jim Otto, Wayne Hawkins, Dan Birdwell and Clem Daniels. For a few months in 1966, Davis took over as the Commissioner of the A.F.L. in the player war with the N.F.L., and his battleplan hastened the peace treaty between the leagues.

Since his departure had resulted in the appointment of Stirling as general manager and John Rauch as coach, Davis returned to the Raiders with a new title—managing general partner. Although confined to the front office, his provocative personality dominated the club, among both the players and the front-office personnel.

Ball Control Key of Oakland Game

Lamonica Counts on Flare Action to Stop Packers

By FRANK LITSKY

BOCA RATON, FLA., *Jan. 10*—A year ago, Daryle Lamonica was second-string quarterback for the Buffalo Bills. Now he is first-string quarterback for the Oakland Raiders, champions of the American Football League, and his success or failure will largely determine the Raiders' success or failure in Sunday's Super Bowl game against the Green Bay Packers at Miami.

"A lot of people say we're going to the slaughterhouse," Lamonica said today at the Raider training base. "I hope not. We feel we can run and throw on them. At least we will try to. If we can't, we'll have to adjust. But teams have beaten them before, and we think we can if we're willing to pay the price. What is the price? Sixty minutes of good, hard-nosed football and holding our mistakes to a minimum."

Lamonica has spent hours watching Packer game films, and he has been duly impressed.

"Their front four gives you a tremendous rush," he said. "The speed of the front four is fantastic. And their linebackers are big and agile. That's something to think about because the best pass defense is a good, hard rush. A quarterback can't throw a pass flat on his back."

Lamonica spoke highly of the Raiders, too.

Ball-Control Teams

"We're a ball-control team, like the Packers," he said. "That's good because when you score off a long drive, you give your defense a good rest and you put added pressure on your opponent.

"The Oakland offense is much more complex than the one at Buffalo. Here, we use a multiple-type offense. We use a lot of flare action, which simply means we utilize our backs as receivers more than any other team."

Until this year, Lamonica has scrambled for a place in the sun. When he completed his college career at Notre Dame in 1962, he was drafted by the Packers in the National League and the Bills in the American. He was "pretty close" to signing with the Packers, but he chose the Bills because he thought they needed a quarterback.

Four Years on Bench

They did—the year before. So they got Jack Kemp, and for four years Lamonica fidgeted on the bench, occasionally getting into a losing game, firing up the Bills and turning a few defeats into victories.

"At times," said Lamonica, "I talked to myself. But I always believed in my ability. I thought I could develop into a leader. Last March, I had a long talk with Coach Joel Collier of the Bills, and he assured me an equal shot at the No. 1 job.

"So 10 minutes before the common draft last March, the Bills traded me to the Raiders."

Davidson, Raiders' Star, Is Mean Without Malice

By FRANK LITSKY

BOCA RATON, FLA., *Jan. 11*—Ben Davidson is a big, rough, tough defensive end for the Oakland Raiders.

His detractors—and there are many—say he is a dirty player (Winston Hill of the New York Jets has called him "the No. 1 cheap-shop artist in the American Football League"). Davidson says people misunderstand him and his motives, that he is just trying to earn a living to support his wife and three daughters.

He defends himself so convincingly that it is difficult to believe this soft-spoken, charming man could do bodily harm to such quarterbacks as Joe Namath and John Hadl. But then you remember that one esteemed judge of character, a writer who goes back to the days of Damon Runyon, describes Davidson as "the greatest put-on in sports."

Davidson has two distinguishing characteristics. First is his size—6 feet 7 inches and 275 pounds. Second is his light brown handlebar mustache, which makes him look like an overgrown lead tenor in a barbershop quartet of walruses.

Not One to Complain

On Sunday, Davidson will play for the Raiders against the Green Bay Packers in the Super Bowl at Miami. Today, at the Raiders' training base here, he talked about the sources of his problem—quarterbacks and offensive linemen. Both, he says, are dedicated to taking the bread from his mouth, and a man must eat, must he not?

"Take that game against the Jets last month," he said. "They say I broke Namath's cheekbone and I drew a 15-yard penalty for roughness. But I was pretty well beat up myself after the game, so maybe I should complain. But as befits my lower position, I just sit in the whirlpool and don't complain and try to come back for the next game."

After a few visits from aggressive defensive ends such as Davidson, quarterbacks supposedly listen for the sound of little feet.

"That's nonsense," said Davidson. "You can't go out and intimidate a quarterback or make him afraid. These guys play every week and don't scare. They have to concentrate on the receiver. I think they feel the pressure, but they don't fear you."

Seeks Job Security

Davidson, like all defensive linemen, complains that his opponents often hold him.

"Offensive guys watch game films," he said, "if they see you are held and don't object, they all pick on you and pretty soon you are looking for a job. I'm just looking for job security. So at times, I don't choose to put up with holding.

"When a guy won't stop holding, you have to resort to illegal tactics, which you hate to do because then you're bringing yourself down to his level. What kind of illegal tactics? Well, you can kick him. Next time, he might think better of it when he's going to hold.

"In a whole game, you're bound to beat your guy once or twice, so you don't begrudge him a couple of holdings. But not time after time, because then it gets to a point when you're not doing your job."

Davidson did his job so well this season that he made the all-league team. Against the Packers, he must overcome the blocking of Bob Skoronski, a smallish (245-pound) offensive tackle but quick, smart and experienced.

In last year's Super Bowl, the Packers teed off on Fred Williamson, Kansas City's braggart of a cornerback. Supposedly, the Packers have a treat in store for Davidson. But as Coach Vince Lombardi of the Packers said:

"My father had a mustache, and I haven't licked him yet."

LOMBARDI HINTS HE WILL RETIRE AS PACKERS' HEAD COACH

Difficulty Cited In Holding 2 Jobs

Lombardi Would Remain as General Manager —Packer Line-Ups Unchanged

By WILLIAM N. WALLACE

MIAMI BEACH, *Jan. 12*—While the athletes continued to work hard in practice—the Green Bay Packers at Fort Lauderdale and the Oakland Raiders at Boca Raton—the main Super Bowl scene shifted to Miami Beach today and the official headquarters at the Doral Hotel.

It was here that Vince Lombardi hinted broadly at a news conference in late afternoon that Sunday's game at the Orange Bowl might well be his last as coach of the Packers. He would stay on in Green Bay as general manager, a post he also holds now. "I haven't decided," he said. "I really have not. I do know that in pro football today it is almost impossible to be a coach and a general manager and to do a good job at both."

Lombardi has been telling friends privately for several weeks that he is giving serious consideration to ending a 30-year coaching career. He is 54 years old.

The Green Bay leader said that his line-ups would remain unchanged, which meant that Chuck Mercein and Donny Anderson would be the starting running backs, with Ben Wilson and Travis Williams in reserve.

Linebacker in Army

One injured Packer, Jim Grabowski, the fullback, will not play and another might not show up for the game. Jim Flanigan, the rookie linebacker, is in the Army in Missouri. "He may not get here," said Lombardi.

Pete Rozelle, the commissioner of pro football, also answered inquiries at an earlier conference. He said that Columbia Broadcasting System officials had indicated a television audience of 50 million was expected to watch the game, the largest ever for a sports event televised over one network.

Last year's Super Bowl event was televised by both C.B.S. and the National Broadcasting Company.

Rozelle also spoke of player unions and alleged television saturation. The commissioner said he had no objection to the two league players' associations declaring themselves to be labor unions, as they did this week, provided their leadership was responsible, their goals realistic and that they truly represented all the players.

Views on Television

Rozelle said he was against the continuation of televised double-headers, but that he and the club owners had been powerless to curb the networks. He did say that he never believed pro football could return to the complete blackout policy of having no game televised locally on the afternoon that a team was playing at home.

At an even earlier conference John Rauch, the quiet, careful Oakland coach, said: "I hope we don't get blown out of the park. We're basically a defensive team. Our defense can do a great job against the Packers but we still have to get points on the score board."

The Packers similarly have a defense more dominant than their offense.

Rauch's comment was a continuation of the Raiders' policy this week to demean themselves in public statements, perhaps in an attempt to make the Packers overconfident.

An informal poll of athletes from other teams, taken at the pro football players' golf tournament at nearby Hollywood, indicated 30 of 36 favored the Packers to win. Said Joe Namath of the Jets: "Green Bay is just better all around. They are one of football's great teams, probably the greatest." Added Tucker Frederickson of the Giants: "I've got to go with my boys—Green Bay. Say 28–14. The Packers are too strong on defense."

In betting circles the Packers remained 14-point favorites.

An insight into how Lombardi operates his team came in a reply to a question about the identity of the players on the club's special teams, the kickoff and punt teams. Said Lombardi with a big smile: "I really don't pay much attention to those teams. I have coaches to do that. All I know is that they'll have the men out there to do the job."

Sunday's game may be played in warm temperatures, possibly 100 degrees warmer than the N.F.L. championship contest in Green Bay Dec. 31 when it was minus 13.

Would this make a difference to the Packers? "No," said Lombardi. "Weather is all in the mind."

Sports of The Times

Our Crowd

By ROBERT LIPSYTE

MIAMI BEACH, *Jan. 12*—The sun hides behind clouds, bathing the sky and water in pale silvery daylight. Flesh reddens slowly, and the aprons of the pools are desolate. In a darkened motel room in Boca Raton, three large young men lie quietly in the air-conditioned cool and watch women wring their hands on afternoon television. Dan Conners, blond and handsome, shifts on his bed and says, "Seek and destroy, how's that for a slogan? It's almost as bad as run for daylight."

Bill Budness, a reserve linebacker, says, "the whole world is N.F.L. orientated."

"Right," says Conners. "Everyone knows about the Minnesota Vikings. Who knows the Oakland Raiders?"

"And if we win," says Ken Herock, a substitute tight end, "they'll say it's a fluke."

"To beat them," says Conners, "we'll have to play basic football, just stick our nose in there. You can't finesse the Green Bay Packers."

Budness makes himself comfortable on a chair and puts his loafered feet up on Conners's bed, near the linebacker's thick, scarred, shaven calves. "Does it ever bother us not being known? Sure, it has to bother us sometimes. We're professionals and we want recognition."

"But you have to understand that the Packers are considered the best in football, and if we beat them . . . ?" Budness's voice trails off. "You know, playing the Packers is like playing our fathers. I'm 24 years old and I grew up in Massachusetts. The Giants were my team. We got their games.

Fathers and Sons

"When I was 12, 13, 14, 15 and starting to play football, I was reading about those Packers. They were breaking in, they were underdogs, they were starting to get better and we grew up together. I never met a Packer personally, but it'll be just like playing our fathers."

A few miles to the south, in Fort Lauderdale, the spiritual fathers of the Oakland Raiders, and their opponents in Sunday's Super Bowl, were roaming through the lobby of their resort hotel, signing their ways through clusters of young autograph collectors. Most of them were older than the Oakland Raiders, and wealthier, and more secure. Last year in Los Angeles, they won the first Super Bowl and took claim to pre-eminence in a sport that is making a lot of men nouveau riche.

"Hey, ho, how are you Bobby-boy" says Fuzzy Thurston, ruining the back and the hand of a man he was meeting for the first time. Packer wives, a pretty and wholesome-looking group, floated through the dining room, and on the top floor, on a stone balcony, Vince Lombardi stood with his back to the ocean and sipped at a glass of scotch.

"A northeast wind," said Lombardi, his big chest thrusting through a white knit sports shirt which bore, over the left breast, a green laurel wreath and the letters V.L. "I think that's going to be bad. A northeast wind means three days of bad weather."

Lombardi, the genial host of this 5 P.M. cocktail hour, asked the guest, "You live near the ocean?"

"I live in New York."

"Waal, where do you think New York is?" snaps Lombardi. "That's right on the ocean."

"Not really," says the guest hastily, feeling skewered by the Lombardi smile and stare. "The buildings change the entire. . . . "

Chill Factor

"Naaah," says Lombardi, jovially.

The talk picks up as Lombardi reflects on the game ahead. Yes, he admits, he has a new psychological ploy ready to spring on his players, a simple one, in fact. The smile intimates that although it is simple, no one will ever guess it, "The history of the Packers is in the future, not in the past," says Lombardi enigmatically.

"That was some speech Jerry Kramer made about you after the game," a guest says, referring to Kramer's eloquent eulogy to his coach after the Packers beat Dallas for the league championship.

"Yes," said Lombardi, grinning, "it counteracted some of that bad publicity I've been getting lately."

"That was some game," said another guest. "So cold."

"Chill factor," says Lombardi, his neck swelling with good humor. "I thought that one up to keep ahead of the press."

"Four Dallas Cowboys got frostbite," said a guest, shivering in the northeast wind despite a jacket. "I read once that troops who were motivated and well conditioned didn't suffer frostbite as often as less motivated troops."

"Same for football players," said Lombardi, proudly. "Well conditioned and well motivated football players suffer less injuries."

"What about Ray Nitschke, he got frostbite," said the man from New York, eagerly.

"No, no, no," snapped Lombardi. "Just a blister, it was only a blister. That's all it was, a blister."

Packers Favored To Down Raiders for Title Today

By WILLIAM N. WALLACE

MIAMI, *Jan. 13*—Because of the drama that pro football built up in the last month over millions of television sets on Sunday afternoons, it would be fitting if tomorrow's Super Bowl game between the Green Bay Packers of the National Football League and the Oakland Raiders of the American were close, hard-fought and full of even more drama. However, the nature of the promotion—the powerful N.F.L. champion against the A.F.L.'s all but untested titleholder—does not guarantee any such proposition.

The Super Bowl, which began last year, is to date an over-dramatized, manufactured affair. It is a spinoff of the six-year war the two leagues fought, a war that ended in an economic peace 19 months ago. The Super Bowl action will begin at 3:05 P.M. in the Orange Bowl tomorrow before a capacity crowd of 75,546 who will have paid as high as $12 for a ticket. Television? Everywhere (Channel 2 in New York) except here in Miami.

The weather forecast is partly cloudy, temperatures in the mid-70's with no mention of rain. It will be up to the Oakland Raiders to make this into a memorable contest or just another football game. They are 14-point underdogs to the Packers, the dominant team in the sport, who made such a dent on football followers by losing to the Los Angeles Rams, 27–24, on Dec. 9; by beating the Rams for the Western Conference title of the N.F.L. on Dec. 23, and by edging the Dallas Cowboys in the last 13 seconds, 21–17, for the N.F.L. title in Green Bay on Dec. 31.

The Raiders won 13 of 14 games this season against A.F.L. opponents. This is a solid team stressing defense and it is better prepared to take on the Packers than were the Kansas City Chiefs in last year's Super Bowl. Why? Because the Raiders make very few mistakes.

A physical problem on the team was exposed here today when it was announced that Carleton Oats would have to start at right tackle on defense rather than Tom Keating whose sore ankle failed to heal completely this week. Keating is the Raiders' best pass rusher and may be their only one. Oats, a third year pro, weighs only 235 pounds and thus gives 20 pounds away to Gale Gillingham, the Packers' left guard opposite him.

Keating will try to play. The Raiders have only one other spare defensive lineman and he hardly counts. He is Richard Sligh, an unused rookie who is 7 feet tall and weighs 300 pounds.

However, the Oakland cause is far from hopeless. In Daryle Lamonica the Raiders have a fine quarterback who can throw the long pass. Since pass receivers and defenders have never played against one another before and have no feel for one another, the receivers should have an edge in the beginning. At least that is what Willie Wood says and he is the Packers' all-pro free safetyman. If Lamonica can strike early for a score; if the Raider defense can hold up against the Packers' offense, which certainly can have its problems, then the game might prove to be a most interesting one.

Mark of Great Team

The Raiders resolved another unsettled personnel problem today. Howie Williams, who four years ago was a Packer himself, was named to be the strong safetyman over injured Rodger Bird and Warren Powers the free safetyman. Dave Grayson will relieve Powers.

Williams had a good comment regarding the game. "We think the Packers are a great team," he said. "We are not awed though. You cannot expect to win if you're awed by somebody. Perhaps the biggest factor is they hate to lose. They win when they're down and out. That's the mark of a great team."

The Packer line-up remains all but unchanged. Ken Bowman, a seasoned hand, will be the center rather than Bob Hyland, a rookie. Donnie Anderson and Chuck Mercein are to be the starting running backs.

There are two interesting matchups in the lines. Big Ben Davidson, the Oakland right end on defense who was briefly a Packer as a rookie in 1961, is matched against Bob Skoronski, a Packer since 1956.

The Green Bay team enjoys knocking off the opponents' wise guy and Davidson is the Raider wise guy although he and all his teammates have been most discreet in interviews this week. "Let sleeping Packers lie," explained Dan Conners, the middle linebacker.

The other matchup of interest will be Henry Jordan, an 11-year pro and the Green Bay right tackle on defense, against Gene Upshaw, the Raiders' rookie left guard. Upshaw is acclaimed the finest new offensive lineman in his league, while Jordan rates as the quickest tackle in his league.

Search for Weakness

The pass matchups are difficult to assess because of no previous exposure. Generally, the Packers like to search for a weakness and they found one a year ago in Willie Mitchell, the Kansas City cornerback, as they beat the Chiefs, 35–10.

This time it might be Kent McCloughan, the left cornerback who must cover Carroll Dale, the Packer flanker. McCloughan has trouble with good deep receivers like Don Maynard of the Jets and Dale is a good deep receiver. Since Bart Starr, the Green Bay quarterback, seems unlikely to be bothered by the Raider pass-rush, McCloughan will be under pressure.

An interesting if unlikely sidelight concerns the possible use of reserve quarterbacks. Both are old men and former teammates, 36-year-old Zeke Bratkowski for Green Bay and 40-year-old George Blanda for Oakland, and their combined pro experience totals 30 years. They were together on the Chicago Bears in 1954, 1956 and 1957.

The Raiders have played one N.F.L. team and in that sense they are better off than Kansas City a year before. The original Super Bowl game in Los Angeles was the first matching of an A.F.L. and an N.F.L. team and the Chiefs did not know what to expect.

Oakland last summer lost to the San Francisco 49ers of the N.F.L., 13–10, in a preseason game. "We lost it on our own mistakes," explained Conners, the middle linebacker. "But we felt good about it. We felt we were better than they were, and they are not so far behind the Packers. Green Bay beat them by only 13–0 in the regular season."

Then there is the football. When the Oakland Raiders are on offense the American League regulation ball will be used and the N.F.L. regulation ball will be used when Green Bay attacks. The A.F.L. ball is slightly—very slightly—thinner and more tapered on the ends than the fatter N.F.L. ball and thus is better for passing. These distinctions are not likely to have much effect on the outcome of the game. The blocking and tackling will.

'Super' Players Talk a Good Game
Packers Respect Raider Defense

FORT LAUDERDALE, FLA., *Jan. 13*—What the Green Bay Packers are saying before tomorrow's Super Bowl football game against the Oakland Raiders at Miami:

Boyd Dowler, flanker: "I believe that Oakland's defense might be a little better conceived than Kansas City's in last year's Super Bowl. For instance, the Oakland linebackers give their defensive backs more help against the pass. I know Oakland's cornerbacks are better than Kansas City's."

Max McGee, reserve split end: "The Oakland defensive backs, as a group, are better than Kansas City's."

Zeke Bratkowski, reserve quarterback: "I think a major problem for us is going to be the Oakland linebacking group. They really are active. They do a fine job of holding up the receivers. They also help out the cornerbacks quite a bit."

Bart Starr, quarterback: "Oakland defensive films I have seen indicate great over-all quickness. They have quick tackles, linebackers and backs, and they seem to work very well as an 11-man unit."

Carroll Dale, split end: "Their cornerbacks are mighty quick. Oakland seems to mix things pretty well on defense—sometimes man for man, sometimes combination, sometimes tight and sometimes loose."

Willie Wood, free safety: "The Oakland receivers rely on moves rather than speed. They don't have a blazer like Bob Hayes, Homer Jones or Pat Studstill, but they run good patterns and they are very quick."

Bob Skoronski, offensive tackle: "Ben Davidson may be the strongest opponent I've ever faced. He reminds me of Doug Atkins a bit in the way he tries to overpower his man. Oakland moves around a lot and tries to confuse you. I've seen films where they actually force offensive linemen into blowing assignments because the blocker cannot find the right jersey number where he figures it should be."

Lionel Aldridge, defensive end: "I'll be against Bob Svihus, and from the films he looks to have good quickness and strength."

Chuck Mercein, fullback who was released earlier in the season by the New York Giants: "Anyone who gets a chance to play with the Packers is fortunate, and no one in his right mind could expect the good fortune I've had this season. I was delightfully surprised at the acceptance I received immediately from the Packers. This team, as you have heard a thousand times, has tremendous unity."

Willie Davis, defensive end: "I guess this season will be remembered as the one when we won when we had to. I guess a 9–4–1 record isn't great, but we had it when we needed it."

Marv Fleming, tight end: "It's a mark of the maturity and poise of this team that our dressing room is relatively quiet after a victory. I just can't imagine us throwing Coach Lombardi into the shower or pouring something over his head."

Oakland Pinpoints Foe's Strengths

BOCA RATON, FLA., *Jan. 13*—What the Oakland Raiders are saying before tomorrow's Super Bowl football game against the Green Bay Packers at Miami:

Dan Conners, middle linebacker: "We camouflage our defenses a lot by moving in and out, listening to audibles of quarterbacks and getting the rhythm down early. After a while, you can feel the cadence and get the tempo of the game. You have to have a feel of the timing. That presents a problem with Bart Starr because Starr is unrhythmic. They stagger a little bit like Kansas City, which makes it more difficult."

Kent McCloughan, cornerback: "Boyd Dowler and Carroll Dale, the Green Bay receivers, are bigger men than we're used to. I've never played against any that big. They have more the size of tight ends, but they have better speed. If our two outside defensive backs can stop their outside receivers, we have a chance."

Willie Brown, cornerback: "The biggest thing about the Green Bay receivers is the very good timing they have with the quarterback. Starr seems to throw on the break, he seems to know exactly when they're going to break."

Dan Birdwell, defensive tackle: "The Packers have been playing together so long that they don't have to hold, if one guy breaks down, another helps out. It's second nature to them. The man I play against, Jerry Kramer, is the finest guard I have ever seen outside, possibly Wayne Hawkins of our team."

Daryle Lamonica, quarterback: "I've been very much impressed with Green Bay's defenses. Whenever they tee off and come, they come as hard as anyone in pro football. It amazes me the penetration the front four gets. They can give a quarterback a lot of trouble. They just beat you with superior personnel."

Gene Upshaw, guard: "I just can't overpower Henry Jordan, I'll have to finesse him to some extent. He doesn't give you a lot to hit. He tries to keep you away from his body. If you get to his body, he's whipped."

Harry Schuh, offensive tackle: "Looking at the films, Willie Davis is awful quick. He is strong on the pass. The game has to be called real good to keep him honest. He plays the situation real well—what down, what yardage. Their front four relies on quickness, and when they run a stunt they run it to perfection. And their defense mixes the plays real well."

Pete Banaszak, running back: "Green Bay's execution is almost perfect every time. Their linebackers are as big as their defensive ends and tackles. They're solid, but they're not invincible."

Hewritt Dixon, running back: "Buffalo's front four reminds me of Green Bay's the most. Since we haven't faced Green Bay, I have no idea which side of their line we might have more success penetrating. It's going to be a touch-and-go thing."

Men Under the Center Are Under the Gun in Game Today

Lamonica Key to Hopes For a Victory by Raiders

Jan. 13, 1968—Daryle Lamonica, the 26-year-old quarterback for the Oakland Raiders, was drafted by the Green Bay Packers during his senior year at Notre Dame in 1962. The Buffalo Bills of the American Football League also drafted Lamonica and quickly signed him, "before we even had a chance to talk to him," according to Vince Lombardi, the Packer coach.

Lamonica comes from Fresno, Calif., and was recruited for Notre Dame by Joe Kuharich, then the coach for the Irish and now the boss of the Philadelphia Eagles.

Lamonica was a star on indifferent Notre Dame teams and for four seasons with Buffalo served as an understudy to Jackie Kemp. He was a "relief pitcher" for Kemp and on five occasions came into games to lead the Bills to victory in their championship season of 1964.

Likes Hunting, Fishing

Lamonica is big as quarterbacks go, 6 feet 3 inches, 218 pounds. He took his degree in business administration and is an avid hunter and fisherman.

Al Davis, the managing general partner of the Raiders so responsible for their success, swung a deal with Buffalo for Lamonica last winter. It was a major transaction, the Raiders giving up Tom Flores, their regular quarterback, and Art Powell, their leading receiver who was unhappy in Oakland.

The trade was somewhat of a risk for Davis because no one knew for sure how good Lamonica might be when established as a regular. He turned out to be very good and had a brilliant season, leading the American League in passing and being named the league's most valuable performer. He threw 30 touchdown passes, an outstanding achievement.

Proved Winning Element

He proved to be the element the Raiders, an otherwise strong club, needed to become champions and they swept through the season, losing only once—to the New York Jets. Then they crushed the Houston Oilers for the A.F.L. title.

Not only can Lamonica throw the long pass, he is noted also as a quarterback who will not hesitate to run with the football when receivers are covered.

He is a modest, quiet type, most polite and guarded this past week in his replies to questions.

Starr Is Held a Reflection Of Coach's Desire to Win

Bart Starr of the Green Bay Packers is said to be the perfect quarter-back for Vince Lombardi, the team's dominant coach. Starr, a mild, quiet man, takes Lombardi's orders and disciplines without question and on the field runs the Packer offense exactly in the way the great man wishes. He also wins and wins and wins.

Starr has been at his best in the big key pressure games and especially on the third down "must" plays. He has been called the best third-down quarterback in pro football.

Starr may not have the strongest passing arm in the game. He is not much of a runner although he will go, and he certainly cannot scramble up to Fran Tarkenton's standards. But he is a complete quarterback and a brilliant signal caller.

Packers Shift Tactics

Starr and Lombardi have been a duo since 1959. That was Lombardi's first year at Green Bay and Starr, who got there in 1956, began the season as a third-stringer. By mid-season he was the regular and has been ever since.

The Packers in the early days were mostly a running team but now they rely on the pass, and on Starr's arm more than on the run.

Starr, 34 years old, is from Montgomery, Ala., although he now lives in Green Bay within sight of Lambeau Field. This season was his 12th in pro football. At the University of Alabama he was just another quarterback and the Packers drafted him way down on the 17th round.

Starr has taken a lot of punishment from defensive linemen through the years but without a whimper. He missed five games in 1963 with a broken hand, for example.

On a team noted for its free spirits, Starr is a conservative family man who holds tremendous respect among his teammates. He is 6-feet 1-inch and weighs 200 pounds but looks smaller than that. This will be his second Super Bowl game and he was the hero of last year's victory when the Packers crushed the Kansas City Chiefs.

Sports of The Times

By ARTHUR DALEY

Not Like Samson

MIAMI, *Jan. 13*—A month after the Super Bowl game last year Jerry Mays had not quite emerged from his state of shock. Jerry is the captain of the Kansas City Chiefs, a 252-pound bundle of youthful energy and a smashing defensive end of considerable skills. But the Green Bay Packers had dissected the Chiefs with such shattering efficiency that they had won the postseason extravaganza, 35–10.

"It's impossible for me to believe," said the still bemused Jerry, "that those baldheaded old men on the Packers could have handled us with such ridiculous ease."

Now it is the turn of the Oakland Raiders to confront the elderly marvels from Green Bay. They will meet in the Super Bowl on the morrow for the championship of the universe, and the hard-faced men who establish the betting odds have indicated another afternoon of frustration for the American Football League winners. The Packers are two-touchdown favorites.

Yet expert observers insist that the Raiders are stronger and better balanced than the Chiefs were. Even inexperts have to be aware of the fact that each Packer is a year older. Furthermore, the Green Bay mercenaries have been so plagued by backfield injuries over the entire season that they have been hitting with reduced firepower. Vince Lombardi's former invincibles have been much more vincible this season.

The Road to Camelot

They even reached the uncharacteristic stage of permitting last-ditch rallies to snatch victory away from them. The Baltimore Colts achieved one seemingly impossible comeback and the Los Angeles Rams violated all laws of probability with an even more fantastic turnabout in the other.

"That Los Angeles loss was such a blow to our pride," Jerry Kramer, the old phrasemaker, was saying the other day, "that it steeled our resolve and made us a better football team. We reached a new peak against the Rams in the return match and climaxed it all with that thriller against the Cowboys."

That was when Kramer offered his now classic postgame remark, "We found Camelot." He even can explain how he hit on so felicitous a phrase.

"We had been in a lifetime situation," he said, "and this was the one shining moment." The glow came after Bart Starr's winning touchdown plunge with only 13 seconds to play.

It fuzzes up the comparative records of the Super Bowl rivals. The Raiders have won 13 games, the last 11 in a row. The Packers have taken nine, only the last two in a row. But they represented so sensational a pair against outstanding opposition that the two seemed to counterbalance the weight of the 11 or even of the 13.

Oakland is a young team. However, age on Green Bay is not measured by years but by the accumulated wisdom that experience alone can supply. Henry Jordan and Ray Nitschke may not have much hair, but they have more savvy than any bushy-haired Raider. They even have more than Ben Davidson, the monstrous defensive end with the reddish walrus mustache.

Davidson is one of Oakland's "Eleven Angry Men," the rousing Raider defensive platoon. He's the guy who broke Joe Namath's cheekbone when the Jets last visited the coast. I have a hunch that the Packers are going to comb Big Ben's mustache with their cleats and that this supposed tower of strength will be an object of primary concentration by the Green Bay attacking forces.

Lombardi insists that the Raiders present so tightly knit and so mobile a defensive unit that they have no weaknesses. But Starr will probe like a surgeon. He'll soon find the spot where he can start slicing. It could be Davidson.

In the Confusion

"To beat them," says Vince, "you have to beat the whole defense, not pick on one man. They don't stand and take the play. They jump around a lot and stunt more than most. They try to confuse you."

"We try to confuse everyone," said Dan Conners, the agile leader of the crew of Raider jumping jacks. He made his observation at a different time from Lombardi but the two statements still fit neatly together.

A year ago the Packers whipsawed the Kansas City cornerbacks to death. But the Raiders have two of the best in their league in Kent McCloughlan and Willie Brown. Neither is big but each is fast enough to help cover those deft Packer pass catchers.

However, Starr, the crafty marksman, has better targets than Daryle Lamonica, his less experienced opposite number. And Green Bay has the game's only true breakaway runner in the spectacular rookie, Travis Williams. He even could emerge as the decisive factor if he can turn loose his blinding bursts of speed.

Unconvinced that the American Football League has yet grown level with the Nationals, I pick the Packers to win. The score? It could be in the neighborhood of 35–16, which is a very nice neighborhood if you happen to be a fan from Green Bay.

Rival Coaches Vary in Temperament

Jan. 14, 1968—There are those in pro football with a sense of history who say that Vincent Lombardi of the Green Bay Packers is the finest coach the sport has ever known. The statistics would support this.

Lombardi arrived in Green Bay from the New York Giants in 1959 as coach and general manager. He had never before been a head coach, let alone a general manager. He took complete charge of a dismal situation and in his second season had a champion. Since 1960 the Packers have never finished lower than second, winning 76 per cent of their games. No other is close to this mark.

The Packers have won five National Football League championships since 1961, the last three in a row. That feat was without precedence.

Lombardi is a disciple of Earl Blaik, the former great Army coach under whom he worked for five years, 1948–53. Blaik in turn was a believer in the Gen. Douglas McArthur credo—"There is no substitute for victory." Lombardi agrees with this premise wholeheartedly.

So do his players or else they do not hang around Green Bay for very long. The coach sets high standards for performance and no one demands more of his athletes. They respond to these demands and an affection for the coach seems to have grown up among them, although everyone still fears his occasional rages.

Lombardi appears to have mellowed this last season. His wife, Marie, says she has never known him to be more calm and relaxed.

His relations with the press, often stormy in the past, reflect this attitude.

His Fordham classmates (1937) have long maintained this was a charming, lovable man and only lately have these characteristics become evident to nonclassmates. "He has finally learned that, because of his team, he belongs to the public," explains an old friend.

Following Green Bay's victory over Dallas for the N.F.L. title on Dec. 31, Jerry Kramer, the Packer guard, gave an eloquent speech of praise about his coach over national television. Lombardi was shown a taped rerun some days later. He broke down and cried—briefly.

John Rauch, the head coach of the Oakland Raiders, assumed that position in 1966 after Al Davis, the prior coach, had moved up to become the commissioner of the American Football League.

Rauch, who is 38 years old, before that had been an assistant coach for 14 seasons, all but three of them in the college ranks. He joined the Oakland organization in 1963.

Unlike Vince Lombardi of the Packers, Rauch was a pro player himself. He had three seasons in the National Football League and was the reserve quarterback behind Bobby Layne on a forgotten team, the New York Bulldogs of 1949. In college, the University of Georgia, Rauch was a star and an all-American in his senior year, 1948.

He was later a college coach at Tulane, Florida, Georgia and Army. Lombardi, too, was an assistant at West Point but a decade earlier.

Rauch says that the strongest influences on his vocation were Wally Butts, the former Georgia coach, and Davis.

Rauch is definitely under the shadow of Davis, now the managing general partner of the Raiders and the man who makes their trades. But Davis does not interfere with the coaching and the arrangement seems to work well.

Rauch has none of the Davis flare and his personality is a bland one compared to that of his boss. His team is Davis's team, especially at the quarterback position. Daryle Lamonica came to Oakland in a trade engineered by Davis and his arrival made a good team into a champion. In Rauch's first season, 1966, his team won eight games, lost five and tied one.

Rauch is patient and hides whatever temper he may have. Said Lamonica, "Heavens knows I made every mistake in the book when I got to Oakland. But the coach was patient with me and I appreciated that."

Rauch's philosophy of football, hardly an original one, he recently expressed this way, "This game is not a game of individuals, although individual effort may count on a single play."

Rauch and his wife Jane have two children, Nancy, 18 years old, and John Jr., 15. The Rauchs live in San Leandro, Calif.

How Rival Teams in Super Bowl Match Up, 1968

OAKLAND ON OFFENSE

No.	Player	Ht.	Wt.	Pos.
89	Bill Miller	6-0	190	SE
76	Bob Svihus	6-4	245	LT
63	Gene Upshaw	6-5	255	LG
00	Jim Otto	6-2	248	C
65	Wayne Hawkins	6-0	240	RG
79	Harry Schuh	6-2	260	RT
33	Billy Cannon	6-1	215	TE
3	Daryle Lamonica	6-3	215	QB
35	Hewitt Dixon	6-1	230	FB
40	Pete Banaszak	5-11	200	HB
25	Fred Biletnikoff	6-1	190	FL

GREEN BAY ON DEFENSE

No.	Player	Ht.	Wt.	Pos.
21	Bob Jeter	6-1	205	RCB
82	Lionel Aldridge	6-4	245	RE
74	Henry Jordan	6-3	250	RT
66	Ray Nitschke	6-3	240	MLB
77	Ron Kostelnik	6-4	260	LT
87	Willie Davis	6-3	245	LE
40	Tom Brown	6-1	190	SS
24	Willie Wood	5-10	190	FS
89	Dave Robinson	6-3	240	LLB
60	Lee Roy Caffey	6-3	250	RLB
26	Herb Adderley	6-0	200	LCB

OAKLAND ON DEFENSE

No.	Player	Ht.	Wt.	Pos.
24	Willie Brown	6-1	205	RCB
83	Ben Davidson	6-7	275	RE
85	Carleton Oats	6-2	235	RT
55	Dan Conners	6-1	230	MLB
53	Dan Birdwell	6-4	250	LT
77	Ike Lassiter	6-5	270	LE
20	Warren Powers	6-0	190	SS
29	Howie Williams	6-1	190	FS
42	Bill Laskey	6-3	235	LLB
34	Gus Otto	6-2	220	RLB
47	Kent McCloughan	6-1	190	LCB

GREEN BAY ON OFFENSE

No.	Player	Ht.	Wt.	Pos.
86	Boyd Dowler	6-5	225	SE
76	Bob Skoronski	6-3	245	LT
68	Gale Gillingham	6-3	255	LG
57	Ken Bowman	6-3	230	C
64	Jerry Kramer	6-3	245	RG
75	Forrest Gregg	6-4	250	RT
81	Marv Fleming	6-4	235	TE
15	Bart Starr	6-1	190	QB
30	Chuck Mercein	6-3	230	FB
44	Donny Anderson	6-3	210	HB
84	Carroll Dale	6-2	200	FL

OAKLAND SUBSTITUTES

No.	Player	Ht.	Wt.	Pos.
11	Mike Eischeid	6-0	190	P
16	George Blanda	6-3	215	K-QB
21	Rodger Bird	5-11	195	SS
22	Larry Todd	6-1	185	HB
23	Rod Sherman	6-0	190	FL
30	Roger Hagberg	6-1	215	FB
45	Dave Grayson	5-10	185	FS
48	Bill Budness	6-2	215	MLB
50	Duane Benson	6-2	215	RLB
52	John Williamson	6-2	220	LLB
62	Bob Kruse	6-2	250	C-G
70	Jim Harvey	6-5	245	G
73	Richard Sligh	7-0	300	DT
74	Tom Keating	6-2	250	RT
78	Dan Archer	6-5	245	G-T
81	Warren Wells	6-1	190	SE
84	Ken Herock	6-2	230	SE
88	Dave Kocourek	6-5	240	TE

GREEN BAY SUBSTITUTES

No.	Player	Ht.	Wt.	Pos.
12	Zeke Bratkowski	6-3	210	QB
13	Don Horn	6-2	195	QB
23	Travis Williams	6-1	210	HB
33	Jim Grabowski	6-2	220	FB
34	Don Chandler	6-2	210	K-P
36	Ben Wilson	6-0	225	FB
43	Doug Hart	6-0	190	DB
45	John Rowser	6-1	180	DB
50	Bob Hyland	6-5	250	C
55	Jim Flanigan	6-3	240	LB
56	Tommy Crutcher	6-3	230	LB
63	Fred Thurston	6-1	245	G
72	Steve Wright	6-6	250	T
73	Jim Weatherwax	6-7	260	DT
78	Bob Brown	6-5	260	DE
80	Bob Long	6-3	205	FL
83	Allen Brown	6-5	235	TE
85	Max McGee	6-3	210	SE
88	Dick Capp	6-3	235	LB

Super Bowl Depth Charts

Green Bay Packers

Offensive Ends—Dowler, Dale, Fleming, McGee, Long.
Defensive Ends—Davis, Aldridge, B. Brown.
Offensive Tackles—Skoronski, Gregg, Wright.
Defensive Tackles—Kostelnik, Jordan, Weatherwax.
Guards—Gillingham, Kramer, Thurston.
Centers—Bowman, Hyland.
Linebackers—Nitschke, Robinson, Caffey, Crutcher, Capp.
Quarterbacks—Starr, Bratkowski, Horn.
Running Backs—Anderson, Mercein, Wilson, Williams.
Defensive Backs—Adderley, Jeter, T. Brown, Wood, Rowser, Hart.
Kicker—Chandler.

Oakland Raiders

Offensive Ends—Miller, Biletnikoff, Cannon, Wells, Sherman, Kocourek, Herock.
Defensive Ends—Lassiter, Davidson.
Offensive Tackles—Svihus, Schuh, Archer.
Defensive Tackles—Birdwell, Oats, Keating, Slight.
Guards—Upshaw, Hawkins, Harvey.
Centers—J. Otto, Kruse.
Linebackers—Conners, Laskey, G. Otto, Williamson, Budness, Benson.
Quarterbacks—Lamonica, Blanda.
Running Backs—Banaszak, Dixon, Todd, Hagberg.
Defensive Backs—McCloughan, W. Brown, Bird, Grayson, Williams, Powers.
Kicker—Eischeid.

Super Bowl Comparison, 1968

OFFENSE

	Raiders	Packers
Total Points	468	332
First Downs	250	243
Rushing.	79	115
Passing	154	112
Penalties	17	16
Net Yds. Gained . .	5,115	4,279
Rushing.	1,928	1,915
Passing	3,187	2,364
Passes Attempted . .	464	331
Completed	236	182
Had Intercepted .	23	27
Fumbles Lost	13	10
Yds. Penalized. . . .	768	531
Times Tackled		
Att. to Pass	40	41
Yds. Lost Att.		
to Pass.	353	394

DEFENSE

	Raiders	Packers
Opponents' Points .	233	209
Opponents'		
First Downs	182	183
Rushing.	80	98
Passing.	83	78
Penalties	19	7
Opponents'		
Net Yards	3,265	3,300
Rushing.	1,100	1,923
Passing.	2,165	1,377
Opponents'		
Passes Att.	454	337
Completed	189	155
Had Intercepted .	30	26
Opponents'		
Fumbles Recov . .	14	10
Times Opponents'		
Dropped Passing .	67	29
Yds. Opponents'		
Lost Att. to Pass .	666	267

INDIVIDUAL PASSING

Oakland	Att.	Comp.	Yds.	Int.
Lamonica . .	425	220	3,227	20
Blanda . . .	38	15	285	3
Green Bay				
Starr	210	115	1,823	17
Bratkowski .	94	53	724	9

INDIVIDUAL RUSHING

Oakland	Att.	Yds.	Avg.
Dixon.	153	559	3.7
Banaszak	68	376	5.5
Hagberg	44	146	3.3
Green Bay			
Wilson	103	453	4.4
Anderson	97	402	4.1
Williams	35	188	5.4
Mercein	14	56	4.0

INDIVIDUAL RECEIVING

Oakland	No.	Yds.	TDs
Dixon.	39	563	2
Biletnikoff	40	875	5
Miller.	38	537	6
Cannon.	32	629	10
Banaszak.	16	192	1
Green Bay			
Dowler.	54	836	4
Dale.	35	738	5
Anderson	22	331	3

INTERCEPTIONS

Oakland	No.	Yds.	TDs
Brown	7	33	1
Powers	6	154	2
Williams	4	96	0
Grayson	4	63	0
Green Bay			
Jeter	8	78	0
Wood.	4	60	0
Adderley.	4	16	1
Robinson	4	16	0

SCORING

Oakland	TDs	EP	FG	Pts
Blanda	0	56	20	116
Cannon	10	0	0	60
Dixon	7	0	0	42
Miller.	6	0	0	36
Wells	6	0	0	36
Biletnikoff	5	0	0	30
Green Bay				
Chandler.	0	39	19	96
Anderson	9	0	0	54
Williams	6	0	0	36
Dale.	5	0	0	30
Dowler.	4	0	0	24

Records of the Teams

GREEN BAY		OAKLAND	
17—Detroit	17	51—Denver	0
13—Chicago	10	35—Boston	7
23—Atlanta	0	23—Kansas City	21
27—Detroit	17	14—New York	27
7—Minnesota	10	24—Buffalo	20
48—New York	21	48—Boston	14
31—St. Louis	23	51—San Diego	10
10—Baltimore	13	21—Denver	17
55—Cleveland	7	31—Miami	17
13—San Francisco	0	44—Kansas City	22
17—Chicago	13	41—San Diego	21
30—Minnesota	27	19—Houston	7
24—Los Angeles	27	38—New York	29
17—Pittsburgh	24	28—Buffalo	21
*28—Los Angeles	7	‡40—Houston	7
†21—Dallas	17		
381	233	508	230

*N.F.L. Western Conference Title　　　　‡ A.F.L. Championship
†N.F.L. Championship

Green Bay Beats Oakland, 33 to 14, In The Super Bowl

Chandler of Packers Kicks 4 Field Goals— Adderley Tallies on Interception

75,546 At Game In Miami

Starr Throws for 62-Yard Score—Lamonica Passes for 2 Raider Touchdowns

By WILLIAM N. WALLACE

MIAMI, *Jan. 14*—The Green Bay Packers, a splendid collection of football players who have made a habit of winning the big games, won another one today and enriched themselves by $15,000 each.

The Packers, champions of the National Football League, trounced the Oakland Raiders of the American League, 33–14, before a crowd of 75,546 in the Orange Bowl and thus exceeded expectations. They had been favored by 14 points.

This was the Super Bowl game, watched by a television audience estimated at 50 million, but only in the first half did it approach being a

Donny Anderson of the Green Bay Packers is about to score a touchdown after a 2-yard run as his team moved to its second straight Super Bowl victory.

super game. The Packers led at half-time, 16–7, and the Raiders had made the mid-afternoon interesting by challenging Green Bay on both offense and defense.

Game Slips Away

But the game slipped away from the American League team in the second half much as it did for Kansas City in the first Super Bowl contest a year ago in Los Angeles when Green Bay routed the Chiefs in the last two periods and went on to win, 35–10.

Although he kicked four field goals, Don Chandler of the Packers was put into position to swing his right leg for $15,000 through the more important contributions of several of his teammates. These were Bart Starr, the impeccable quarterback; Gale Gillingham, the guard who neutralized Tom Keating, the outstanding Oakland tackle; plus Herb Adderley, Ron Kostelnik and Ray Nitschke of the magnificent defensive unit. Chandler's field goals, which ranged in length from 20 to 43 yards, came at the end of Green Bay drives in the first, second and third periods. These 3-point kicks gave the Packers leads of 3–0, 6–0, 16–7 just before half-time, and 26–7.

Adderley, the cornerback, stepped into a weak pass thrown by Daryle Lamonica toward Fred Biletnikoff, intercepted and streaked 60 yards for a touchdown. That was the final Packer score and along the way Adderley was aided by two tremendous blocks by Henry Jordan and Kostelnik.

Lamonica was a producer for Oakland, which had a limited offense, on two touchdown passes. He passed twice for 23 yards to Bill Miller, a slot back lined up on the strong side inside of Biletnikoff. This somewhat unorthodox offensive formation was the only Oakland weapon that bothered the Packers.

The Super Bowl prize money was set at $15,000 for each of the winners and $7,500 for each of the losers. Keating, one of the losers, certainly warranted every dollar. Playing with a sprained ankle, this small-sized (247 pounds) defensive tackle from Michigan was the only Raider to put pressure on Starr, who was Mr. Cool as usual.

Starr Sprains Thumb

Starr completed 13 of 24 passes for 202 yards and one touchdown (62 yards to Boyd Dowler in the second period) before leaving the game in the last quarter because of a sprained thumb. Starr also made good on six of 11 third-down plays while Lamonica gained the first down only four times on nine third-down situations.

Lamonica found his receivers covered most of the time and completed 15 of 34 attempts. He did enjoy good pass protection until late in the game, when Kostelnik and Willie Davis of Green Bay began to bore into him through tiring linemen.

The Oakland defense, as with Green Bay the strongest half of the team, put up a stout fight. But the Packers nibbled away at this defense, as is their custom, and put the points on the scoreboard in every quarter. The Packers' only big offensive play was the strike by Starr to Dowler that made the score 13–0 in the second period. Dowler, who is 6 feet 5 inches tall, ran to the inside and past Kent McCloughan, the covering cornerback. Dowler was beyond the last man when he caught the ball.

Outcome Sealed Early

Oakland then courageously mounted a quick two-minute touchdown drive of 78 yards in nine plays. Four plays were completed passes, two to Miller.

The Raiders did not score again until almost six minutes had passed in the fourth quarter and Green Bay was ahead, 33–7. The outcome had by then been sealed by the wealthy minions of Coach Vincent Lombardi.

One of the troubles of Lamonica and his coach, John Rauch, was their insistence in trying to run around Green Bay flanks. No teams do this successfully and Nitschke, the ferocious middle linebacker, wound up tackling Hewritt Dixon, the Raider fullback, for no gain.

Starr moved his plays around the Oakland defense and found no glaring weakness, but he did find several little inadequacies. It was a typical, thorough Packer job and if this was Lombardi's last game as a coach, he went out with a good one to remember.

Green Bay Packers (33)

Ends—Dowler, Dale, Fleming, Davis, Aldridge, Long, McGee, Capp, B. Brown.
Tackles—Skoronski, Gregg, Kostelnik, Jordan, Weatherwax.
Guards—Gillingham, Kramer, Thurston.
Centers—Hyland, Bowman.
Linebackers—Robinson, Nitschke, Caffey, Crutcher, Flanigan.
Quarterbacks—Starr, Bratkowski.
Offensive Backs—Anderson, Wilson, Williams, Mercein.
Defensive Backs—Adderley, Jeter, T. Brown, Wood, Rowser, Hart.
Kicker—Chandler.

Oakland Raiders (14)

Ends—Miller, Biletnikoff, Cannon, Lassiter, Davidson, Wells, Kocourek, Herock, Oats.
Tackles—Svihus, Schuh, Birdwell, Keating, Kruse, Archer, Sligh.
Guards—Upshaw, Hawkins, Harvey.
Center—J. Otto.
Linebackers—Laskey, Conners, G. Otto, Williamson, Budness, Benson.
Quarterback—Lamonica.
Offensive Backs—Banaszak, Dixon, Todd, Hagberg.
Defensive Backs—McCloughan, W. Brown, Grayson, Powers, Williams, Bird.
Kickers—Blanda, Eischeid.

Green Bay Packers .... 3 13 10 7—33
Oakland Raiders...................................... 0   7   0 7—14

  G.B.—FG, Chandler, 39.
  G.B.—FG, Chandler, 20.
  G.B.—Dowler, 62, pass from Starr (Chandler, kick).
  Oak.—Miller, 23, pass from Lamonica (Blanda, kick).
  G.B.—FG, Chandler, 43.
  G.B.—Anderson, 2, run (Chandler, kick).
  G.B.—FG, Chandler, 31.
  G.B.—Adderley, 60, return of interception (Chandler, kick).
  Oak.—Miller, 23, pass from Lamonica (Blanda, kick).

Individual Statistics

RUSHES—G.B.: Wilson, 17 for 65 yards; Anderson, 14 for 48; Williams, 8 for 36; Starr, 1 for 14; Mercein, 1 for 0. Oak.: Dixon, 12 for 52; Todd, 2 for 37; Banaszak, 6 for 16.

PASSES—G.B.: Starr, 13 of 24 for 202 yards. Oak.: Lamonica, 15 of 34 for 208.

RECEPTIONS—G.B.: Dale, 4 for 43 yards; Fleming, 4 for 35; Anderson, 2 for 18; Dowler, 2 for 71; McGee, 1 for 35. Oak.: Miller, 5 for 84; Biletnikoff, 2 for 10; Banaszak, 4 for 69; Cannon, 2 for 25; Dixon, 1 for 3; Wells, 1 for 17.

Statistics of the Game

	Packers	Raiders		Packers	Raiders
First downs	19	16	Interceptions by	1	0
Rushing yardage	163	105	Punts	6-39	6-44
Passing yardage	162	186	Fumbles lost	0	2
Return yardage	144	139	Yards penalized	12	31
Passes	13-24	15-34			

LOMBARDI SHUNS QUESTIONS ON RETIREMENT AFTER PACKERS WIN BIG ONE AGAIN

Future Will Get 'Real Hard Look'

Too Early for Any Decision, Lombardi Says— Blitzing Of Raiders Unexpected

By JAMES TUITE

MIAMI, *Jan. 14*—Green Bay's super-happy fans carried Vince Lombardi off the field today, caring not that he was surly and burly, but only that their football team had won the big one.

The 54-year-old martinet of the National Football League champions smiled the expected smile and said the expected things—without really saying anything.

Did he plan to retire, now that the American Football League foes were ground into the dust of the Orange Bowl?

"It's much too early to do anything like that. I'm going to give Vince Lombardi a real hard look."

More Blitzing Than Expected

Did Oakland provide any surprises on defense?

"They blitzed more than we expected, but I wouldn't say I was surprised. I've been in this business too long for anything to surprise me."

The Packer dressing room was decorous with the composure of professional champions.

Ray Nitschke, the defensive star of the club, walked down the line of benches, hugging and kissing his teammates. The amenities of victory over, he plopped 240 linebacking-pounds on the hard wooden bench and casually inspected muscular legs sore with welts. Dried blood caked over his knee bandages.

"I knew we were going to win the first time we got the ball," he said.

But the glory belongs to the touchdown-makers and Bart Starr was the center of attention. His thin, sandy hair was moist over a serious face. Packer players are as methodical as a locomotive, and Starr was the engineer on this trip.

"We made as few mistakes as possible," he drawled with the aplomb of a surgeon explaining his latest heart transplant.

"The game was very important to me," he continued. "I felt I was

Boyd Dowler, one of Green Bay's key receivers, scampers past Oakland defenders with a Bart Starr bomb on his way to a 62-yard touchdown.

representing every quarterback in the National League in this game, just as the Raiders were representing every player in their league. You play for everybody in this kind of a game."

No touchdown-maker but the heaviest contributor in points was Don Chandler, the former New York Giant who contributed 15 points via four field goals and three extra points.

The baldish Oklahoman grinned when someone suggested that his line-drive field goal that bounced off the crossbar was not "a work of art."

"I don't give a damn what they look like," he said, "as long as they go over."

Did he, at age 34, plan to retire?

"No sir, I've got a few good years yet."

Herb Adderley was in a happy mood, as befitted a Packer who had scooted 60 yards with a fourth-period interception.

Reward Important, Not Site

Did you prefer playing in Miami over playing in Los Angeles, where the last Super Bowl was held, someone asked.

"For $15,000," he said, like a real pro, "I'd play anywhere."

Adderley dissected his grandstand play.

"Oakland was using a slot formation all day, so I had been covering

Fred Biletnikoff all the way. On this play, he made a turn-in pattern, but I managed to get up quickly inside of him, went for the ball and picked it off cleanly."

Adderley also revealed that he had played most of the early part of the season with an arm injury. He said that he had suffered a muscle separation against the Minnesota Vikings.

He continued to play despite what he called several "bad" games early in the season. He thought that the last three games were his best.

The Packers all said the proper things, about how well the Raiders had played, and all that. With visions of $15,000 checks for an afternoon of work, the words came out easily.

McGee Catches One Pass In Final Game of Career

MIAMI, *Jan. 14 (AP)*—Max McGee closed out his 12-year National Football League career in typical fashion today as the Green Bay Packers whipped Oakland.

With a third and one situation on the Green Bay 40, Bart Starr flipped a third-down pass to McGee, who raced to the Oakland 25. The play set up a field goal. It was the only pass he caught during his final game.

He probably wouldn't have been on the field if Boyd Dowler hadn't been hurt. "I really didn't expect to play," he said. "I kiddingly told Boyd to get hurt so I could catch a pass and darned if he didn't."

Man in the News: Kicker in Packer Deck

Don G. Chandler

Jan. 14, 1968—In producing 15 points on four field goals and three conversions for the Green Bay Packers in yesterday's 33–14 Super Bowl victory, Don G. Chandler continued to return the two favors that Vince Lombardi, the Packer coach, had done for him during his 12-season career as a professional football player. In the summer of 1956, when Chandler was a discouraged rookie with the New York Giants, Lombardi, then a Giant aide, talked him out of going home. In 1965, when Chandler was in disfavor with the Giants, Lombardi acquired him for the Packers.

"I owe my career to that man," Chandler said after the triumph over the Oakland Raiders. "I owe him everything."

Lombardi owes the Oklahoma rancher quite a bit, too. In three championship seasons, Chandler has provided a total of 261 points for the Packers. Unlike the soccer-style kickers who have infiltrated the pro leagues in recent years, the 33-year-old Chandler is a traditionalist. He uses a square-toed shoe. But, like all place-kicking specialists, he practices in obscurity.

"When the other players finish practice, that's when I start," he said, "because until then Bart is too busy."

His ball-holder is Bart Starr, the Packer quarterback.

Practice has made Chandler a solvent rancher who also dabbles in real estate and insurance to provide for his wife, Pat, their two daughters, 9 and 6, and 7-year-old son. Asked if he planned to tutor his son into becoming a place-kicker, he laughed and replied, "No, I'm going to buy him golf clubs."

Now a loosely muscled 215-pounder at 6 feet 2 inches, Chandler was born in Council Bluffs, Iowa, on Sept. 9, 1934 but he grew up in Tulsa, Okla., where he was graduated from Will Rogers High School. At the University of Florida, he was an outstanding halfback, but his punting ability attracted the pro scouts. He led the nation's major-college punters as a senior.

During his career with the Giants, he was a punting specialist for seven seasons. Following the retirement of Pat Summerall, the Giants' place-kicking duties also were assigned to Chandler.

Beginning in 1962, Chandler sat on the Giant bench with two right shoes close by—the square-toed place-kicking shoe, and the normal-type shoe used for punting. During the 1963 season, he led the N.F.L. in scoring with 106 points, including 18 field goals. Prior to the 1964 season, he disenchanted the Giant hierarchy when he requested permission to commute from Oklahoma.

"We're not going to have a part-time place-kicker," snapped Allie Sherman, the coach of the Giants.

Chandler, called Babe when with the Giants, had hoped to practice at home, then arrive on weekends. He quickly changed his mind and joined the Giants fulltime, but shortly after the season—a dismal one for the Giants—he was traded to the Packers for a third-round draft choice.

Although he says his middle initial "doesn't stand for anything," G. as in Good would seem to be symbolic.

Raiders Remain Calm In Defeat
Coach Rauch Lauds Rivals for Fine Team Effort

By FRANK LITSKY

MIAMI, *Jan. 14*—All last week, the Oakland Raiders had been spouting the party line, saying how good the Green Bay Packers were and how great an honor it would be just to be on the same field with them in the Super Bowl.

Today, after the Packers whipped the Raiders, 33–14, there was another party line, but this one totally unrehearsed.

In their steamy, freshly painted dressing room, the Raiders talked about what they had learned in combat against the Packers, and four points kept coming up in conversation—(1) Bart Starr's uncanny play selection, (2) the Packers' lateral pursuit on defense, (3) their experience and (4) their lack of mistakes.

The Raiders also felt that the Packers were mere mortals and could be defeated. And the Raiders felt they could defeat the Packers the next time they played.

Mistakes Hurt Oakland

When the Packers beat the Kansas City Chiefs a year ago in the first Super Bowl game, the Chiefs were stunned. The Raiders were not stunned today. They were calm and analytical. They were disappointed, but there were no tears and no one kicked a locker or threw a helmet in disgust.

"You're always disappointed when you lose," said Coach Johnny Rauch, as unemotional as ever. "It's tough in life to accept defeat, and we're not used to it. We made mistakes, like a breakdown in pass coverage that gave Boyd Dowler a touchdown and that fumble that gave them a field goal at the end of the first half. But that's why people win or lose.

"They have a fine blend of talent. They compensate for each other. Their linebackers can play looser because their front four is tougher to get around. Their secondary can take more chances on interceptions because they know their linebackers will help out."

Day for Learning

"It was a day of learning," said Daryle Lamonica, the Raider quarterback. "I learned an awful lot. I didn't have a great day, but I think we did better when I started rolling out in the second half. But we got untracked a little too late."

Rauch and Lamonica thought the Raiders would have greater success on sweeps. But the Packer linebackers were so quick and the over-all pursuit so good that the Raiders had to run inside.

"Maybe," said Jim Otto, the Raider center, "we should have run more right at them. One reason we had trouble on sweeps was that we could pull only one guard. One had to stay behind to block Henry Jordan because he was so fast."

"They had good offensive blocking," said Tom Keating, the Raider defensive tackle. "Good, but nothing to hold you in awe. But that execution was great. On paper, I don't think they are any better than us. But I wouldn't want to play Kansas City on paper, either."

Keating was a surprise starter. He had a pulled and inflamed Achilles tendon in the right foot.

"I was afraid to get a shot of Novocaine," he said, "because then I might have torn it and not even known it. But I bugged them until they let me start. I didn't see any sense sitting on the bench until someone else got hurt. My foot is sore as hell right now. It's really going to hurt when I take the tape off. That's why I'm drinking this Coke so slowly."

"We played below par," said Dan Birdwell, the Raiders' other defensive tackle. "If we played them every day of the week, we'd split. Jerry Kramer threw one good block at me all day. I told him when he did it."

"How good was their blocking?" said Ben Davidson, the Raider defensive end with the walrus-like handlebar mustache. "Well, you saw how big those holes were, didn't you? They were just big, quick and smart. But they're not as good as last year."

Davidson laughed a nervous laugh, as if the joke were on him. Then he rubbed a fresh purple welt on his left cheek. Where did it come from?

"Maybe," said the man who had been accused of being the American Football League's dirtiest player, "they're dirty players."

Davidson laughed again. The joke was still on him.

Sports of The Times

Let's Rack the Pack

By ROBERT LIPSYTE

MIAMI, *Jan. 14*—In the deep, dark, moist past, only a few weeks before the Chicago White Sox dumped the 1919 World Series, some burly youths in Green Bay, Wis., formed a football team and named it after a local meat packing company. Ten years later, in the year of the crash, the Green Bay Packers won their first championship. Thirty years after that, in a year that produced jet travel, Vincent Lombardi went to Green Bay, by now a nonprofit corporation owned by football fans. All this week, speaking cordially through tombstone teeth obviously hacked out for a larger graveyard, Lombardi intoned, "The history of the Packers is in the future, not in the past." It is the measure of Lombardi that only his teeth are really vulnerable to criticism.

Today, in a handsome, orange-trimmed ballpark called the Orange Bowl, the Packers defeated the Oakland Raiders, 33–14, for the championship of all football in a game that was only sporadically interesting. It was an anticlimactic game in the sense that the millions spent to televise the game, the thousands to promote it, and the enormous emotion and work spent preparing for it, were not rewarded by either sustained drama or even moments of great excitement. Days before, an Oakland Raider had said that playing the Packers would be like "playing our fathers." The boys from the Golden West were not quite ready yet.

Perhaps that should have been obvious early in the week. While Raider players were complaining mildly that no one knew their names, that dinners were held in Oakland and Raiders weren't invited, the Packers were pondering deeper problems, such as dressing room decorum. Said the tight end, Marv Fleming, "I just can't imagine us throwing Coach Lombardi in the shower or pouring something over his head."

From the beginning of today's game, when the Raiders were unable to move the ball one inch on their first three plays, there was that sense of superior Packer power, grown strong, but not fat, on history. They seemed to spring from the sun-dappled turf, yellow helmets ablaze, bringing down Raider runners like big wolves on a deer. They hit hard, and by the end of the first quarter there was sometimes the feeling that Oakland players were looking around.

One Play Ruins Raiders

At the end of that quarter, in the play that led to Don Chandler's second field goal and a 6–0 lead, Bart Starr, the physical extension of Lombardi's mind, destroyed the Raiders with a gesture of utter contempt. On the Raider 36-yard line, on a fourth down with 1 yard to go, Starr called a running play. Even if it had failed, the play would have snapped the Oakland mind. But Ben Wilson went for 5 yards, and after that it was over except for little, personal wars.

Some of the little wars were gallant ones. Tom Keating, one ankle wobbly, one arm dripping blood, bucked and slugged in the trenches with Green Bay's Gale Gillingham, and once boiled through to come down with Starr on his lap like a baby. Dan Conners, the Oakland middle linebacker, made 10 tackles, turning and whirling and never stopping. But the Packers rolled on, and they went into the second half leading, 16–7.

The Packers can be beautiful in a precise sort of way. In the third quarter, when they moved 69 yards in 10 plays, they flashed some breathtaking glimpses of 11 men in trained unity, cracking through Oakland, and over, in wondrous combinations that still left room for a Max McGee, aging and a reserve at 35, to reach over his head like a dancer for a ball that seemed destined to meet only him in time and space.

Dedicated to the End

But the Packer pleasure is in hitting hard enough to please Lombardi, hard enough to shake loose footballs from men. They never relaxed, bald, old Henry Jordan throwing a block to free Herb Adderley for a 60-yard touchdown run with an interception, old Willie Davis, with 1 minute 1 second left in the game, picking up Daryle Lamonica and hurling him down on the now-shadow-blotched field like a sack of rotten meal.

And then it was over, even for the fans who screamed for one more Oakland touchdown and a point-spread of less than 13½, a gambler's victory. History had been served and the fathers had kept the sons at bay for yet another year.

Sports of The Times

By ARTHUR DALEY

Clear-Cut Superiority

MIAMI, *Jan. 15*—If the gap between the two leagues is narrowing, it is not yet visible to the naked eye. The Green Bay Packers manhandled the Oakland Raiders in the Super Bowl as scandalously as they had treated the Kansas City Chiefs in last year's first Super Bowl contest. The score yesterday was 33–14 as compared with 35–10 a season ago. Only a professional hair-splitter would quibble about the difference.

The status seekers in the American Football League are hungry for acceptance as the equals of the National Football League. But those Packers keep disillusioning them with such disheartening emphasis. It is quite possible that the youthful Raiders will someday become the first team in the A.F.L. to win a Super Bowl game. But no one can begin to guess when that day—or that year—will arrive.

It didn't seem that the Packers were anywhere near as impressive against the Raiders in Miami as they had been against the Chiefs in Los Angeles last January. But all they do is win, a habit that's hard to knock. Nor were they as impressive as they had been in their homestretch thrillers against the Los Angeles Rams and Dallas Cowboys. Maybe Green Bay had used up its quota of emotional exhaustion.

There was nothing emotional about this one. It was a cold-blooded execution that almost seemed to lack inspirational fervor. Only the importance of the game saved it from bordering on dullness, much like a heavyweight fight, which has a built-in aura of glamour because it's for the championship of the world. Jack Dempsey, Joe Louis and Cassius Clay always brought along their own electric excitement. Green Bay is in the same class.

The Safety Factor

"It's quite possible," said one National Leaguer, "that the Rams, the Cowboys or the Colts would have beaten Oakland by an even bigger margin. But I always feel safer with the Packers in there for us. We know that they won't make the mistakes that give anything away."

The Packers didn't even give the Raiders the right time. They even took away from them the best Oakland ground gainer, the power sweeps. Ray Nitschke and company smothered them with fierce finality. Later in the fray Hewritt Dixon ripped off some handsome yardage down the middle, but it didn't mean much, except statistically, and the Raider running game remained well contained.

Daryle Lamonica did hit for two touchdown passes but inward pressure seemed to hurry his throws until near the end when Willie Davis, Ron

Kostelnik, Henry Jordan and friends supplied outward pressure as well.

When the game ended, there was one admirable gesture that few even noticed. The crowd swarmed on to the field. Dogtrotting from the Packer bench with his characteristic mincing steps came Bart Starr, threading his way through the multitude.

Lamonica was heading for the dressing room, head bowed. He looked up just in time to see Starr approaching him, hand outstretched in sincere greeting to a worthy foe. It was heartwarming and the grin on the face of the Raider quarterback showed how much he appreciated it.

Starr won the Corvette as the outstanding player in the game but the least he should do is let Don Chandler borrow it on weekends. The one-time Giant kicker was really the key performer. When the first Packer drive bogged down, Chandler kicked a 39-yard field goal. When the second one faltered, he kicked a 20-yarder. He later had field goals of 43 and 37 yards.

In fact, his kicks opened the way to Packer success. When Green Bay led by a none too secure 13–7 margin a few seconds before the end of the second quarter the placement expert hammered home his longest, the 43-yarder, to drive down the last firm nail in the Raider coffin.

The Bomb

The Raiders were the strongest defensive team in their league and they did reasonably well until Starr exploded the bomb in the second quarter.

They suffered shellshock the rest of the way. Starr called for a long pass with Carroll Dale as the primary receiver. Oakland fired in a blitz and Starr, instantly sensing that Boyd Dowler would be open, changed direction and lofted a perfectly timed pass to Dowler in the clear. It was a 62-yard touchdown romp.

Herb Adderley also read a play correctly, recognizing an Oakland pass pattern and intercepting the ball for a 60-yard gallop to the end zone. Jordan and Kostelnik cleared the way for him with gorgeous blocks, an eye-catching display of Vince Lombardi football at its efficient best.

When it all was over, Raider players kept repeating the same refrain, "I learned a lot today." It was an expensive lesson. The cost was $7,500, the difference between a winning and losing share for each player. It may yet prove a good investment for the future but impatient American Leaguers can't help but wonder when in the world they'll ever be able to cash in on it.

Starr Gets Second Super Bowl Car

Packer Passer Says He Feels Lombardi May 'Step Up'

By JOSEPH DURSO

Jan. 17, 1968—Bart Starr said yesterday that the Green Bay Packers had a "feeling" that this could have been Vince Lombardi's last season as coach, although Lombardi had not disclosed his plans to the players.

"It's an awesome job being both coach and general manager," the 34-year-old quarterback declared. "He hasn't said anything to us, but the players have been aware of the speculation and there was a feeling before the Super Bowl game that this could be his last year as coach.

"I think that's one more reason we wanted to wrap up this third straight championship this year."

Starr made his comment during a brief visit here to gather more of the spoils of the Packers' 33–14 victory over the Oakland Raiders in the Super Bowl last Sunday. He received a Corvette convertible from Sports magazine as the outstanding player in that game.

Corvettes Are Extras

Since he also won the award last year, he now has two Corvettes and about $50,000 in playoff money as his share of the treasure that has flowed to the Packers during the last 13 months.

He also earns around $50,000 a season for masterminding the Packers on the field and holds two offseason jobs as a representative of both the Pepsi-Cola Company and Lincoln-Mercury in Green Bay.

Nevertheless, during the award luncheon at the New York Hilton yesterday, Starr managed to surround this affluence with modesty, a sense of humor and an impressive vocabulary.

Speaking in a soft southern accent, he referred to himself diffidently as "we" instead of "I." He said it seemed "inappropriate that you can't invite the whole 40-man squad here," because he wasn't "oblivious" to the Packers' togetherness. Then he vouched a little joke on Lombardi, the patriarch of the Packers.

"Coach planned to be here today," he said, suppressing a grin. "But he had an accident down in Miami. He was out for his morning stroll and was struck by a speedboat."

When somebody asked at what point in his 12-year career at Green Bay he would dare to make such gibes at the coach, he replied: "Fifteen minutes ago."

Starr acknowledged that the Packers' road to the Super Bowl had been arduous because of injuries early in the season. He suffered so many injuries, he related, that he had been "ready to give it up." But a turning point was reached about the time the Packers played the Giants in New York Oct. 22.

"The Giants," he said, leaving no diplomatic stone unturned, "are a fine young football club. You moved the ball on us so much that you scared us."

Starr became the second football player to win two Corvettes since the award was established in 1958. John Unitas of the Baltimore Colts monopolized the award the first two years. Since then, though, the Packers have put five Corvettes on the streets of Green Bay, Wis.—Paul Hornung in 1961, Ray Nitschke in 1962, Jim Taylor in 1965 and Starr the last two years.

Until the first Super Bowl game last year, the prize was given for excellence in the National Football League championship game. A similar bauble is given for baseball players in the World Series. Last year's winner was Bob Gibson of the St. Louis Cardinals, also for the second time.

Chapter 3

Super Bowl III—1969

In retrospect, it is easy to make a case that Super Bowl III was the most important football game ever played, in terms of its consequences. But even in anticipation, it had something special, something the first two games lacked: Joe Namath. Rarely in any sport had a single athlete generated so much magnetism, entirely out of proportion to his admittedly outstanding playing ability. There was a time, older people could remember, that Dizzy Dean had that effect in baseball, and contemporaries knew that Cassius Clay, who had become Muhammad Ali, had stirred such feelings in boxing. Namath was a charismatic personality, beyond any accurate definition or description, who made millions of people feel strongly about his existence, for or against, and as the central character in 1969's better-advertised-than-ever melodrama, he aroused interest even in those whose devotion to pure football was well contained.

And it was plain enough that new forces were in motion. The Packer dominance of the N.F.L. had ended, and Baltimore was the new established champion and prohibitive favorite. The legal obstacles to a full merger of the N.F.L. and A.F.L. had all been cleared, but the practical re-alignment that had to be made was still up in the air. The question of separate identities of the two leagues had yet to be decided, and the nature of the schedules they would play was a topic as the clan gathered in Miami for Super Bowl III.

It was a serious problem. The A.F.L. owners had payed heavily for acquisition of their share of the N.F.L. label, which still held all the prestige. The first two Super Bowls had only increased that prestige, and as soon as Baltimore crushed the current A.F.L. champion, Namath's New York Jets, that prestige would be higher than ever. The essence of a merger was inter-league play during the regular season —but how would the public accept continued relations between a demonstrably inferior league and an established product?

Of course, if the Jets could win . . . Namath "guaranteed" they would.

That made it memorable even before it happened.

And after it happened, attitudes were wholly changed. Three N.F.L. teams—Baltimore, Pittsburgh and Cleveland—found themselves willing to move into an "American Conference" with the 10 A.F.L. teams, making two 13-team conferences that comprise the present system.

If nothing else, Super Bowl III unlocked the re-alignment impasse, and gave us the pro football pattern we now have. For that alone, it would have been a historic event.

No Auld Lang Syne for Ewbank As He Watches Colts in Action

Jan. 1, 1969—Weeb Ewbank renewed his acquaintance with some friends yesterday, and the meeting was not an especially happy occasion.

The coach of the New York Jets and his assistants began the task of dissecting the Baltimore Colts, a team he once coached, on film. The Jets have a date with the National Football League champions in the Super Bowl in Miami on Jan. 12.

Hour after hour slipped by as Ewbank and his staff studied motion pictures of a Baltimore team that has become a veritable powerhouse.

The films showed Baltimore routing the Browns in Cleveland last Sunday to win the N.F.L title. And the manner in which the Colts' defensive unit shackled Leroy Kelly, the league's leading rusher, presented Ewbank with perhaps his biggest problem.

If Kelly could not gain appreciably against Baltimore's defensive line, how will the Jets spring Matt Snell and Emerson Boozer loose?

Stronger than Packers

The Colts, in beating Cleveland, 34–0, posted their fourth shutout of the season and kept the opposition from scoring a touchdown for the sixth time during the 1968 campaign. Not even the once-mighty Green Bay Packers were that strong.

The Colts that Ewbank once coached are Tom Matte, Jerry Hill, Jimmy Orr, Dan Sullivan, Ordell Braase, Billy Ray Smith, Don Shinnick, Bobby Boyd and Lenny Lyles.

He saw them all yesterday on the screen, performing against Cleveland with almost 100 per cent efficiency under Coach Don Shula, a former defensive back for Ewbank.

If the Jet coaches had any ideas of how to break through the Baltimore defenses, they were keeping quiet.

Ewbank would say only that, other than bumps and bruises in the American Football League championship victory over Oakland, his players were all right. All, that is, except Don Maynard, the flankerback whose hamstring muscle still bothered him.

The medical word from Baltimore was not so encouraging. Matte, Bubba Smith, and Mike Curtis were reported injured, although not seriously.

Matte to Be Ready

Matte, who scored three touchdowns against Cleveland suffered a slight concussion in the fourth quarter and a contusion of the lower back. After a whirlpool bath and a massage yesterday, Matte declared he would be ready for the Super Bowl game.

Smith, the 6-foot-7-inch, 295-pound defensive end, came out of Cleveland with a slightly sprained ankle. After ice treatment and a tight tape job, Smith left for Beaumont, Tex., to visit his family.

Asked if he were looking forward to playing against Joe Namath, the Jets' quarterback, Smith replied, "I'm looking forward to winning $15,000, and I don't care who's playing."

Curtis, the Colts' left linebacker, reinjured his sprained wrist against the Browns. He had injured it the previous week in the Western Conference playoff against Minnesota but did not report the injury. Bob Vogel, an offensive tackle, also has a chip fracture in his left wrist and will continue to wear a cast in the Super Bowl game.

The Colts, off the last three days, resume practice tomorrow in Baltimore.

Jets to Restart Season Today, Getting Ready for Super Bowl

By GERALD ESKENAZI

Jan. 1, 1969—The New York Jets will have their first look at their greatest victory today, but tomorrow it will be July 15 all over again.

The New Yorkers, who fly to Miami tonight, will work out—hard— tomorrow, Saturday and Sunday as they prepare for the Baltimore Colts and the Super Bowl game on Jan. 12.

"They haven't done any work for a few days," Coach Weeb Ewbank said yesterday, taking a few minutes off from viewing the cascade of collegiate bowl games on television."So we have to get the stiffness out. It will be just like training camp again in Miami."

Ewbank and his players will watch the films of their 27-23 victory over the Oakland Raiders that gave them the American Football League championship last Sunday.

Not Too Much Too Soon

"On Monday, I'll go over our offensive plans with the coaches," said Ewbank. "Then I'll tell the boys about it on Tuesday. I don't want to fill up their minds with it just yet. They'll have too long to think about it."

Ewbank is concerned that, at this stage of the season, or postseason, the Jets may have had too much mental preparation for football. "After all, we started training camp July 15. That's a long time."

So he is trying to pace them, feeding them as much information as he thinks they ought to know, and still working them so they will be at a physical peak for the game.

The coach saw only a few of his players at Shea Stadium yesterday. They were taking sauna baths. Ewbank was working, though, with his assistants.

He thought that at Miami the Jets would have the crowd on their side.

Miami is the home of the Dolphins, an A.F.L. club. And Joe Namath, whom Ewbank hasn't seen since Monday, has been a Miami darling since he starred in the Orange Bowl in his final game with Alabama.

Always New Wrinkles

Ewbank, of course, knows the Colts. "I know so many of those players from when I was coaching them, I hope I line my boys up on the right side of the field," he said.

Would he spring some surprises? "Oh, there's always a few new wrinkles we have." He recalled the Statue of Liberty play—a hoary tactic that every boy who ever picked up a football tried on the sandlots—that Emerson Boozer used against the Raiders.

"He would have gotten free, too, if he hadn't run into his own man," Ewbank recalled, with a chuckle. "Then we tried that play I call a flea-flicker." The flea-flicker came against the Dolphins at Miami, and worked. Matt Snell took a Namath handoff on an apparent draw play, but suddenly flipped the ball backward to Namath. The quarterback then threw a pass good for 71 yards.

"But generally," Ewbank conceded, "you're better off sticking with what you know."

JETS FIND ROLE OF 17-POINT UNDERDOGS UNFITTING

Namath Expects Team to Triumph

Players Respect Colts but Are Confident—Jets Land in Florida for Drills

By DAVE ANDERSON

FORT LAUDERDALE, FLA., *Jan. 2*—Amusement or annoyance typified the reaction of the New York Jets to their role as a 17-point underdog as they arrived here tonight to prepare for the Super Bowl game with the Baltimore Colts, a week from Sunday in Miami.

"I didn't know we were that bad a football team," Joe Namath said.

The quarterback of the American Football League champions sounded slyly sarcastic. He believes the Jets can deflate the monarchs of the National Football League despite the reputation of the Colts' defensive unit as one of the best in the game's history.

"It's going to be a challenge," Namath continued, "but it's going to be a challenge on their part, too. I might sound like I'm boasting and bragging, and I am. Ask anybody who's played against us in our league. The Colts are good, but we're good."

During their flight on a chartered Northeast Airlines jet, other players were asked to comment on the underdog role.

Favorite's Role Backfires

"It's great," said Paul Rochester, the experienced defensive tackle. "It's better than being a 19-point favorite. We blow those games."

As a 19-point favorite against both Buffalo and Denver, the Jets were upset during the regular season.

"Our season would have been easier," said Winston Hill, the offensive tackle, "if our opponents had looked to see how much we were favored."

"It doesn't make any difference," said George Sauer, the split end. "When we go out on the field, the scoreboard is going to read 0 to 0."

"I think being an underdog," said Emerson Boozer, the offensive halfback, "gives you something to work for."

"I don't think any team in pro football can be called a 17-point underdog, especially in the Super Bowl," said Larry Grantham, the linebacker who calls the defensive signals. "Football is an emotional game, and the Super Bowl is the most emotional game."

"It's the greatest thing for us," said Gerry Philbin, the defensive end. "I'd rather be an underdog."

"The Colts deserve to be favored," said Matt Snell, the fullback. "They've won 15 games, we've won 12."

'Psychological Advantage'

"It's a little ridiculous to be a 17-point underdog," said Johnny Sample, the cornerback who is the captain of the defensive unit. "It gives us a psychological advantage."

"I felt we'd be the underdogs, but not that much," said Ralph Baker, the linebacker. "It makes you want to beat 'em that much more."

Typically cautious was Weeb Ewbank, the head coach. After choosing his words carefully, he commented:

"From what I've seen on the films, I'd say I think that the Colts are a great team, a real great team."

Five players were excused from the chartered flight—Don Maynard, Jim Hudson, Bill Baird, Carl McAdams and Jim Richards. Maynard, Hudson and Baird received permission to drive here. McAdams returned to Texas on business and Richards registered for postgraduate studies at Virginia Tech.

After three days of rest and recreation, the team had assembled at noon at Shea Stadium to view films of the 27-23 victory over Oakland for the league title.

With screeching sirens and flashing red lights, an escort of three motor-cycle policemen guided the team's two chartered buses from Fort Lauder-dale Airport to the Galt Ocean Mile Inn, where they will be lodged throughout their stay.

After having escaped from the subfreezing temperatures in New York, the players appeared to enjoy the swaying palms and the adjacent beach all the more.

Joe Namath: Man of Defiance Faces Biggest Challenge

By DAVE ANDERSON

FORT LAUDERDALE, FLA., *Jan. 4*—Joe Namath had been lobbing passes on the practice field when Emerson Boozer appeared, the last of the New York Jets to emerge from the locker room.

"I told you, Weeb," yelled Namath, grinning. "I told you Emerson would practice this week."

"Well," said the coach, Weeb Ewbank, "it's nice of you to do us a favor today, Emerson."

The three of them laughed. The halfback had been delayed in the trainer's room where his surgical knee requires taping. Ironically, the true humor of the situation was that Namath, who is excused from the team calisthenics because of his surgical knees, usually is the last Jet out to practice. But not these days.

Joe Namath is preparing to challenge the superiority of the National Football League next Sunday in the Super Bowl game with the Baltimore Colts.

And when Joe Namath is confronted with a challenge, beware. As a $400,000 rookie he challenged the salary structure of pro football, but he proved to be a bargain. With his Fu Manchu mustache, he challenged the tonsorial tradition of American athletics, but he shaved it off for a $10,000 fee.

As the symbol of the American Football League, he is confronted with the challenge of penetrating the Colt defense.

His attitude is significant. Occasionally he presents a droopy appearance, but not now. He's alive and alert. When he saw the Jets' white uniforms, which they will wear in the Super Bowl, hanging in their lockers here, he reacted immediately.

"We're wearing the white uniforms," he shouted to his teammates. "That must mean we're the good guys."

He's anxious to face his moment of truth. But he's not awed by it or by the Colts.

"When the Colts lost to the Browns at midseason," he was saying on the Jets' chartered flight last Thursday night, "they didn't get beat by any powerhouse. I'm not going to take what I read about their defense. I'm going to go with what the one-eyed monster shows me." The one-eyed monster is the projector that shows films of the Colts.

"The one-eyed monster doesn't lie," he said. "He shows it like it is."

In his blue turtleneck shirt and maroon corduroy slacks, he was sitting, as he usually does, on the left side of the aisle. That way he can extend his tender right leg into the aisle. But on this flight the seat in front of him was empty. He had folded the back rest and his right leg was stretched across it.

"When we won our title last Sunday, I said that Daryle Lamonica of the Raiders was a better quarterback than Earl Morrall, and now that's supposed to fire up the Colts.

"I said it and I meant it. Lamonica is better. If the Colts use newspaper clippings to get up for a game, they're in trouble. And if they're football players they know Lamonica can throw better than Morrall. I watch quarterbacks, I watch what they do.

"You put Babe Parilli with Baltimore," he continued, referring to the Jets' backup quarterback, "and Baltimore might have been better. Babe throws better than Morrall.

"There are more teams in the N.F.L. so they should have more good teams, but you put their good teams and our good teams together, or their bad teams and our bad teams together, and it's 50-50, flip a coin. And we've got better quarterbacks in our league—John Hadl, Lamonica, myself and Bob Griese."

Hadl directs the San Diego Chargers, while Griese is with the Miami Dolphins.

"I read where some N.F.L. guy joked about Lamonica and me throwing 100 passes last Sunday," he said. "We threw 97, but what's so terrible about that? How many N.F.L. teams have a quarterback who could complete many passes to their wide receivers. In our league, we throw much more to our wide receivers.

"I completed 49 per cent of my passes this season, but I could have completed 80 per cent if I dropped the ball off to my backs like they do in their league. For wide receivers the Jets have the best. George Sauer has the best moves, nobody can cover him one on one, and Don Maynard is the smartest.

"The best thrower in the N.F.L. is Sonny Jurgensen of the Redskins. I've said that if Jurgensen had been with the Packers or the Colts or the Rams the last few years, he would have won the championship for any of them. But if you put any pro quarterback on our team, only a few would not be on third string.

"That's my opinion, and I don't care how people value my opinion. But I value it very highly, especially when I'm talking about football."

The stewardess approached with a steak dinner, but Namath lifted the platter into the row behind him where John Schmitt, the Jets' 245-pound center, took it.

"He's had dinner," the stewardess protested. "He's a growing boy," Namath said winking.

In his fourth season, Namath is considered to have matured as a quarterback, notably after two early-season games when the Buffalo Bills and the Denver Broncos each intercepted five of his passes to achieve upset victories. During his last 10 games, including the title game, he had six interceptions.

"I don't feel matured, if that's the word, over last year," he said. "People might think I've matured now, but that's because we've been winning. And the reason we've been winning is defense."

Another reason was that Namath directed a winning touchdown or a winning field goal in the final minutes of three regular-season games. In the opener, he provided the poise that made the Jets realize they could win the league title by guiding a ball-control offense to preserve a 20-19 victory through the final six minutes.

"But after those games with the five interceptions," he acknowledged, "I disciplined myself as to throwing the ball. I was overcautious at times. I remembered an old rule: The only way to win is to keep from losing."

In the league title game an interception positioned the touchdown that put the Oakland Raiders ahead, 23-20, midway in the final quarter. But it did not deter Namath from connecting for three consecutive completions in moving the Jets 68 yards in 55 seconds for the winning touchdown of the 27-23 triumph.

"After that interception," he said, "I just told myself, 'you got eight minutes and you got to score.' That's all."

Three days before the title game, pain had seared his marvelous passing arm for the first time in his career.

Pulled Muscle in Arm

"I pulled a muscle in it," he disclosed. "Nothing like that had ever happened to my arm before. It must have been my 50th pass of the day. I was warmed up, but I felt the long muscle go, and I was afraid to throw hard that day and the next. But on Saturday, it worked itself out and I was all right."

His arm has been his great gift, but he mentioned the luck factor for an athlete.

"Any player has to be lucky," he said. "Take our kicker, Jim Turner —suppose he had to have an operation on his right knee when he was playing quarterback at Utah State. If he did, he'd never be kicking now. I was lucky because I was trained good by my brothers, Bob and Frank, and I've had good coaches.

"Larry Bruno, my coach at Beaver Falls High School, he was terrific. We had 13 guys go on scholarships to college, 13 guys from one team. And to go from a coach like that to Coach Bear Bryant at Alabama, a kid has to be lucky. He made me feel proud to be a part of his team. I learned a lot from Coach Bryant.

"And then coming here, with Weeb, was lucky for me. Until this season, I don't think I really appreciated Weeb, but now I realize how hard he works.

"Something the trainer, Jeff Snedeker, said one day made me realize it. He told me that when he got to the locker room at 8 o'clock one morning Weeb already was there taking a whirlpool bath. I mean Weeb's an old man, he's about 60, and he was in the locker room before 8 o'clock in the morning.

"And the day we came back from San Diego after just about cinching our division. Weeb and the coaches got off the plane at 7 in the morning and went straight to the stadium. They could have taken a break, but they didn't."

Hassle Over Champagne

"I've had my disagreements with Weeb, I probably always will. I'm that kind. Like last Sunday, after we won the championship, there's a league rule that you're not supposed to have champagne in the clubhouse. But I told Weeb to break it out, and that all of us were three times seven and that I'd pay the fine out of my pocket.

"And later Mr. [Milt] Woodard, the league president, came over to talk to me about it and I told him that I thought it's a stupid rule, that all of us were three times seven and that it was the biggest day of our lives.

"Mr. Woodard tried to tell me that it was bad for the image of football, that it was bad for the kids to see it. You know what the real image of football is, it's brutality. Why don't they tell the kids like it is? Tell the kids that this guy is trying to hurt that guy and knock him out of the football game.

"Like the letters I get from people who hope some guy cripples me because of my mustache."

Namath swirled the ice in his plastic up and glanced at his right knee across the folded seat.

"Some of those letters," he said, "I read for entertainment because those people are sick. Or maybe I'm the sick one, but I'm happy the way I'm sick."

Colts Riding a Crest

N.F.L. Crown Caps Decade of Success Despite Many Shifts in Personnel

By WILLIAM N. WALLACE

Jan. 4, 1969—In the opinion of many, the Baltimore Colts probably are the best team in the history of professional football. What they do next Sunday against the Jets in the Super Bowl game at Miami will support or weaken this contention, of course.

The Colts have been one of the most successful teams in the National Football League since 1957. That was the year the team, which had been founded in 1947 as a part of the old All-American Conference, had its first winning season in the N.F.L. Its quarterback, significantly, was John Unitas.

Since that year the Colts have never had a losing season, although they dipped to .500 in 1960 and 1962. The latter year was Weeb Ewbank's last as Baltimore's head coach. Since 1957, the team has won 116 games and lost 53, for a remarkable percentage of .686.

This proves that Carroll Rosenbloom, who directs operations as the president and sole owner, has accomplished one of the most difficult feats in the game. Under Rosenbloom, the Colts have replaced their personnel position by position one or more times and continued to win.

In the recent season the club won for the first time without Unitas, as Earl Morrall, an undistinguished journeyman, took his place.

Five years ago the Colts lined up like this on offense:

E—Ray Berry	John Mackey—TE
LT—Bob Vogel	Unitas—QB
LG—Jim Parker	Tom Matte—RB
C—Dick Szymanski	J. W. Lockett—RB
RG—Alex Sandusky	Jimmy Orr—FL

Here is the Club's Super Bowl line-up on offense:

SE—Orr	Mackey—TE
LT—Vogel	Morrall—QB
LG—Glenn Ressler	Matte—RB
C—Bill Curry	Jerry Hill—RB
RG—Dan Sullivan	W. Richardson—FL
RT—Sam Ball	

So in five years the club replaced its interior line with the exception of the talented Vogel, plus one wise receiver in Richardson and Morrall.

The defense five years ago lined up this way:

E—G. Marchetti	D. Shinnick—LB
T—Jim Colvin	Lenny Lyles—CB
T—Fred Miller	Jim Welch—CB
E—Ordell Braase	Andy Nelson—S
LB—J. Burkett	W. Harris—S
MLB—B. Pellington	

On Sunday a much better defense, especially in the secondary will start, as follows:

E—Bubba Smith	Shinnick—LB
T—B. Ray Smith	Lyles—CB
T—Miller	Bobby Boyd—CB
E—Braase	Rich Volk—S
LB—Mike Curtis	Jerry Logan—S
MLB—D. Gaubatz	

This shows that 7/11ths of the defense has been replaced in half a decade. With the disappearance of Unitas, because of his tendonitis of the elbow of his passing arm, this remarkable defense took it upon itself to be even better. It now is gaining recognition long overdue.

Says Billy Ray Smith, "People used to think this team was all John Unitas. That never was so. And now we're proving it."

Of the new regulars since 1963 all but Curry, Morrall, Billy Ray Smith and Gaubatz were drafted by the Colts. The others came by trade and they were darn good trades. Gaubatz, for example, came from the Lions in exchange for Joe Don Looney.

The Green Bay Packers, in the time of Vince Lombardi, were said to be a dynasty. These dynasties in professional sports seldom last a decade. The Baltimore Colts are a dynasty and their Super Bowl appearance is the climax to one that has endured beyond a decade.

Former Second Stringer Calling Tune

MIAMI, *Jan. 4 (AP)*—It was late in August after another long—and disheartening—training grind that Earl Morrall was told that he had been traded by the New York Giants to the Baltimore Colts.

Hardly disillusioned since he had been down the same street before, Morrall nevertheless thought about trying a new avenue.

In assessing the situation, Morrall put the facts in perspective.

He was 34 years old. He was a 12-year experienced player. He was still a second fiddle.

Maybe it was time to leave the band.

"I had had it up to here with being a backup quarterback," Morrall recalls. "You start to reach the conclusion that everybody's given up on you. You start to question your own ability."

Just An 'Insurance' Man

Even the Colts did that.

In acquiring Morrall they gave up a reserve tight end named Butch Wilson, and admittedly were latching on to him only as insurance since Jim Ward, the regular backup quarterback for Johnny Unitas, had been injured.

But Morrall decided to pick up his bow once more.

"Everything," he says, "would have been wasted if I turned tail and went home. I knew I could help any club I'd be with."

And so, after stops at San Francisco, where he had been a backup quarterback, and Pittsburgh, where he had been a backup quarterback, and Detroit, where he had been a backup quarterback, and New York, where he had been a backup quarterback, Morrall went to Baltimore to be a backup quarterback. Then something in Unitas's arm popped.

Now, 16 games and 15 victories later, Morrall is Baltimore's No. 1 field general, Morrall is the National Football League's No. 1 quarterback and

Morrall is the No. 1 reason the Colts will be favored to grab the $15,000-a-man prize that goes to the winners in next Sunday's Super Bowl game against the New York Jets here.

And now instead of being called "Rag Arm," he's being called "Earl the Pearl." And instead of having his name mispronounced morale he's being called properly moral.

For Morrall, the bushy-eyed, dark-haired, crew-cut star had statistically—as well as personally—earned the praise and respect of teammates and opponents alike after all those years he learned to live with, although never enjoy, his backup role.

Statistically, Morrall was rated the No. 1 quarterback in the N.F.L. after completing 182 of 317 passes for 57.4 per cent, third best in the league; 2,909 yards, second best, and 26 touchdowns, No. 1, while leading the Colts to a 13–1 won-lost regular season record.

He added to his statistics, and his accolades, by bringing the Colts to the threshold of the world championship by engineering a 24–14 victory over the Minnesota Vikings in the Western Conference playoff and a 34–0 victory over Cleveland in the N.F.L. title game.

Unitas, the unquestioned golden arm of pro football, who sat out almost the entire season while Morrall directed the club to its first championship since the 1958–1959 club led by the man he replaced, is one of Morrall's biggest supporters.

"He's a real nice guy," says Baltimore's center, Dick Szymanski. "When he came to us in training camp he went around the dining hall introducing himself to all the players. He's a top gentleman, has good sense and is well-liked."

Made Good in a Hurry

It was a short training camp, because Morrall immediately was thrown into the regular season, against the San Francisco 49ers.

After only three weeks with the club, Morrall led the Colts to a 27–10 victory and was awarded the game ball—a move probably more symbolic of his acceptance than his achievements, under the circumstances.

But you couldn't prove that to a 49er linebacker, Matt Hazeltine, a 14-year player.

"I don't see," said Hazeltine, "how Unitas could have done much better. I didn't see any great difference defending against Earl and defending against John."

Neither did the other teams on the schedule.

Now, there's only the Super Bowl and the Jets left. And where Morrall is standing in for Unitas, he is standing up against Joe Namath, the heir apparent to Unitas's throne.

Quarterback, Boozer and Snell Are Fined for Missing Photo Day

By DAVE ANDERSON

FORT LAUDERDALE, FLA., *Jan. 6*—Among the command performances for participants in the Super Bowl game is "photo day" when the players are ordered to be available in uniform for newspaper cameramen and television crews.

But when the New York Jets assembled today at 10 A.M. in a drizzle at Fort Lauderdale Stadium, three of their stars were sleeping—Joe Namath, Emerson Boozer and Matt Snell.

Namath's roommate, Jim Hudson, had attempted to awake the quarterback, without success. Boozer and Snell, the running backs who are roommates, had ignored a wake-up phone call from the Galt Ocean Mile Hotel switchboard.

Coach Weeb Ewbank later announced that "appropriate disciplinary action" had been taken against the trio. The fine for each player was believed to be $50.

A Tardy Reputation

Namath's absence was a surprise, but he has a reputation for being late to many team appointments, such as meetings, planes and buses. Ordinarily, he is not required to appear until noon, the time of the team's daily meeting.

When he finally emerged from his room in the early afternoon, Namath explained:

"I always sleep in the morning, that's the thing to do. You've got to get your rest."

Boozer and Snell had been aware of the photo-day appointment but, in their slumber, forgot.

"When the wake-up call rang," Boozer said, "we didn't answer it. We both thought it was just another call. We forgot about the picture-day thing. I know it'll cost us."

Another fine-provoking situation, this one in the extravagant amount of $5,000, went into effect tonight.

Ewbank, as he had planned before the photo-day absences, installed a midnight curfew. Any player not in his room at that hour would be subject to the $5,000 levy. The curfew will be changed to 11 P.M., beginning Thursday.

Tomorrow the Jets' workout will be delayed. To accommodate cameramen who missed Namath, Boozer and Snell today, Ewbank has promised their availability before the 2:30 P.M. practice.

Namath Is Twice Slapped: For Nap and Rap at Morrall

Shula Is Critical of Jet Star's Downgrading of Colts' Passer

By WILLIAM N. WALLACE

FORT LAUDERDALE, FLA., *Jan. 6*—Joe Namath makes news even while sleeping. As the Jets' quarterback rested at the Galt Ocean Mile Hotel, he was the major subject of a news conference held by Don Shula, the 39-year-old coach of the Baltimore Colts, at the Statler Hilton Hotel, one mile up the road.

"I don't know how Namath can rap Morrall," said Shula. "He can say whatever he wants to say, but I don't see how he can rap a guy who led the league in passing. We're very happy with Earl."

Shula's retort followed Namath's earlier published opinions about Earl Morrall, who will be the Colts' quarterback in the Super Bowl game against the Jets in Miami on Sunday.

Namath had said that Daryle Lamonica of the Oakland Raiders was better than Morrall and so was Babe Parilli, the Jets' second-stringer, and that the American League had better quarterbacks than the National.

Praise For the Passer

Shula, displaying briefly his renowned but controlled temper, questioned Namath's position as an authority of N.F.L. quarterbacks, whom Joe sees on television. And then the coach went on to praise Namath, the passer, rather than Namath, the critic.

His praise was lavish. "A great arm, strong and accurate . . . great when throwing to the outside . . . moves quickly . . . has what we call fast feet . . . hard to get to him . . . back-pedals when he sets up to pass so he can see everything . . . sees the blitz when it's coming . . . recognizes defenses and can pick them apart . . . knows where to go with the football."

In the afternoon the Colts were stuffed in two buses and driven for 45 minutes north to a private boys' school at Boca Raton, named St. Andrew's, where much of the football movie, "Paper Lion," was filmed last spring. They will practice there daily henceforth in isolated secrecy. But today was photo day and the Colts lounged among the dozens of spectators, getting photographed and interviewed for television. Busy, obliging Earl Morrall was present and accounted for.

Report of Fight Denied By Namath

He Calls an Encounter With Lou Michaels 'Just Talk'

FORT LAUDERDALE, FLA., *Jan. 7*—Reports of an altercation between Joe Namath of the New York Jets and Lou Michaels of the Baltimore Colts were denied today by the two players on the rival Super Bowl teams.

"It was just talk," the Jets' quarterback said. "I even drove Lou back to his hotel."

Namath and his Jet roommate, Jim Hudson, became acquainted with Michaels, the Colts' field-goal kicker, during their travels Sunday night. Michaels is the youngest brother of the Jets' defensive coach, Walt Michaels.

"When we were introduced," Michaels recalled, "Joe told me the Jets were going to kick the heck out of us."

Michaels acknowledged that he was annoyed by Namath's boast, but that Hudson succeeded in calming him.

"Joe walked away to meet some people," Michaels said, "and while he was gone, Hudson told me, 'don't pay any attention to Joe, you've got to understand him.' When he came back, I told Joe, 'suppose we kick the heck out of your team,' and Joe said he'd 'sit in the middle of the field and cry.'"

Sports of The Times

By ARTHUR DALEY

Mutual Admiration

BOCA RATON, FLA., *Jan. 7*—It would have been an awkward, perhaps even impossible situation if their personalities had been different from what they actually are. But Earl Morrall and Johnny Unitas happen to be a couple of great guys in an antihero era when such old-fashioned types are sneered at as squares. But because both have a whatever-is-best-for-the-team un-selfishness, the Baltimore Colts are preponderant favorites to defeat the New York Jets in the Super Bowl on Sunday.

It was Morrall, the gypsy quarterback, who came to the rescue of the Colts just before the start of the season. Not only did he take over for the injured Unitas to lead Baltimore through a hugely successful championship year but he also replaced the incomparable Johnny U., as the most valuable player in the league. Who gave Morrall the most help? It was Unitas, of course.

"Before I joined the Colts," said Earl, his crew cut demonstrating how square he still is, "I knew Johnny in a general way and had heard what an outstanding person he was. My respect for him has increased. I found out what a really big man he is. There's no way of measuring the help he has given me. I'll always be grateful to him."

"Give Earl all the credit," said Unitas, the other half of the mutual admiration society. "He's a good fellow and success doesn't change good people. You can't say enough complimentary things about him. He knows the ins and outs of football and no one can underplay the importance of experience at the quarterback position. He's cool and calculating, knows how to handle an offense and mixes his plays well. Like I say, give him all the credit."

Slow Progress

When Morrall was purloined from the Giants, just before the start of the season, Coach Don Shula assumed that it would be for a backup role. Everyone thought that the lame-armed Unitas would return in a couple of weeks.

However, the weeks passed and Unitas sat unhappily on the bench as Morrall performed miracles on the field. Johnny played only parts of four games but has started to come along in the last month until he now is considered to have regained 80 per cent of his effectiveness. Even on a reduced scale, he is considered superior to almost every other quarterback in the sport.

"It's no fun being a spectator," says Johnny.

Being an eminently fair-minded man, Unitas cannot quarrel with Shula's conclusion that Earl deserves to start in the Super Bowl. But Johnny's eyes widened when it was mentioned that Earl also would rate a starting spot in the game against the College All-Stars next August. It really jolted him because he's long taken for granted that he's No. 1. So he expressed a thought that never before had entered his mind.

"If it means that I have to win the job back," he said, groping for words that came hesitantly to his lips, "then if I have to, I will."

Morrall doesn't even think about next season. This one was troublesome enough for him, even though he contrived to reach undreamed of heights. In fact, he accomplished one thing that Unitas, great as he always has been, never has achieved. Earl also won the passing championship of the league.

"The toughest adjustment I had to make," he said, gracious as always, "was getting used to the numbering system. It was the exact opposite of what I'd grown used to in those long years at Detroit and with the Giants. They had odd-numbered holes to the right and even-numbered holes to the left. But the Colts have odd to the left and even to the right.

Not Ambidextrous

"It was as if someone told you after all these years that your right hand is your left and your left hand is your right. Early in the year I'd have to eat the ball sometimes because I'd turn the wrong way and the backs were going in the opposite direction, away from my handoff.

"I remembered that Y. A. Tittle had the same problem when he came from San Francisco to the Giants because those two teams had opposite numbering systems. He got in the habit of looking around to see where his fullback was placed so that he'd know in what direction he was going.

"I learned to do the same, taking my cue from our formations where we were going because the formation dictated whether I wanted a 34 or a 35. Tom Matte was a big help to me in huddle from the start and he also would flutter his right hand. It kept me thinking.

" 'You're doing a good job,' I said to him one day, 'by fluttering your hand.'

" 'I'm glad it helps,' he said. 'But it's a nervous habit I have. I also do it when Johnny U. is in there.'

"Sure, I was hurt when the Giants traded me to Baltimore but it has worked out for the best. Here I am in the Super Bowl. I have no complaints."

Sports of The Times

By ARTHUR DALEY

The Sanitation Man

FORT LAUDERDALE, FLA., *Jan. 9*—Alex Karras, the hulking defensive stalwart of the Detroit Lions, gave vent to his irritation and frustration after trying to stop Tom Matte of the Baltimore Colts one unhappy afternoon.

"He's just a garbage-can runner," growled Alex.

What he meant was that Matte goes out on the gridiron, picking up a few yards here and a few yards there until he has accumulated more scraps than anyone else before the festivities are over.

"If he's a garbage-can runner, he's goldplated," snapped Coach Don Shula in quick rebuttal.

"I'm no superstar," says Matte, an innocent look on that handsome choir-boy face. "I'm an average ballplayer with average speed and average skills. But I get the job done."

He sure does. He outgained the flashier Leroy Kelly of Cleveland by 60 yards in the championship playoff a fortnight ago. Tom scored three touchdowns. He caught passes. He threw deadly blocks. He is the complete football player and he'll be the guy giving the crunch to the Colt attack in the Super Bowl game against the New York Jets on Sunday.

Instant Hero

The only time celebrity status descended on Matte was late in the 1965 season when he became an instant hero. Johnny Unitas broke a leg and Gary Cuozzo, the back-up quarterback, suffered a shoulder separation. The Colts were without a quarterback. So Matte, the handyman, moved in for the final game with the Rams and for a tie-breaking playoff with the Packers. It was his first whirl at the job since his sophomore season at Ohio State seven years earlier.

"I didn't have time to get scared," said Tom with his quick, rippling laugh. "I also didn't have time to prepare because I came down with the flu that week and had to jam everything into the last couple of days. I had all our plays written on adhesive tape around my wrist, a crib sheet of sorts.

"But our guys rose to the occasion. They played super and they never let any tackler through on me. With me in there at quarterback the Rams didn't know what we were going to do. The trouble was that we didn't know, either. We beat them, 20–17. But I needed all the help I could get.

"I remember one time when we were in trouble. We were backed up to the 1-yard line and I called a play that I hoped would spring Lenny Moore loose. Just as we lined up, Dan Sullivan turned around to me.

" 'Better change that play, Tom,' he said, 'you're aiming Lenny smack into the goal post.' So I changed it, steering him to the other side.

"Don Shula was sending in most of the plays from the sidelines, but once I carried myself out of bounds in front of our bench. So he gave one to me directly. I stared at him and he repeated it. Then he repeated it again, each time louder than the time before.

" 'Don't you hear me, Tom?' he finally said.

" 'Sure,' I said, 'but so does the entire Ram team.' "

Like all the Colts, Tom is a worshiper at the Johnny Unitas shrine.

"What a man John is," he said reverently. "Let me give you an example that sticks in my mind for several reasons. The Vikings were beating us by 4 points with eight seconds to play. A field goal would do us no good and we had one time-out left. In the huddle, Alex Sandusky spoke up.

" 'John, make sure you call a time-out right away,' he said.

" 'Shut up, Alex,' said Dick Szymanski.

" 'After the next play, John, please don't forget,' said Sandusky.

" 'Shut up, Alex,' said Szymanski, stomping on Alex's foot with his cleats. 'Now will you shut up?'

"I laughed so hard that I hardly could carry out my assignment. What happened? Just what you might expect. John passed for the winning touchdown.

The Crutch

"John has been our crutch over the years. We leaned on him for everything because he was the best ever, the finest passer, the greatest guy. Now we have Earl Morrall, another great guy, running the show.

"He's different. He uses more running plays and he mixes them up more than John did. So we have been capitalizing on what Earl does best. Basically it makes no difference to me. We have more plays, more formations and I don't care whether I'm catching passes or carrying the ball on runs. I just want to get my hands on the ball.

"Our offensive line and our blockers have been fantastic. When they're bad, I'm bad. Fortunately they rarely are bad. Jerry Hill, the unknown fullback, is the best blocker of all and I do have the knack of following my blockers. As a team we make a minimum of mistakes.

"And our defense—wow! They're so good that every night when I say my prayers, I just thank the good Lord that I don't have to play against them."

A Big Man Belittles a Big Talker

Bubba Smith Terms Namath's Remarks Far Out of Line

Colt End Says Stars Should Be Seen and Not Heard

By FRANK LITSKY

FORT LAUDERDALE, FLA., *Jan. 9*—When a man is 6 feet 7 inches tall (or maybe 6-8) and weighs 280 pounds (or maybe 295) discretion dictates that he be treated kindly.

Bubba Smith has not been treated kindly. His sense of propriety has been hurt, and he may take out his anger on the New York Jets in Sunday's Super Bowl game in Miami.

Bubba is the left end on defense for the Baltimore Colts, the National Football League champions. He is only 23 years old, but he has definite ideas on how football players should conduct themselves. He thinks they should not criticize other players, even future opponents, and he thinks Joe Namath's putdowns of Earl Morrall, the Baltimore quarterback, and his other criticisms of the Colts have been out of line.

"I have a bundle of respect for Joe," Bubba said before today's workout here. "He is a damned good quarterback, an exceptional quarterback. But a football player who's real good doesn't have to talk. The Green Bay Packers were real champions. They never talked. They never had to. This is the way I visualize all champions—solemn, dignified, humble.

"My father coached me at Charlton Pollard High School in Beaumont, Tex., and he taught us to be humble off the field. Inside, I've got to feel I'm the best, but if I tell you I'm the best, then I'm a fool.

"All this talk by Namath isn't going to fire us up. You're a man. You're a professional. You're playing for $15,000. So you don't have to be fired up. But this gives us a little more incentive to get to him—understand, not try to hurt him, but to get to him like any other quarterback.

"My job is to get to the quarterback, whether I hurt him or not. But

I don't try to hurt anybody, no matter how strong I am. How strong am I? I don't know what my strength is."

Smith has one immediate concern. His left ankle was badly sprained two weeks ago, but the swelling is down and he is running again.

"I lie in bed at night with my foot in a plastic boot," he said. "There is air pressure around the foot, just like in a blood-pressure machine. It makes the ankle feel better, but it doesn't do anything for my sleep."

In 1967, Bubba had hoped to become National League rookie of the year. He had been pro football's first draft choice, and he had everything going for him. But the Colts shifted him to defensive tackle, he sprained a knee in preseason and the year was a loss.

Now he is back at his old position, and he is becoming a legend in his time. As Weeb Ewbank, the Jet coach said:

"The way people talk about him, you'd think he's the greatest thing since peanut butter."

Or as Ogden Nash wrote:

"When hearing tales of Bubba Smith,
You wonder is he man or myth."

Or as Jeff Richardson of the Jets, his Michigan State roommate, said:

"In college, he was just a great player. Now he's learned to play like Superman."

ROZELLE INDICATES TOMORROW'S SUPER BOWL CONTEST COULD BE NEXT TO LAST

Realignment Due After '69 Season

One-League Format Looms—Clubowners to Decide at Meeting in March

By WILLIAM N. WALLACE

MIAMI BEACH, *Jan. 10*—Pete Rozelle, the commissioner of pro football, indicated today that because of a possible realignment beginning with the 1970 season, Sunday's Super Bowl game might be the next to last under the format matching the champions of the two pro leagues.

Speaking at a news conference in the Hilton Plaza Hotel, Rozelle described two plans for realignment that would complete the merger of the American and National Leagues. A decision is expected at a meeting of the owners beginning March 17 in Palm Springs, Calif.

Under one plan there would be a complete mixture "involving present members of both leagues." New divisions would be formed, based on such considerations as geography, established rivalries and stadium capacities. Several A.F.L. principals, such as Paul Brown of Cincinnati and Ralph Wilson of Buffalo, support this idea.

"Then there are those who believe the existing rivalry between the N.F.L. and A.F.L., which has been built up since 1960, should be preserved," Rozelle said. "A new mix would eliminate much of this rivalry."

If the identity of the leagues is wiped out, the Super Bowl contest would become merely a title game in a 26-team league.

N.F.L. Would Stand Pat

National League owners in general are known to favor the two-league structure.

"To make it fairer economically," said Rozelle, "a great many inter-league games would be played. In this way, a mix could be achieved through scheduling."

The Giants and the Jets, for example, would play each other and play eight to 10 games with league rivals and four to six against teams in the other league.

Pro football's joint committee is working on the alternative. Any agreement requires a three-fourths vote in both leagues. Rozelle will be pushing hard for a decision.

"That's why we chose an attractive spot like Palm Springs," he said. "We might be there a while."

It is important that a decision be reached, because the commissioner will be negotiating this year for television contracts for 1970 and beyond.

The Columbia Broadcasting System, which televises the N.F.L. games, and the National Broadcasting Company, the A.F.L. network, have rights of first refusal with regard to continuing pro football telecasts, Rozelle said.

Beginning in 1970, all television income, he said, is to be divided equally among 26 teams. In order that N.F.L. teams, now getting about $200,000 more than A.F.L. teams from television, do not receive less, Rozelle feels that more income must be generated from TV.

He said he favored elimination of double-header broadcasts on Sunday afternoons, which were begun by the networks and not football. In place of the double-headers, Rozelle seeks a telecast of a Monday night game through the season. He said an independent network, such as the Sports Network Company recently purchased by the Howard Hughes interests, might be used to broadcast such games should C.B.S. and N.B.C. refuse them.

Rozelle said the extended baseball schedule beginning this year posed serious scheduling problems for football because of stadium availability.

He said the owners, meeting here tomorrow, would take up the matter.

"We have the shortest season of the four major sports," he said. "Baseball's will be about two months longer than ours."

Rozelle said he believed most sports stadiums would have synthetic surfaces "within 10 years, and maybe five."

He said that although the city of Miami was a wonderful host for the Super Bowl, a policy of rotating the game around the country might be adopted by the owners. New Orleans, which made a feeble bid last year for the game, is bidding again in a more formidable manner.

For the athletes, practice continued today despite light rain. There is a chance of rain for Sunday's game, but neither coach, Weeb Ewbank of the Jets and Don Shula of the Baltimore Colts, thought that would hinder his team.

"Some of our best games this year were played on a damp field," said Ewbank.

Two Colts, Lenny Lyles and Don Shinnick, collided in yesterday's practice and have bruised legs. But both will play. Timmy Brown, a Baltimore kick-returner, pulled up lame while running pass routes and if he cannot play Sunday, Terry Cole will replace him on kickoffs and Rick Volk on punts.

Both coaches said that if they won the coin toss, their team would receive the opening kickoff.

"I think my players would run me out if I didn't," said Ewbank.

JETS BANK ON NAMATH'S ARM AGAINST COLTS TODAY, BUT RAIN POSES A NEW THREAT TO PASSER AT MIAMI

Wet Field Likely

Possibility of Upset Draws 75,000 to Super Bowl

By WILLIAM N. WALLACE

MIAMI, *Jan. 11*—A tough kid from Beaver Falls, Pa., named Joe Namath, who was born to be a football player, will try to make something good come out of the third annual Super Bowl game tomorrow. Namath's team, the New York Jets, is an 18-to-20-point underdog to the Baltimore Colts, who represent the alleged superiority of the National Football League over the American.

The plot of this contest will be very simple. Namath, a great passer on a team without much excellence in other areas, will match himself against a Colt defense that is the sport's strongest. But it is inherent in the nature of football that a great passer can work miracles. That is why there will be 75,354 spectators filling the Orange Bowl and 30-million more around television sets across the land.

Cloudy Skies Expected

If Namath is to work miracles, he may have to do so on a wet field. Today's forecast was for cloudy skies, temperature in the 70's and a strong possibility of rain during the game. But the possibility of an "off" field did not disturb the Jets' coach, Weeb Ewbank, who said yesterday that "some of our best games this year were played on a damp field."

The game will begin at 3:05 P.M. Eastern Standard Time and Channel 4 will televise it in New York.

This is the money game. The gross receipts, counting the $2.5-million the National Broadcasting Company is paying for television and radio rights, will come to $3.3-million. Each winning player is to receive $15,000, each loser $7,500 for three hours on the field. About $1-million will go into the player pension funds and close to another $1-million will go to the two competing franchises, the league and the commissioner's offices.

The Super Bowl, matching the champions of the American and National Leagues, began two years ago. The Green Bay Packers won the first game by 25 points over Kansas City and the second game by 19 over Oakland. Almost everyone expects Baltimore to continue the N.F.L. dominance, although a great many hope Namath can "get on the board," meaning score points, with some touchdown passes.

The first two Super Bowl games were so one-sided as to be dull and that is not the goal for professional football's showcase event.

Although good, the Colts can be dull. They were both in beating the Cleveland Browns, 34–0, for the league title two Sundays ago. On the same day, the Jets played an exciting game to down Oakland, 27–23, for the A.F.L. title in New York.

Namath Seeks to Be Best

Namath, a truthful and therefore outspoken athlete, has said the money does not interest him. He is playing the game so as to become the best quarterback on the best team. Because he is unconventional and tells it like it is, Namath seems to infuriate a number of people, some of whom will be dressed in the blue-and-white Baltimore uniform. "Someday he'll learn a little humility," Billy Ray Smith of the Colts has said of Namath.

There will be very little mystery to the action. The first 10 minutes are likely to forecast the game's direction. Jet fans hope that Namath can move the ball not only by passing but also by running. His lightning strikes to the outside receivers, George Sauer Jr. and Don Maynard, are of vital import. But the passing game must be complemented by some effective running from Emerson Boozer, with Matt Snell, the fullback, blocking for him.

The match-ups, always fascinating in championship games, find Lenny Lyles, a 32-year-old cornerback not quite as rough as he used to be, covering Sauer, and bald Bobby Boyd on Maynard.

If Namath cannot establish a well-rounded offense he is just going to have to heave the ball and hope for the best. Should the Jets fall behind early, Namath may wind up throwing as many as 50 passes as he plays catch up. (He threw 49 against Oakland and completed 19, 13 of them to Sauer and Maynard.)

Bubba Smith Looms

An area of concern for the Jets rests on the right side of their offensive line. Smallish Dave Herman (6 feet 1 inch, 255 pounds), a guard now playing tackle, will be pitted against the giant end, Bubba Smith, 6-7, 295.

Smith, Mike Curtis, a linebacker, and John Mackey, a tight end, are acknowledged to be the Colts' three truly great athletes.

At right guard the Jets will have Randy Rasmussen, a second-year man who lost his regular status early in the season. He will oppose the quick and mobile Billy Ray Smith, seasoned and smart after a decade in pro football.

The Baltimore offense is unspectacular and its line is its best feature. Earl Morrall, the old New York Giant, is not in Namath's class as an all-round quarterback, but Morrall can do what the Colts expect—call the plays competently, throw the deep pass occasionally and keep the team moving.

The Colts have two fine wide receivers in Jimmy Orr and Willie Richardson. Randy Beverly, relatively inexperienced, will be covering Orr, and John Sample, a cheeky, talky former Colt, will worry about the fleet Richardson. The Jets may be vulnerable at these cornerback positions.

Fortunately, they have one of their best athletes, Jim Hudson, covering Mackey, who can be a game breaker. A big man, he runs through and over people.

All tickets have been sold and scalpers are asking $100 apiece along Miami Beach.

Baltimore has been designated the home team and will wear blue jerseys while the Jets wear white. As in past Super Bowls, the American League ball will be used when the A.F.L. team is on offense and the N.F.L. ball when the Colts attack. The two balls are slightly different in shape. The A.F.L. optional 2-point rule for conversions after touchdowns will not be used.

Should the score be tied after four periods, the game will go into sudden-death overtime, with the first team to score the winner. Namath's number is 12. Look for it.

The Coaches: Their Success and How They Made It

MIAMI, *Jan. 11*—The coach and the quarterback help form the character of professional football teams. For contrasts, take the Baltimore Colts and the New York Jets, opponents tomorrow in the Super Bowl.

Wilbur Charles (Weeb) Ewbank, the short, rotund, 61-year-old coach of the Jets, does not resemble an athlete. An easy-going Hoosier, Ewbank has been swept up by the tide of circumstances in pro football and finds himself at the top once again.

No one ever doubted that Don Shula, a strong, forceful man who coaches the Colts, would be anything but successful as a head coach in this sport. He has tremendous command and a tremendous temper which he forcefully controls. He is 38.

Joe Namath, at 25, has a small piece of the world in his hands. The Jet quarterback has fame and fortune and is the subject of much adulation. But these qualities require some responsibility. Namath sometimes finds it hard to be responsible and live up to several images others have created for him. He is a bachelor and a free spirit.

Morrall the Good Guy

Earl Morrall, the 34-year-old Baltimore quarterback, has only one image and it never changes. He is the American good guy, the bland, steady even-tempered family man. Morrall reflects adoration rather than adulation. He has had a number of failures in his pro football career and those who know him are delighted at his recent good fortune.

The Jets then are a team with a wild and highly skilled quarterback who has carried them to heights that few believed possible. The coach has been carried along.

The Colts, showing the mark of their dominant coach, have been so successful they were able to absorb a new quarterback, who had been a failure elsewhere for almost a dozen years, as a replacement for their great but injured star, John Unitas.

Ewbank began his football career slowly. He spent 14 years as an assistant coach at his alma mater, Miami University of Ohio. During World War II he joined a Miami contemporary, Paul Brown, in coaching the Great Lakes Naval Training Station team. Following two short stops at Brown University and Washington University of St. Louis, Ewbank joined Paul Brown on the coaching staff of the Cleveland Browns.

Brown brought a number of new techniques and depths to coaching. Ewbank absorbed them all. He very much reflects Brown's thinking and methods, which have not changed in 15 years.

Ewbank's chance to become a head coach came in 1954 when he took over the Baltimore team. Shula was one of the players. The Colts won two league championships, 1958 and 1959, and then went down. Ewbank was dismissed as coach in 1962 and joined the Jets the next year.

Shrewd and occasionally devious like most coaches, Ewbank is gregarious and well-liked and has a mild sense of humor.

Shula, a native of Painesville, Ohio, was a fine athlete at John Carroll University in Cleveland. A defensive back, Shula played seven seasons in pro football and then went into coaching.

He attracted notice in building the great defensive teams of the Detroit Lions beginning in 1960. After Ewbank was dismissed, Carroll Rosenbloom, owner of the Colts, chose Shula to take charge.

Smalltown Boy Makes Good

Don's record has been outstanding, the Colts winning 65 games, losing 18 and tying three. Until this season the biggest prize of all, a league championship, has eluded him.

Shula does not let many people get close to him. But he certainly knows how to motivate athletes and he does it through inspiration rather than fear.

Namath left Beaver Falls, Pa., where he was brought up in humble circumstances, to play football. His grades were poor and so he went to the University of Alabama to become famous. Then he was projected into the New York scene with tremendous publicity.

Becoming a great quarterback takes a while, even for one so talented as Namath, whose knee injuries held him back. In his fourth season, he emerged as the best and was voted the most valuable player in the American League.

Morrall won the same award in the National League. Morrall graduated from Michigan State, where he was an all-America choice with a degree in industrial engineering. He has another career apart from football as a sales executive for Garwood Industries. His specialty is wheel covers, and he sells to Chrysler and Ford in Detroit.

He and his wife and four children live in suburban Bloomfield Hills. Morrall played for the San Francisco, Pittsburgh, Detroit and New York teams for a dozen years before going to Baltimore last August. In only three of those seasons was he a regular. He admits he cannot quite grasp the fact that Earl Morrall will be the starting quarterback in the Super Bowl for what probably is the best team in football.

What Ewbank and Shula Have to Say
Concerning Rival Teams

MIAMI, *Jan. 11—Here are some of the things Coach Weeb Ewbank of the New York Jets has said this week about the Jets, the Baltimore Colts and tomorrow's Super Bowl game:*

On the importance of the game: "It's just another game. You can't play it any other way. You have to prepare for this one exactly the way you've prepared for all those other games you've played all season."

On preparing his team for the game: "I don't think you have to ever get a player ready for a game. If you do, you don't want him."

On the difference between the Jets and Colts: "They have a great football team, but we don't have their experience."

On the Colts: "They've had a fine football team for three years and this year they've had the determination not to let it get away from them."

On the Jets: "We are the best American League team to play in the Super Bowl. I wouldn't have said it earlier in the season, but I'll say it now."

On the Jets' chances: "I think we have a better chance of winning the Super Bowl than Kansas City or Oakland the last two years. We have Joe Namath and we have the receivers. The big question is whether we can keep our poise. I don't want to happen to us what happened to Kansas City and Oakland."

On what it takes to get into the Super Bowl: "You not only have to be good, but you have to be a little lucky. We had five operations on our team this year, but somehow we always seemed to have the man ready to step in."

On the difference in the Jet and Colt systems: "There is little difference. There are just a few basic plays you can use in football. The difference is in the execution, the experience, the injuries and the organization."

On the difference between the National and American Leagues: "I think we are closing the gap, but if we are so fortunate as to win, I wouldn't say we had passed them. Little by little, the discrepancy has been overcome. There's nothing mysterious. We could probably trade playbooks. The only thing you don't tell them is when you're going to use some particular play."

On whether the Jets would rather kick off or receive: "If we win the toss, we'll receive unless there's a hurricane blowing. In all the years I've been around, I've never done anything but receive. I think the players would run me out of the ball park if I didn't get the ball when I had the chance."

On quarterbacks: "They have two great quarterbacks and I think we have two great quarterbacks. Getting Babe Parilli has helped us. I would never have the slightest doubt about sending him in if I had to."

On comparing a young Joe Namath with a young Johnny Unitas: "They're pretty much the same except John had good wheels. Both can pass long. Some quarterbacks can throw long, but can't pass long."

On the basic approach to a game: "It's all a matter of matching men and getting the execution."

On Super Bowl strategy: "We'll add maybe a wrinkle here and there, a change or two on defense, but that's about it. You do the things you know best."

MIAMI, *Jan. 11—Here are some of the things Coach Don Shula of the Baltimore Colts has said this week about the Colts, the New York Jets and tomorrow's Super Bowl game:*

On the outcome: "I like the Colts."

On the danger of overconfidence: "We've had some discussion with the team. All season is riding on this game. I'd hate to see all the good go down the drain because of one poor effort."

On what the game can prove: "There are not too many ways to judge the relative strength of the two leagues other than this game and the preseason games. I think this game has a lot of bearing."

On the Colt defense: "I haven't seen a better one. We had a good defense last year and I think it has improved this year."

On 11th-hour preparations: "I pretty much leave my players alone. I don't go for anything false. I feel that it has to come from inside a player to get ready for a game."

On withdrawing himself emotionally for a game: "I discipline myself so as not to allow anything to interfere with my responsibilities on the day of a game, which is the most important day. There are many decisions to make that day, like whether to stick with your game plan or what adjustments to make. I work hard to control myself and my temper. I don't want anything to cause me to lose track of what is going on."

On changes for the Super Bowl: "We have installed some new plays, but nothing drastic. We enter every game with a few little changes—the same basic plays with little wrinkles. I don't think this game will be won or lost with any gimmicks. Good solid football will determine who wins."

On the Jets' improvement: "My impression of the Jets through the years has been that they always had a good offense. This year, the defense seems to have arrived, and that's probably the big reason why they are where they are now."

On Joe Namath: "He's the one who moves their offense. His aim is very strong and accurate and quick. He's a heckuva thrower."

On blitzing Namath: "Blitzing him is tough, because he has such quick release and his receivers are taught to change patterns if there's a blitz."

On comparing Namath to National League quarterbacks: "He has quick release like Sonny Jurgensen, but I think first of Norm Van Brocklin, who got back very quickly."

On the Jet receivers: "They've been with Joe four years. Earl Morrall has been with ours four months."

On the sideline duties of Johnny Unitas: "John has no set duties. He's always available. Often, when the receivers come off the field and think they can get open to the outside and Earl isn't sure of the best play to employ, they will talk about it."

On John Mackey, the Colt tight end: "The best I've ever seen."

On Tom Matte, the Colt halfback: "Show me a better runner."

On Jerry Hill, the Colt fullback: "The best blocker in football."

Sports of The Times

By ARTHUR DALEY

The Showdown

MIAMI, *Jan. 11*—"Everything we've done so far is nothing if we don't win this one," said Don Shula. There was urgency in the words and intensity in the voice of the Baltimore Colt coach as he made ready to hurl his heroes against the New York Jets in the Super Bowl on the morrow for the football championship of the blinking universe.

"We've had too many disappointments, too many frustrations of recent years," he continued. "We just couldn't stand another. We're overdue to take it all."

The Cleveland Browns upset the Colts for the 1964 championship, a title show that was generally acknowledged as settling No. 1 rating in pro ball. A year later, Baltimore lost both quarterbacks, Johnny Unitas and Gary Cuozzo, and had to go with a reformed halfback, Tom Matte, in the clutch games. But even then it took a disputed, dubious field goal for the Packers to beat them in sudden-death overtime, 13–10. The season before last, the Colts were eliminated by the Rams in the only game they dropped all year.

This will be the extra motivation that Baltimore will carry into the Super Bowl, not that this showdown game requires any artificial pump-priming. But the Colts are convinced they are the best there is and they are determined not to fluff so matchless an opportunity for proving it. Agreeing with them in this self-esteem is the bookmaking gentry, whose opening price established the National Football League champions as 17 points better than the Jets.

The Big Gun

But the Jets have Joe Namath and they always will have a scoring hope so long as he can remain vertical enough to throw the ball. But never in his young life has he faced as ferocious and as smothering a defense as the Colts can mount. Baltimore pressure on him and his receivers might even be shattering to the point of demoralization, an item that has not been overlooked by those shrewdies, the professional oddsmakers.

No one expressed the situation better than Al Davis, the front-office genius of the Oakland Raiders. This firebrand is still burning inwardly at the way Namath snatched away the Super Bowl assignment from the Raiders in the American Football League title game, but he is still realistic enough to recognize the extra qualities that Namath brings into a game.

"He can throw," Davis conceded. "On his good days he can lift a ball club, just as Sandy Koufax used to do in pitching shutouts to win for a team that maybe wasn't as good over all as the other one."

Strictly speaking, Namath alone has brought the element of uncertainty and excitement to a game that might be regarded as a prosaic romp for the Colts otherwise. He will attract a record television audience, a loudmouthed antihero like Cassius Clay, who also drew those hoping to see him get his block knocked off. Yet Cassius—at least in his pre-Muslim days —had more charm, personality and likability.

"Funny thing about this game," said Davis musingly. "It brings together the two finest passers in football, Namath and Unitas—except that Unitas won't play."

In a way that's one of the extraordinary facets of the match. Unitas was sidelined by an injured arm for the entire season and the Colts still won 15 of 16 games with Earl Morrall running the show with unexpected surehandedness and skill.

The great Johnny U. is almost ready to return, but he will sit it out nonetheless, provided no emergency develops. If Unitas were at the peak of his powers, this would be no contest. National Leaguers, however, are not yet totally convinced that the unbelievable Morrall can do the same. Hence the faint flickers of doubt.

Character Switch

Morrall has brought about a change in the character of the Colt attack because he relies more on running plays than Unitas did. So they now have excellent offensive balance. Because of Namath, the Jets rely more on passing, especially the bomb. But he will have to throw against a defense that will hound him to death—the Colt defenders have produced four shutouts this season. Meanwhile, Don Maynard, George Sauer and Pete Lammons, Namath's primary receivers, will filter into the adhesive coverage of a tightly knit, marvelously coordinated secondary.

It's a better secondary than the Jets'. John Mackey, a bull of a man, along with the fleet Willie Richardson and the wily Jimmy Orr, may be too hot for the New York secondary to handle, with Johnny Sample picked as the likeliest pigeon. Furthermore, the workmanlike Matte and Jerry Hill can grind out running yardage because Colt blocking is fiendishly efficient.

The Green Bay Packers won the first two Super Bowl games, 35–10 and 33–14. Namath may make it closer. On an exceptional day he may even win it. Contrariwise, though, this also could blow up into a lopsided score, especially if Joe the Jet is forced into the desperation straits of having to play catch-up football.

A week ago, in a long-distance look, I picked Baltimore to win, 24–12, the dozen points being for Jim Turner field goals. I haven't seen anything here to change my opinion. I'll stay with the original call.

How Rival Teams in Super Bowl Match Up

NEW YORK ON OFFENSE

No.	Player	Ht.	Wt.	Pos.
83	George Sauer, Jr. . .	6-2	195	SE
75	Winston Hill	6-4	280	LT
61	Bob Talamini	6-1	255	LG
52	John Schmitt	6-4	245	C
67	Dave Herman	6-1	255	RG
71	Sam Walton	6-5	276	RT
87	Pete Lammons. . . .	6-3	233	TE
12	Joe Namath	6-2	195	QB
41	Matt Snell	6-2	219	FB
32	Emerson Boozer. . .	5-11	202	HB
13	Don Maynard	6-1	179	FL

BALTIMORE ON DEFENSE

No.	Player	Ht.	Wt.	Pos.
43	Lenny Lyles	6-2	204	RCB
81	Ordell Braase. . . .	6-4	245	RE
76	Fred Miller	6-3	250	RT
53	Dennis Gaubatz . .	6-2	232	MLB
74	B. R. Smith.	6-4	250	LT
78	Bubba Smith	6-7	295	LE
20	Jerry Logan.	6-1	190	SS
21	Rick Volk.	6-3	195	FS
32	Mike Curtis.	6-2	232	LLB
66	Don Shinnick. . . .	6-0	228	RLB
40	Bob Boyd.	5-10	192	LCB

NEW YORK ON DEFENSE

No.	Player	Ht.	Wt.	Pos.
42	Randy Beverly. . . .	5-11	198	RCB
86	Verlon Biggs	6-4	268	RE
80	John Elliott	6-4	249	RT
62	Al Atkinson	6-2	230	MLB
72	Paul Rochester . . .	6-2	250	LT
81	Gerry Philbin	6-2	245	LE
22	Jim Hudson	6-2	210	SS
46	Bill Baird.	5-10	180	FS
51	Ralph Baker	6-3	235	LLB
51	Larry Grantham . . .	6-0	212	RLB
24	Johnny Sample . . .	6-1	204	LCB

BALTIMORE ON OFFENSE

No.	Player	Ht.	Wt.	Pos.
28	Jimmy Orr	5-11	185	SE
72	Bob Vogel	6-5	250	LT
62	Glenn Ressler. . . .	6-3	250	LG
50	Bill Curry	6-2	235	C
71	Dan Sullivan	6-3	250	RG
73	Sam Ball	6-4	240	RT
88	John Mackey	6-2	224	TE
15	Earl Morrall	6-2	206	QB
41	Tom Matte.	6-0	214	FB
45	Jerry Hill	5-11	215	HB
87	Willie Richardson .	6-2	198	FL

NEW YORK SUBSTITUTES

No.	Player	Ht.	Wt.	Pos.
11	Jim Turner.	6-2	205	K-QB
15	Vito Parilli	6-0	190	QB
23	Bill Rademacher. . .	6-1	190	DB
26	Jim Richards	6-1	180	DB
29	Bake Turner	6-1	180	FL
30	Mark Smolinski . . .	6-1	215	FB
31	Bill Mathis	6-1	220	HB
33	Curley Johnson . . .	6-0	215	P-TE
43	John Dockery	6-0	186	DB
45	Earl Christy	5-11	195	DB
47	Mike D'Amato. . . .	6-2	204	DB
48	Cornell Gordon . . .	6-0	186	DB
50	Carl McAdams. . . .	6-3	245	DT
56	Paul Crane	6-2	204	LB
63	John Neidert.	6-2	230	LB
66	Randy Rasmusses . .	6-2	255	G
74	Jeff Richardson . . .	6-3	250	T
85	Steve Thompson . .	6-5	240	DE

BALTIMORE SUBSTITUTES

No.	Player	Ht.	Wt.	Pos.
16	Jim Ward	6-2	195	QB
19	John Unitas	6-1	196	QB
25	Alex Hawkins . . .	6-1	186	FL
26	Preston Pearson . .	6-1	190	HB-DB
27	Ray Perkins	6-0	183	E
34	Terry Cole	6-1	220	HB-P
37	Ocie Austin.	6-3	200	DB
47	Charles Stukes . . .	6-3	212	DB
49	David Lee.	6-4	215	P-K
52	Dick Szymanski . .	6-3	235	C
55	Ron Porter	6-3	232	LB
61	Cornelius Johnson .	6-2	245	G
64	Sidney Williams . .	6-2	235	S-LB
75	John Williams . . .	6-3	256	G
79	Lou Michaels. . . .	6-2	250	DE-K
80	Gail Cogdill.	6-2	200	E
84	Tom Mitchell. . . .	6-2	235	TE
85	Roy Hilton	6-6	240	DE

Super Bowl Comparison

OFFENSE

	Jets	Colts
Total Points	419	402
First Downs	249	258
Rushing	80	110
Passing	144	131
Penalties	25	17
Net Yds. Gained	5,047	4,681
Rushing	1,608	1,809
Passing	3,439	2,872
Passes Attempted	436	359
Completed	217	196
Had Intercepted	19	22
Fumbles Lost	10	11
Yds. Penalized	742	655
Times Tackled Att. to Pass	18	29
Yds. Lost Att. to Pass	135	222

DEFENSE

	Jets	Colts
Opponents' Points	280	144
Opponents' First Downs	178	207
Rushing	59	71
Passing	104	119
Penalties	15	17
Opponents' Net Yds.	3,363	3,377
Rushing	1,195	1,339
Passing	2,168	2,038
Opponents' Passes Att.	403	432
Completed	187	224
Had Intercepted	28	29
Opponents' Fumbles Recov.	9	12
Times Opponents' Dropped Passings	43	45
Yds. Opponents' Lost Att. to Pass	399	367

INDIVIDUAL PASSING

New York	Att.	Comp.	Yds.	Int.
Namath	380	187	3,147	17
Parilli	55	29	401	2
Baltimore				
Morrall	317	182	2,904	17
Unitas	32	11	139	4

INDIVIDUAL RUSHING

New York	Att.	Yds.	Avg.
Snell	179	747	4.2
Boozer	143	441	3.1
Mathis	74	208	2.8
Smolinski	12	15	1.3
Baltimore			
Matte	183	662	3.6
Cole	104	418	4.0
Hill	91	360	4.0
Brown	39	159	4.1
Mackey	10	103	10.3

INDIVIDUAL RECEIVING

New York	No.	Yds.	TDs
Sauer	66	1,141	3
Maynard	57	1,297	10
Lammons	32	400	3
Snell	16	105	1
Boozer	12	101	0
Baltimore			
Mackey	45	644	5
Richardson	37	698	8
Orr	29	743	6
Matte	25	275	1
Hill	18	161	1

INTERCEPTIONS

New York	No.	Yds.	TDs
Sample	7	88	1
Hudson	5	96	0
Beverly	4	127	1
Baird	4	74	0
Baker	3	31	0
Baltimore			
Boyd	8	160	1
Volk	6	154	0
Lyles	5	32	0
Logan	3	9	0

SCORING

New York	TDs	EP	FG	Pts.
J. Turner	0	43	34	145
Maynard	10	0	0	60
Snell	7	0	0	42
Mathis	6	2	0	38
Boozer	5	0	0	30
Baltimore				
Michaels	0	48	18	102
Matte	10	0	0	60
Richardson	8	0	0	48
Orr	6	0	0	36
Mackey	5	0	0	30

Facts on Third Super Bowl

At Stake—World professional football championship.

Participants—Baltimore Colts, champions of National Football League, and New York Jets, champions of American Football League.

Colts' Season Record—Regular-season won-lost record of 13–1, losing to Cleveland Browns, then defeated Minnesota Vikings, 24–14, for Western Conference championship, then defeated Browns, 34–0, for league championship.

Jets' Season Record—Regular-season record of 11–3 (losing to Buffalo Bills, Denver Broncos and Oakland Raiders), then defeated Raiders, 27–23, for league championship.

Odds—Colts favored by 18 to 20 points.

Site—Orange Bowl, Miami, seating capacity 75,354.

Kickoff time—3:05 P.M., New York time.

Television—Nationwide (Miami area blacked out) by the National Broadcasting Company, Channel 4 in New York at 2:30 P.M. Announcers—Curt Gowdy, Kyle Rote, Al DeRogatis and Jim Simpson.

Radio—Nationwide (including Miami area) by the National Broadcasting Company, WNBC in New York at 2:45 P.M.

Network Television-Radio Receipts—$2.5-million.

Players' Shares—$15,000 to each member of winning team, $7,500 to each member of loser.

Where the Money Goes—After deduction of expenses, taxes and players' shares, remainder of gross receipts is distributed among the competing teams, the 24 noncompeting teams in the National and American leagues, the two league offices and the commissioner's office. The 26 teams will contribute a "substantial portion" to the player benefit (pensions, etc.) plans.

Uniforms—The Colts will be the home team and will wear blue jerseys. The Jets will wear white jerseys.

Rosters—Each team is allowed to activate one or two players any time before the start of the game, but must stay within 40-player limit. Players on hand from the Jet taxi (reserve) squad are Harvey Nairn (flanker), Karl Henke (defensive end) and Ray Rayes (defensive tackle). Players on hand from the Colt taxi squad are Gail Cogdill and Don Alley (wide receivers), Bob Grant (linebacker) and Jim Duncan (defensive back).

Trophy—The winning team will receive a sterling silver World Championship Game Trophy, created by Tiffany, mounted on a three-sided base.

Game Ball—The National League ball will be used when the Colts are on offense, the American League ball when the Jets are on offense. The balls differ in three ways: (1) the National League ball has a naturally tanned-in tack, while the American League ball is sprayed with a tacky substance after manufacture; (2) the American League ball, like the college ball, has a more pointed ogive (the arch from the laces to the nose of ball), while the National League ball is more rounded at the ogive, and (3) the lacing on the National League ball is 4¼ inches long, on the American League ball 4½ inches long.

Conversions—The conversion after each touchdown is worth 1 point. The American League rule allowing a 2-point option for conversion by run or pass is not in effect.

Sudden Death—If the game is tied after the regulation 60 minutes it will continue in sudden-death overtime. The team that scores first in overtime (by touchdown, field goal or safety) wins.

Game Officials—Referee, Tom Bell, Lexington, Ky., National League; umpire, Walt Parker, Denton, Tex., American League; head lineman, George Murphy, Los Angeles, National League; line judge, Cal Lepore, Chicago, American League; field judge, Joe Gonzales, Los Angeles, National League; back judge, Jack Reader, Edison, N. J., American League.

Official Time—Scoreboard clock will be official.

Previous Results—The Green Bay Packers won both previous Super Bowl games, 35–10, from Kansas City Chiefs in 1967 and 33–14 from Oakland Raiders in 1968.

Jets Upset Colts By 16–7 for Title in the Super Bowl

A.F.L. Club Wins for First Time as Namath Pierces Baltimore Defense

Millions Watch Game

Morrall Is Harried Into 3 Interceptions by Rushers—Snell Is Standout

By DAVE ANDERSON

MIAMI, *Jan. 12*—In a memorable upset that astonished virtually everyone in the football realm, the New York Jets of the American League conquered the Baltimore Colts, the supposedly impregnable National League champions, 16–7, today for the Super Bowl prestige and paycheck.

Joe Namath, the quarterback whose optimism proved to be contagious to his teammates, directed the Jets to a 4-yard touchdown run by Matt Snell, the workhorse fullback, and field goals by Jim Turner from 32, 30 and 9 yards.

Equally important, the Jet defensive unit dominated the Colt offense. Led by Gerry Philbin, the Jet pass-rushers harried Earl Morrall, selected as the N.F.L.'s most valuable player, into throwing three interceptions in the first half.

Namath Best Quarterback

Midway in the third quarter, Morrall was benched and Johnny Unitas, the sore-armed master, took over at quarterback. With about 3½ minutes remaining in the game, the Colts scored on a 1-yard run by Jerry Hill, but by that time the Jets were in command.

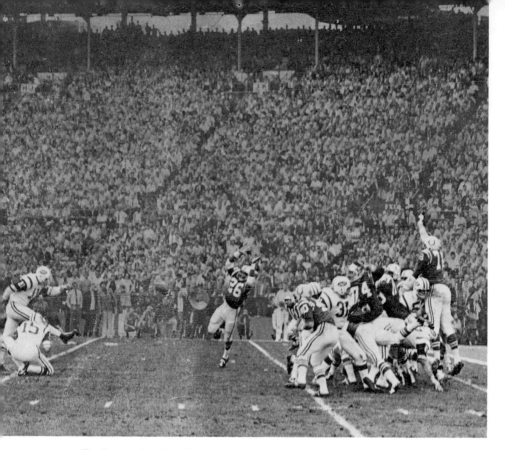

Jim Turner of the Jets kicks an extra point after a second-period touchdown as Babe Parilli Holds. Turner's three field goals, from the 32-, 30- and 9-yard lines gave New York its margin of victory.

In the A.F.L.'s ninth season, the Jets convinced 75,377 stunned spectators in the Orange Bowl and a television audience of perhaps 60 million that they deserved parity with the best teams in the N.F.L. and that Namath had developed into pro football's best quarterback.

In the two previous Super Bowl games, the Green Bay Packers had maintained the N.F.L. aura of invincibility by decisively defeating their A.F.L. opponents—35–10 over the Kansas City Chiefs two years ago, 33–14 over the Oakland Raiders a year ago. And the Colts had been expected to continue that supremacy.

In the point-spread type of betting, the Colts were favored by 18 to 20 points. Without a point spread, the Colts were a 7-to-1 choice.

The outcome put the Jets on a plateau with such other famous upset-makers in sports as Cassius Clay, knocking out Sonny Liston for the world heavyweight title as an 8–1 underdog in 1964, and the racehorse, Upset, defeating Man o' War in 1919 for that thoroughbred's only loss.

But the upset did not surprise Namath, the Jets' positive thinker. Despite his reputation as a playboy, he also is a serious student of football. As he observed the Colts in game films during the week, he noticed weaknesses in their vaunted zone pass-defense that he hoped to exploit. It is one thing to see the weaknesses as the film is flashed on a hotel-room wall, it is quite another to penetrate that defense on the field.

Namath accomplished it with his lariat arm, a scientific split end named George Sauer Jr. and a fullback, Snell, whose power running established the ground game that enabled the celebrated $400,000 quarterback to keep the Colts uncertain as to what play he would call next.

Namath, Sauer and Snell accumulated impressive statistics, but the members of the Jets' offensive line—Winston Hill, Bob Talamini, John Schmitt, Randy Rasmussen and Dave Herman—provided the blocking that produced those statistics.

Protected from the vaunted Colt pass-rush as if he were a rare jewel, Namath completed 17 of 28 passes for 206 yards. Sauer caught eight for 133 yards, a significant statistic because the Jets' other wide receiver, Don Maynard, was shut out. Snell rushed for 121 yards and caught four passes for 40 more.

Jets Keep Poise

In earning $15,000 apiece, double the reward for each Colt, the Jets kept their poise in moments of crisis as demanded by their coach, Weeb Ewbank, once dismissed by Baltimore.

Late in the scoreless first quarter, Sauer fumbled a sideline pass when tackled by Lenny Lyles, and the loose ball was pounced on by Ron Porter, a Colt linebacker, at the Jets' 12-yard line. On third down at the 6, Morrall's pass bounced high into the air off his intended receiver, Tom Mitchell. Randy Beverly, the Jets' cornerback who had been outmaneuvered by Mitchell, intercepted. Touchback. Jet ball.

Starting at the Jets' 20, Namath used Snell on four consecutive running plays aimed at the Colts right side. Ordell Braase, the end, and Don Shinnick, the linebacker, were victimized for a total of 26 yards, providing Namath with a first down at the Jets' 46, good field position.

After an incompletion and a short pass to Bill Mathis, a third-and-4 situation confronted Namath, but he drilled a 14-yard pass to Sauer, who had fooled Lyles, for the first down.

Another pass to Sauer moved the Jets to the Colts' 23. Then a 2-yard gain by Emerson Boozer, a 12-yard pass to Snell, a 5-yard gain by Snell and Snell's sweep produced a touchdown.

Sample Makes Interception

Not long after that, Tom Matte, who ran for a total of 116 yards, put the Colts at the Jets' 16 with a 58-yard dash down the right sideline.

On first down, Morrall threw toward Willie Richardson, his flanker, but Johnny Sample, once a Colt, zipped across to intercept the pass at the 2.

In the final minute of the first half, Morrall committed his worst mistake. At the Jets' 45, he handed off to Matte, who turned and tossed a backward pass to Morrall as the split end, Jimmy Orr, drifted beyond Beverly toward the end zone.

Orr was alone near the goal-line, with no Jet within 20 yards, but Morrall apparently never saw him. He threw toward Jerry Hill, his fullback, who was in front of the goal posts, but Jim Hudson, the Jets' strongside safetyman, intercepted at the 12, assuring a 7–0 half-time lead.

Another mistake, a fumble by Matte on the first play from scrimmage of the second half, turned the ball over to the Jets at the Colts' 33, in position for Turner's first field goal.

After three unsuccessful passes by Morrall on the next Colt series, Namath hit Sauer for two 14-yard gains to set up Turner's second field goal for a 13–0 lead with about 4 minutes remaining in the third quarter.

When the Colt offensive took the field, Unitas had replaced Morrall. Unable to throw long because of his tender right elbow, Unitas misfired twice on short passes to Matte and Orr.

When the third quarter ended, Namath was guiding the team to Turner's final field goal and the Colts had been limited to only eight plays, including two punts, in that period.

But early in the final quarter, Matte and Hill moved the Colts to the Jets' 25, but Unitas was unable to deliver. After overthrowing Richardson, the 35-year-old quarterback found Orr in the end zone, but the pass was intercepted by Beverly.

In his next opportunity, Unitas generated an 80-yard drive, sparked by a fourth-down pass to Orr from his own 20.

After the Colts avoided a shutout on Hill's touchdown, they recovered an onside kick-off at the Jets' 44. When Unitas hit Orr and Richardson to move the ball to the 24, the Jets began to wonder if Unitas would work the magic he had performed for so many years when his right arm was healthy.

But again, the Jet pass-defenders, not the Colt pass-receivers, made the big play. Sample tipped away a pass intended for Richardson. After the Jet rush harassed Unitas into throwing short to Orr and then too longs a fourth-down pass intended for Orr was batted beyond his reach by Larry Grantham, the linebacker.

After that, Snell carried on six consecutive plays, providing a needed first down that enabled the Jets to exhaust the final 2 minutes 21 seconds and frustrate the Colts.

Namath was awarded a Dodge Charger by *Sport* magazine as the game's most valuable player, but Snell appeared to be equally deserving. So did all the offensive linemen. In the most significant victory in A.F.L. history, the battle had been won where it usually is in football—in the trenches.

Super Bowl Scoring

New York Jets (16)

Ends—Sauer, Maynard, Lammons, B. Turner, Rademacher, Philbin, Biggs.
Tackles—Hill, Herman, Richardson, Walton, Rochester, Elliott, McAdams.
Guards—Talamini, Rasmussen.
Centers—Schmitt, Crane.
Linebackers—Baker, Atkinson, Grantham, Neidert.
Quarterbacks—Namath, Parilli.
Offensive Backs—Boozer, Snell, Mathis, Smolinski.
Defensive Backs—Sample, Beverly, Hudson, Baird, Christy, D'Amato, Richard, Dockery.
Kickers—J. Turner, Curley Johnson.

Baltimore Colts (7)

Ends—Orr, Richardson, Mackey, Perkins, Hawkins, Mitchell, Bubba Smith, Braase, Michaels.
Tackles—Vogel, Ball, J. Williams, Billy Ray Smith, Miller, Hilton.
Guards—Ressler, Sullivan, Cornelius Johnson.
Centers—Curry, Szymanski.
Linebackers—Curtis, Gaubatz, Shinnick, S. Williams, Porter.
Quarterbacks—Morrall, Unitas.
Offensive Backs—Matte, Hill, Brown, Pearson, Cole.
Defensive Backs—Boyd, Lyles, Logan, Volk, Stukes, Austin.
Kicker—Lee.

New York Jets .... 0 7 6 3—16
Baltimore Colts .... 0 0 0 7— 7

N. Y.—Snell, 4, run (Turner, kick).
N. Y.—FG, Turner, 32.
N. Y.—FG, Turner, 30.
N. Y.—FG, Turner, 9.
Balt.—Hill, 1, run (Michaels, kick).
Attendance—75,377.

Statistics of the Game

	Jets	Colts		Jets	Colts
First downs	21	18	Interceptions by	4	0
Rushing yardage	142	143	Punts	4-39	3-44
Passing yardage	206	181	Fumbles lost	1	1
Return yardage	34	139	Yards penalized	28	23
Passes	17-29	17-41			

Super Bowl Comparison

INDIVIDUAL PASSING

New York	Att.	Comp.	Yds.	TDs	Int.
Namath 28	28	17	206	0	0
Parilli. 1	1	0	0	0	0
Baltimore					
Morrall. 17	17	6	71	0	3
Unitas 24	24	11	110	0	1

RECEIVING

New York	Caught	Yds.
Snell	4	40
Lammons	2	13
Mathis	3	20
Sauer.	8	133
Baltimore		
Mackey	3	35
Mitchell	1	15
Richardson	6	58
Matte.	2	30
Hill	2	1
Orr	3	42

INDIVIDUAL RUSHING

New York	Att.	Yds.	Avg.	TDs
Boozer. 10	10	19	1.9	0
Snell 30	30	121	4.1	1
Mathis 3	3	2	0.7	0
Baltimore				
Morrall. 2	2	-2	-1.0	0
Matte. 11	11	116	10.5	0
Hill 9	9	29	3.2	1
Unitas 1	1	0	0.0	0

Interceptions—Beverly, N.Y., 2; Sample, N.Y., 1; Hudson, N.Y., 1.

Man In the News: Football's Super Star

Joseph William Namath

Jan. 12, 1969—People talk about Joe Namath. He excites comment. Today he is provoking more than ever, because after an all-America career at the University of Alabama and four years as the quarterback of the New York Jets, he sits supreme at the top of the hard-nosed world of professional football. Namath, the ultra-publicized individualistic quarterback from Beaver Falls, Pa., yesterday led the New York Jets to an astounding 16–7 victory over the Baltimore Colts in the Super Bowl game at Miami. He intended to do it and, last week, in preparation for the game, said he would do it. Few believed him.

The victory, which elevated the American League to an equal level with the older National League, marks the high point of Namath's success-studded career.

"What we like about him is that he is a winner, he doesn't know about losing," commented Weeb Ewbank, the coach of the Jets, a few seasons ago.

Sonny Werblin, the former owner of the Jets, who signed Namath for a bonus of $387,000 and a Lincoln convertible, found another quality in Namath that he thought valuable. He said, on signing the sleepily handsome 6-foot-2-inch black-haired star:

"Namath has the presence of a star. You know how a real star lights up a room when he comes in. Joe has that quality."

Namath, who sparkled on the football field for Beaver Falls High School and at Alabama has become a legendary figure since moving to New York in 1965.

His penthouse apartment at 76th and First Avenue with its famous white llama rug is often the scene of get-togethers and parties. ("A get-together is when the guys come over to eat steaks and play cards; a party is when there are girls," he has said.)

Namath has pursued pleasure in the saloons and discotheques of the East Side, often in the company of beautiful young women. During one early-morning jaunt, he allegedly had a dispute with a sports writer that is still awaiting legal adjudication.

Joseph William Namath, the fifth child of a Hungarian steelworker, was born in Beaver Falls on May 31, 1943, and started playing football with his three older brothers when he was hardly able to hold the football.

The Golden Arm

After a splendid career in high school, he was offered scholarships by 52 colleges and universities. He also was offered $50,000 to play baseball with the Chicago Cubs.

Under Coach Paul (Bear) Bryant, Namath developed into one of the most sought-after passers in college football. Bryant called him, "the greatest athlete I ever coached."

His signing by Werblin and the Jets represented a great triumph for the A.F.L. and many observers contend led the way for the merger of the A.F.L. and N.F.L.

Although many people scoffed at the huge investment in the weak-kneed Namath and predicted he might never be able to complete one season because of his delicate underpinnings, he quickly established himself as one of the greatest passing quarterbacks.

Although the Jets were not able to win a league championship with Namath until this season, he set a pro record for the most yardage in a single campaign in 1967 by passing for 4,007 yards.

This year, although he threw significantly fewer passes for fewer touchdowns, he was voted the most valuable player in the A.F.L.

At Miami, while training for the Super Bowl, he was bedeviled by sports writers, who eagerly quoted him saying that the Jets would win the game, that the A.F.L. was equal to the N.F.L., that Earl Morrall of the Colts was not as good a passer as several in Namath's league. Most writers expected Namath to eat his words yesterday.

Instead, Namath said of the writers in a post-game interview: "I hope they all eat their pencils and pads. We won!"

Game's Star Felt Relaxed at Start

Namath Told A Teammate Arm Was 'Real Loose'

MIAMI, *Jan. 12 (UPI)*—Some of the New York Jets were a bit edgy going into their showdown today with the highly touted Baltimore Colts in the Super Bowl, but not Joe Namath.

Before trotting out on the field for the start of the game, he turned to one of his teammates and said: "I feel loose, real loose. My arm is so loose I think it's gonna fall off."

A pre-game ceremony was capped by the appearance of the three astronauts who had circumnavigated the moon. The trio—Capt. James A. Lovell, Col. Frank Borman and Lieut. Col. William A. Anders—recited over the loud-speaker system the Pledge of Allegiance. Their appearance must have further inspired Namath to put the Jets into orbit.

Probably no one on the Jets savored their 16–7 upset victory more than Larry Grantham, the weary 30-year-old linebacker who first signed nine years ago with the club when it was known as the New York Titans and something of a laughing stock throughout the A.F.L.

"Not in my wildest dreams did I ever imagine anything like this happening to me when I signed with the Titans in 1960," said Grantham. "We didn't know of any Joe Namath then, but things got different when he came along. I don't see how any team can defense against him. He hits you where it hurts."

Another happy member of the Jets was Walt Michaels, their defensive backfield coach. Michaels's brother, Lou, is the Colts' place-kicking specialist and was involved in a near-fight in a Fort Lauderdale restaurant a week ago. But Walt smilingly had no comment about that incident.

"It was simply two hardheaded Pennsylvania ballplayers getting together," Michaels grinned, referring to Namath and his brother.

EWBANK CALLS NAMATH FABULOUS, SAYS JETS MADE NO ERRORS IN BEATING COLTS

Feat Acclaimed as Team Victory

Players Label Themselves as "the Greatest" and Praise Each Other

By FRANK LITSKY

MIAMI, *Jan. 12*—In case anyone watching in person or on television failed to get the message, the New York Jets left no doubt how they felt after beating the Baltimore Colts in today's Super Bowl game.

"We are a great team and this is the start of a new era," a happy Coach Weeb Ewbank said. "Ball control did it. We didn't make any errors. Joe Namath called a great game. He was fabulous, and he had great pass protection."

Johnny Sample, the Jet cornerback, defensive captain and No. 1 cheerleader, agreed.

"We're the greatest team," said Sample. "We put the Baltimore offense and defense to shame. When Earl Morrall released the ball, our defensive backs were racing to the ball. We read him pretty good. And I'll tell you, I feel pretty good. I've been thinking about this game for three years—every day."

Many Heroes on Club

Sample, with one interception and fine coverage of the dangerous Willie Richardson, was one of the many Jet heroes. So was Namath and Randy Beverly and Gerry Philbin and Matt Snell and George Sauer and so many others. The victory, as so many Jets pointed out, belonged to them all.

"It was execution," said assistant coach Walt Michaels, the architect of the Jet defense, "and great play by our safetymen. And I can't say enough about our linebackers. We sacrificed by letting the linebackers help out against passes. We didn't think their runners could go all the way. And they didn't."

"It was the offensive line with that straight-ahead blocking," said Snell, who had a big day at fullback.

"It was our defense," said Emerson Boozer, the halfback. "Our defense broke their backs."

"How about our defensive backs?" said John Elliott, the defensive tackle. "They played one hell of a game. I want to know who's got the No. 1 defense now."

Ewbank, too, had great praise for the defensive unit. "When our defense had to come through, it did, with the big play, with interceptions," he said.

Jets Are Jubilant

The Jets were not exactly humble in victory, and they didn't feel they had to be.

"We taught them out there," said Larry Grantham, who has been with the Jets since 1960; when they were the laughable Titans. "Now we're the first American League team to be taken seriously."

"I just hope," said Philbin, "this changes some people's minds about our league."

"It was a long time coming," said Namath, "a long time coming for the whole league."

Namath has a flair for the dramatic off the field, too. The team voted him the game ball. He promptly said he would give it to the American League. Sport magazine said it would give him a Dodge Charger, its prize for the game's outstanding player.

"Is that one of those things I have to give back after a year?" Namath asked.

"You keep it forever," he was told.

"That's more like it," Namath said.

Namath sat in the trainer's room cutting the yards of tape off his legs and knees. His wet hair flopping over his face, the wisecrackers coming fast and easily, he was as usual, king of the hill.

"Are you more exhilarated than usual after winning a big game?" he was asked.

"That's a big word," he said. "They didn't teach us that in school."

Did his right thumb, injured in the third quarter, hurt?

"Nothing hurts now," he said.

Was he really so confident of victory when he "promised" earlier in the week that the Jets would win?

"I always had confidence we would win," he said. "But I didn't know what to expect. But I had a good time. When you go out and play football, you're supposed to have a good time. When you're losing, you're not having a good time, so we went out and won."

Nearby, Babe Parilli, Namath's seldom-used substitute, raved about the job Namath had done.

"He caught them off balance," said Parilli, who has been a pro quarterback for 15 years. "He called the right play at the right time. He read the safety blitz, and he read their pass coverage. What else is there?"

Joe's Father Not Surprised

John Namath, Joe's father, said he wasn't excited because "I was sure they would win." A. M. Mathis, the father of Bill Mathis, the Jet halfback, said he tried to stay calm because of his heart condition, but his throat was sore from hollering.

Unexpectedly, there was little hollering in the Jet dressing room. The players had believed they would win, so they were not as surprised as almost everyone else. "We didn't make us three-touchdown underdogs," said Philbin.

Through it all, the Jets were looking forward to their winners' checks of $15,000 a man. The favored Baltimore players wound up with only $7,500 as the losers' shares.

"I just hope the Colts didn't spend theirs," said Philbin.

"My wife," said Sample, "spent mine already."

COLTS, DEJECTED BY THEIR SHOWING, CITE MISSED CHANCES

Defense Accepts Blame for Loss

Rushers 'Couldn't Quite' Get to Passer— 'Didn't Make Big Plays,' Says Shula

By WILLIAM N. WALLACE

MIAMI, *Jan. 12*—The many moods of the Baltimore Colts, following their loss today to the Jets in the Super Bowl, were in this order:

Disgust at themselves for having played a disappointing game, sky-high praise for Joe Namath and begrudging admiration for the other Jets.

Namath was the man the Colts remembered best. Said Billy Ray Smith, who before the game had suggested that Joe Willie might learn a little humility:

"He did it all. He threw the ball short a little. He threw the ball long a little. He ran the ball a little. He had it all going and so they won. I just couldn't quite get to him."

Smith was sitting half-undressed on a locker bench, perspiration on his upper body and dirt around his eyes. Ordell Braase, who like Smith, could not get to Namath, said, "He was everything we expected."

Blitz Fails in 3d Period

Don Shula, the Baltimore coach, echoed his two pass-rushers.

"He was all we had heard," he said. "A fine football player."

"The story of the game was simple," added Shula. "We didn't do it and they did. We had all the opportunities, especially in the first half. We didn't make the big plays we've had all season. We had a lot of dropped balls. We just didn't do it. They deserved it.

"We'll have to be men enough to do it."

In Shula's estimation Namath clearly won the battle of the blitz. The Colts, beginning in the second period, began to blitz Namath, charging with one of the safetymen, Rick Volk or Jerry Logan, in combination with Dennis Gaubatz or Mike Curtis of the linebacking corps. It was no good.

"He beat us," said Shula. "He beat our blitz three or four times and we beat him only once."

Unloaded Ball Quickly

Namath beat the blitz by unloading the ball quickly, usually to George Sauer, before the attackers could reach him.

Smith, at 33 years of age an old-timer on the highly praised Colt defense, blamed that unit for the defeat.

"It was us," he said. "We let down our teammates and the entire National Football League. My pride is bent."

Bill Curry, the center, said the Colts in their league had played "10 or 12 teams as good as the Jets."

"I don't mean that as sour grapes," he said, "but we didn't play our game. The turnovers were the story of the game. We had them. They didn't."

Curry's reference was to the four interceptions of Baltimore passes.

A downcast Earl Morrall repented for a missed opportunity at the end of the second period.

On a "flea flicker" play, in which he took a lateral pass from Tom Matte, then threw deep downfield, Morrall picked the wrong receiver, Jerry Hill.

He Didn't See Orr

Jim Hudson of the Jets stepped in front of Hill and intercepted the pass. Jimmy Orr, the Colt split end, had been wide open elsewhere.

Said Morrall: "The way I caught the ball from Matte, I was turned to the right and didn't see Orr."

Earlier in the second quarter, Morrall's pass bounced off Tom Mitchell's shoulder into the hands of Randy Beverly of the Jets for an end-zone interception. It would have been a tough touchdown catch for Mitchell.

"I think a linebacker tipped the ball and I think I threw it too hard," said Morrall.

John Unitas was not as visibly upset as Morrall. Said Unitas:

"I've been in football a long time. You always hate to lose. But a football player can't feel sorry for himself."

Shula said he had planned at half-time, after the Colts had gained only 71 yards passing and three of Morrall's passes had been intercepted, to replace Morrall with Unitas following one series of downs in the third period.

"I wanted to try to get something going," he said, "but we had a fumble (by Matte) on the first series and I kept Earl in."

In action for the final 19 minutes, Unitas completed 11 of 24 passes, but only two were beyond 20 yards and tested the power of his ailing arm. Neither was complete. The first went toward Jim Orr and was intercepted in the end zone by the ubiquitous Randy Beverly. The second, Unitas's final pass of the game, was overthrown to Orr in the end zone on fourth down.

"That's what happens when you don't practice much," said Unitas.

Sports of The Times

Broadway Joe is No. 1

By ROBERT LIPSYTE

MIAMI, *Jan. 12*—Five years ago, a few miles from here, a young, loud-mouthed, confident charmer named Cassius Clay prepared to meet Sonny Liston for the world boxing championship. Hardly anyone would bet on the fight because Clay was at least a 7–1 underdog, and there was some harsh talk about the greediness of a sport and of a television industry that would allow such a good-natured kid to risk his life against the most powerful puncher of all time.

Sonny the Bear would let Cassius hit him a few times, a rubber ball against a brick wall, then beat the boy blue.

People were not terribly upset by this prospect because Liston, ex-convict, labor goon, intimidator, represented the kind of solid, silent brutality they had come to expect, even demand, in a champion. Clay was a pop-off, he was gay, he was magical, he went his way and told the truth. He said he was sorry for Liston, built up so big he would fall a long way and he said he was going to win. Incredibly, he did.

And last Thursday night, with a double scotch in his hand, Joe Namath of the Jets said: "We'll win. I guarantee it." It was neither the first nor the last time he promised victory, provoking laughter from fans of the Baltimore Colts, of the National Football League, of the Columbia Broadcasting System, of history, nostalgia, propaganda, logic and from the gamblers who made the Colts at least a 16-point favorite.

Clay told the world how he would win: he was going to jab and move and cut the beast to pieces. Namath said he was going to establish a running game so the Colts could not concentrate entirely on stopping his vaunted "bomb," the game-busting pass to his wide receivers, George Sauer and, especially, Don Maynard. Clay warned the world not to sell his defenses short, Liston would never touch him. And Namath said that the Colts' second-string quarterback, Earl Morrall, was not the best the Jets had faced, and would not do well against their defense.

Packaging the Smith Brothers

Ultimately, the talk had to stop, and it did on a mild and breezy afternoon in the Orange Bowl. The Jets won the toss and elected to receive, and Namath ran his fullback, Matt Snell, twice into the right side of the Colts' line. Snell gained 3 yards the first time, 9 the second, and knocked Rick Volk, the right safety, rubber-legged. Namath had established his running game.

Morrall did little against the Jets' defense, as predicted. A journeyman quarterback, thrust into fame by an injury to Johnny Unitas, long considered the greatest, Morrall did not seem able to get the grinding, inexorable Baltimore touchdown machine moving. As the game moved into the second quarter, scoreless, the air began to visibly seep out of the Baltimore balloon. The Baltimore defense, including the Smiths, Bubba and Billy Ray, who are supposed to rise out of the turf on game days to swallow quarterbacks whole, was being contained. And Snell, playing the greatest game of his pro career, was bucking through that right side.

After the big boxing match, with Liston hurt and sitting on his stool, people said the Bear was a quitter. No one will say the Colts quit, but there came a time when the snap and crack were gone from their game. It may have happened sometime in that second quarter when Namath, in the midst of an 80-yard drive, gave Snell a breather and went to his receivers.

He passed to Sauer for 14 yards, and Lenny Lyles, the Colts' right cornerback, brought Sauer down. Namath, on the very next play, went to Sauer again, and Lyles took a chance. He flashed in front of Sauer in a wild attempt to pick the pass out of the air. He missed. Volk brought Sauer down with only a 1-yard gain, but it was another first down, and it was only a few minutes before Snell ran through that Colts' right side again and gave the Jets a lead they never lost.

Who Is the Greatest?

The game was not over, but it sometimes threatened to disintegrate into the kind of taunting with which Clay maddened Liston. Johnny Sample, the Jets' cornerback, intercepted a pass in that second quarter and tapped the intended receiver, Willie Richardson, on the head with it. No such nonsense for Namath, cool and professional and well-protected. It was deep into the third period before Bubba Smith finally got through. But it hardly mattered by then.

And then, with the score 13–0, John Unitas went into the game. If anyone in the world could turn it around and stop the upstarts and push

Broadway Joe down for another few years, it would be Johnny U., even with that swinging chain of a right arm now a rag.

But the kid hadn't lied. Johnny U., his passes wobbly and short, managed to get the Colts moving and even onto the scoreboard. And with about 3 minutes left, trailing, 16–7, the Colts recovered their onside kick and threatened again. But time was against them, and Namath jogged off the field, his right forefinger waggling over his head. The Jets were world champions, and he was No. 1.

In the locker room, like Clay that magical night, Namath hectored a press corps that had predicted him a loud-mouthed loser.

Those men of little faith could now eat their words, as they were told to five years ago. Or they could go across town and eat hamburgers. In the great new athletic rendition of the American dream, both Namath and Clay have their fast-food shops in Miami. Namath has his Broadway Joe's, and, not too far away, Clay has his Champburgers.

Super Bowl's Status

Game Rated in Class With World Series After American League's Major Upset

By WILLIAM N. WALLACE

MIAMI, *Jan. 13*—Norm Van Brocklin, a noted wisecracker, who was a great quarterback himself, delivered an opinion when asked about Joe Namath a few days before the Super Bowl game. You should understand that Van Brocklin, now the coach of the Atlanta Falcons, is an establishment man who believes in the National Football League and the status quo of 1950–60, his great decade.

"I'll tell you what I think about Namath on Sunday night," he said, "after he has played his first pro game."

It was a typical remark. The Norm Van Brocklins and the Bill Wallaces crept out of Miami today, silent and unseen.

Because of what Joe Namath accomplished in the Super Bowl yesterday, pro football will never quite be the same again. First, Joe Willie made the Super Bowl into a true competitive contest with stature equal to the World Series, the Kentucky Derby, the Masters golf tournament, or any other recurring, established sports events.

The Super Bowl was contrived. Its artificiality had begun to show because the National League's champion, Green Bay, won the first two dull games so convincingly.

•

Until Namath proved yesterday afternoon at around 3:40 o'clock that Lenny Lyles, the Baltimore cornerback, could be had, the Super Bowl belonged to the N.F.L. The A.F.L. champion was merely a punching bag. Namath put competition, anticipation and equality into an extravaganza that needed a justification for its continued existence.

Second, Namath gave his league, the American, a much stronger position from which its team owners can bargain in March. And bargain they will when the joint meeting of the leagues is held at Palm Springs, Calif., to plan the new structure of this rich and vibrant business-sport for 1970 and beyond.

The N.F.L. owners, who thought they were so superior by reason of having come to pro football first, extracted a price bordering on extortion when they agreed to let the A.F.L. co-exist in their merger agreement of 1966.

Broadway Joe destroyed their posture in less than three hours yesterday.

These words will be said at Palm Springs. The A.F.L. owner will say to the N.F.L. one, "Look, we don't need you quite as badly as you've been telling us for so long. We've got him and you don't." This him, this Namath, is the most valuable, talked-about property in pro football, if not in all sort of sports. And the A.F.L. is going to get O. J. Simpson, too.

Even the National Broadcasting Company stands to benefit. It might make some money off of pro football for a change next season when its cameras will be staring at O. J. and Broadway Joe. Its unrealistic, status-motivated television contract with the A.F.L. dates to 1964, a time when Namath was still trying to beat Bear Bryant's curfew at the University of Alabama.

•

A third point is that Namath proved a single athlete can take a mediocre cast of characters a long way. There is nothing special about the Jets in the office or on the field. The club has had three presidents in the last year and has no particular direction. Beloved Weeb Ewbank, the coach and general manager, ran such a sloppy ship last season that the club was fined by the commissioner's office about $2,500 for demeaning game officials. And if you took 35 of the 40 Jets and put Denver Bronco uniforms on them, who could tell the difference?

In the wake of pro football's greatest upset, the purpose of sport—these games we play—gains clarity. The reason for having such games, these Super Bowls, is so that once in a while the impossible can happen, the Jets can beat the Colts. If it could never happen, the great talent of Joe Willie Namath would be pumping gas in Beaver Falls without rhyme or reason.

N.F.L. Pretensions Analyzed: Super Status of Jets Confirmed

By DAVE ANDERSON

Jan. 15, 1969—Anyone phoning the New York Jets' offices now is greeted with the salutation, "Hello, world champions."

Although some National Football League-oriented observers consider Joe Namath to be a torch in the darkness of the American Football League, his teammates proved in their Super Bowl victory over the Baltimore Colts that they form the best young squad in pro football. Only two starters, Don Maynard and Johnny Sample, will be as old as 32 before next season, and Sample might retire.

Of the other 20 Jet starters on offense and defense, the average age will be about 26 on offense, 27 on defense.

If an N.F.L. team were to have won the Super Bowl with that young a squad, it would be acclaimed as the start of a dynasty. Instead, the Jets have been compared with the Denver Broncos except for a handful of players, presumably Matt Snell, George Sauer, Jim Turner, Gerry Philbin and Maynard, in addition to Namath, the suddenly accepted passer, play-caller and psychologist.

But if Namath was the only Jet of any consequence in the Super Bowl, his blockers must have been invisible and he forgot to stay on the field when the defensive unit took over.

Namath, Snell and Sauer provided the theatrics on offense. But somebody must have been blocking Bubba Smith and Billy Ray Smith, and the Jet defensive unit limited the Colts to one touchdown, and that occurred in the final 3½ minutes. Throughout their N.F.L. season, the Colts were unable to score at least 20 points only once, in a 16–3 triumph over the Green Bay Packers, as Earl Morrall was hailed as their savior at quarterback.

But against the Jet defense, Morrall was so hurried that he threw three interceptions near the goal-line, a development that recalled his travels as a journeyman quarterback with the 49ers, Steelers, Lions and Giants.

•

On defense, the Colts showed their age. Namath pierced three experienced defenders—Ordell Brase at right end; Don Shinnick at right linebacker, and Lenny Lyles at right cornerback—thereby proving that N.F.L. players get another year older each year, too. Some day the Jets will be old, but they're young and approaching their peak now, and Joe Willie has only begun to pass. The defensive unit has only begun to say . . . shall not pass.

Perhaps the most succinct tribute to Weeb Ewbank's coaching was delivered by Namath at the team's victory party.

"We didn't win on passing or running or defense," the quarterback said. "We beat the Colts in every phase of the game."

For that to happen, a team must be solid, particularly on defense, where a weak link can be exploited so easily.

Another excuse offered by N.F.L. advocates was that since the common college draft began following the 1966 peace treaty, all the A.F.L. teams have been strengthened. But only one Jet starter, Randy Rasmussen, the right guard who erased Billy Ray Smith's pass-rush, was a product of the common draft.

And here is a thought for Giant devotees. If the Giants had outbid the Jets for Snell in 1964, they would have had the big back they needed the following season when they chose Tucker Frederickson instead of Gale Sayers—or Joe Namath.

•

Dave Herman, the Jet tackle who handled Bubba Smith, also was a Giant draftee. But as he tells it, the Jets showed more interest in him. Philbin and Verlon Biggs were chosen by the Detroit Lions, Al Atkinson by the Colts, Ralph Baker by the Pittsburgh Steelers, to name a few young Jets who have had to live with a stigma because they preferred A.F.L. money.

In their embarrassment, some N.F.L. advocates condescend to agree that the Mickey Mouse League, as they've called the A.F.L., has developed into the Mighty Mouse League.

But perhaps the most important development of the Jet triumph is that it has increased, rather than decreased, the controversy between the followers of each league, particularly in New York where the arguments are reminiscent of the old Giant-Dodger baseball rivalry.

Arguments, and a modestly friendly wager, are what sports is all about. For those N.F.L. believers who can't wait for another crack at Joe Namath in next year's Super Bowl, he'll be ready and so will his teammates.

Chapter 4

Super Bowl IV—1970

The potential for anti-climax, always built in and at some point inevitable, threatened to overwhelm Super Bowl IV.

The old issue of comparative league strengths had been played out. Not only had the Jets made it irrelevant after Super Bowl III, but the whole separate existence of the leagues had become irrelevant. The public had been informed (oh, so thoroughly) that starting next season the new alignment would take effect, all under the N.F.L. banner, with two hybrid conferences divided into three divisions each.

Kansas City, the last A.F.L. champion, was in effect a lame-duck champion, further tarnished by the not-yet-accepted idea that it wasn't even a divisional champion. And Minnesota, representing the N.F.L. proper, wasn't exactly a member of the historic elite: it was an expansion team itself, actually one year younger than the A.F.L., having started up in 1961.

If the Chiefs, humbled by Green Bay only two years before, could now beat the Vikings, it would only prove that Minnesota wasn't Green Bay; and if the Vikings, as was generally expected, polished off the last A.F.L. champion, it wouldn't prove anything at all, since the A.F.L. as a separate entity had already agreed not to exist any longer.

Because of that background, Super Bowl IV forced itself on the full public not on the strength of its combatants, but oddly enough through a subject all sports promoters dread: the hint of a gambling scandal.

As it turned out, the hints and allegations had no substance, nor even the power to stir serious suspicions. But they did make the pregame week headlines more intriguing and created more interest than would have existed if the subject matter had consisted strictly of football.

It was a fine demonstration of the most cynical adage of the callous publicity man: "I don't care what you say about my client as long as you spell the name right." It certainly wasn't the way the masterminds in Commissioner Rozelle's office had planned things, and they hated every moment of it, but the net result was undeniable: once again, the Super Bowl held the full attention of 60 million or so Americans, and at the very least slightly annoyed most of the rest.

Vikings are Made 13-Point Favorite

Minnesota is 7-2 to Defeat Chiefs in Super Bowl

Jan. 6, 1970—In the closest betting spread of the four Super Bowl games, the Minnesota Vikings were installed yesterday as a 13-point favorite over the Kansas City Chiefs by Jimmy (The Greek) Snyder, the Las Vegas odds-maker.

For those wishing to wager without a point spread, the Vikings are a 7-to-2 favorite.

The New York Jets had been a 17-point underdog to the Baltimore Colts last year, while the Green Bay Packers were a 14-point choice over the Chiefs three years ago and a 15-point choice over the Oakland Raiders two years ago.

In computing the difference between the teams in order to "equalize the game for betting purposes," as Snyder said, he was influenced mostly by the Viking offensive line.

2-Point Edge on Running

"The Vikings have the greatest offensive line I've ever seen," Snyder said. "They will control the ball on the Chiefs, and I gave them a 3-point edge. I gave their running offense 2 points, and that includes Joe Kapp as a runner. Anybody who can knock out a linebacker on a tackle is a strong runner."

Kapp flattened Jim Houston of the Cleveland Browns for several seconds in the National Football League championship game.

"And you have to give Kapp a 1-point edge over Lenny Dawson as a quarterback," Snyder said. "Kapp has a knack for touchdown passes."

The Vikings earned 3 points on defense—1 for their defensive line, and 2 for their defensive backs.

Injuries Slow Chiefs

"The Chiefs have a good front four, that's why the Vikings are only worth one point more," Snyder said. "But the Viking cornerbacks and safeties are much better. Kenny Robinson is hurt for the Chiefs, and so is Jim Marsalis. I've never seen a team take such a physical beating as the Chiefs did. They must have a lot of minor injuries."

Robinson's status as the Chiefs' free safety man is uncertain. His replacement would be Willie Mitchell.

"And if Mitchell plays, he's a weak spot," Snyder said. "Robinson being out is a very big thing."

The other 4 points in Snyder's calculations come from Bud Grant's superiority over Hank Stram as a coach and the fact that the game will be played in New Orleans, an N.F.L. city.

NAMATH, DAWSON REPORTED AMONG THOSE TO BE CALLED IN GAMBLING INQUIRY

Rozelle Assails Naming of Stars

Says U.S. Regards Inquiry as in 'Embryo' Stage—Lammons Also on List

By CHARLES FRIEDMAN

Jan. 7, 1970—Joe Namath of the New York Jets and Len Dawson of the Kansas City Chiefs will be asked to appear before a Federal grand jury in Detroit investigating sports gambling, the National Broadcasting Company reported yesterday.

The report by Bill Matney, a network correspondent, came on the Huntley-Brinkley television show. It said that Bill Munson of the Detroit Lions and Karl Sweetan of the Los Angeles Rams also would be called.

All four are quarterbacks. They are to be questioned on information compiled by inquiry investigators, the report said.

In addition, the report said, the jury will call in Pete Lammons, the Jets' tight end, and Bob Devaney, head football coach at the University of Nebraska.

Namath, who has an apartment in New York, had left for a vacation in Florida and could not be reached for comment.

Dawson Holds Conference

Dawson, in New Orleans with the Chiefs for Sunday's Super Bowl game with the Minnesota Vikings, said at a news conference he had not "been contacted by any law enforcement agency or been apprised of the reason my name has been brought up.

"The only reason I can think of is that I have a casual acquaintance with Mr. Donald Dawson of Detroit, who I understand has been charged in the investigation," he said in a prepared statement. "I have known Mr. Dawson for about 10 years and have talked to him on several occasions.

"My only conversation with him in recent years concerned my knee injuries and the death of my father. On these occasions, he contacted me to offer his sympathy. His calls were among the many I received."

Donald Dawson, who comes from Birmingham, Mich., was arrested last Friday at a Birmingham motel as part of a statewide raid by Federal agents. Cashier's and business checks totaling $450,000 were found in his possession and gambling records were found in his car, the agents said.

James E. Ritchie, assistant United States Attorney in Detroit, characterized him as "one of the largest bookmakers in the Midwest."

Munson and Sweetan could not be reached for comment.

Pete Rozelle, the Commissioner of pro football, denounced the report as "totally irresponsible." In a statement from New Orleans, he declared:

"We have been advised by the Justice Department that the investigation is in its embryo stages and before any decisions are reached, the entire matter is going to be very carefully evaluated in the Department of Justice."

Chiefs Know of Report

Rozelle said that "rumors had circulated regarding Dawson" during the 1968 season.

"At that time," he said, "Dawson cooperated fully with our office and volunteered to take a polygraph [lie-detector] examination to establish innocence in regard to the rumors.

"The test and our own independent investigation proved to our satisfaction that the rumors were unsubstantiated. We cooperated with a Federal investigative agency throughout the course of that investigation."

Then the commissioner, referring to the present case, emphasized:

"While the entire matter has been under investigation by our security department for several days, we have no evidence to even consider disciplinary action against any of those publicly named.

"It is most unfortunate," Rozelle went on, "that any sports figures' names be mentioned loosely with an investigation of other persons, particularly the name of Len Dawson just prior to his playing in the world championship game."

Coach Hank Stram said in New Orleans that the Chiefs were aware of the report.

"I apprised the squad of certain rumors," he said, "and I am positively sure they will not have an adverse effect on the attitude of our squad."

The Chiefs were 13-point underdogs in the game.

At the team's workout earlier yesterday, Dawson had been asked his reaction to the large point spread.

"I don't know who makes the odds," he replied. "It wasn't Hank Stram."

No Warrants Issued

DETROIT, *Jan. 6*—James Brickley, the United States Attorney in Detroit handling the case, said tonight no warrants or subpoenas for sports figures had been issued. But he wouldn't "include or exclude" Namath, Dawson, Munson, Sweetan, Lammons or Devaney as possible witnesses before a grand jury.

Devaney's name had appeared in an affidavit, filed in Federal Court here, as part of the gambling case. In the affidavit it was said a Michigan businessman-gambler had tried to telephone the Nebraska coach.

Internal Revenue Service and Justice Department agents attacked the gambling syndicate New Year's Day, arresting 10, nine of them in Michigan, and confiscating $620,000 in cash and checks. Over the weekend, four more—three in Mississippi and one in New York City, all alleged bookmakers—were arrested.

Brickley said when the first arrests were made that "the Government now has in its possession a great deal of records and additional evidence linking with this conspiracy a number of additional people, including well-known figures in the sports and horse-racing world."

But he and other Federal officials would not say whether the connections were gamblers trying to associate with sports figures, athletes betting, or efforts to fix games or point spreads. And they noted that the questioning of sports figures did not mean they were guilty of any crimes.

The best-known sports figure formally mentioned has been Jerome (Dizzy) Dean, a star pitcher for the St. Louis Cardinals in the nineteen-thirties. Federal agents searched Dean's hotel room in Las Vegas seeking gambling records, but said they found none.

Brickley noted this week that Dean was cooperating and that information he gave led to other arrests. Affidavits filed in Federal courts also connect Dean to betting but Brickley has said there was no plan to arrest him.

After the N.B.C. report this evening, Brickley said that "if and when it should become necessary to have to formally proceed against any sports figures, the press will be duly advised.

"I think it is unfortunate that some news media have seen fit to speculate on some sports figures," he said.

ROZELLE QUOTES U.S. ATTORNEY AS SAYING HE HAS NO CHARGES AGAINST PLAYERS

Some Are Facing Call To Testify

'Have No Information Any Player Has Bet on Game,' Pro Football Head Says

By DAVE ANDERSON

NEW ORLEANS, *Jan. 7*—Pete Rozelle, the Commissioner of pro football, said tonight that the United States Attorney in Detroit investigating nationwide sports gambling had told him that no information had come to his attention to warrant preferring charges against any pro football players.

"I talked to James Brickley, who is supervising the investigation," Rozelle said, "and some players may or may not be subpoenaed. But we have no information that any player has bet on a game."

A National Broadcasting Company report circulated yesterday and branded as "totally irresponsible" by Rozelle said that four quarterbacks —Joe Namath of the New York Jets, Len Dawson of the Kansas City Chiefs, Bill Munson of the Detroit Lions and Karl Sweetan of the Los Angeles Rams—would be questioned in the investigation.

Pete Lammons, the Jets' tight end, and Bob Devaney, coach at Nebraska University, also would be called, according to the report.

At Super Bowl headquarters here, Rozelle acknowledged that his security agents were not aware until last Saturday of Dawson's "casual acquaintance," as the quarterback described it, with Donald Dawson, a Michigan restaurateur implicated in the investigation.

Donald Dawson's name had not entered the commissioner's investigation of Len Dawson following gambling rumors about the Chiefs during the 1968 season.

In regard to Namath, who was forced to sell his half share of the Bachelor's III restaurant in New York last year because it allegedly was frequented by "undesirable" customers, the commissioner said he had "total confidence" in the Jets' quarterback "in regard to this investigation."

Rozelle said he informed Namath of the imminent N.B.C. report yesterday and the quarterback had reacted by saying, "Here we go again."

According to Rozelle, the 26-year-old Namath "cooperated totally" with the commissioner's security agents who visited him today in Florida.

Rozelle said that Donald Dawson and Munson were "neighbors" in the Detroit suburb of Bloomfield Hills.

Earlier today Len Dawson would not elaborate on the extent of his long acquaintance with Donald Dawson.

Outwardly calm and with a soft smile, the 34-year-old Dawson appeared at a news conference at the Fontainebleau Hotel, where the Chiefs are lodged for the Super Bowl game with the Minnesota Vikings on Sunday.

After saying he had been shocked at a report yesterday that he would be asked to appear before a Federal grand jury, Dawson was asked if his acquaintance with the 48-year-old Dawson, no relation, had occurred only in telephone conversations or in personal meetings.

"Are we going to get into all this?" he said, turning to Hank Stram, his coach.

"Gentlemen," said Stram to about 125 newsmen at the conference, "we'd like to keep this on the football game."

Earlier Dawson had agreed that the commissioner's office had a "responsibility" to concern itself with gambling so as to protect the game's integrity.

"I'm sure they have their job to do," Dawson said. "I understand it."

Stram said Rozelle was not consulted in advance of Len Dawson's statement acknowledging his acquaintance with the other Dawson, labeled by a Federal attorney as one of the biggest bookies in the Midwest.

However, Lamar Hunt, the Chiefs' owner, said he had discussed the inquiry with Jim Kensil, Rozelle's executive assistant.

In his statement last night Dawson said he had known the Michigan man for "about 10 years" and he had talked to him several times. Their only conversations in recent years, the quarterback said "concerned my knee injuries and the death of my father," which occurred last month.

When the Chiefs assembled for breakfast today, Stram had Dawson read his statement to them. The players had not been informed of Rozelle's statement yesterday that Dawson volunteered to take a lie-detector test in 1968 when rumors prompted the commissioner to investigate why the Chiefs had often been taken "off the boards," meaning the bookies would not accept bets on their games on suspicion of a fix. Rozelle said then his inquiry in 1968 had found Dawson innocent of any wrongdoing.

In describing the breakfast, Jerry Mays, the defensive co-captain, said:

"Lenny got a big hand when he got up, like a speaker at a banquet. He read his statement and coach Stram asked, 'Are there any questions about this' like he always does in a meeting, and nobody said anything, and then he said, 'Are there any questions about anything?' and E. J. Holub asked if our tickets were in."

Mays added that when Dawson had taken the lie-detector test, his teammates "were not aware of it generally, but a few knew about it."

Stram reportedly advised his players to take the attitude that the incident would provide an "added incentive" for the game because the players would be "rallying round" their suddenly controversial quarter-back.

In questioning several members of the team, this reporter found that attitude prevalent.

"Right now we're the closest we've ever been," Mays declared.

Johnny Robinson, the safetyman, who is Dawson's roommate, said the players thought the case was "ridiculous."

Mike Garrett, the leading running back, said: "We laughed about it; it won't affect us at all."

Willie Lanier, the middle linebacker, commented: "It doesn't bother me. The Justice Department is doing its job. It won't add to our incentive, the incentive is being here."

As for the game, Stram said that Robinson, who is considered a doubt-ful starter because of damaged ribs, would try to work out tomorrow.

Robinson got a pain-killing injection today as a test. The 30-year-old defensive back, an all-league performer most of his 10 seasons, said, "I can play if they eliminate the pain."

Witnesses Won't Be Indicted

DETROIT, *Jan. 7 (AP)*—A Justice Department spokesman said today that witnesses called before a Federal grand jury investigating nationwide gambling in sports probably would not be indicted.

"Justice Department policy clearly prohibits calling anyone as a witness when there is an indication that you are going to indict them," the spokesman said.

James Ritchie, head of the Justice Department Task Force handling the gambling inquiry said here the persons called to appear before the grand jury were more likely to be "prospective witnesses than prospective defendants."

Vikings Try Out the Game Plan; They'll Know Sunday if It Fits

By WILLIAM N. WALLACE

NEW ORLEANS, *Jan. 7*—Apart from game day, Wednesday is the most important day in the pro football week. It is the day the team drills on the game plan—the defenses and plays the coaches believe will work on Sunday.

The Minnesota Vikings set their game plan today in secrecy on a practice field in suburban Metairie for Sunday's Super Bowl game here against the Kansas City Chiefs. They felt at home—it was windy, with the temperature at 34 degrees and the natives apologizing for the cold.

Thirty-nine Vikings worked out. The 40th, Lonnie Warwick, again rested his sprained left ankle.

"His condition is good, but we're keeping him off his feet," said Coach Bud Grant.

It is not too hard to guess the Viking game plan. Joe Kapp, the quarterback, will be throwing the ball against a Chiefs' secondary weakened by the injury to the most experienced man, Johnny Robinson at free safety.

Grant reviewed the day.

"We've given the players our game plan," he said, "and told them exactly what we want them to do. Now we'll show them the Kansas City game films and, most important, tell them why we want them to do things our way. Our job is a selling job. These players are basically intelligent people. They want to know why and we feel they can do a better job if they understand our reasons."

Various Vikings had comments. Jim Vellone, who with Milt Sunde makes up the little-publicized Minnesota guard contingent, reflected on the Chief he will play opposite: Buck Buchanan, 6 feet 7 inches and 275 pounds.

"How do I move Buchanan? With a tank, I guess," he said.

At 255 pounds, Vellone is the heaviest of the relatively light Viking offensive linemen who will go against pro football's largest defensive line.

Vellone played at Southern California with Mike Garrett, the Chiefs' star halfback. It is another of the entwining relationships that run through pro football.

"He was a very close friend of mine," said Vellone. "He's a trememdous individual and athlete. We called him 'Superduck.' I played defense and I don't think I ever did tackle him."

Wally Hilgenberg, the linebacker the Vikings obtained from Pittsburgh for the $100 waiver fee last year, spoke of the screen pass.

"It's one of my responsibilities," he said. "In the statistics, Garrett is their leading receiver. That means the screen is an effective part of their offense. Besides, our opponents went to the screen often in the last part of the season."

With little success, he might have added.

Bill Brown, the fullback who has been a Viking since 1962, said of Grant: "He has greatly influenced our way of thinking. He has emphasized to each player to come up with the big play when we get a chance and also to cut down on penalties."

Under Grant's predecessor, Norm Van Brocklin, the Vikings were a rough team often hurt by penalties. But Van Brocklin also made the Vikings into hitters.

"He [Grant] stopped the penalties without taking away our enthusiasm or hustle or our reputation as a hard-hitting team, which we still are," said Brown. "He's given us poise and control of our reactions. We think a little more."

Van Brocklin traded draft choices to Cleveland in 1961 for Jim Marshall among others. Marshall, the defensive end, and Grady Alderman are all that remain of the cast of '61.

"Most of the fellows then were outcasts," said Marshall. "We have slowly evolved into a champion. The organization has selected the right personnel much the same way any successful company would."

GRANT FORESEES RUGGED DEFENSIVE BATTLE AND CLOSE SCORE IN SUPER BOWL

Coach of Vikings Cites Foes' Depth

13-Point Spread is Called Unrealistic—Cold Weather Continues at New Orleans

By WILLIAM N. WALLACE

NEW ORLEANS, *Jan. 8*—Although his team is favored by 13 points, Coach Bud Grant of the Minnesota Vikings predicted today that Sunday's Super Bowl game here between the Minnesota club and the Kansas City Chiefs would be close.

"Neither team is going to get knocked out of the ball park," said the 42-year-old white-haired, blue-eyed Grant. "Also, I expect a low-scoring game."

Grant brushed aside a suggestion that the Vikings might wish to run up a score on the Chiefs, the American Football League champions, to "revenge" last year's victory by the New York Jets, the A.F.L. title team, over Baltimore, the National League entry.

He said he would be "delirious" with a 1-point victory.

Rivals' Depth Is Cited

Although it would be politic for Grant to envision a close, exciting game, this man has convictions behind his opinions. He minimized the probable loss through injury of Johnny Robinson, the seasoned Kansas City safety. "All teams who come this far have good depth," he reasoned. Similarly, he said the Vikings lost their regular cornerback, Bobby Bryant, but replaced him with Ed Sharockman.

Many analysts foresee the passes of Joe Kapp, Grant's quarterback, destroying a confused Kansas City secondary playing with Willie Mitchell in place of Robinson and this is the reasoning behind the 13-point favorite role.

But Grant is dubious. "Nobody here sets the point line," he said as he addressed a group of sports writers at the Hilton Inn Motel, the Viking headquarters near the airport. In adjoining rooms the players were in meetings run by assistant coaches.

The weather remained cold, 35 degrees, which Grant saw as no advantage for the Vikings, who came out of the frozen North on Tuesday.

"After what we've been through the past three weeks," he said, "we wouldn't complain if it was 75 degrees."

Not only will the Vikings be ready for the Chiefs but also for the National Anthem. Grady Alderman, the only Viking player remaining from the stocking pool that got the expansion franchise going in 1961, disclosed the squad had had National Anthem drills.

Just Like the Army

"We let Milt Sunde run them," said Alderman. "He's a sergeant in the National Guard." Sunde, the right guard, taught the players how to line up evenly on the field, to stand at attention and how not to wiggle or scratch.

League headquarters has made a fuss over this issue in the last sensitive year, and a member of Commissioner Pete Rozelle's staff, Bob Cochran, was appointed vice president in charge of the National Anthem.

Max Winter, the president of the Vikings, said today, "Most of the credit for this team's development should go to two men: our general manager, Jim Finks, who coordinates everything, and Bud Grant, who has done a tremendous job. This year our players have this '40 for 60' slogan, and our success has come from the coordination of these fellows rather than individual stardom."

The Vikings shout this togetherness phrase on the field and in the locker room. The reference is to 40 players, the number on the active squad, and the 60 playing minutes in every game.

Kicker Could Be Sunday's Hero
Tight Game Looms, So Stenerud, Cox Hold Key Roles
By GEORGE VECSEY

NEW ORLEANS, *Jan. 8*—Bud Grant doesn't go around tossing predictions and declarations all the time. But when he has something to say, he has been known to be right.

The tall and reserved coach of the Minnesota Vikings predicted two weeks ago that the Western title game with Los Angeles would produce a relatively high score for a playoff game. When his Vikings won, 23-20, people congratulated Grant on his prediction.

The coach refrained from giving such an analysis of last week's game, but he came out today with a view of Sunday's Super Bowl game with Kansas City.

"The defenses are good enough," Grant said. "With those big lines, you won't see either team getting knocked out of the ball park."

If the offenses cannot produce touchdowns, the two kickers could decide the game. Jan Stenerud of Kansas City and Fred Cox of Minnesota have won games before.

Stenerud a High Scorer

Stenerud finished second to Jim Turner of the Jets in American League scoring with 38 extra points and 27 field goals for 119 points. He missed only eight field-goal attempts. Born in Oslo, Norway, he came to this country for the skiing, but tried kicking a football at Montana State. He is 27 years old and has scored over 100 points in all three professional seasons.

Cox led the National League in scoring with 121 points on 43 extra points and 26 field goals in 37 kicks. A former running back at Pittsburgh, the chunky 31-year-old Cox has been kicking for the Vikings since 1963. He studies to be a chiropractor in the offseason.

Both men are also used for the kickoffs. Cox varies his kicks, sometimes booming long, sometimes aiming for the weaker return man. The Vikings had the fifth best defensive average against kickoff returns this year, allowing only 20.8 yards a kickoff, a tribute to the specialty team. Stenerud's kickoffs were returned for 24.3 yards, the second worst figure in the A.F.L.

The punting will also be increasingly important in a tight game. The Chiefs use Jerrel Wilson, 28, who was third in the A.F.L. with a 44.4-yard average this year. But his punts were returned for 11.7 yards a carry, the worst defensive average in the league.

Both the punter and the specialty squad must take the blame in such a case—the punter for not getting the ball high enough, the suicide squad for not tackling the runner.

Minnesota's punter is Bob Lee, a young red-haired quarterback from the University of the Pacific. He was 10th in the N.F.L. with an average of 40 yards and his teammates were 11th in covering his punts, allowing 7 yards a return.

However, the efficiency of the specialty squads could improve in playoff games because the coaches may decide to use some of their better athletes from the regular platoons.

He'd Rather Call Kicks

Lee thinks of himself as a quarterback, not just a punter, and he was used toward the end of several games this season. His earliest experience with football came when he accompanied his father, Paul Lee, an assistant bureau chief for the Associated Press in San Francisco, to college games at Berkeley or Palo Alto.

"There was one game in 1958 when my father's assistant didn't show up," Lee recalled today, "so my father asked me to go to the California dressing room and bring him back some quotes."

The 13-year-old boy later relayed quotes from the California quarterback, an hombre named Joe Kapp.

"I tell Joe I used to watch him play when I was a kid," Lee said today. "He was 22 years old in 1958. I tease him that there's no way he can be 31 now. Like he says he is."

VIKINGS ARE 13-POINT FAVORITES OVER CHIEFS TODAY; SUPER BOWL OUTCOME HINGES ON KAPP AND DAWSON

80,997 To Attend

50-50 Chance for Rain in Pro Title Game at New Orleans

By WILLIAM N. WALLACE

NEW ORLEANS, *Jan. 10*—A covey of 3,000 pigeons and one turtle dove will fly out of Tulane Stadium tomorrow afternoon, while Pat O'Brien, the actor, is reading the words of the national anthem backed by a chorus and band from Southern University. A few moments later, either Fred Cox of the Minnesota Vikings, an aspiring chiropractor with a bad back, or Jan Stenerud of the Kansas City Chiefs, a Norwegian-born ski-jumper, will kick off and the Super Bowl game will be under way.

Professional football's extravaganza matches the Vikings, the National League champions who are favored by 13 points, and the Chiefs, the American League champions. A capacity crowd of 80,997, occupying $15 seats, will see the game here and perhaps 60 million will watch on television.

The game will be televised by the Columbia Broadcasting System, which is paying $2.5-million for the rights. The outlet in New York is Channel 2, with the kickoff set for 3:35 P.M., New York time.

$15,000 Each to Winners

There is a 50-50 chance that the game will be played in the rain, a matter of indifference to both sides.

Each player on the winning team will receive $15,000 and each loser $7,500. The contest will be played to a decision in overtime should a tie exist at the end of the usual four 15-minute periods. The sudden-death method will be used—the first team to score in the 15-minute overtime period, or periods, will be the winner.

This is the fourth Super Bowl game, but the first in New Orleans, a city that generated excitement over the event in the last two days despite a numbing cold spell. Because of the customary 75-mile television blackout, many fans will drive north and east to Baton Rouge, La., or Biloxi, Miss., to watch the game on TV in motels and hotels.

Apart from enjoying another payday, the players will perform for prestige and pride. Gary Cuozzo, a reserve quarterback for Minnesota, summed it up: "You're nobody if you lose. You are relegated to another year of trying to get here."

Cuozzo plays behind Joe Kapp, who will be the key figure. Kapp, a brawler who enjoys his nickname of Zorba the Viking, apparently has made a deep impression on the Chiefs. Their coach, Hank Stram, cited "the ability of Kapp to throw on the run" as a key factor.

The Vikings like to roll Kapp out of the passing pocket so he can threaten to run or throw. Since he enjoys running into and over people, this threat terrorizes the defensive backs.

The Chiefs hope their excellent defense puts so much pressure on Kapp that their quick cornerbacks, Jim Marsalis and Emmitt Thomas, can intercept his unartistic passes. Thomas led the A.F.L. in interceptions with nine and had three off Daryle Lamonica in the league championship game.

Marsalis, defensive rookie of the year in the A.F.L., intercepted two passes by Joe Namath and one by Lamonica in the playoffs.

Kapp had 13 of his 237 passes picked off in the regular season, a frequency slightly higher than the league average for quarterbacks.

The other quarterback, Len Dawson, will be playing under a small cloud of suspicion because earlier this week he admitted to a casual friendship of 10 years' standing with a Detroit man recently arrested in a Federal investigation of gambling. The Chiefs hope Dawson can move his team by completing passes to Otis Taylor, an outstanding receiver, against the coverage of Ed Sharockman, an average cornerback.

Another Kansas City cloud is the physical condition of Johnny Robinson, the free safety with 10 years' experience, who has a torn rib cartilage. Stram will decide if Robinson is to play just before the kickoff. His substitute, Willie Mitchell, said: "I want to play, but I think Robby should be in there."

Mitchell was the covering back when Max McGee of the Packers caught a 37-yard touchdown pass to open the way for Green Bay's 35-10 victory over Kansas City in the first Super Bowl game on Jan. 15, 1967.

"The Chiefs," says their owner, Lamar Hunt, "are much improved over the team that lost to Green Bay. We have seven new starters on defense."

Big Man, Big Words

Buck Buchanan, the largest of the enormous Chiefs at 6-feet-7 and 275 pounds, adds, "Our defense is 80 per cent stronger than in the first Super Bowl. Overall, our team is 50 per cent improved."

The original Super Bowl game was the first between N.F.L. and A.F.L. teams and the Chiefs admit they were awed by the Packers' reputation. But since then, interleague games have become commonplace and Kansas City has played N.F.L. teams nine times in preseason games, winning seven. Among their victims were the Vikings, who were beaten by 13-10 in the summer of 1968. Says Dawson: "The mystery is gone as far as the N.F.L. is concerned."

The point spread, 13, is the lowest yet in any Super Bowl game. The Packers were 15-point favorites over Kansas City and 14 over Oakland the next year. The Colts were 17-point favorites when upset by the Jets last year.

The Chiefs reached the Super Bowl in an unusual way, because they were a second-place team at the end of the regular 14-game season. They won 11 and lost three and finished 1½ games behind Oakland in the Western Division. But divisional second-place teams qualified for the A.F.L. playoffs last season for the first time. The Chiefs then beat the Jets, the Eastern winners, and then the Raiders for the league championship. Counting preseason and postseason games, their over-all record is 19-3, the same as the Vikings.

Minnesota lost its opening and closing games, but won 12 straight in between and beat the Los Angeles Rams and the Cleveland Browns in the playoffs.

The Chiefs have a tricky offense, utilizing 18 basic plays disguised by a multiplicity of backfield formations or sets.

"Recognition is the biggest problem we face," said Bud Grant, the Viking coach, "because of the many sets they use. But once the football is snapped, it's the same game. I'm impressed by what I've seen of them in the films. It is not hard to see why they are here."

The Heat Is on Lenny the Cool

By DAVE ANDERSON

NEW ORLEANS, *Jan. 10*—In tomorrow's Super Bowl game, Len Dawson will be playing in the shadow of a doubt.

Inside his red Kansas City Chiefs' helmet the 34-year-old quarterback's blue-gray eyes will dominate his boyishly handsome features. His expressionless face will add to the strange stare of those eyes. His teammates have called him "Lenny the Cool" for years, but tomorrow the heat will be on his cool as never before.

Dawson has acknowledged a "casual acquaintance" for 10 years with a Michigan restaurateur, Donald Dawson, who was arrested by Federal agents a week ago with $450,000 in checks and various gambling records. The restaurateur, no relation to the quarterback, has been implicated in a nationwide investigation into sports gambling.

Since then, the quarterback has been defended by his friends as a "perfect gentleman" and even as a "Puritan," but tomorrow before a capacity crowd of 80,997 and a television audience of perhaps 60 million, his integrity will be judged not so much by his reputation as by his performance.

If he is intercepted or if he fumbles, the suspicions of the cynics will be nourished. Even an incompletion, if the pass-receiver is in the clear, will be viewed with a smirk by some. To avoid criticism, he must produce an almost flawless game and that is difficult for the best of quarterbacks under the best of circumstances.

"But if there's anybody who can handle this situation," Johnny Robinson said, "it's Lenny Dawson."

Robinson, an experienced defensive back, was in the room he shared with Dawson at the Fontainbleau Hotel, where the Chiefs were lodged all week.

"He keeps a lot to himself," Robinson continued. "He doesn't have a lot of emotion. He keeps his cool."

Although his passes have guided the Chiefs to three American Football League championships, Dawson's aloof manner has contributed to his relatively insignificant niche among pro football's leading quarterbacks. He doesn't possess the flair of Joe Namath or Joe Kapp, or even the somewhat silent stature of Johnny Unitas or Bart Starr.

But during his eight A.F.L. seasons, Dawson has thrown 182 touchdown passes, the most of any pro quarterback during that span.

At a slender 6 feet and 190 pounds, he not only is among the smaller quarterbacks, but he also is not really muscular.

But despite his slender physique, he has fiber. He has been playing on a damaged left knee that kept him out of six games during the season.

And when the Chiefs opened their 1969 schedule, he had a broken bone in his passing hand.

"I'll be all right," he told Coach Hank Stram, "but we've got to change the snap so it doens't hit my right hand."

In the victory over the San Diego Chargers that day, Dawson completed 19 of 34 passes for 224 yards and two touchdowns.

His manner can be as tough as his mechanical style. He was asked once why he chose to throw a pass on a critical third-and-1 situation.

Basketball Not His Cup of Tea

"I knew it would work," he said.

When he was an all-American at Purdue, an assistant coach wished him "good luck" on the sideline.

"Luck won't win the game," he said.

When he was being recruited by Purdue after an outstanding schoolboy career in Alliance, Ohio, the basketball coach attempted to entice him by saying that Len "might be a big help" in that sport as well.

"You don't know that," Dawson said. "You've never seen me play."

And when he stopped smoking a few years ago, somebody asked him how he was able to do it so easily.

"I just wanted to," he said.

He didn't particularly want to play football, but he had six older brothers who had played it. As he has said, "If I didn't go out for football, I couldn't have gone home." He became a quarterback because, at 110 pounds, he knew he wouldn't be able to play anywhere else.

"When you play the game as long as I have," he said not long ago, "you get to like it, but actually I should've been a golfer."

But among his teammates, he has developed into a quiet leader of their offensive unit and a loyal friend in time of need.

"I've never heard him raise his voice," said Ed Budde, one of the guards. "When you do something wrong he just gives you that look and you know you had better shape up. Lenny's the same way and I love this guy like I loved my father."

Budde recalled the time several years ago when he was hospitalized suddenly.

"Lenny was the first guy to offer to have him and his wife take care of my three children while my wife was at the hospital with me," Budde said. "They've got two kids of their own, but my kids stayed with them for about three days until my mother arrived."

Fred Arbanas, the tight end, remembered a similar situation.

"When I had my eye injury," said Arbanas, who lost the sight of one eye in a mysterious assault, "I needed somebody to throw passes to me to redevelop my depth perception. Lenny worked out with me for half an hour a day, five days a week, for a couple of months. He didn't have to do it, but that's the way he is."

Dawson does four daily radio spots and a nightly TV show in Kansas City and his face "lights up on TV," a teammate said.

"But he needed an offseason weekend replacement on his TV show," said Willie Lanier, the middle linebacker, "and he recommended me for the job."

"That's right," Dawson said, overhearing Lanier and smiling. "I wanted to make sure they didn't have anybody as good."

The quarterback smiled again and Lanier laughed, enjoying the typical locker-room repartee. But behind that rare smile, the quarterback has a frozen frankness. Such as the time when he was asked about the five seasons he had spent in the National League.

Five Years in a Wasteland

"I wouldn't say that I spent five years in the N.F.L.," he said. "I'd say I wasted them."

Although he had been the Steelers' first-round draft choice in 1957, he was seldom used. Earl Morrall was the Steelers' quarterback that year, then Bobby Layne was acquired. After two years of being frustrated by Layne's experience, he was traded to the Browns, but there he watched Milt Plum play. After two years of that, he requested his release.

When he joined Hank Stram, who had been an aide at Purdue, he soon developed into a winning quarterback.

When he was reunited with Stram, his passing arm was weak from inactivity.

"It took him a couple of years to get back in the groove," Stram has said. "He was like sterling silver. The silver was there, but it was tarnished."

But despite his success, the aloofness remained, even when the Chiefs celebrated their entry into the first Super Bowl game.

"I remember we had a party in Buffalo after we won the championship game," said Jim Schaaf, the assistant general manager, "and all the players were in the banquet room at the hotel execpt Lenny, who was out in the lobby, talking to somebody from his family who had come up from Ohio. He was happy, but he was celebrating in his own way. That's the way he is."

But the way he is was perhaps best demonstrated last September when he defied five orthopedic surgeons who had advised knee surgery.

"The sixth one said I didn't need an operation," Len Dawson said at the time. "He was the one I was looking for. And besides, I wanted to find out what I'm made of."

He'll find out more about that tomorrow.

Vikings Thrive on Kapp's Fight

Quarterback's Toughness Leads to Super Bowl

NEW ORLEANS, *Jan. 10*—The Fight, as his teammates refer to it, was what won for Joe Kapp the acceptance and admiration of the Minnesota Vikings that led to a place in the Super Bowl tomorrow. He will be the quarterback of the favored team, the Vikings, against the Kansas City Chiefs.

The Vikings had become accustomed to a different kind of quarterback. Fran Tarkenton, a slight, slick diplomat, had run the team and made himself famous by running away from the defensive giants. He was The Scrambler.

Kapp arrived on the Minnesota scene in 1967, a much larger and more physical quarterback. He was a tough guy with a reputation as a barroom brawler.

The other tough character on the Viking team is Lonnie Warwick, the middle linebacker out of the West Virginia mines who once worked as a section hand on a railroad.

Drinking tequila together after the team lost to Green Bay in 1967, Kapp and Warwick argued. Kapp wanted to take the blame for the defeat because of his fumble. Warwick said it was the fault of the defense for allowing too many points.

Although the issue was absurd, the two apparently were destined for combat. They went outside the bar and fought in the moonlight, Warwick winning by a technical knockout when he was pulled off Kapp who was lying on the ground with a rapidly closing left eye.

"The point was that Joe did fight him," said Clinton Jones, the halfback. "He's not afraid of anything."

The Vikings then rallied behind their new leader and found themselves, two seasons later, in the Super Bowl as the National League champions.

Defensive players generally are tougher and more physical than offensive ones whom they often hold in disdain. Like John Unitas, Kapp hangs out with the defense. "He rides in the back of the bus with the boys," says Coach Bud Grant.

Kapp depreciates the role of the quarterback. "You sportswriters emphasize the quarterback too much," he says. "Football games are won up front."

Born in New Mexico of German and Mexican parentage, Kapp and four other children were raised by his mother, a waitress, in Salinas, Calif. "I played in the lettuce fields," he said.

He was recruited to play football at the University of California in Berkeley. He was an all-American quarterback and played on a team that lost to Iowa in the Rose Bowl. Drafted 18th by the Washington Redskins in 1959, Kapp, instead, accepted a contract of $13,000 salary and $2,000 bonus to play for the Calgary Roughriders of the Canadian Football League.

"The Redskins never contacted me and the Calgary money at the time was terrific," he said.

The man who signed him was Jim Finks, the present general manager of the Vikings. Faced with a quarterback surplus, Finks two seasons later traded Kapp to Vancouver where he led the British Columbia Lions to their first C.F.L. championship.

Seeking more money in the wealthier United States leagues, Kapp played out his option in Canada and signed with Minnesota in 1967. Grant, a coach for 10 years at Winnipeg, was beginning with the Vikings and knew Kapp well. He was not exactly enchanted, because Kapp was hardly the polished pocket passer. He still is not, although Grant has convinced him to run less.

"We signed Kapp because he was better than what we had," said Grant. The Viking quarterbacks at the time were Bob Berry, now the regular at Atlanta; Ron Vanderkelen and John Hankinson.

Kapp struck a tremendous psychological blow for himself in the National Football League championship game last Sunday when he ran into and over Jim Houston, Cleveland's 240-pound linebacker, knocking Houston out of the game. It was a tremendous shot seen on national television and also by the Kansas City Chiefs, whose respect he has also gained.

"There's not another guy like him," said Jim Lynch, the Chiefs' linebacker. "He's such a threat as a passer and a runner he puts pressure not only on the pass rush but on the linebackers and secondary as well."

Sports of The Times

By ARTHUR DALEY

The Super Bowl

NEW ORLEANS, *Jan. 10*—It has been a miserable week in this supposedly gay and charming city. An embarrassing cold wave even produced a low of 22 degrees one day, a level that hadn't been reached since 1879. Worse than that, though, is the possibility that the Super Bowl game on the morrow between the Kansas City Chiefs and the Minnesota Vikings may be played in a chill rain.

An all-weather sport, football can endure that even if unprepared spectators find the going a lot more rugged than expected. But the one thing that cast a mighty pall over the proceedings was the television news report last Tuesday that four football players would be subpoenaed by a grand jury to give whatever information they had regarding a Federal investigation of a gambling ring.

Although this totally unsubstantiated news item would have jarred the football establishment at any time, it hit this Super Bowl city with shattering impact because one of those so carelessly named was Len Dawson, quarterback and key operator for the Chiefs. He was shaken to his shoetops. What effect would it have on him and his teammates? Would they be spurred to extra effort to "win this for Lenny" as a mark of their confidence in him? Could this distracting shocker be turned into a Kansas City advantage?

That last question was put to Dawson the other day. His troubled blue-gray eyes stared into space, almost as if he were trying to peer into the future.

"I hope so," he said slowly, "but we really won't know until the game is played on Sunday."

Football is such an emotional sport that the Chiefs rallied fiercely to Dawson's support even though distressed by the wretched timing that snapped their intense concentration on the task ahead. Before the week was out they were quoting the blunt reaction to the implications of the newscast by Joe Namath, one of the four quarterbacks named. Karl Sweetan of the Rams and Bill Munson of the Lions were the other two.

"Hell," said Namath, "a subpoena? That's nothing. All it means is that they want to talk to you. The bad part is that people read about it and think you're guilty."

The shadows of this mischievous pronouncement still will hang over the Super Bowl. They already have obscured the preparations of Vikings and Chiefs. Yet the game is still the main thing, even though there is no way of calculating the effects on Dawson & Co.

Even without the mental anguish that has enveloped Dawson there never was a guarantee that the Chiefs could topple those rugged Vikings. But Kansas City has been to the Super Bowl before, bowing to the Green Bay Packers in the first one, 35-10. However, the Chiefs feel this will be different: They won't be plunging into the great unknown.

"The Packers were a legend when we met them in 1966," said Mike Garrett, the main Kansas City gound-gainer. "They awed us then. But we've since played enough National League teams to have a common ground for comparisons and we're not awed by anyone—including the Vikings."

"The mystery is gone," said Dawson.

So the unmysterious Vikings will play the Chiefs. Oddly enough, Minnesota operates in the same basic style as the Packers. But the Vikes have a tougher, better defense. For that matter, so do the Chiefs, as compared with their 1966 model.

In fact, these are the two most physical teams ever to perform in the Super Bowl. Both are huge in size—Kansas City is bigger—and each led its league in defense. The expectation is that scoring will be difficult and the point totals will be low. Both have excellent field-goal kickers—Fred Cox for the Vikes and Jan Stenerud for the Chiefs.

The quarterbacks offer sharp contrasts. Dawson is cool, calculating, intelligent and conservative. Ironically enough, he is a nongambler. His opposite number, Joe Kapp, is a reckless, hell-for-leather operative who doesn't hesitate to take chances and, unlike Dawson, loves to run into people. Each has a catcher of bombs: Otis Taylor for Dawson and Gene Washington for Kapp. Garrett is the lone breakaway-type back. But Dave Osborn and Bill Brown of the Vikes have such great second efforts that they're forever picking up extra yards.

Super Bowl week has had everything go wrong and a dull game would be a proper climax. Dull or lively, though, I still pick the Vikes.

Facts on Super Bowl Game, 1970

Title at stake—World professional football championship.

Participants—Minnesota Vikings, champion of the National Football League, and Kansas City Chiefs, champion of the American Football League.

Date—Today.

Place—Tulane Stadium, New Orleans.

Kickoff—3:35 P. M. (Eastern Standard Time).

Seating capacity—80,007.

Television—Nationwide by the Columbia Broadcasting System
        (Channel 2 in New York) with New Orleans area blacked out.

Radio—Nationwide by Columbia Broadcasting System.

Players' shares—$15,000 to each member of winning team, $7,500 to each loser (approximately $1.2-million total for personnel of contesting teams).

Division of game receipts—After deduction of taxes, expenses and guaranteed players' shares, remainder will be distributed among the competing clubs, A.F.L. and N.F.L. league offices, the commissioner's office and to member clubs of both leagues, who will contribute approximately $1.3 million of these receipts to player benefit plans.

Player uniforms—A.F.L. will be home team and will wear colored jerseys. N.F.L. will be the visiting team and will wear white.

Game ball—N.F.L. ball will be used when N.F.L. team on offense, A.F.L. ball when A.F.L. team on offense. A.F.L. is college-type ball with a more pointed arch from the laces to nose and has lacing 44¼-inches long.

Conversions—The teams will kick, run or pass for 1 extra point after touchdowns. The A.F.L. 2-point rule will not be in effect.

Sudden death—If the game is tied after regulation 60 minutes, it will continue in sudden-death overtime. The team scoring first by safety, field goal or touchdown will win. Play will continue by 15-minute periods until there is a score.

Officials—Three from each league in this order: referee, A.F.L.; umpire, N.F.L.; linesman, A.F.L.; back judge, N.F.L.; field judge, A.F.L.; line judge, N.F.L. The scoreboard clock will be official

Trophy—A world championship game silver trophy will be presented to the winning team for permanent possession.

Records of the Teams

MINNESOTA		KANSAS CITY	
23—New York	24	27—San Diego	9
52—Baltimore	14	31—Boston	0
19—Green Bay	7	19—Cincinnati	24
31—Chicago	0	26—Denver	13
27—St. Louis	10	24—Houston	0
24—Detroit	10	17—Miami	10
31—Chicago	14	42—Cincinnati	22
51—Cleveland	3	29—Buffalo	7
9—Green Bay	7	27—San Diego	3
52—Pittsburgh	14	34—New York	16
27—Detroit	0	24—Oakland	27 ,
20—Los Angeles	13	31—Denver	17
10—San Francisco	7	22—Buffalo	19
3—Atlanta	10	6—Oakland	10
Conference Playoff		**Inter-division Playoff**	
23—Los Angeles	20	13—New York	6
N.F.L. Championship		**A.F.L. Championship**	
27—Cleveland	7	17—Oakland	7

How Rival Teams in Super Bowl Match Up, 1970

KANSAS CITY ON OFFENSE

No.	Player	Ht.	Wt.	Pos.
89	Otis Taylor.....	6-3	215	WR
30	Gloster Richardson	6-0	200	WR
84	Fred Arbanas ...	6-3	245	TE
73	Dave Hill......	6-5	260	RT
76	Mo Moorman ...	6-5	252	RG
55	E. J. Holub.....	6-4	236	C
71	Ed Budde	6-5	260	LG
77	Jim Tyrer	6-6	270	LT
16	Len Dawson	6-0	190	QB
45	Robert Holmes ..	5-9	220	FB
21	Mike Garrett....	5-9	190	HB

MINNESOTA ON DEFENSE

No.	Player	Ht.	Wt.	Pos.
45	Ed Sharockman ..	6-0	200	RCB
46	Earsell Mackbee ..	6-0	195	LCB
29	Karl Kassulke....	6-0	195	SS
81	Carl Eller	6-6	255	LE
77	Gary Larsen	6-5	255	LT
59	Lonnie Warwick ..	6-3	235	MLB
88	Alan Page......	6-4	255	RT
70	Jim Marshall	6-3	248	RE
22	Paul Krause.....	6-3	188	FS
60	Roy Winston	5-11	228	LLB
58	Wally Hilgenberg..	6-3	231	RLB

KANSAS CITY ON DEFENSE

No.	Player	Ht.	Wt.	Pos.
18	Emmitt Thomas..	6-2	192	RCB
40	Jim Marsalis	5-11	194	LCB
46	Jim Kearney	6-2	206	SS
75	Jerry Mays.....	6-4	250	LE
61	Curley Culp	6-1	265	LT
63	Willie Lanier....	6-1	245	MLB
86	Buck Buchanan ..	6-7	275	RT
87	Aaron Brown ...	6-5	265	RE
42	Johnny Robinson .	6-1	205	FS
78	Bobby Bell.....	6-4	228	LLB
51	Jim Lynch	6-1	235	RLB

MINNESOTA ON OFFENSE

No.	Player	Ht.	Wt.	Pos.
84	Gene Washington .	6-3	208	WR
80	John Henderson ..	6-3	190	WR
87	John Beasley	6-3	233	TE
73	Ron Yary......	6-5	255	RT
64	Milt Sunde	6-2	250	RG
53	Mick Tingelhoff ..	6-2	237	C
63	Jim Vellone.....	6-3	255	LG
67	Grady Alderman..	6-2	245	LT
11	Joe Kapp	6-3	216	QB
30	Bill Brown	5-11	230	FB
41	Dave Osborn	6-0	205	HB

KANSAS CITY SUBSTITUTES

No.	Player	Ht.	Wt.	Pos.
3	Jan Stenerud....	6-2	187	K
6	Warren McVea...	5-9	182	RB
10	Mike Livingston ..	6-4	212	QB
12	Tom Flores.....	6-1	200	QB
14	Ed Podolak.....	6-1	204	RB
20	Goldie Sellers ...	6-2	198	DB
22	Willie Mitchell ...	6-0	185	DB
24	Ceaser Belser...	6-0	212	DB
25	Frank Pitts.....	6-2	199	WR
32	Curtis McClinton .	6-3	227	TE
38	Wendell Hayes...	6-1	220	RB
44	Jerrel Wilson....	6-4	222	P
60	George Daney ...	6-4	240	G
65	Remi Prudhomme.	6-4	250	C
66	Bob Stein	6-6	235	LB
74	Gene Trosch	6-7	260	DE
82	Ed Lothamer ...	6-5	270	DT
85	Chuck Hurston ..	6-6	240	LB

MINNESOTA SUBSTITUTES

No.	Player	Ht.	Wt.	Pos.
14	Fred Cox	5-10	200	K
15	Gary Cuozzo	6-1	195	QB
19	Bob Lee.......	6-2	195	P-QB
21	Jim Lindsey ...	6-2	210	RB
26	Clint Jones	6-0	200	RB
27	Bob Grim......	6-0	197	WR
32	Oscar Reed	6-0	222	RB
35	Bill Harris......	6-2	204	RB
40	Charlie West ...	6-1	190	DB
49	Dale Hackbart ...	6-3	205	DB
50	Jim Hargrove....	6-3	233	LB
55	Mike McGill	6-2	235	LB
57	Mike Reilly.....	6-3	235	LB
62	Ed White	6-2	252	G
71	Doug Davis.....	6-4	255	T
74	Steve Smith.....	6-5	250	DE
76	Paul Dickson ...	6-5	250	DT
89	Kent Kramer	6-5	235	TE

Kansas City Beats Minnesota by 23-7 in The Super Bowl

Dawson of Chiefs Shatters Vikings' Defense, Passes for 46-Yard Touchdown

Stenerud Also Excels

Kicks Three Field Goals as A.F.L. Representative Wins 2d Year in Row

By WILLIAM N. WALLACE

NEW ORLEANS, *Jan. 11*—Kansas City was all Chiefs and no Indians on the field today as the American League champions upset the Minnesota Vikings, 23-7, in the Super Bowl game before 80,998 fans at Tulane Stadium.

The mightiest Chief of all was Len Dawson, the quarterback who attacked and cracked the Vikings' defense that had yielded only 10 points a game in winning the National Football League title.

Dawson, 34 years old and a failure with two N.F.L. teams early in his career, triumphantly ended a season in which he had missed six games because of a knee injury and had been tenuously linked five days ago with a gambling investigation in Detroit. Completing 12 of 17 pass attempts, Dawson exploited the perimeters of the Minnesota zone defense and pitched one 46-yard touchdown pass to Otis Taylor.

That was the big play of a game that was never close but full of expectation that the Vikings might finally bestir themeslves. They did, just once.

Behind, 16-0, and thoroughly outplayed in the first half, the Vikings drove 69 yards for a touchdown, scored by Dave Osborn early in the second half, showing their offensive talents for the first time. But hope was short-lived.

With a first down on the Minnesota 46 in the following series, Dawson started his play on a short count without the usual shift out of the I formation. He quickly threw a pass to Otis Taylor, who was covered alone at the sideline by Earsell Mackbee, the Viking cornerback.

Playing Taylor closely and without help from the inside, Mackbee attempted a tackle as the receiver caught the ball. It was not good enough. Taylor broke free and ran 40 yards for a score.

Mackbee said, with reference to Taylor's pass pattern: "He had used a hitch [a pause] and go earlier. This was just a hitch. I had gone up tight on him a lot. Earlier I had a pinched nerve in my shoulder and as I hit him my shoulder went numb and I lost him."

The play had come with 82 seconds remaining in the third quarter and it was apparent that the Vikings, down by 16 points, would not have time to catch up against a defense as strong as the Chiefs', even if everything went right.

Nothing went right in the final quarter for the Vikings. Joe Kapp, the heralded Minnesota quarterback, threw two poor passes that were intercepted and his successor, Gary Cuozzo, threw one.

Kapp, an admitted tough guy believed to be indestructible, was knocked out of the game when tackled hard by Aaron Brown, the Kansas City defensive end. The Chiefs liked that added touch.

"We socked it to them," said Mike Garrett, the little Kansas City halfback. "We felt if we could outhit them we could beat them," added Jerry Mays, the giant defensive end.

In the first half the Chiefs came close enough to the Minnesota goal so that Jan Stenerud, their Norwegian-born soccer-style kicker, could kick field goals of 48, 32 and 25 yards.

After the third field goal, Charlie West of the Vikings fumbled the kickoff and Kansas City recovered at the Minnesota 19-yard line.

Dawson ran Wendell Hayes on a draw play past the overeager Alan Page, the charging Minnesota tackle, and then threw a pass to Taylor, who beat Mackbee at the 5. On third down Garrett scored behind a block by Mo Moorman that split Page and Paul Dickson of the goal-line defense. It was only the fifth touchdown the Minnesota defense had given up on the ground in 17 games.

The touchdown was doubly significant because the Vikings were not moving the ball. They had crossed midfield only twice and never past the Kansas City 38. About that fumble, Coach Bud Grant of the Vikings later said: "They got a break and scored. We played a great team and they beat us. Why? They made the big plays and didn't make any errors."

The victory for the Chiefs proved that there is some value in being second in pro football as in automobile rentals. Kansas City, which had an 11-3 regular-season won-lost record compared with Minnesota's 12-2, finished 1-1/2 games behind the Oakland Raiders in the Western Division of the A.F.L.

(Oakland fans paraded here near the end of a game with a banner reading, "Raiders Still No. 1".)

Then the Chiefs began the uphill climb defeating the Jets, the Eastern winners, in New York and the Raiders in Oakland for the league title. For the first and last time, the second-place team in each division qualified for the A.F.L. playoffs. Kansas City thus won three pressure games in a row and no wonder Hank Stram, the coach, said, "I'm really proud of our team."

The Chiefs were well rewarded. Each will receive $15,000 for today's victory to go with the $7,000 apiece they gained in the A.F.L. championship. The Vikings settle for $14,800, $7,500 from today's contest and about $7,300 for the N.F.L. title game.

It would be hard to single out individual Chiefs, but Dave Hill, an offensive tackle, plus the two cornerbacks, Emmitt Thomas and Jim Marsalis, deserve citations. Hill played Carl Eller, the feared defensive end, to a standstill, which means a victory for the offense. "He's good but not that good," said Hill.

Hill, Moorman and the others on the offensive line—Ed Budde, E. J. Holub and Tim Tyrer—were stubborn in protecting Dawson. Eller and the other Viking end, Jim Marshall, were often double-teamed. The Viking pass defenders had always been suspect but N.F.L. quarterbacks had a hard time working against Mackbee and Sharockman because they were always so harassed by the Minnesota pass rush that could not reach Dawson today.

Marsalis and Thomas covered the Viking wide receivers all the way and held Gene Washington, the best one, to one catch. Thomas, Johnny Robinson, who played despite sore ribs, and Willie Lanier, the middle linebacker, made the interceptions.

The game brought to an end the rivalry between the National and American Leagues because next season all 26 pro teams will be under one umbrella, the newly constituted N.F.L.

The Super Bowl score ended at two victories for each league but the A.F.L. won the last two in a row. Not only did the American Leaguers end up even with the National, they got in the last punch.

Kansas City Chiefs	3	13	7	0—23
Minnesota Vikings	0	0	7	0— 7

    K.C.—FG, Stenerud, 48.
    K.C.—FG, Stenerud, 32.
    K.C.—FG, Stenerud, 25.
    K.C.—Garrett, 5, run (Stenerud, kick).
    Minn.—Osborn, 4, run (Cox, kick).
    K.C.—Taylor, 46, pass from Dawson. (Stenerud, kick).
    Attendance—80,998.

Individual Statistics

RUSHES—K.C.: Garrett, 11 for 39 yards; Pitts, 3 for 37; Hayes, 8 for 31; McVea, 12 for 26; Holmes, 5 for 7; Dawson, 3 for 10. Minn.: Brown, 6 for 26; Osborn, 7 for 15; Reed, 4 for 17; Kapp, 2 for 9.

PASSES—K.C.: Dawson, 12 of 17 for 142 yards. Minn.: Kapp, 16 of 25 for 183; Cuozzo, 1 of 3 for 16.

RECEPTIONS—K.C.: Taylor, 6 for 81 yards; Pitts, 3 for 33; Garrett, 2 for 25; Hayes, 1 for 3. Minn.: Henderson, 7 for 111; Brown, 3 for 11; Beasley, 2 for 41; Osborn, 2 for 11; Reed, 2 for 16; Washington, 1 for 9.

Statistics of the Game

	Chiefs	Vikings		Chiefs	Vikings
First downs	18	13	Interceptions by	3	1
Rushing yardage	151	67	Punts	4-49	3-37
Passing yardage	122	172	Fumbles lost	0	2
Return yardage	79	97	Yards penalized	47	67
Passes	12-17	17-28			

DAWSON KEEPS HIS COOL AFTER GAME, TOO, AS WEEK OF INNER TORMENT ENDS

Passer Survives Inquiry Effects

Denies Outside Events Had Effect on His Motivation or Concentration

By DAVE ANDERSON

NEW ORLEANS, *Jan. 11*—When the Super Bowl game ended, Len Dawson was the first of the Kansas City Chiefs to enter their locker room. Typically, his boyish face was expressionless.

A moment later, a club official told him, "Great game, Lenny," and shook the quarterback's right hand. Dawson "cracked a smile," as the club official said later, but continued in silence toward his open wooden cubicle.

In recent days, the 34-year-old Dawson has been living with an inner turmoil. He had acknowledged a "casual acquaintance" with a Michigan restaurateur, Donald Dawson, no relation, who was arrested 10 days ago in a Justice Department investigation into nationwide sports gambling.

But throughout the 23-7 victory over the Minnesota Vikings today, the quarterback had performed almost flawlessly. He had justified his nickname of "Lenny the Cool" with icy precision, and at no time in the moments of celebration after the triumph did he stray from his mechanical manner.

"The entire week was quite an ordeal for me," he acknowledged. "But I didn't win the game, the whole team did."

Not long after that, following a television interview, Dawson was told that President Nixon wanted to speak to him by telephone and he entered a trainer's office.

"Mr. President," he said during their conversation, "I hope that we'll always try to exemplify what's good in football."

When their conversation ended, the quarterback was asked if the victory had been a "vindication" for him.

"I don't look at it in that vein," he said softly. "Unfortunately, it put a great deal of stress and strain on me, and more so on my family, but I asked the Good Lord to give me the strength and the courage to play my best, and asked him to let the sun shine on my teammates today."

Dawson disclosed that he had received "thousands of telegrams from all over the country," especially the Kansas City area.

Moments later, in the mob scene that surrounded him, Dawson was

Roy Winston of the Vikings hurtles toward Len Dawson, who managed to
withstand this physical pressure as well as emotional pressure from
off-the-field entanglements to lead Kansas City to victory in Super Bowl IV.

informed that he had won an automobile from Sport magazine as the Super
Bowl game's most valuable player. But in the commotion, the quarterback
either didn't hear it, or didn't understand it, because he stared through his
benefactor.

Suddenly, his 10-year-old son, Leonard Jr., joined him and they
hugged. Soon they were together atop a trainer's table, where the quarterback's quiet voice would be heard easier.

"When the team came in at the half," he said, "we had a 16-0 lead,
and we knew there were only 30 minutes left. We wanted to keep our
composure. We wanted to make sure we didn't give away anything, and we
didn't."

Asked if the gambling investigation had provided an additional incentive, Dawson stared at his questioner.

"No," he said. "It's such a big game, an opportunity to be the best,
that you don't need outside motivation."

Asked if the "strain and stress" of the "ordeal," to use his words, had
affected his concentration, he said:

"No, when you're out on that field in a football game, you're concentrating on your job, and you do it."

Perhaps his "coolest" moment occurred when Mike Garrett slashed
across the goal-line on a 5-yard touchdown run after taking a handoff. With

his back to Garrett, the quarterback heard the roar, realized the touchdown had been scored, and slapped his hands quickly.

Without another display of emotion, Dawson turned and told the referee that the Chiefs wanted the line of scrimmage for the extra point attempt to be the 4-yard line, rather than the usual 2-yard line.

"You've got an option on that," the Chiefs' center, E. J. Holub, said. "If the ball had been snapped from the 2, it would've had to be spotted at the 9, where it was slippery with mud. But back at the 11, it was dry. That's how cool Lenny was, but he's always like that."

In the morning, the quarterback had appeared equally relaxed. Sprawled on his bed, Dawson had a thin smile as he watched his roommate, Johnny Robinson, prowl the room in anticipation.

After the victory, Dawson summed it all up:

"The best thing about this game is that we don't have to answer for it for the next three years, like we did the last time." He was referring to the loss of the first Super Bowl game to the Green Bay Packers three years ago. "This time, we're the champions."

Dawson Receives Hail From Chief

Nixon Calls to Congratulate Kansas City on Victory

NEW ORLEANS, *Jan. 11 (AP)*—Lenny Dawson had to spell his name twice for the long-distance operator and hold a finger in his right ear to hear the President of the United States after the Chiefs' Super Bowl victory today.

"Thank you, Mr. President, I really appreciate it," the Kansas City quarterback said in a low voice. "But it wasn't me, sir, it was the whole team that did it."

Dawson had to fight his way into a little anteroom of the team's dressing quarters to receive the call from the White House.

There was a delay and several times the connection was broken.

"D-A-W-S-O-N," he spelled to an operator. "D-A-W-S-O-N, Lenny Dawson."

Then the President came on.

Dawson held the telephone in his left hand as he talked quietly to Mr. Nixon.

"Who is this?" he said. "Oh, yes sir, thank you, Mr. President."

"I appreciate it, Mr. President," he repeated four times.

It was a $2.68 call—six minutes—from the White House.

Later, Dawson explained that Nixon had congratulated him and his teammates for playing so well under such adverse conditions.

"He told us we did a great job and said the youth of the world looks up to pro players for courage," Dawson related.

"I told him we try to exemplify what is good in professional football."

Dapper Disciplinarian Gains Acceptance Among His Peers

Stram's Skill as Organizer, Tactician and Innovator Previously Slighted

By FRANK LITSKY

Perhaps the 25 to 30 suits, 15 sports jackets and 22 pairs of shoes, which are part of his four-closet wardrobe, made him appear a dude. Perhaps his instant charm alienated older and less-polished fellow coaches. Perhaps his failure to win with talent often called the best in the sport left his abilities suspect.

Whatever the reason, the football world had never fully accepted Henry Louis Stram as a great leader. Yesterday, when his Kansas City Chiefs upset the Minnesota Vikings in professional football's Super Bowl, Hank Stram won acceptance.

In a sport bathed in publicity, the 47-year-old Stram is not among the most publicized. Yet he is a master organizer, tactician and innovator.

He is the only man who has been a head coach in all 10 seasons of the American Football League. He was the first A.F.L. coach to use the moving pocket, I formation and stack defense. In 12 years as a college assistant at Purdue, Southern Methodist, Notre Dame and Miami of Florida, he developed such outstanding quarterbacks as Len Dawson, Dale Samuels, George Izo and Fran Curci.

When the American League began, he became a head coach for the first time—with the Dallas Texans. In 1962, the Texans won the league title. Then the Texans moved (1) to Kansas City and (2) out of contention.

"One day," said a former American League coach, "I saw those Chiefs run onto the field against us and I buried my head in my hands. I thought they would beat us, 40-0. Instead, we beat them."

Stram's players were usually bigger, stronger and better, but they were inconsistent. People said Stram wasn't a winner.

The Chiefs' success yesterday meant vindication for Stram, a round man with a round face. He stands 5 feet 7 inches and weighs 205 pounds, a result of his craving for candy and desserts (a friend described him as a "dessertnik").

He is fastidious ("If a man doesn't have a shoeshine," he said, "he isn't well-dressed"), and he wants his players to be the same (no mustaches, no sideburns below midear). He is a man of strong beliefs ("I've seen many football coaches at mass the day of a game," said Msgr. Vincent J. Mackey of Boston, a close friend, "but Hank is the only coach I've seen at mass the day after a game").

The principles were instilled years ago. Stram was born in Chicago on

Jan. 1, 1923, and raised with a younger sister in Chicago and Gary, Ind. His father was Polish-born Henry Wilczek, who wrestled professionally under the name of Stram. His mother is the former Nellie Butz of Carbondale. Pa.

At Lew Wallace High School in Gary, Stram lettered in football, baseball, basketball and track. At Purdue (Class of 1948), he played football and baseball and met Phyllis Pesha, a drum majorette. They were married in 1953. Mrs. Stram has become an excitable and vocal football fan.

The Strams have six children—Hank Jr., 15; Dale, 14; Stu, 10; Julie, 9; Gary, 8, and Mary Nell, 6. They live in Prairie Village, Kan., in a six-bedroom, early Colonial brick house with 4,700 feet of living space and a backyard pool.

Like most football coaches, Stram's life from July to January is almost all football. He seldom reads a newspaper beyond the sports pages. He drinks socially (scotch) but does not smoke. In the offseason, he plays golf (75 to 82), tennis and handball.

He is a happy, outgoing man. He is also a disciplinarian.

"In his own way," said a man close to the Chiefs, "he is just as tough as Vince Lombardi. If Lombardi does it with a hammer, Hank does it with a velvet hammer."

After suffering Super Bowl defeats in 1967 and 1968 Hank Stram and his Kansas City Chiefs finally got their championship when they beat Minnesota in Super Bowl IV.
WIDE WORLD PHOTOS

SOUND OF DEFLATING FOOTBALLS ACCENTUATES GLOOM IN VIKINGS' DRESSING ROOM

Kapp's Shoulder Is Due for X-Rays

Quarterback Retreats to the Trainer's Table— Losers Praise Foes' Toughness

By GEORGE VECSEY

NEW ORLEANS, *Jan. 11*—Joe Kapp's tan suit was hanging on a hook in the corner of the dressing room, but the Minnesota quarterback was out in a trainer's room having his injured left shoulder inspected. He is expected to take X-rays tomorrow morning before flying home.

The only sound in Kapp's corner of the clubhouse was the hissing sound of escaping air.

Bobby Lee, the bright, young punter-quarterback was letting the air out of his footballs, to make it easier to ship them home to Minnesota. The deflation of the footballs seemed the final act for the Vikings, who had been similarly punctured by the Kansas City Chiefs all afternoon.

"All that work," Lee muttered, "and this is the way it ends." It was sure over. The score was 23-7 and the defeat included one injured quarterback, "Hennepin Joe" Kapp, this year's magnetic personality of Super Week, the man who was to Minneapolis's Hennepin Avenue what Joe Namath was to Broadway

A Painful End to Season

But when Aaron Brown of Kansas City clobbered Kapp with four minutes to go, the season was over, and painfully.

As the Vikings trudged off the field, 39 of them hunched their shoulders against the scattered boos of the fans, but Kapp did not seem to hear. He was close to crying from the pain and he needed support as he stumbled toward the clubhouse. Then he disappeared into the trainer's room.

"It's the left shoulder," said Coach Bud Grant. "It's not dislocated and they don't think it's broken, but they'll need X-rays anyway. Joe's in too much pain to talk."

The rest of the Vikings had their psychic pains, but they tried to talk about the loss. The front line of the defense, so magnificent all season, was asked about Kansas City's diversified offense.

"I don't think they hurt us mentally," said Alan Page. "We knew about their formations. They were one of the most physical teams we've faced. They came out tough right from the start. We weren't surprised about anything. We were told it would take our best effort to beat them."

'As Well as We Could'

There was some question whether the Vikings had shown their best effort. Coach Grant said, "Maybe we could play better tomorrow, but today we played as well as we could."

The coach praised Len Dawson, the Kansas City quarterback, calling him "underrated among so many stars." Grant said he hadn't gone for a field goal from the Chiefs' 41-yard line early in the game because of a strong wind against the Vikings.

While Grant was talking, an assistant flitted into the clubhouse and gathered all of Kapp's clothes. They dressed the quarterback in the private room in the back and sent him to their hotel to rest.

Although he couldn't meet the press, Kapp later relayed a few of his remarks through his publicity man.

Chiefs' Defense Cited

"The Kansas City defensive line looked like a redwood forest," he said. "I don't remember that one individual stood out—they were all very active. They took the running game away from us. We went into the game wanting to run the ball, and they were able to take it all away with a great defensive play.

"The big thing was the fact that we couldn't come up with the big play when we had to. That's what got us here, but we couldn't do it today."

Grant Analyzes Defeat of Team

Chiefs 'Came Up With the Big Play, Didn't Fumble'

NEW ORLEANS, *Jan. 11 (AP)*—Coach Bud Grant had a simple explanation on the loss of his Minnesota Vikings today to the Kansas City Chiefs in the Super Bowl.

"We played a great football team," the Minnesota coach said after Kansas City's 23-7 victory. "They beat us. It's as simple as that.

"They came up with the big play, didn't fumble, moved the ball when they had to and were not hurt by the interception.

"I can't say Kansas City is the toughest team we've played this year. But productionwise and pointwise, they outplayed us the toughest."

The Vikings shuffled into their dressing room with their heads bowed in an attempt to cloak their emotions.

A Vikings' cornerback, Earsell Mackbee, sustained a pinched nerve in his left shoulder.

The Vikings, 13-point favorites, lost all chance of winning in the fourth period when the Kansas City quarterback, Len Dawson, combined with Otis Taylor for a 46-yard touchdown pass to produce the final margin.

"When they get that touchdown," said Minnesota's defensive end, Carl Eller, "that put them three scores out. That's what changed the game."

Grant said the Vikings also had to abandon hopes for developing a strong rushing attack when the Chiefs took a 16-0 half-time lead.

"When they get that far ahead, they could afford to run for five or six first downs and be satisfied not to score," Grant said. "We couldn't afford to do that. They ate up the first five minutes of the second half like that.

"They just beat us with fine personnel. No secrets. We put our best on the line. They put their best on the line and they were a better football team . . . today."

Mackbee said when he hit Taylor on the touchdown play, "My arm was numb and I did not even feel it."

Taylor also broke away from Karl Kassulke's attempted tackle before going in standing up for the touchdown.

"We made a batch of mistakes," said Kassulke. "We made more mistakes today than we made in 23 games."

Eller, Marshall 'Double-Teamed'

Stram Discloses How Chiefs Stopped Vikings' Ends

NEW ORLEANS, *Jan. 11*—Hank Stram, the coach of the Kansas Chiefs, disclosed today that their game plan consisted primarily of passing "in front of the cornerbacks" while double-teaming the Minnesota Vikings' defensive ends.

"With that double-team," Stram said, "they didn't have time to interfere with the flight of the ball on our short passes."

Stram used Fred Arbanas, the tight end, in addition to Dave Hill, the right tackle, to stop Carl Eller, the Vikings' celebrated defensive end. Jim Tyrer, the Chiefs' left tackle, was aided by one of the running backs in halting Jim Marshall, the other Viking end.

"There were no wrinkles put in for this game," Stram said. "The end-around from the I formation might have been new to them, but we used it before. But it wasn't in any of the films the Vikings had seen of us."

On the end-around play, Frank Pitts, a wide receiver, carried three times for a total of 37 yards, producing a first down each time.

His first run, of 19 yards, aided the drive that led to Jan Stenerud's third field goal. His last preceded Otis Taylor's touchdown reception.

Hill, the 260-pound right tackle on offense, handled Eller with relative ease, but was annoyed when the Vikings' defensive star pounced on Len Dawson after a handoff.

"He was trying to hurt Lenny," Hill said, "because he had to know that the ball had been handed off. That was a cheap shot, and we let him know it now. Another time Alan Page punched Lenny when Lenny was down. That's high school stuff. I was ashamed of them doing that."

Defensively, the Chiefs limited the Viking runners to only 67 yards, about half of their game average during the National Football League season.

"We knew," explained Willie Lanier, the middle linebacker who calls the defensive signals, "that if we could take away their running game, it would be a big factor. We used a tackle head-on with their center, either Buck Buchanan or Curley Culp, and it confused them."

STRAM SEES STRONG INTERLEAGUE RIVALRY CONTINUING DESPITE PROS' MERGER

Coach of Chiefs is Proud of A.F.L.

Recalls Previous Derogatory Comparisons With N.F.L., Finds Parity Achieved

By DAVE ANDERSON

NEW ORLEANS, *Jan. 12*—In a glow of satisfaction, Hank Stram, coach of the world champion Kansas City Chiefs, predicted today that there would always be a strong rivalry between the American and National League teams despite the merger of the 26 pro football clubs under the National League banner next season.

"There is a strong attachment among the people who have been in the American Football League from the beginning," he said. "I think there always will be a strong rivalry because football is such an emotional game."

After its All-Star game on Saturday in the Houston Astrodome, the A.F.L. as such will disappear. Its 10 teams will be joined officially on Feb. 1 by the Cleveland Browns, Baltimore Colts and Pittsburgh Steelers in the American Conference of the merged league while the 13 other teams in the N.F.L. will form the National Conference.

Stirred by First Game

"We're proud of our league," Stram said. "We're the proud champions of a proud league."

When the New York Jets surprised the Colts, 16-7, for the A.F.L.'s first Super Bowl triumph a year ago, many N.F.L. loyalists considered it a fluke. But with their decisive 23-7 defeat of the N.F.L. champions, the Minnesota Vikings, in yesterday's game, the Chiefs proved the parity of the leagues.

"I hope Joe Namath and the Jets are as proud of us as we were of them last year," said E. J. Holub, the center.

To add to the A.F.L.'s enjoyment, the Chiefs were not even a division winner during the regular season. They finished second to the Oakland Raiders in the Western Division before qualifying for the Super Bowl with playoff victories over the Jets and Raiders.

"Just imagine," an A.F.L. official said with a chuckle, "what one of our first-place teams would have won by."

Another factor in the Chiefs' triumph was the memory of their 35-10 loss to the Green Bay Packers in the first Super Bowl three years ago. After that game, Vince Lombardi, then the Packer coach, commented that the Chiefs were not on the level of the N.F.L.'s best teams.

Alludes to Lombardi

"There were a lot of things said after that game that were uncalled for," Stram said in an allusion to Lombardi. "I've felt for several years that we could play with anybody. An insignia on your hat or jacket doesn't make any difference. Football is a game of people, not of emblems."

Among those converted to the parity of the leagues was Jimmy (The Greek) Snyder, the Las Vegas oddsmaker who had installed the Vikings as 13-point favorites. Last year the Colts were his 17-point choice.

"My number was 13 and it hardly changed," Snyder said, "so apparently it was the proper number for betting purposes and that's my primary role. But I'm convinced now that if the Chiefs and the Vikings played a series of 10 games, each would win five, or one would win six and lose four. They're on the same level."

It Was a Super Day For Television, Too

The Columbia Broadcasting System estimated yesterday that 57 million people watched at least part of Sunday's Super Bowl football telecast.

According to overnight figures provided by National Arbitron, on which the estimate was made, the game had a 70 per cent share of the over-all television audience.

For last year's Super Bowl, televised by the National Broadcasting Company, figures from the A.C. Nielsen Company indicated that more than 60 million had watched. The Nielsen rating for Sunday's game will not be announced for a week.

Sports of The Times

By ARTHUR DALEY

History Lesson

"Not many people realize," said a smiling Billy Sullivan, the president of the Boston Patriots, "the extra measure of satisfaction that all American Football League owners got when one of our teams beat the Minnesota Vikings in the Super Bowl. It was great for us a year ago, of course, when the Jets beat the Colts, but there wasn't the same undercurrent that was running against the Vikings, the same deep feelings.

"To put it in proper perspective I'll have to backtrack 10 years to when we were organized as an eight-team league and our eighth team was the Minnesota Vikings. A few days earlier, though, the Vikes agreed to jump to the National Football League and our dinner meeting was somewhat on the tense side when we had a confrontation with Max Winter, the president of the Vikes.

"We all were upset, no one more than Harry Wismer of the then New York Titans. You know Wismer—mercurial, flighty and explosive. At sight of Winter, Harry really exploded. He even got slightly sacrilegious.

" 'Max,' he said, 'when I see you at the supper table, I can't help but think how admirably you fill the role of Judas.'

"They almost had a fistfight. But after the A.F.L. lost the Vikings we filled in the gap at the last minute with Oakland. At our first meeting with Wayne Valley, the president of the Raiders, he described our desperate situation best.

" 'Gentlemen,' he said, 'welcome to the Foolish Club.' "

Mickey Mouse League

It was truly a joke league, so scorned by the N.F.L. owners that they hung on it the tag of "Mickey Mouse League." The players were bad and the playing sites second-rate—or maybe even fifth-rate. The N.F.L. merely sat back, waiting for the A.F.L. to collapse from its own dead weight.

The late Wismer was all sound and no substance—and no money, either. He supposedly had the flagship franchise in New York and he quickly ran it into the ground before running it into bankruptcy. His apartment also served as his office with his publicity man operating out of the bathroom and the ticket manager out of the pantry. At least the ticket manager didn't do much business because customers were so few as to be almost invisible.

The Raiders played at either Kezar Stadium or Candlestick Park in San Francisco across the Bay from Oakland. "Follow the Raiders," exhorted the signs. It was difficult to find them, much less follow them. The Dallas Texans couldn't buck the Dallas Cowboys and fled to Kansas City to become the Chiefs. The Los Angeles Chargers, playing regularly before 89,000 empty seats, couldn't buck the Rams and skeedaddled to San Diego.

The league was a mess, inches from total collapse, until Sonny Werblin, the showman supreme, moved in with his associates to buy the Titans and rename them the Jets. He made two major contributions that saved the league.

Aware of the fact that the National Broadcasting Company was gazing enviously on the way the Columbia Broadcasting System was devouring the entire pro football pie with its exclusive rights to N.F.L. games, Sonny swung a package deal with N.B.C. In effect, the space cadets subsidized the A.F.L., advancing sufficient cash to all poverty areas so that the Mickey Mouse League finally had the wherewithal to outbid its established rivals for draft choices.

Then Sonny hit the headlines by starring a personality with star quality, Joe Namath, the well-advertised $400,000 bonus baby. The N.F.L. tried to ignore the A.F.L. but couldn't. The war for talent was on in earnest, and bonuses became so outrageous that all teams were soon tumbling down the hill to the poorhouse.

The Dynamo

The A.F.L. commissioner had been Joe Foss, a war hero, who seemed forever off hunting or on safari whenever his services were most needed. So he was replaced by Al Davis of Oakland, described by his many enemies as a "gutter fighter." He began raiding the N.F.L. where it hurt most, the top quarterbacks. Suddenly, the N.F.L. began to listen to merger propositions and the amalgamation was effected under the sole rule of Commissioner Pete Rozelle.

The Super Bowl series evolved from this. The Nationals won the first two and the Americans the next two, with the Kansas City victory over the Vikings being the sweeter to the American League old-line owners.

Beginning next month the A.F.L. dissolves into the American Conference, balanced by the addition of three N.F.L. teams—Cleveland, Baltimore and Pittsburgh. The remaining 13 teams will become the National Conference, while the over-all legal entity will be the National Football League.

Survival had seemed impossible when the A.F.L. first was organized. But the original Foolish Club now numbers men with wisdom, stability, stature and success.

Chapter 5

Super Bowl V—1971

For Super Bowl V, all pretense at special mystique was an outright impossibility. This was the new National Football League champion-ship game, no more, no less, no matter what you called it.

The participants, Dallas and Baltimore, were both "old" N.F.L. teams even though Baltimore had moved over into the newly created American Conference. To reach this final game, each had survived a fantastically complicated set of regular-season possibilities leading to an eight-team playoff. Baltimore, it turned out, did have the best record in the American Conference; Dallas had the second-best record in the National Conference, and had by-passed Minnesota (which had the best mark) during the intricate playoff. In the first year of the 26-team conglomerate, a Super Bowl, by any name, was merely the end of the road—a rough road, a royal road, to a prize richly deserved and dearly cherished, but purely and simply a championship game.

Did that make it any less of a football game, or less desirable a title? Certainly not. Did it make it less of a "unique, unforgettable, once-in-a-lifetime, game-of-the-century" experience? And how.

Of course, that would have happened in any case. The fifth in-stance of anything can't be as "unique" as the first. But Super Bowl V had so little of the unique about it that it revealed, almost perversely, how truly established the football establishment had become. The Super Bowl, once so fertile a source of speculation, had taken its place in the sports firmament, as dependable and as important as the vernal equinox, and in the same fashion an annual festival rather than a periodic cataclysm.

Tickets for Super Bowl Are Rarer Than Snowflakes in Miami

MIAMI, *Jan. 9*— The Super Bowl game was nearly sold out before the tickets went on sale.

All 79,000 available Orange Bowl seats are gone for next Sunday's pro football war between the Baltimore Colts and Dallas Cowboys. Scalpers are already rubbing their palms in anticipation.

"Ticket pressure is mounting," said Jim Kensil, assistant commissioner of the National Football League. "There's a dozen ways to get Super Bowl tickets, but you've got to act before the supply evaporates."

Season ticket holders of the host Miami Dolphins scoop up the largest batch of tickets—about 25,000. They are allowed to buy on a 1-for-1 basis for their regular-season commitments.

The Colts and Cowboys get team assignments of 10,000 tickets apiece. Neither the fans in Baltimore nor Dallas allowed any to be returned to the N.F.L. clearing house.

Twenty-four remaining N.F.L. franchises claim 500 tickets each, which accounts for another 12,000. The news media are allowed to purchase a total of 1,000. Persons with the right political connections are allocated another 1,000.

Nobody gets free tickets to the Super Bowl. If you enter without paying and won't be performing on the artificial turf, chances are you're indebted to somebody looking for a favor.

That accounts for some 60,000 of the 79,000 available seats in the Orange Bowl's giant horseshoe. Remaining pasteboards are split among three TV networks, N.F.L. TV-radio sponsors, N.F.L. players and participants, such as bandsmen.

This year, tickets for the end zone sold faster at $15 than they did three years ago at $6.

"Those cheaper seats always went last," Kensil said this week. "When the first Super Bowl drew only 61,000—about 25,000 under capacity—in 1967, most unsold tickets were the lowest in price."

The last time the Super Bowl game was played in the Orange Bowl, the tickets were scaled from $12 to $10 to $8 to see the underdog New York Jets beat the Colts.

League officials raised the tariff to $15 all around for last January's event in New Orleans.

"We cannot get into the mail-order business," said Kensil, who was busy setting up a half-dozen temporary offices in the Americana Hotel in Miami Beach.

"That would mean disappointing about 98 per cent of those who applied. It would also mean sending back all that money."

Actually, there are only 1,000 no-strings-attached tickets sold where the "little guy" can line up and buy space without a connection with some team or somebody. Those were peddled in a very few minutes one Sunday in November at an Orange Bowl ticket window.

NBC-TV will show the game to much of the world, but it is to be blacked out in the Miami area. The network will use 11 color cameras and a crew of 200.

News media representatives will occupy a 98-seat main pressbox, a 65-seat old pressbox and more than 500 stand seats. Those relegated to the stands will be provided clipboards to help cover the game.

Unitas, Superstar, Facing a Supertest

By WILLIAM N. WALLACE

Jan. 10, 1971— Sid Luckman, the Hall of Fame quarterback for the Chicago Bears, spoke recently at a dinner honoring John Unitas. Said Luckman, "Sammy Baugh and I made an agreement a long time ago. He would always call me the greatest pro football player of all time and I would always call him the greatest. I called Sammy this morning and told him I was sorry, but I had to break the agreement because I was going to a dinner to talk about a man who surely is the greatest pro football player of all time, Johnny Unitas."

Next Sunday, Unitas will come up to another memorable event of his long career as quarterback of the Baltimore team. This will be the Super Bowl game matching the Colts against the Dallas Cowboys, who have a defense formidable enough to test the greatest of all time.

Although 37 years old, Unitas is healthy and can still throw the long touchdown pass, as he demonstrated last Sunday in the American Conference championship game against Oakland. Such was not the case two years ago when a sore-armed Unitas tried to rally the Colts against the Jets in a prior Super Bowl contest.

•

There was no Super Bowl, and no idea of a second league, in 1958 when Unitas approached the first great event of his career. That was the National Football League championship game matching the Colts, the Western champions, and the Giants, the Eastern titleholders, in Yankee Stadium on Dec. 28.

The Giants, like the Cowboys, had a great defense. Unitas, in the sudden-death period, cracked the defense by leading the Colts to a touchdown drive. He used his star receiver, Raymond Berry, and his runner, Alan Ameche, in perfect balance.

This year's receiver is Roy Jefferson and the power runner is the rookie, Norm Bulaich.

•

The research department of the National Broadcasting Company has estimated that 67 million people will view the Super Bowl game on television.

The game alternates each year between N.B.C. and the Columbia Broadcasting System. Last year's audience was estimated to be 62.28 million viewers in 30.83 million homes.

If the 67 million estimate holds up, the audience would be the largest for any sports event.

Sports of the Times

By ARTHUR DALEY

In Good Voice

FORT LAUDERDALE, FLA., *Jan. 11*— At least Craig Morton now knows he won't have to use sign language to call the plays for Dallas against the Baltimore Colts in the Super Bowl. The Cowboy quarterback has filled the role of a strong, silent man for a week. Last night he was able to whisper. Today he talked normally. By Sunday he'll be barking out the numbers.

"It was a strange thing," he said this morning, hurrying contentedly in the 75-degree sunshine at the baseball park the football people have borrowed from the New York Yankees. "The night before the San Francisco game my throat was feeling peculiar. I noticed nothing during the game—maybe it was the excitement—but after it I couldn't talk. I'd lost my voice.

"I rested in bed from Tuesday until yesterday and I realize now that I needed the rest. I'll be O.K. by game time. I'll tell you one thing, it would be pretty hard to play unless I could talk. Take that San Francisco game. I called more audibles than at any time in my life, and I expect Baltimore will move around so much that I'll also have to change the plays at the scrimmage line again. But I dunno. With our multiple sets, they may have to standardize their defenses more."

Adversity's Child

Morton raised his arms on high and brought them down as if he was affectionately embracing the sunshine. "I love hot weather," he said. He was standing near first base on the well-manicured diamond that is ready for the arrival of the Yankees a month hence. But the chalklines of the gridiron were in the outfield, with everything set for secret practice sessions starting on the morrow.

"It's hard to believe we're here," said Craig happily, "but beating San Francisco for the championship ended our frustrations and made us a real proud team. I've been through it all, too. Tom Landry says, 'adversity brings success.' I believe it, and I'm satisfied with the results.

"I know I've been criticized pretty harshly at times, but the only bad game I had of the last seven we played was against Detroit. My statistics don't look fancy against San Francisco with only seven of 22 completions. But I had a few good passes dropped and I deliberately threw away the ball a half-dozen times. That's one thing I learned this year, how to dump the ball. As long as I know what I'm doing, I'm not worried.

"I have to feel that Baltimore should have worries. The Colts must concern themselves with stopping the running of Duane Thomas, Walt Garrison and Calvin Hill. At all times they must also watch Bob Hayes. And they'd better keep an eye out for Reggie Rucker, too. To cover Hayes and stop Thomas they can't help but weaken themselves some place."

If there is such a weakness, the likelihood is enormous that Landry will spot it and exploit it.

"Landry is smarter than everybody," once said an admiring Alex Webster of his old Giant teammate.

"My theory of defense," Landry was saying today, "is to play responsibility as contrasted with the hit-and-react theory which is much more natural and instinctive. That's why it takes two or three years to teach it. But it has to be sold to every player, and he has to bow to the discipline it demands.

"I started it when I became player-coach of the Giants in 1954 and it became a reality in 1956 when the Giants won the world championship, with defense playing a major role. It's an attempt to destroy Vinnie Lombardi's run to daylight theory. Guys have to believe they can control an area, shutting out the daylight.

Rugged Salesmanship

"I'll grant you that it's difficult to sell a fellow like Bob Lilly the idea that he should hold a position when his every instinct tells him to leave it and make a play. But a super player like Lilly can be privileged to free-lance a bit, just as Rosey Grier was permitted to do with the Giants, because their teammates will cover up for them. Dick Nolan is still selling this theory to the 49ers and he'll turn them into champions, too."

Once many years ago Nolan was a defensive back on the Giants under player-coach Landry. Tom outlined an enemy pass play on the blackboard and marked a big X.

"That's where you'll intercept the ball," said Landry.

"But suppose they don't throw it there," said Nolan.

"They will," said Landry. They did. Nolan intercepted for a touchdown.

Seven games ago, when the Cowboys were tailspinning out of contention, Landry relieved Morton of the burden of deciding on what plays to call. Using messengers, Tom calls all plays from the sideline and the Cowboys haven't lost since. The voice that will direct the Dallas offense on

Sunday will be the regained voice of Craig Morton. But it will emerge from the high-powered brain of Tom Landry.

Adderley Expects to Be Busiest

Back to Guard Jefferson, Star Baltimore Receiver

By WILLIAM N. WALLACE

FORT LAUDERDALE, FLA., *Jan. 11*—Herb Adderley, a vital link in the Dallas Cowboy defense at left cornerback, expects that John Unitas, the Baltimore Colt quarterback, will be picking on him in the Super Bowl game on Sunday. Adderley is ready.

"Brodie [John Brodie of the 49ers] threw 40 passes against us last week," said Adderley today. "We figure Unitas will throw at least as many. If we shut off their running like we've been doing against other teams, it might be more."

The Super Bowl matches a running team, the Cowboys against a passing one, the Colts with Unitas. The most dangerous Baltimore receiver, Roy Jefferson, usually is flanked to the right, opposite Adderley. It will be a great matchup.

Opposing quarterbacks find themselves throwing passes in Adderley country. It is a weak option. No one dares throw much at the opposite cornerback, Mel Renfro, an all-league choice and a game-breaking interceptor. Cornell Green and Charlie Waters playing safety with help from the quick linebackers are no easier on the inside.

At Peak of His Game

Adderley said: "I'm 31 years old and I think I'm at the peak of my game. I'm so glad to be here for a third time. It's unbelievable what happened to me. I feel sorry for all the great players who never get to be on one championship team."

Adderley is an old Green Bay Packer. He starred on five championship Packer teams, two of which won in the Super Bowl. Then Adderley got mad at Vince Lombardi's successor, Phil Bengston, and forced the Packers to trade him—to the Cowboys for Malcolm Walker, a center, and Clarence Williams, a spare defensive end.

The trade did not come until last September. With three days' practice, Adderley played against the Jets in the final preseason game in the Cotton Bowl. "I didn't know my teammates; I didn't know the defenses which are plenty complicated; I wasn't in top shape, and I had never played on artificial turf before," he said.

The Jets won and Richard Caster, their rookie receiver, had a big night at Adderley's expense. But Herb went on to have a good season.

"One of my best," he said. "I gave up only one touchdown, to John Gilliam in St. Louis. And they sure threw at me a lot."

Adderley noted that the Dallas pass defense went from 11th place last year to third best this season in the National Conference. He was the sealer where the Cowboys always had a problem, at left cornerback.

Two of Adderley's Packer teammates, Bart Starr and Doug Hart who were representing a Green Bay television station, interviewed him. "Congratulations," said Starr.

The sun has set in Green Bay, with the Packers now a losing team in search of a coach to replace Bengston, who resigned.

Adderley said later: "I don't want to talk about what happened to me in Green Bay. It's over and Phil Bengston is gone."

Adderley was upset a year ago because a teammate, Bob Jeter, was voted to the pro bowl team and he was not. He blamed Bengston for lack of support.

"It wasn't only that," he said. "It was a whole lot of things."

His two winning Super Bowl experiences as a Packer made Adderley $50,000 richer. A Dallas victory Sunday would add $15,000 more. "I'm so fortunate," he said and then turned his attention to Mr. John Unitas five days away.

HILL WORKS OUT IN COWBOYS' BACKFIELD, WITH THOMAS TAKING GARRISON'S SPOT

Injured Fullback Vows He'll Play

But Ex-Yale Star, on Bench for Last Part of Season, Likely to Be Used More

By WILLIAM N. WALLACE

FORT LAUDERDALE, FLA., *Jan. 12*— The Dallas Cowboys began their final series of practices today for Sunday's Super Bowl game against Baltimore, and Calvin Hill, all but forgotten the last two months, was back in the spotlight. Hill, the Yale alumnus voted the National League's rookie of the year in 1969, was running in the first backfield with the 1970 rookie who took his job away, Duane Thomas.

With Hill at halfback, Thomas moved a step or two into the fullback position filling in for the injured Walt Garrison, the regular who worked gingerly under sunny skies in 80-degree temperatures. Garrison caught the winning touchdown pass when Dallas beat San Francisco for the National Conference championship. But he came out of that game with a badly twisted ankle to go with his previously strained knee and chipped collar bone.

Garrison May Start

Garrison, a gung ho type, said today, "I'll play." His coach, Tom Landry, backed him up. "He'll play if he's ready," said Landry. But the Cowboys, like all pro teams, play the people on Sunday who were the heaviest practice workers during the week. This week that will be Hill and Thomas rather than the limping Garrison.

The prediction now is that Garrison may start the game but that Hill will be an early replacement.

What difference can it make to the Colts? Not much, because Thomas, Hill and a healthy Garrison are first-class backs running behind an offensive line that has become devastating of necessity in blocking for the run. On account of mediocre passing, the Cowboy style is to run and the Colts must stop the run, regardless of the identity of the ball-carrier.

But the Thomas-Hill alignment is intriguing from the Dallas standpoint because for the first time it would put two big fast game-breaking runners together. Hill played the first five games for Dallas, gained over 500 yards, hurt a shoulder and Thomas took over for the last nine. He gained 803 yards.

Game Plan Given Out

The Cowboys got a total of 1,380 yards from these two in one position, a figure that would have led the National League by far if contributed by one player.

This was the day Landry and his coaches gave the Cowboys their offensive game plan for Sunday. The game plan came in a 45-page blue notebook containing dozens of plays. Because the Baltimore defenses are so varied in appearance, the Cowboys feel they need a full repertoire.

But once the game begins, Landry, who calls the plays from the sidelines, will eliminate plays by the handful. "You keep cutting down," explained Jim Myers, an assistant offensive coach. "You find out what's going to work against their defenses and you throw out what won't work. And you repeat what does work. That's a big factor, to repeat."

Sports of The Times

It's Only a Game?

By ROBERT LIPSYTE

Jan. 16, 1971— Historians have written that the weeks leading up to that ancient American religious spectacle, the Super Bowl, were filled not only with song and celebration, but with mass national seminars. In 1967, before the event was officially called Super Bowl (supposedly after a child's high-bounce black ball), the entire country was divided into two antagonistic factions, called the National Football League and the American Football League. Followers of each league argued endlessly in journals and on street corners. They argued not only the relative merits of the competing teams, but about the Larger Issues that would be resolved by The Game. N.F.L. fans believed it essential that the Green Bay Packers win to uphold tradition, orderly change and basic national values. A.F.L. fans came to believe that if the Kansas City Chiefs won, all mankind would realize that youth, new money and inferior talent were no handicaps in the battle for the top. After Green Bay won, N.F.L. fans, with noblesse oblige, said: "It's only a game." A.F.L. fans, realizing there would be always youth, new money and inferior talent making life tense for everyone else, seemed willing to wait for success until they got older. They, too, said: "It's only a game."

They waited rather patiently through Super Bowl II, whose issue was simple: Could Vince Lombardi, on the brink of becoming the nation's authority figure, coach the Packers to their second straight Super Bowl victory, a feat hitherto impossible? After he beat Oakland, he graciously led the nation in the chant: "It's only a game."

The Fundamentalists

In 1969, a long-haired, weak-kneed, booze-loving, active young man said: "And we're going to win Sunday—I'll guarantee it." The national seminars were very troubled. N.F.L. fans argued that the crewcut, tight-lipped, grim-visaged Baltimore Colt quarterbacks would uphold the values and decency by beating the Jets, while their defensive line beat up on Joe Namath. Some A.F.L. fans also hoped this would happen although they felt it was time for the leagues to merge as equals. So most of them merely expressed fear that Joe's brashness would inflame the Colts, that the Jets would have had a chance if Joe kept silent. When it was all over, everybody agreed that the habits of American adolescence were much too important to be dependent on the outcome of a 60-minute sporting event. After all: "It's only a game."

Super Bowl IV, the last before the A.F.L.-N.F.L. rivalry was blurred by reorganization, was very complex. By then, even some N.F.L. fans wanted the Chiefs to win, closing the circle and proving the merger was sensible. A broader ideology began to appear in the seminars, although it was masked by football metaphors: Would the basic brute strength and rote execution of Minnesota, the fundamentalists, be able to withstand the new technocracy, K.C.'s Stram-lined formations? Chief fans, who sensed that Joe Kapp had nothing but personality, worried lest their quarterback, Len Dawson, be unduly upset by pregame reports alleging his involvement with gamblers. Or, worse yet, that he be arrested early in the game. But it all worked out and the metallic voice of K.C.'s computer said, after: "It's only a game."

Super Bowl V, played in 1971, provided a glimpse of the genius of the game's managers. The teams that met that year were both from the old N.F.L. The only celebrity on either team was the Colts' quarterback, Johnny Unitas, who, when asked if chills ran up and down his spine when thinking about playing again in the Super Bowl, kept answering: "It's only a game."

Infiltrators

If Unitas wasn't turned on, what about the country? So former football players infiltrated the mass national seminars to bring up the question. Is this game a moral event? A philosophy professor at the University of Guelph, John McMurtry, who played linebacker for the Calgary Stampeders, looked southward and wrote in The Nation: "The connections between the politics of fascism and the mania for football are too many to be ignored: both ground themselves on a property-seizing principle, apotheosize struggle and competition, publicly idolize victory and the powerful, make authority absolute and relate to opposing groups by violent aggression."

A former St. Louis Cardinals' linebacker, Dave Meggysey, published the book, "Out of Their League," just before Super Bowl V and stumped the country saying such things as: "The fan in the stand is saying to the players, 'I'm hostile and angry, you get it off for me.' Football acts as a bread and circus and ultimately cheats the public of really getting down to the basis of what is bothering them."

Historians of the times fail to appreciate the extraordinary scheme: If McMurtry and Meggysey prove right, pro football would say, "They're our boys," and if they prove wrong, "Well, weren't you listening? It's only a game."

DALLAS IS A ONE-POINT CHOICE IN SUPER BOWL TODAY; STRATEGIC TEST LOOMS BETWEEN UNITAS AND LANDRY

Weather Seen as No Factor

By WILLIAM N. WALLACE

MIAMI, *Jan. 16*—The Dallas Cowboys are the favorites—but by only one point in the latest odds quoted here—over the Baltimore Colts in the Super Bowl game tomorrow. The championship of pro football will be seen by 80,000 persons in the Orange Bowl stadium and an estimated 64 million on televison.

The kickoff will be at 2:10 P.M. and the telecast in New York will be on Channel 4. Weather will be no factor. The playing field has an artificial surface; temperatures are expected to be in 60's with variable cloudiness.

If the teams are as evely matched as the odds suggest, then the game is likely to be a cerebral battle between a field performer, John Unitas of the Colts, and a coach standing one yard out of bounds, Tom Landry of the Cowboys.

They will run this game.

Unitas, the Baltimore quarterback and strategist, is 37 years old. His coach, Don McCafferty, who gives him full rein, said of John: "His arm isn't as strong as it used to be, but his head is much stronger."

Jimmy Orr, a Unitas receiver for 10 years, said Unitas "has never thrown better than this week."

Landry will call all the offensive plays for his quarterback, Craig Morton, and will have a say in the defensive alignments.

"No one can touch Tom when it comes to football," said Lee Roy Jordan, the Dallas linebacker.

Hello, John—I'm Tom Landry

Unitas and Landry have clashed before at the championship level. The Colts, with Unitas, beat the New York Giants for the National Football League championship in 1958 and 1959 when Landry was the Giants' defensive coach.

"That was execution," said Landry.

Although they have been a significant part of the pro football scene for 14 years, Unitas and Landry are almost strangers.

"We've met a couple of times to say hello," said Landry. "But we've never really talked."

It may take Unitas a couple of offensive series to comprehend the Dallas defensive strategy. Meanwhile, the Colts will have to hold off the powerful Cowboy running attack.

An opening Dallas touchdown drive of 75 yards or so in a dozen plays on the ground would severely handicap the Colts, a passing team.

"The key," said Jordan, "will be to make John read our defense as he's going back to pass. We can't let him read at the line of scrimmage."

There will be camouflage so Unitas cannot know until the last second which Cowboys are covering which Colts where and at what strength.

The Unitas targets will be the wide receiver tandem of Roy Jefferson and Eddie Hinton, covered by the Dallas cornerbacks, Mel Renfro and Herb Adderley.

"We can leave our corner people, Mel and Herb, man for man because we know they can play it," said Jordan. "But we'll change up to keep John off balance."

"We expect he'll throw at least 40 passes," said Adderley.

The Dallas defense is formidable. It has given up only one touchdown in the last 25 periods covering seven games. The Cowboys are hard to run against and Baltimore will try a little with Norm Bulaich, a rookie, as the carrier and Tom Nowatzke, the fullback, as the lead blocker.

"The Colts don't do anything fancy. Their line is just physical," said Bob Lilly, the Cowboy defensive tackle. Lilly is one of the best in the business and the Colts, like other teams, will put two blockers on him, John Williams the right guard, and Bill Curry, the center.

In running situations the Cowboys will set one of the defensive linemen two feet off the scrimmage line and he will wait before moving to the ball-carrier. It is called the "flex" defense.

"I hate that," said Curry. "It really louses up our blocking."

This will be the fifth Super Bowl game and the third for both Adderley and Curry, who were teammates on the first winner, the Green Bay Packers of 1967. The victors will receive $15,000 each, the losers $7,500.

Both teams had a hard time getting here and played some feeble football along the way. Baltimore beat Chicago, 21–20, in the 11th game only because Dick Butkus, the Bears' linebacker, garbled an oral defensive signal so that his defensive backs played two different pass coverages. That left John Mackey open for a touchdown pass and left the Colts shaken.

The players then held a secret meeting and berated one another for playing poorly. Five straight victories followed.

The Cowboys were demoralized after losing their ninth game, 38–0.

"We stopped to think," said Morton. "We seemed to be going separate ways."

Landry suggested they play touch football together on their days off. Togetherness begot seven straight victories. Both coaches say their teams are still "peaking" as they get set for their 23d and final game tomorrow.

Artificial Turf Could Be a Factor

By DAVE ANDERSON

MIAMI, *Jan. 16*—For the first time, the Super Bowl game will be played on artificial turf tomorrow and an artificial controversy has been swept out from under the green rug.

Will the Dallas Cowboys have an edge because of their greater experience on artificial turf?

Of their 22 games, the Cowboys have played 14 on an artificial surface —nine during the regular season (including seven in their Cotton Bowl stadium), one in the playoffs and four in preseason. By comparison, the Baltimore Colts have performed only three times on artificial turf—twice during the season, once in the preseason.

But if a big play is influenced by a player slipping or stumbling, the outcry won't be artificial.

"As a quarterback," says John Unitas of the Colts, "you have to learn to pick up your feet more when you set up to pass. I generally slide my feet along, but on this stuff you can't do that."

"It moves you fast," says Bob Hayes, the Cowboys' wide receiver who is fast enough by himself. "But I don't like the burns."

"I like it," said Mike Curtis, the Colts' middle linebacker. "You have to be careful you don't get your feet snagged in it. But after the game, your fingernails are clean, for one thing."

Mention artificial turf and many people assume that it's AstroTurf, the original. But in the Orange Bowl stadium, the site of the Super Bowl game, Poly-Turf is the surface. Developed by the American Biltrite Company, it's softer than either AstroTurf or Tartan Turf, the other artificial surfaces used for football fields.

"But even if the same firm makes them, each field is different," says Bob Lilly, the Cowboys' defensive tackle. "That's the only thing I have against it."

But the Colts, oddly, are more accustomed to the Poly-Turf surface in the Orange Bowl than the Cowboys are. The Colts played here twice and lost to the Miami Dolphins each time—once during the regular season, once in the preseason.

"We won on the AstroTurf in the Houston Astrodome," says Unitas, "but we didn't play well there. I prefer the regular ground."

As the first artificial football field, the surface in the Astrodome is considered by most players to be the worst of them. The field there is firmer than the other newer ones. When a player falls there, the bumps and bruises last longer.

"The turf in the Astrodome is too hard," says Chuck Howley, the Cowboy linebacker, "and so is the AstroTurf in St. Louis because they play baseball on it. But our AstroTurf in the Cotton Bowl is good and so is the Poly-Turf they have here."

The Cowboys requested only one brief practice here, but the Colts held two fullscale workouts to readjust to the Poly-Turf surface.

"I like it," says Norm Bulaich, the Colts' best running back. "It gives my legs more spring, they don't get as tired on it as they do on grass or dirt."

"I like it, too," says Roy Jefferson, perhaps the Colts' most dangerous wide receiver. "It feels good to me when I run on it."

"I love it as a kickoff-return man because it's built for straight-ahead speed," says Jim Duncan, a Colt cornerback who will cover Bob Hayes. "On defense, Bob Hayes will have to slow down on his cuts, but he'll be faster straight at me."

"In tackling," says Mike Curtis, "you have to get down lower so you don't slip. But you can change direction fast."

But several other Colts appear unsure of their footing, which is so important in a game where a missed assignment can mean a difference of $7,500 per player.

"As a guard," says Glenn Ressler, "if your foot slips for a split second while you're blocking, you can blow the whole play."

"I need a base to push off," said Bubba Smith, the huge defensive end. "And a lot of times, I'll slip. It's like a wet field."

"I like grass," says Jim O'Brien, the Colt place-kicker. "On grass, if your foot is too low, you'll tear out grass. But if you're too low on artificial turf, your foot will be stopped by it. I've also shanked a couple on it."

Mike Clark, the Cowboy place-kicker, is more accustomed to working on artificial turf.

"To me, it's a lot easier," Clark says. "It's better because it's more uniform. There are no potholes, no bumps you have to kick from. But if the ball isn't spotted perfectly straight up, it'll kind of walk off the spot. Like if you dropped a hairbrush on a tile floor it'll move on you."

All the players, of course, wear special shoes, mostly with a round rubber soccer cleat instead of the usual football cleat.

But like it or not, artificial turf is here to stay. Of the 26 stadiums that will be used by National Football League teams next season, nine will have artificial turf. But the Orange Bowl is one of the few with a turtle-back shape to air drainage. The stadiums that also house major-league baseball teams are restricted to a virtually flat field.

Shea Stadium, the home of the Jets, needs artificial turf in order to have a decent football field, but the baseball Mets have vetoed it.

"In time," says Tex Schramm, the Cowboys' president, "economics will dictate that the baseball teams agree to install it. Not only does it reduce the expense of having a large ground crew, but it might save as many as 5 or 10 dates that might ordinarily be rained out. If it stops raining an hour before the game, you can play on this stuff."

Should it rain tomorrow morning, the Orange Bowl field can be drained in several minutes by pulling plugs as if in a bathtub.

When the Dolphins played an early-season game, a downpour drenched the Poly-Turf surface during the first half. But during the intermission, the ground crew pulled the rain plugs, turning the field from a lagoon into a virtual desert in a matter of minutes.

But artificial turf also is affected by a hot sun because the surface holds the heat.

"If the temperature is in the 80's, the field will be a lot hotter," says Tom Landry, the Cowboy coach. "The heat will drain the players. I might tend to substitute running backs and receivers more often than I would on a grass field."

With that in mind, the Colts will wear lightweight nylon-mesh jerseys.

"This field gets hot," Bubba Smith says. "On the sideline I don't even like to kneel down, because you're that much closer to the surface and it feels like it's burning your face."

But the most serious burn might scar the losing players. Would they have lost on a grass field?

Sports of The Times

By ARTHUR DALEY

Family Affair

MIAMI, *Jan. 16*— In its original conception the Super Bowl was built on mutual loathing and deep-seated animosity. The aristocrats of the National Football League had regarded the nouveau riche upstarts from the American Football League with such contempt that they referred to them as "the Mickey Mouse League." The newer A.F.L. resented its second-class citizenship and correctly blamed all its troubles on those supercilious snobs in the N.F.L.

The war between the leagues had been not much more than a light skirmish in the early years from 1960 on. The N.F.L. had all the firepower, all the prestige and virtually all of the best players. But it heated up when the Americans began using dollars for ammunition in a bidding battle for talent. This grew so costly that a merger had to be projected as the only salvation. Part of the price was the Super Bowl bringing together the champions of each league.

Up to now it worked out beautifully, although it was to produce twin surprises of shattering dimensions. With scornful ease the Green Bay Packers, honed to perfection by Vince Lombardi, demolished the Kansas City Chiefs one year and the Oakland Raiders the next. Badgered into making a comparison between the two leagues after the first showdown, Vince uncharacteristically lost his restraint.

"They're not as good as any of the top teams in our league," he said. A year later he made a slight concession. "The A.F.L. is making progress," he said.

Heating Up

Every disparaging word that was tossed in the direction of the Americans over those years was gasoline on the flames. The rivalry grew hotter and hotter. It was sizzling just before the New York Jets, supposedly hopeless 17-point underdogs, met the lordly and overconfident Baltimore Colts in the third of these postseason classics. The Colts played badly, the Jets played great and the New Yorkers won, 16–7.

An unhappy accident, stunned and unbelieving N.F.L. owners kept saying to one another. Mickey Mouse could not possibly have grown that much. But he had. Then the Minnesota Vikings, proud paladins of the N.F.L., were 13-point favorites over Kansas City, and yet were helpless against the swift-striking Chiefs, 23–7 winners. And still the die-hards in the N.F.L. refused to concede that parity had arrived.

For the season just completed, three N.F.L. teams were transferred to the old A.F.L., which became the American Football Conference. But to the considerable embarrassment of this group, the Baltimore Colts became their champions almost before they had replaced National with American on their letterheads. Hence the Super Bowl is not a bitter internecine war this time. It's the equivalent of a family fight.

Admittedly family fights can be brutal. If you also want to check back as far as Cain and Abel, you can learn that they sometimes can be fatal. But they just don't seem to generate as much excitement and interest as a brawl between strangers. Hence the fifth Super Bowl matchup between the Dallas Cowboys, representing the Nationals, and the Colts, now representing the Americans, has little of the impact and suspense the others had.

When Commissioner Pete Rozelle entered the Jets' dressing room after the Jets had engineered their monstrous upset in 1969, Bake Turner sang out a greeting that was really a taunt.

"Welcome to the American Football League," shouted Turner.

Spreading the Glory

To him and to all his teammates this was not a Jet victory alone. It was a victory for an entire league. It was an end of humiliation and a beginning of self-respect. And Kansas City was to feel pretty much the same way last year. But Baltimore never had to suffer as the others did while waving the banner of the Americans. In fact, the Colts haven't waved it long enough to have loyalties awakened.

"We don't care what conference we're in," said Johnny Unitas the other day. "My allegiance is to the Baltimore Colts."

The emotionalism of the first four Super Bowls is missing from the fifth. Some cynics even are inclined to regard it as no more than an old-fashioned N.F.L. championship game, even if it does have extra fancy trappings.

Neither Colts nor Cowboys can be ranked as a super team, as were the Packers in the first two of these affairs and possibly the Chiefs last year. Baltimore has the aging Unitas, still a matchless strategist and often a deadly passer. Dallas has runners, defense and passing that's suspect.

Oddly enough, though, this could be the closest and most exciting Super Bowl of all. I'm on record as picking Dallas by 3 points, which means I'm going against Unitas, a money player beyond compare. It's a risky business but I guess I'm stuck with it.

66 Double Bow-Out: Colts Ready With Big Pass Play

Jan. 16, 1971—When the Baltimore Colts are confronted today with an obvious passing situation, such as third down with 8 yards to go for a first down, the Dallas Cowboy defensive unit will be alert for the big play that put the Colts in the Super Bowl game.

In the Colt playbook, it's known as "66 Double Bow-Out," meaning that the pass pattern run by two receivers resembles a bow.

Four wide receivers are employed. Jimmy Orr and Raymond Perkins join Roy Jefferson and Eddie Hinton, the usual wide receivers.

In the American Conference championship game two weeks ago, John Unitas, the Colt quarterback, collaborated with Perkins for a 68-yard touchdown that assured the 27–17 victory over the Oakland Raiders.

"We thought Orr would be open on the play," Don McCafferty, the Colt coach, said in diagramming the play, "but Perkins was."

Orr had replaced John Mackey, the tight end, and Perkins had been inserted for Norm Bulaich, the Colts' best running back. Jerry Hill, the best pass-blocker among their running backs, was Tom Nowatzke's substitute. Hill was Unitas's only bodyguard.

As the four receivers lined up, Orr was near the tight end's usual location, but in a slot formation, about 2 yards out from the right tackle and set back slightly from the line of scrimmage. Perkins was in a slot formation inside Hinton, flanked left.

"Since we'd disguised Orr as the tight end," McCafferty said, "we thought the Raiders would cover him with a linebacker and that he'd be able to get open easier. But they moved up a safetyman to cover him and inserted a fifth defensive back, Nemiah Wilson, to cover Perkins while Jefferson and Hinton ran patterns underneath."

Unitas looked for Orr, who was covered. Perkins, however, had eluded Wilson and was in the clear at midfield.

"I got the ball to him," Unitas said that day in explaining the play. "It turned out to be a good play for us."

Ironically, it was the first time that the Colts had used the play throughout the current campaign. If a similar situation develops today, watch for it. The Cowboys will be watching.

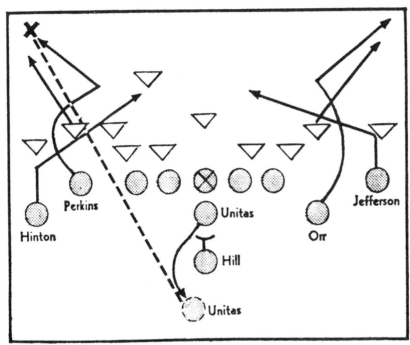

JAN. 17, 1971

The Colts' game-breaking play, known as 66 Double Bow-Out, utilizes four wide receivers and only one running back, who blocks for the passer. The idea is to get Raymond Perkins or Jimmy Orr, the slot men, in the clear.

Slant Lead 45: The Cowboys' Run-to-Daylight Play

Jan. 16, 1971—Televiewers of the Super Bowl Game are certain to see this play by the Dallas Cowboys more than once.

"We'll use it anywhere on the field, especially down near the goal line," said Jim Myers, the Dallas assistant offensive coach.

The play features the halfback, Duane Thomas, who is the team's leading ground-gainer. In the last two playoff games, against Detroit and San Francisco, Thomas gained 135 and 143 yards. He scored on this play, called Slant Lead 45, from 13 yards out against the 49ers.

The halfback is the No. 4 back and he slants toward the No. 5 hole, right tackle, with the fullback, Walt Garrison, leading. Should Thomas, who is also a fine blocker, be playing fullback, Calvin Hill would be the ball-carrier at halfback. The play begins from the I formation.

The Dallas offense is known for its complexities. Although this play appears to be a simple one, its variations and flexibility can make it complex according to how the line-blocking develops.

In the illustration, the play is drawn against a standard 4–3 defensive alignment (four linemen, three linebackers). This is the basic Baltimore formation, although the Colts move around a lot.

Thomas has the option to go wherever he sees an opening. The defensive middle linebacker, left tackle and end are likely to move to their left to close on Garrison and Thomas, who start out that way.

In that event, look for Thomas to cut sharply to his left to find the opening.

"He is an instinctive runner," said Myers. "He never hesitates, never breaks the flow of his rhythm. And he always finds the hole. This is no 3-yard play. It's a run-to-daylight play, one designed to go all the way."

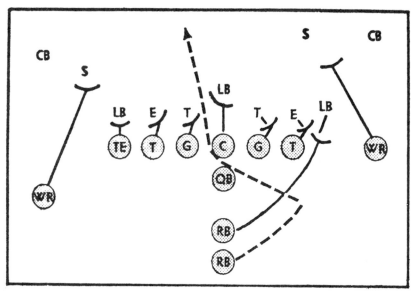

THE NEW YORK TIMES   JAN. 17, 1971

The Cowboys' big play, known as Slant Lead 45, sends the flow of the offense to its right. However, the ball-carrier will probably cut sharply to his left. The running back farther from the quarterback is Duane Thomas, the halfback and the man who carries the ball on this play.

FLORIDA JUDGE CALLS SUPER BOWL BLACKOUT ILLEGAL BUT LACKS POWER TO RULE

Trust Violation Found by Franza

State Court Cannot Rule on Federal Issues, He Says—Rozelle Is Firm

FORT LAUDERDALE, FLA., *Jan. 16, (UPI)*—State Circuit Judge Arthur Franza ruled today he had no jurisdiction to lift the Super Bowl television blackout, but said the blackout violated Federal antitrust law.

"I find the N.F.L. commissioner has no authority to decree a blackout," the Broward County judge said. "I further find that such a decree violates the Sherman Antitrust Act."

Franza said it would be a nice gesture for Pete Rozelle, Commissioner of the National Football League, to lift the blackout voluntarily for tomorrow's game. But Rozelle refused. Franza called the blackout "a transgression and usurpation of the airwaves and the people who own them."

But he said he could not order Rozelle to lift it because the state circuit court lacked jurisdiction on Federal issues and acts of Congress.

Ellis Rubin, a Miami Beach attorney, in challenging the blackout contended that the Federal law permitting local blackouts applied only to a 75-mile radius of the "home" team's city. Neither the Baltimore Colts nor the Dallas Cowboys could call themselves the home team, he argued.

The rejection of his latest effort meant that 2.5-million South Floridians living within 75 miles of Miami could not see the telecast of the pro championship game.

Franza appealed to Rozelle to lift the blackout, noting that the Orange Bowl's 80,000 seats were sold out. But Rozelle, who had been subpoenaed to appear in court, said afterward that lifting it would set a dangerous precedent.

Removing the blackout this year may affect future Super Bowls and division championship playoffs, Rozelle said. Proceeds from those games go entirely to the players' pension fund, he added, and televising them locally would ultimately reduce attendance.

He said blackouts were partly responsible for pro football's large attendance and popularity.

"There's never been in the history of professional football a championship game televised locally," he said. "I think that's one of the reasons that they continue to be sellouts."

Rubin brought an antitrust action against the N.F.L. last month in Federal Court, but was rebuffed because he could not show that the league's action affected his personal business or income. He also lost a civil suit in Dade County circuit court last Wednesday. In that suit he contended that the blackout "discriminates" against South Floridians, whose tax money, he said, provided $115,000 in promotional funds for the game.

Rubin said he would begin work now to prevent a blackout next year.

"We will start at the proper level this year, and some day they're going to realize that you can't come into an area, take money from the public, tell them to go to hell and still maintain that you are a clean, respectable sport," he declared.

The Coaches: McCafferty, First-Year Success, vs. Landry, Patient Old Pro

MIAMI, *Jan. 16*—In both intercollegiate and professional sports, coach after coach expresses the new need for understanding and explaining in dealing with the athletes. Motivation seems to follow compassion. Going, if not gone, are Vince Lombardi's shouting, militant ways.

Don McCafferty belongs to the new breed of "good-guy" coaches, although he is hardly new to the profession. Now 49 years of age, McCafferty began coaching 22 years ago as an assistant to Kent State in his native Ohio.

McCafferty's style is quite different from that of his predecessor, Don Shula, now with the Miami Dolphins. Shula was caustic and critical. Many of the seasoned players, especially such blacks as John Mackey and Bubba Smith, were not sorry to see Shula go. They are among McCafferty's stronger supporters. "He treats you like a man," said Smith. "Not like a dog."

The Colts had an uneven season and an easy schedule. But they came on strong at the end. One of the motivations of the players was to show that the team could win under McCafferty as well as Shula.

McCafferty has reached the Super Bowl in his first year as head coach. No one has ever done that before. He had a lot of preparation. He had spent 11 seasons as an assistant coach on the Baltimore staffs of both Weeb Ewbank and Shula. Before that came the 10 years at Kent State; one year as a player with the New York Giants and, prior to World War II, as a collegian at Ohio State under Paul Brown.

Tall, 6 feet 5 inches, and graying at the temples, McCafferty is pleasant, easygoing and open. As an assistant, he was the offensive coordinator up in the press box talking on a field phone to the quarterback during games.

He and John Unitas have always done well together. Says Unitas of his coach, "Don has a great knowledge of football. He is a calm, collected individual. He doesn't shout and scream. He is able to look at football objectively without getting carried away emotionally."

McCafferty lives in the Baltimore suburb of Timonium and is the father of four children.

McCafferty's popularity with his players served him well. After Shula skipped off to Miami with a better offer, the infuriated owner of the team, Carroll Rosenbloom, thought about hiring a successor with a big reputation.

McCafferty was finally chosen. His position was not an enviable one and his team lost two out of three games to Shula's Dolphins. But the Colts did reach the Super Bowl and that was what really mattered.

Tom Landry was a smalltown Texas boy who went to New York and made good as a football player 21 years ago. He was a player and assistant coach for the Giants for a decade, then he went back to Texas and took command of the Dallas Cowboys, a brand new team, in 1960.

After four false starts in that direction, Landry has finally brought his Cowboys to the Super Bowl and they are the favorites to beat Baltimore here tomorrow. In a profession famous for insecurity, Landry along with Hank Stram of the Kansas City Chiefs has lasted longer in his present position than any other coach in pro football.

The Cowboys have made the post-season playoffs five seasons in a row, but always before they lost in the playoffs. In the past five seasons, they have won more games, 52 out of 68, than any other team in pro football.

Those who have played for him or coached against him have a common opinion about Landry's football ability. "Tom Landry is smarter than anybody," said Alex Webster, the Giant coach and a former teammate.

Landry will call all the plays for his team tomorrow. He does this to relieve the pressure on his quarterback, Craig Morton.

One of his assistants, Jim Myers, says, "Not only is he thinking about what play to call next, he is also thinking ahead a series or two. Then he is involved with the defenses. He stands down there on the sidelines, which is the worst possible place to see anything and with all that turmoil around him. But he sees everything, misses nothing."

Landry is 46 years old, tall (6 feet 3 inches) and as slim as when he played defensive back for the Giants. He is balding and usually wears a small brown porkpie hat. He never raises his voice. His smile is tiny and he has been called "old stoneface" or "the next candidate for Mt. Rushmore."

Hobbies? None. Golf? Next to never. Interests apart from football? Family and church. His wife Alicia is a striking woman. Tom Jr., a student at Duke, had to give up football on account of injuries. There are two teenage daughters, Kitty and Lisa.

Landry's life began in Mission, Tex., an agricultural town near the Mexican border. He flew 30 missions as a B-17 bomber pilot in World War II and then returned to the University of Texas, the launching pad for his professional career.

The Quarterbacks: Unitas the Pass Master Goes Against Morton the Enigma

MIAMI, *Jan. 16*—John Unitas is 37 years old and owns all the career passing records possible in pro football after 15 seasons.

The Baltimore Colts have been grooming successors for Unitas for several seasons, and the latest is Sam Havrilak, age 23. But if Unitas has his way, Havrilak will be old and gray before he will play.

Unitas has succeeded in removing from football a great part of the emotional factors in a game with a full tank of emotions. Asked what he thought about the Jets' dramatic upset of the Colts in the Super Bowl two years ago, Unitas merely shugged and repeated the score, "16–7."

Asked about tomorrow's Super Bowl encounter against the Dallas Cowboys, Unitas said this week, "It's another game. The money makes it different." His reference was to the high stakes, $15,000 for each of the winners and $7,500 for each loser.

Boos Don't Penetrate

Speaking before dozens of reporters here last Monday, Unitas was asked if he had any feelings when fans boo him, which they have occasionally. He replied:

"I don't care. I can't care. I don't care what people say and I don't care what you write. All that matters is the team, the game and winning."

A reference was made to the popular magazine, Sport, which has carried his picture on the cover as often as anyone else's.

He didn't know Sport. He certainly had never read it.

Unitas lives in Lutherville, a suburb of Baltimore, with his wife and five children. It's a casual, easy household. One time Unitas said revealingly:

"I like kids better than adults. I better, I've got enough." And he grinned the great Unitas toothy grin.

If there is a youth who was ever refused a John Unitas autograph, he should step forward for a one-of-a-kind award.

Rejected as Skinny

Unitas grew up in a poor neighborhood of Pittsburgh and went to the University of Louisville on a scholarship. He wanted Notre Dame, but was said to be too skinny. He was 6 feet 1 inch and weighed 145 pounds. Indiana turned him down for the same reason.

A good small-college passer, Unitas was drafted by the Steelers. But the coach, the late Walt Kiesling, ignored him and Unitas played catch with the owner, Art Rooney, and his sons, Art Jr. and Dan.

When he was dropped, the Colts picked him up the next year as a free agent, following an 85-cent phone call of discovery. The great career was launched.

Can Unitas still throw the long touchdown pass after sieges of elbow tenderness? Yes, he can. Missing perhaps is the quick snap on the sideline passes that he made famous with Raymond Berry, the receiver. But Unitas still finds ways to win games.

In speaking of Craig Morton, the Dallas Cowboy quarterback for the Super Bowl game tomorrow against Baltimore, the seasoned coach of the San Diego Chargers, Sid Gillman, observed recently, "He can only improve."

In the Dallas playoff victories over San Francisco and Detroit, Morton came as close as possible to being a nonparticipating quarterback. In those two games, he completed only 11 of 40 passes, and the rest of the time he handed the ball off to his running backs and stepped out of the way.

Although pro football defies generalities, the sages like to point out that hardly any teams have ever won a championship without a great quarterback. The often-cited exception is the Chicago Bears team of 1963 with Billy Wade.

The Cowboys could become another exception tomorrow. Or Morton might have a great day. He is an enigma with a history.

Morton is a big (6 feet 4 inches, 215 pounds) handsome bachelor, an all-American at the University of California at Berkeley, and a No. 1 draft choice in 1965. Now 27, Morton has a less-than-positive personality and seems indifferent enough to pass through all kinds of difficulties.

He has been maligned in the press for his poor performances, but he passes them off and points to periods when he had very good statistics. He admits to a series of injuries—a shoulder separation which required surgery, finger and hand ailments—but does not offer them as excuses.

His preseason efforts were so poor that his coach, Tom Landry, benched him in favor of Roger Staubach as the season began. Morton was reinstated, but looked feeble when the Cowboys lost their fourth game in nine starts, 38–0, to St. Louis.

Landry decided to call the signals for Morton after that, and Craig, who seemed to carry the whole burden of the team on his shoulders, did better. He completed 60 per cent of his passes as the Cowboys won five straight.

"After the St. Louis game," he said, "the only thing that gave me any kind of a lift was when Ralph Neely gave me a Spiro Agnew watch as a gift."

Morton's problems in pressure playoff games began when he relieved Don Meredith in Cleveland in 1968. The Browns beat the Cowboys, 31–20, but it was not that close.

As the regular the next year, Morton contributed to failure as the Browns again beat the Cowboys decisively in the Eastern championship game.

Yet Morton has demonstrated many times in lesser games that he has as many good physical qualities as any other quarterback. He is the No. 1 mystery surrounding this year's Super Bowl.

How the Super Bowl Rivals Match Up, 1971

DALLAS ON OFFENSE

No.	Player	Ht.	Wt.	Pos.
22	Bob Hayes	5-11	185	WR
88	Reggie Rucker	6-2	190	WR
84	Pettis Norman	6-3	220	TE
70	Rayfield Wright	6-6	255	RT
61	Blaine Nye	6-4	251	RG
51	Dave Manders	6-2	250	C
76	John Niland	6-3	245	LG
73	Ralph Neely	6-6	265	LT
14	Craig Morton	6-4	214	QB
33	Duane Thomas	6-1	220	HB
32	Walt Garrison	6-0	205	FB

DALLAS ON DEFENSE

No.	Player	Ht.	Wt.	Pos.
20	Mel Renfro	6-0	190	RCB
26	Herb Adderley	6-1	200	LCB
34	Cornell Green	6-3	208	SS
63	Larry Cole	6-4	250	LE
75	Jethro Pugh	6-6	260	LT
55	Lee Roy Jordan	6-1	221	MLB
74	Bob Lilly	6-5	260	RT
66	George Andrie	6-6	250	RE
41	Charlie Waters	6-1	193	FS
52	Dave Edwards	6-1	225	LLB
54	Chuck Howley	6-2	225	RLB

DALLAS SUBSTITUTES

No.	Player	Ht.	Wt.	Pos.
10	Ron Widby	6-4	210	P
11	Bob Belden	6-2	205	QB
12	Roger Staubach	6-3	197	QB
23	Margene Adkins	5-10	183	WR
24	Dennis Homan	6-1	181	WR
30	Dan Reeves	6-1	220	RB
35	Calvin Hill	6-4	227	RB
36	Joe Williams	6-0	199	RB
42	Claxton Welch	5-11	203	RB
43	Cliff Harris	6-0	184	S
45	Richmond Flowers	6-0	180	S
46	Mark Washington	5-10	188	CB
50	D. D. Lewis	6-1	225	LB
56	Tom Stincic	6-4	230	LB
60	Steve Kiner	6-0	218	LB
62	John Fitzgerald	6-4	250	T
64	Halvor Hagen	6-5	253	C
65	Doug Mooers	6-6	245	DE
67	Pat Toomay	6-5	244	DE
72	Tony Liscio	6-5	255	T
77	Ron East	6-4	242	DT
78	Bob Asher	6-5	250	T-C
83	Mike Clark	6-1	205	K
89	Mike Ditka	6-3	225	TE

BALTIMORE ON DEFENSE

No.	Player	Ht.	Wt.	Pos.
35	Jim Duncan	6-2	200	RCB
47	Charlie Stukes	6-3	212	LCB
20	Jerry Logan	6-1	190	SS
78	Bubba Smith	6-7	295	LE
74	Billy Ray Smith	6-4	250	LT
32	Mike Curtis	6-2	232	MLB
76	Fred Miller	6-3	250	RT
85	Roy Hilton	6-6	240	RE
21	Rick Volk	6-3	195	FS
56	Ray May	6-1	230	LLB
83	Ted Hendricks	6-7	215	RLB

BALTIMORE ON OFFENSE

No.	Player	Ht.	Wt.	Pos.
33	Ed Hinton	6-0	200	WR
87	Roy Jefferson	6-2	195	WR
88	John Mackey	6-2	224	TE
71	Dan Sullivan	6-3	250	RT
75	John Williams	6-3	256	RG
50	Bill Curry	6-2	235	C
62	Glenn Ressler	6-3	250	LG
72	Bob Vogel	6-5	250	LT
19	Johnny Unitas	6-1	196	QB
36	Norm Bulaich	6-1	218	HB
45	Jerry Hill	5-11	217	FB

BALTIMORE SUBSTITUTES

No.	Player	Ht.	Wt.	Pos.
14	George Mira	5-11	190	QB
15	Earl Morrall	6-2	206	QB
17	Sam Havrilak	6-2	195	RB
25	Tom Curtis	6-1	196	DB
27	Ray Perkins	6-0	183	WR
28	Jimmy Orr	5-11	185	WR
29	Paul Maliska	6-1	190	DB
30	Ron Gardin	5-11	180	DB
34	Tom Nowatzke	6-4	230	K-P
40	Jack Maitland	6-1	210	RB
42	Tom Maxwell	6-2	195	DB
49	David Lee	6-4	230	K
51	Bob Grant	6-2	225	LB
52	Robbie Nichols	6-3	220	LB
53	Tom Goode	6-3	245	C
55	Dale McCullers	6-1	215	LB
60	George Wright	6-3	260	DT
61	Cornelius Johnson	6-2	245	G
67	Lynn Larson	6-4	254	T
73	Sam Ball	6-4	240	T
80	Jim O'Brien	6-0	195	K-WR
81	Billy Newsome	6-4	240	DE

Facts on Super Bowl Contest, 1971

Title at Stake—World professional football championship.

Participants—Baltimore Colts, champion of the American Football Conference, and Dallas Cowboys, champion of the National Football Conference.

Site—Orange Bowl Stadium, Miami, Fla.

Date—Today.

Starting Time—Kickoff 2:10 P.M. (New York time).

Seating Capacity—80,035.

Television—Nationwide by the National Broadcasting Company (Channel 4 in New York), with Miami area blacked out. Air time 2 P.M., preceded by pregame show at 1:30 P.M.

Radio—Nationwide by the National Broadcasting Company. Air time 1:50 P.M.

Players' Shares—$15,000 to each member of the winning team; $7,500 to each member of the losing team. Approximately $1.2-million total for the personnel of the two competing clubs.

Division of Game Net Receipts—After deduction of taxes, expenses and players' shares, remainder will be distributed to the competing clubs and the player pension fund.

Uniforms—Dallas will be the home team, will wear colored jerseys and use the South bench. Baltimore will be the visiting team, will wear white and will use the North bench.

Game Ball—The standard N.F.L. ball, adopted before the 1970 season and in use in all games this past season, will be used.

Sudden Death—If the game is tied at the end of the regulation 60 minutes, it will continue in sudden-death overtime. The team scoring first, by safety, field goal or touchdown, will win.

Officials—There will be six officials and two alternates appointed by the Commissioner's office.

Official Time—The scoreboard clock will be official.

Trophy—The winning team receives permanent possession of the Vince Lombardi Trophy, a silver football mounted on a three-sided base.

Regular-Season Figure Comparisons

PASSING

Baltimore	Att.	Comp.	Pct.	Total Yds.	TDs	Int.
Unitas	321	166	51.7	2,213	14	18
Morrall	93	51	54.8	792	9	4
Dallas						
Morton	207	102	49.3	1,819	15	7
Staubach	82	44	53.7	542	2	3

RUSHING

Baltimore	Att.	Total Yds.	Avg. Gain	Long Gain	TDs
Bulaich	139	426	3.1	15	3
Nowatzke	73	248	3.4	14	1
Maitland	74	209	2.8	24	1
Havrilak	54	159	2.9	26	0
Dallas					
Thomas	151	803	5.3	47	5
Hill	153	577	3.8	20	4
Garrison	126	507	4.0	18	3
Staubach	27	221	8.2	25	0

RECEIVING

Baltimore	No. Caught	Total Yds.	Avg. Gain	Long Gain	TDs
Hinton	47	733	15.6	40	5
Jefferson	44	749	17.0	55	7
Mackey	28	435	15.5	54	3
Mitchell	20	261	13.1	44	4
Nowatzke	16	93	5.8	17	0
Dallas					
Hayes	34	889	26.1	89	10
Garrison	21	205	9.8	36	2
Hill	13	95	7.3	21	0
Reeves	12	140	11.7	23	0
Thomas	10	73	7.3	17	0

INTERCEPTIONS

Baltimore	No.	Total Yds.	Long Gain	TDs
Logan	6	92	33	2
Curtis	5	50	18	0
Volk	4	61	31	0
Stukes	3	52	47	0
Dallas				
Waters	5	45	20	0
Renfro	4	3	3	0
Adderley	3	69	30	0

PUNTING

	No.	Total Yds.	Avg. Punt	Long Punt	Had Blkd.
Lee, Balt.	63	2,819	44.7	62	1
Widby, Dall.	69	2,847	41.3	59	1

PLACEKICKING

	Con.	Att.	FG	FGA	Pts.
O'Brien, Balt.	36	36	16	29	84
Clark, Dall.	35	35	18	27	89

Records of the Teams

DALLAS		BALTIMORE	
17—Philadelphia	7	16—San Diego	14
28—N.Y. Giants	10	24—Kansas City	44
7—St. Louis	20	14—Boston	6
13—Atlanta	0	24—Houston	20
3—Minnesota	54	29—N.Y. Jets	22
27—Kansas City	16	27—Boston	3
21—Philadelphia	17	35—Miami	0
20—N.Y. Giants	23	13—Green Bay	10
0—St. Louis	38	17—Buffalo	17
45—Washington	21	17—Miami	34
16—Green Bay	3	21—Chicago	20
34—Washington	0	29—Philadelphia	10
6—Cleveland	2	20—Buffalo	14
52—Houston	10	35—N.Y. Jets	20
5—Detroit	0	17—Cincinnati	0
17—San Francisco	10	27—Oakland	17
321	231	365	251

Baltimore Field Goal in Last 5 Seconds Defeats Dallas in Super Bowl, 16 to 13

By WILLIAM N. WALLACE

MIAMI, *Jan. 17*—The Baltimore Colts beat the Dallas Cowboys, 16–13, and won the Super Bowl game today. The National Football League headquarters will soon be sending the winners their $15,000 checks. But it will be difficult to convince the Cowboys and many of the viewers that anybody won this game, the climactic contest of the pro football season.

The contest was full of errors made by both offensive teams and one Baltimore touchdown play, a 75-yard pass-run, John Unitas to John Mackey, was controversial if not illegal.

The winning points were scored with only five seconds to play when Jim O'Brien, a Baltimore rookie, kicked a 32-yard field goal, breaking a 13–13 tie and eliminating the possibility of a sudden-death overtime period.

It might have been a good idea to start all over again with everyone even.

The Cowboys led, 13–6, at half-time, but the Colts scored a touchdown and a field goal in the fourth quarter. Interceptions set up both scoring opportunities. Those were two of the 11 turnovers, resulting from an intercepted pass or a lost fumble, in the game, seen by 80,055 in the Orange Bowl and an estimated 64 million on television.

The Colts lost four fumbles to the Cowboys and had three passes intercepted. Two of these were thrown by Unitas and one by Earl Morrall. Unitas was hurt (bruised ribs) in the second period and Morrall took over.

Earl Morrall holds as Jim O'Brien kicks the Colts to victory with a field
goal five seconds from the finish.
UNITED PRESS INTERNATIONAL

There is an adage that a team cannot win when it turns the ball over
to its opponent half a dozen times or more. But this game defied a lot of
adages. Three Cowboy passes, all by Craig Morton, were also intercepted,
and Dallas lost a fumble on the Baltimore 1-yard line. The ball was knocked
loose from Duane Thomas's grip in a pile-up.

"We beat ourselves," said Tom Landry, the Dallas coach. "The fumble
and two interceptions killed us."

So did some kind of fate. The Dallas defense was outstanding, and the
Colts, with Unitas, made no early progress. Then Unitas threw a pass 20
yards deep and high to Eddie Hinton, who got his finger tips on the ball
but could not hold it or stop it. The ball passed over or through a Dallas
player's finger tips and into the hands of Mackey, who ran 45 yards for a
score that tied the game at 6–6 in the second quarter.

A pass is incomplete if two offensive players touch the ball successively without a defensive player intervening. The ruling on this play was that a Dallas defender had touched the football. Which defender?

"Not me," said Charlie Waters, the safetyman. "I was 10 yards away," said Cornell Green, the other safety. "I don't know," said Mel Renfro, the cornerback. "I didn't think I did," he added, and then to another questioner, he said, "maybe my finger nail."

The replay shown on television was inconclusive because of a poor camera angle. The official's instant decision was that the ball had been touched by a Cowboy and the call will stand.

Another pass grazed the finger tips of Walt Garrison, the Cowboy fullback, when Dallas was ahead, 13–6, in the fourth quarter and comfortably in control.

Rick Volk, the Colts' safety, made the interception on the Dallas 33 and ran to the 3. Tom Nowatzke scored on second down and the game was tied, 13–13, with half the period still to play.

With a minute left more fingers came into play. Morton's pass to Dan Reeves, the halfback, bounced off his hands when he was hit by Jerry Logan. The football careened into the hands of Mike Curtis, the Baltimore linebacker, and he returned this interception 13 yards to the Dallas 28.

The Colts ran two plays and then O'Brien, a nervous 23-year-old, came in and kicked his field goal. It represented the $7,500 difference between a winning and losing share for himself and his 39 teammates.

The Colts failed on three prior scoring chances. Hinton fumbled after catching a pass from Sam Havrilak, a halfback, in the final period. The ball rolled from the Dallas 5 through the end zone and out of bounds. Because the Colts were the last team to have possession, the play resulted in a touchback and Dallas took over at its 20.

Chuck Howley intercepted a pass by Morrall in the Cowboy end zone at the start of the fourth quarter and the Colts failed to score in four downs at the Dallas 2 just before the half-time intermission.

Dallas missed its touchdown chances early in the game. Recovery of a Baltimore fumble—Ron Gardin dropped a punt—put the Cowboys on the Colt 9, but Morton overthrew Reggie Rucker in the end zone. Dallas settled for a field goal by Mike Clark.

Morton missed on two more passes a little later from the Baltimore 7 and, following a penalty, Clark kicked a 30-yard field goal for a 6–0 lead.

The Colts tied the game when Mackey scored on the controversial play and O'Brien's attempted conversion kick was blocked by Mark Washington.

A fumble by Unitas at his 28 set up the Cowboy touchdown, scored on a 7-yard pass by Morton to Thomas in the second period.

The Colt defense tightened in the second half and the Cowboys' big runner, Thomas, gained only 37 yards in all.

Curtis was the outstanding defender.

Morton again left much to be desired as a passer. So did Unitas, who completed only three of nine passes and made only two first downs. Morrall was the best quarterback, although he had little to do with winning the game apart from holding the ball for O'Brien's field goal.

Somebody upstairs seemed to take care of the winning and losing. "You can say that again," said Renfro.

Baltimore Colts. 0   6   0   10—16
Dallas Cowboys. 3   10   0   0—13
    Dallas—FG, Clark, 14.
    Dallas—FG, Clark, 30.
    Baltimore—Mackey, 75, pass from Unitas (kick blocked).
    Dallas—Thomas, 7, pass from Morton (Clark, kick).
    Baltimore—Nowatzke, 2, run (O'Brien, kick).
    Baltimore—FG. O'Brien, 32.
    Attendance—80,055.

Statistics of the Game

	Colts	Cowboys		Colts	Cowboys
First downs	14	9	Interceptions by	3	3
Rushing yardage	69	104	Punts	4-42	9-39
Passing yardage	260	113	Fumbles lost	4	1
Return yardage	159	65	Yards penalized	44	120
Passes	11-25	12-26			

Individual Statistics

RUSHES—Balt.: Nowatzke, 10 for 33 yards; Bulaich, 18 for 28; Unitas, 1 for 4; Havrilak, 1 for 3; Morrall, 1 for 1. Dal.: Garrison, 12 for 65; Thomas, 18 for 37; Morton, 1 for 2.

PASSES—Balt.: Morrall, 7 of 15 for 147 yards; Unitas, 3 of 9 for 88; Havrilak, 1 of 1 for 25. Dal.: Morton, 12 of 26 for 127.

RECEPTIONS—Balt.: Jefferson, 3 for 52 yards; Mackey, 2 for 80; Hinton, 2 for 51; Havrilak, 2 for 27; Bulaich, 1 for 5; Nowatzke, 1 for 45. Dal.: Reeves, 5 for 46; Thomas, 4 for 21; Garrison, 2 for 19; Hayes, 1 for 41.

Man in the News: Riding High With Colts

Dale Carroll Rosenbloom

Jan. 17, 1971—Two years ago, the controversial but benevolent multimillionaire who owns the Baltimore Colts planned a big Super Bowl celebration party at his home in Golden Beach, Fla.

Baltimore lost that game to the New York Jets, but Carroll Rosenbloom had the party anyway. The Colts were back in Miami yesterday, but this time Rosenbloom and his employees came out of the Super Bowl with something to celebrate.

When the rugged-looking, 5-foot-11-inch Rosenbloom has reason to celebrate no one does it more lavishly. And when he has other good reasons to spend his money, he does that without skimping, too.

For example, in the team's early, struggling years, he presented his players with practically unheard of postseason bonuses. Later he helped players get started in off field business ventures. There was, for example, the $100,000 loan he gave three players to begin what has become a successful, fast-food franchising operation.

Generous to Unfortunate

More recently, Rosenbloom donated $50,000 each to Marshall and Wichita State universities following plane crashes that killed many of their football players.

No amount of money, though, could have soothed the gray-haired executive's feelings after his team's stunning loss to the Jets in 1969.

"We felt we had as fine a football team as had ever been put together, and then you wake up and find that you're a bunch of bums," he said of the defeat. "It's not the most pleasant thing in life. It's like finding your wife running around with another guy."

Rosenbloom never really got over the game. In fact, the desire to play the Jets again led to his decision to move the Colts from the National to the American Conference in the realignment of the merged National and American Football Leagues.

The move was not popular with the zealously faithful Baltimore fans, but now that the wayward "wife" has stopped running, they may look more approvingly at the man who helped bring them the Colts.

Dale Carroll Rosenbloom (he never has used his first name) was one of five men who brought the Colts to life in 1953, when the N.F.L. was seeking a franchise to replace the floundering Dallas team, which originally was the New York Yankees.

He was born on March 5, 1907, as one of nine children of Solomon Rosenbloom, a work-clothes manufacturer. Rosenbloom became involved in pro football because of Bert Bell, the man who had been his backfield coach when he was a halfback at the University of Pennsylvania in the late nineteen-twenties.

Bell was commissioner of the N.F.L. in 1953 and prevailed upon Rosenbloom to buy 51 per cent of the Baltimore franchise for a reported $200,000 (he now owns 100 per cent of the club, which could be worth 10 times that).

Since then, the Colts have become one of the most successful teams, financially and artistically, and Rosenbloom has become one of the most powerful and influential owners in the game.

His tenure has not been without controversy. He was accused of betting on N.F.L. games early in his pro football career, but he was absolved of the charges. Last year, he became involved in a bitter dispute with the Miami Dolphins, who, supposedly without Rosenbloom's permission, induced Don Shula to leave his coaching job with the Colts and go to Miami.

Rosenbloom has turned over the day-to-day operation of the Colts to his 27-year-old son, Steve. But he still goes to all the games.

And no matter when it is, he's always ready to throw a victory celebration.

One Cowboy Wins: Howley Gets Award

MIAMI, *Jan. 17*—Chuck Howley, the Dallas Cowboys' linebacker, was the surprise winner today of Sport Magazine's award of a 1971 Dodge Charger as the outstanding player in the Super Bowl game.

"The award is tremendous, but I wish it were the world championship," Howley said. "They go hand in hand."

Howley made two interceptions and also jarred loose a fumble by John Unitas, the Colt quarterback, early in the game.

"Howley was in on everything on defense," Al Silverman, editor of Sport, explained. "We thought he was the best over-all player."

Unitas Could've Played 'If They Needed Me'

MIAMI, *Jan. 17*—Johnny Unitas was injured today when George Andrie, a Cowboy defensive end, tackled him in the act of passing.

"With my right arm up, my ribs were open," Unitas said. "He got me with his helmet or his shoulder, I don't know which. They hurt, but they're not broken. They took X-rays right here to find that out immediately. I could've gone back if they'd needed me.

"I'm happy for Earl, he did a fine job," Unitas said. "I did not mind not going back in. That was the coach's decision. Earl was down in the dumps after our other Super Bowl, and it was great that he could come back."

Don McCafferty, the coach, explained that he had kept Morrall in the game even though Unitas was available because "Earl was doing a fine job and I saw no reason to make a change."

Interception by Curtis Turning Point: Colts

By DAVE ANDERSON

MIAMI, *Jan. 17*—Jim O'Brien learned today the meaning of a dream he had about 10 days ago.

"Right after we got down here," the Baltimore Colts' place-kicker said, "I had a dream that a long field goal was going to win this game. I didn't know who was going to kick or how far or when it would happen, but now I know."

O'Brien, a rookie, kicked the 32-yard field goal that won the Super Bowl game, 16–13, with 5 seconds remaining.

"All the guys had confidence in me, that was the big thing," the 23-year-old bachelor said. "When we went out there, Earl Morrall, my holder, just told me to kick it straight through, that there was no wind— just to kick it."

The Tension Makers

But after the Colts had taken a time out with 9 seconds to play, the Dallas Cowboys took a time out, hoping that the additional time would add to O'Brien's tension.

"We expected that," O'Brien said. "In fact, all season, whenever we're practicing field goals, Billy Ray Smith will yell 'time out, time out,' just to get me ready for something like this. And that's the way it worked."

As the Colts exulted, O'Brien wore a dark blue baseball cap with a Colt emblem over his long black hair.

"Hey, rookie," yelled Fred Miller, the captain of the defensive unit. "I just took a survey. You can keep your long hair."

O'Brien laughed and recalled that in the Colts' season opener, he had kicked a winning field goal with about a minute to play.

"It was in San Diego and I'd missed a couple of field goals early in the game," he recalled. "But the one at the end made up for it. Just like this game when I missed the extra point after our first touchdown."

A Bad Call

His conversion attempt had been blocked by Mark Washington, preventing the Colts from taking a 7–6 lead.

"I don't know what happened," O'Brien said, "but I either took too much time or my foot caught in the artificial turf. After that I couldn't blame the coach for not letting me try a field goal from up close near the end of the half."

Don McCafferty, the Colt coach, chose to let Morrall throw a fourth-down pass that was incomplete.

"If we'd lost," McCafferty later acknowledged," it would have been the worst call I made this year. But someone has to make the decisions. I made it and it was a bad one."

Instead of being co-goats, O'Brien and McCafferty received a game ball apiece.

"But the turning point of the game had to be Mike Curtis's interception," McCafferty said. "That set up the winning field goal for us. We had a lot of bad breaks in the first half but we hung in there. These guys are just fantastic."

Curtis, the Colt middle linebacker, explained that his interception occurred in a new defensive alignment.

"We'd just put it in three weeks ago," Curtis said, referring to the strategy designed by Bobby Boyd, the Colts' defensive coach. "I had a deep drop to help out the safety on the deep pattern, and when Jerry Logan hit Dan Reeves as he was catching the pass, the ball popped up and I caught it."

The Colts attributed the frequent turnovers to the punishing defensive units.

"It may have looked sloppy," Logan said, "but it was a great defensive football game."

"Maybe it wasn't a good game for the fans," Curtis said, "but it was a good physical game."

Morrall had been bothered for two years by the loss to the Jets in Super Bowl III and had answered numerous questions about it during the week. Inserted after the injury to Johnny Unitas, Morrall completed seven of 15 passes for 147 yards, in addition to holding the ball for O'Brien's winning field goal.

Mrs. Marie Lombardi, widow of the coach of the Green Bay Packers and Washington Redskins, who died of cancer last year, presented the silver Super Bowl trophy to Carroll Rosenbloom, owner of the Colts, in the Baltimore dressing room following the game.

"There is only one Vince Lombardi," said Rosenbloom in acceptance, "and there'll never be another like him."

Cowboys: Thomas Fumble Hurt

MIAMI, *Jan. 17*—When the Dallas Cowboys returned to their dressing room today, what did Tom Landry say to them?

"You can't say anything," their coach explained. "I tried, but I can't say anything after a game like this."

Landry branded Duane Thomas's lost fumble at the Colts' 1-yard line early in the third quarter as the "big play" of the game from the Cowboys' viewpoint. The fumble occurred on first down. Had the Cowboys scored a touchdown, they would have opened a 20–6 lead.

"If he'd scored," Landry said, "they would've had a lot of catching up to do. We would have been in firm control. But he fumbled because of his second effort on the play."

Passing the Credit

Jerry Logan, a Colt safetyman, was credited with the tackle on Thomas, the Cowboys' star runner. But the Colt cornerback, Jim Duncan, who recovered the loose ball at the 1-yard line, thought that Ray May, the Colt linebacker on that side, had caused the fumble with a jarring tackle.

"I hit him," May said, "but I think Billy Ray Smith jerked the ball loose."

"If he says I jerked the ball loose, then I guess I did," Smith said, smiling.

Thomas was unavailable for comment. He dressed and departed before newsmen were permitted to enter the dressing room.

"We beat ourselves," Landry said. "The fumble and the two interceptions killed us."

Landry said the interceptions that enabled the Colts to rally with a touchdown and field goal in the final quarter were the result of deflected passes, and so was the Colts' first touchdown on the controversial deflection of a pass from John Unitas to John Mackey.

"The ball was bouncing off us, instead of them," Landry said. "That's a hard way to lose."

Quietly, the Cowboy coach discussed his disappointment in the hushed atmosphere.

"We were emotionally up, we were working and hustling," Landry said. "It was just one of those games. So many penalties."

Not far away, Lee Roy Jordan, a Cowboy linebacker, also discussed officiating.

"We had to overcome a lot of people today," Jordan said, "including the officials."

Craig Morton, who completed only 12 of 26 passes for 127 yards, was deflated by the defeat.

"We just made too many mistakes," said Morton, perhaps thinking of his three last-quarter interceptions.

"Their defenses didn't do anything we didn't expect. But they shut down our run, especially in the second half. And we've been a running team. I don't know what they did—maybe they changed up front."

Landry sent in virtually all the Cowboy plays to Morton, but not the pass play on which Mike Curtis intercepted to position the Colts' winning field goal.

"We were in our 2-minute offense at the time, Craig knew what plays I wanted. This hurts pretty bad. We fought uphill for eight weeks—nobody could play defense the way we have for the last eight weeks. You can't measure our disappointment."

Landry, who was finally able to bring the Cowboys into the Super Bowl after years of frustration, said: "We had our opportunities to control the game in the first half, but we missed the big plays on a couple of occasions and had to settle for field goals. In the third period we moved the ball well downfield only to be stopped by Thomas's fumble."

Dan Reeves, a player-coach with Dallas, said: "This was the biggest game we ever played. I just wish we could have won it. What hurts most was giving up 10 points on two tipped plays."

Reeves explained as follows the pass that tipped his fingers only to be caught by Curtis, setting up the Colts' victory: "A back fresh out of college could have caught it. I went as high as I could, but it went through my hands.

"I don't take the blame for the loss. We lost it as a team. O'Brien did a great job. I didn't think a rookie could make a kick like that under such pressure."

Sports of The Times

By ARTHUR DALEY

Not Very Super

MIAMI, *Jan. 17*—According to the advance billing this was the Super Bowl, a titanic contest between two super teams playing super football. But this one came up strictly from hunger, a sandlot exhibition between a couple of ball clubs of Lilliputian dimensions and miniscule skills. The Baltimore Colts defeated the Dallas Cowboys in the final 5 seconds, 16–13.

It was a merciful coup de grace because these ball clubs were so bad that they might have gone into sudden-death overtime and the game might still be continuing. That would have been cruel and inhuman treatment to the 80,055 spectators in the Orange Bowl and the millions of televiewers. At least the TV watchers could have escaped if they so desired. The folks here were trapped.

Maybe the ferocious defenses of the combatants nullified each other and forced fumbles, interceptions, penalties and all the dreadful misfeasances that marked this slightly less than epic struggle. There probably weren't as many screwball plays and crazy happenings as there seemed to be. But an observer got numbed after a while and permitted an over-all impression to stand without even attempting to justify it.

It was a game that followed no preconceived patterns. Johnny Unitas, the marvelous passer, passed badly but still threw for a touchdown when the ball bounced off finger tips in volleyball style to nestle in the arms of John Mackey for 75 yards and a touchdown. But Jim O'Brien had his conversion attempt blocked.

After Unitas went out for repairs, in went Earl Morrall, who was handling the controls when the victory arrived. And who should contribute the winning points? It was O'Brien, a rookie from Cincinnati, who had goat horns hung on him for having an extra-point attempt blocked and then cast aside for a starry diadem by booting the clinching field goal. Suddenly the missed extra point had lost all significance. Yet it had loomed so large for so long.

•

From as far back as anyone can remember, the tinkerers and the let's-make-a-change boys have been scoffing at the conversion of extra points after touchdowns. It was a waste of time, they said, because the professionals are so expert they never miss. Oh, yeah. . . .

O'Brien, later a hero, failed unheroically to supply the extra point when Baltimore had a chance to take a 7–6 lead in the second quarter. Mark Washington of Dallas slipped through to smother the ball and this was to haunt the Colts for a long while thereafter.

Just before the first half ended, Baltimore was on the Cowboy 2½-yard line with a first down and a glorious opportunity to pick up 7 points and thus gain a 13–13 tie. But that tough Dallas defense yielded a total of only one-half yard in three assaults.

That's what made for the strategic squeeze. Because of the foozled conversion, Baltimore no longer could settle for a field goal then and perhaps another later. It still would be a point short. So the Colts went for a touchdown and emerged with no points at all.

This was at a stage in the proceedings when old Super Bowlers were wondering if poetic justice would rear its pretty head and give Morrall something long overdue. A couple of years ago against the Jets an end-of-the-half touchdown opportunity confronted Morrall and he also missed that chance, too.

•

Against the Jets the Baltimore play that failed was a flea-flicker. Doggone if the flea-flicker didn't reappear in this daffy game. Morrall flicked the ball to Sam Havrilak, who threw a forward to Ed Hinton, heading for the end zone. Suddenly things happened.

Cornell Green of Dallas hooked the ball from Hinton's grasp just as Mel Renfro tackled him. Hinton stopped abruptly. The ball didn't, it kept scooting blithely into the end zone with players from both sides in hot pursuit. No one caught up with the ball as it bobbled right through for a touchback. Thus no one got any points.

•

That is to say that no one got any points out of it unless you want to count indirection. Dallas took over at the 20-yard line and almost immediately threw an interception that Rick Volk carried to the goalmouth. This time the Colts didn't miss, Tom Nowatzke going over for the tying touchdown that was to set up the grandstand finale by O'Brien.

Come to think of it, though, this was not the last time the Colts were to get points by indirection. The Cowboys made too bold an effort to free themselves from the tie. With less than 2 minutes to go, Craig Morton threw a pass for his third interception, the ball bouncing off the fingers of Dan Reeves into the hands of Mike Curtis. It set up the winning field goal.

According to Coach Don McCafferty, "This was the turning point." It was an accurate estimate. It also was a lot more accurate than something else McCafferty said.

"The players gave us good football," he said, carried away presumably by the euphoria of winning. Sorry, Don. They all were lousy.

Sports of The Times

By ARTHUR DALEY

Which Viewpoint Counts?

MIAMI, *Jan. 18*—Maybe the experts are too expert. Most of them were so appalled by the bush-league performances displayed by both teams in the Super Bowl yesterday that they were inclined to regard this unfunny comedy of errors as not only a smear on football but as an inadvertent boost for baseball.

Yet a surprising number of starry-eyed folks seemed to think it had been a great and exciting game. It was neither. Any contest that is determined by a field goal just five seconds short of being plunged into sudden-death overtime has a certain amount of built-in excitement. But it was the tail wagging the dog. The rest of the dog was dead weight because of mountainous esthetic and technical imperfections.

Hence this was a badly played game that the Baltimore Colts won from the Dallas Cowboys, 16–13, on a 32-yard field goal by Jim O'Brien, a rookie. It had six fumbles, six interceptions, 11 turnovers and more flukes, freaks and funnies than any other important championship contest in memory.

It brought to mind Warren Brown's classic crack when asked to pick between wartime baseball clubs in one World Series.

"I don't think either can win," he said. This was a football game that both teams seemed to be trying to give away through incompetence. It will endure in memory, though, because it was jam-packed with controversy.

Fickle Form

The club that was supposed to have the overpowering running attack, Dallas, couldn't run a lick and the unstoppable Cowboy ball-carrier, Duane Thomas, could gain only 37 yards in 18 tries. The club that was supposed to have the deadly passing attack, Baltimore, couldn't mount an aerial game when Johnny Unitas, the old master, was in action. He completed only three of nine and one of these may have been illegal.

It was a crusher, though. It also was a prize sample of the way footballs bounced off finger tips all afternoon in utterly crazy deflections, constantly turning the tide of battle. On this particular one Unitas passed over the middle to Ed Hinton and the ball caromed off his finger tips. Eventually it settled in the arms of big John Mackey, who fumbled on a 75-yard touchdown play.

The key question, though, is this: Was the ball touched by a Cowboy before it reached Mackey? All three Cowboys in the general area of the play deny that it also caromed off any of their reaching fingers. If none of them touched the ball, the pass was illegal because it was handled by two receivers. But if any Dallas player as much as grazed the ball, legality was restored. The instant replay was too fuzzy to prove anything. Maybe the official movies eventually will eliminate this disputatious point—or fan it to full flame.

The amount of mistakes made by both sides was unbelievable. Perhaps the defenses were so smothering that they negated all offensive efforts. That would be the kindest way to look at it. Assuredly the opportunities were there and it has to seem that Dallas blew more of them than did Baltimore. After recovering one fumble on the 9-yard line very early in the game, the Texans had to settle for a field goal.

Later on—and this was the killer—Thomas seemed to wriggle over for a touchdown in the third quarter from pointblank range. The officials hesitated for a moment and then signaled frantically that it was Baltimore's ball on the 1-yard line. Thomas either fumbled or had the ball stolen from him. But if he had scored, the Cowboys would have led by 19–6 or 20–6, and it would have been all over.

"What hurts so much," moaned Dan Reeves, the Dallas player-coach, "is that we gave up 10 points on two tipped plays."

He miscalculated. He had forgotten the early tipped pass that Mackey caught for the touchdown. That added up to 16 points on tips. What Dan had in mind were a pair very late in the proceedings. A Craig Morton pass skidded off the fingers of Walt Garrison and Rick Volk intercepted to set up the tying touchdown. Then a Morton toss skidded off the fingers of Reeves himself and Mike Curtis intercepted to set up the winning field goal.

It's almost impossible to remember all the screwball things that happened in yesterday's Super Bowl game. There was Hinton grabbing a pass from Sam Havrilak (who had got the ball from Earl Morrall) and heading confidently for a touchdown. One Cowboy hooked his arm and another belted him. The ball squirted all the way through the end zone for a touchback. How often do you see that? Or there was an embarrassed Mel Renfro letting a kick roll dead on the 1-inch line.

Oh, well. It's over. Most of the other coaches in the league were probably mumbling to their owners, "Geez, we could have beaten both of them." Maybe so, but more likely not. The Super Bowl did not produce good football yesterday, even though it was good theater.

Super Bowl 'Overcome' by Success

By WILLIAM N. WALLACE

MIAMI, *Jan. 18*—Pro football's Super Bowl promotion has become so big, so successful that it has developed problems on three levels: tension, tickets and television.

In yesterday's game, won by Baltimore over Dallas, the players showed the tension. Two weeks of preparation, build-up and clamor seemed to affect their ability. There were 16 major errors, meaning fumbles, interceptions and dropped or badly thrown passes, and also 14 penalties. The Colts led in mistakes, 10–6, and the Cowboys in penalties, 9–5.

Lamar Hunt, president of the American Conference and the Kansas City Chiefs, said, "I was surprised at how tight those two teams were. They seemed more nervous than any of the teams that have played in the other Super Bowl games."

The errors did not detract from the entertainment and excitement generated by the game. It was zany and fun.

•

As an event, the Super Bowl has a few problems. Tickets are one. Most of the tickets are distributed on a V.I.P. basis, meaning very important people. Businessmen use it as an entertainment vehicle. There were not enough tickets this time and a lot of people had to be turned down, including V.I.P.'s This caused disappointment, embarrassment and anger.

"Nobody likes to say no," said a member of Commissioner Pete Rozelle's staff. "I think we made as many enemies as friends this time."

It is estimated that the Super Bowl generates $20-million worth of business in terms of hotel, restaurant and travel. Cities vie for it and Miami has it for now. But will Miami keep the Super Bowl? There were minor problems and abrasions this time.

The National Football League owners, at their March meeting in Palm Beach, will decide whether to bring the game back here or try some place else, like going to Los Angeles.

Many of Miami's citizens became exercised at the television blackout and there was a lot of caustic comment in the press.

Apart from the benefits of the $20-million the tourists spend, the Super Bowl does little for a Miamian. He cannot go to the game unless he knows someone who can get him a ticket and he cannot see it on TV.

If the Miami Dolphins, the popular local team, should qualify for the Super Bowl the problems of tickets and television would become utterly impossible.

•

Rozelle was annoyed and angered by the legal moves taken by a local lawyer, Ellis Rubin, to try to force a lifting of the blackout. Rozelle, who hid out two extra days in the Bahamas last week to avoid subpoena papers being served on him, called the actions "harassment."

Rozelle might recommend to his owners a departure from Miami on that issue alone—too much local harassment to have the blackout lifted. Even though the game is sold out, the N.F.L. wants to keep its blackout rule as a matter of principle and policy. If it is breached now, Rozelle reasons, it would become a target of politicians for all kinds of other games.

Nixon Finds Bloopers In Super Bowl Super

WASHINGTON, *Jan, 18*—Like most American males, President Nixon watched the Super Bowl game on television yesterday and had an opinion on the caliber of the contest.

"Somebody asked me about it and I said 'I hope I don't make that many mistakes in one day,' " the President told a group of visitors to his office today.

Film Shows Renfro Deflected Ball on Colts' First Score

By DAVE ANDERSON

In the film viewed yesterday of the Super Bowl game's most controversial play, Mel Renfro of the Dallas Cowboys clearly deflected the football to John Mackey when the Baltimore Colts scored the first touchdown last Sunday in their 16–13 victory.

The film, from an end-zone camera and supplied by National Football League Films, Inc., will be seen Saturday on the American Broadcasting Company's "Wide World of Sports" TV show, beginning at 5 P.M. here on Channel 7.

On the play, John Unitas, the Colt quarterback, threw a high pass to one of his wide receivers, Eddie Hinton, who leaped and touched the ball with his left hand. As the ball floated end over end, Renfro, also leaping touched it with his right hand, increasing its spin.

The ball then dropped into the hands of Mackey, who completed a 75-yard touchdown play.

Had the pass been deflected from Hinton to Mackey without having touched a Cowboy defender, it would have been an illegal play. But the film shows that the official, Hugh Gamber, the back judge, made the correct call.

After the game, Renfro denied having deflected the ball, but acknowledged that "I might've touched it with my fingernail." Many of the Cowboys contended it had been an illegal touchdown.

On the Super Bowl segment of the "Wide World of Sports" show, the commentators are Howard Cosell and Joe Namath, the New York Jets' quarterback. When the controversial play was screened during yesterday's video-taping at an A.B.C. studio, Namath said:

"Watch the trajectory, you'll see that Renfro clearly hits the ball."

The film also showed that Tom Mitchell, a Colt tight end, stumbled over Jethro Pugh, a Cowboy defensive tackle, on his way into the end zone for Earl Morrall's incomplete fourth-down pass shortly before the half-time intermission.

On the vital fumble by Duane Thomas of the Cowboys at the Colts' 1-yard line early in third quarter, Mike Curtis, the Colts' middle linebacker, appears to have jarred the ball loose.

During his commentary, Namath mentioned that "both teams made too many mistakes to win" and estimated that "six or eight teams could've beaten either team on that particular day if they'd avoided errors," meaning the total of 11 interceptions and lost fumbles.

Regarding the decision of Don McCafferty, the Colt coach, to disdain a virtually sure field goal for Morrall's fourth-down attempt at a touchdown, Namath was shocked.

"I didn't think there was any considering to do. I thought it was a field goal. But coaching is a peculiar thing. When they went for the touchdown, I jumped three feet off the couch, but that," Namath said, laughing, "was because I had a good bet on Baltimore."

"Some people may even believe that," Cosell said.

What might have been the key play of 1971's Super Bowl rested on the rotation of the football. John Mackey (88) was on the receiving end of a Johnny Unitas 75-yard touchdown pass, but before he got the football it had been touched by a fellow Colt and, as this photo sequence shows, Mel Renfro of the Cowboys, who barely touched the ball as the altered trajectory of the football indicates. A rule states that two offensive players may not touch the ball consecutively once it leaves the passer's hand.

WIDE WORLD PHOTOS

Chapter 6

Super Bowl VI—1972

A pattern was emerging.

Experience counted.

In Super Bowl I, of course, both teams were in it for the first time, but Green Bay had been through more intense championship fires than Kansas City had. (It had better players, too.)

In Super Bowl II, Green Bay was a repeater and Oakland was a newcomer. Green Bay won.

In Super Bowl III, both teams, the Jets and the Colts, were at the summit for the first time.

But in Super Bowl IV, Kansas City was back for a second shot (for most of its key players) while Minnesota was there for the first time. Kansas City won.

And in Super Bowl V, the Baltimore Colts who had lost to the Jets only two years before were back against a Dallas team that had made it that far (after much frustration) for the first time.

And Baltimore won.

Now, in Super Bowl VI, Dallas was back, essentially unchanged from the previous year, against a team that was not only new in identity but young in personnel: the Miami Dolphins, whose franchise was only six years old. It was an expansion team from an expansion league, 25th among the 26 teams in date of origin. (Only the Cincinnati Bengals came later.)

So it was a sound enough hunch that Dallas should win, right? Especially since it seemed that Dallas had better players.

And perhaps the fact that one could have such a hunch, based on such a pattern, was the most significant feature of Super Bowl VI. Imperceptibly, history had accumulated. There were things to compare. The game was part of a series. It had continuity. The playoff system that led to it seemed less bizarre the second time around, and the "special" quality of two-league days was simply forgotten.

It was a championship game, football's "World Series," and what more did the fans of America want?

Coach Nixon Sends In a Play to the Miami Dolphins

By DAVE ANDERSON

MIAMI, *Jan. 3*—President Nixon gave Don Shula, coach of the Miami Dolphins, a suggestion today for the American Football Conference champions' game plan in the Super Bowl with the Dallas Cowboys at New Orleans on Jan. 16.

"The President alerted me that the Cowboys are a real good football team," the coach said after receiving a congratulatory telephone call from Mr. Nixon. "But he told me, 'I still think you can hit Warfield on that down-and-in pattern against them.'"

Paul Warfield, sleek wide receiver, caught a long pass from Bob Griese, the Dolphin quarterback, on a down-and-in pattern for a 50-yard gain that positioned the final touchdown in the 21–0 victory over the Baltimore Colts here yesterday in the title contest. Earlier, on a down-and-out, Warfield caught another long pass for a 75-yard touchdown.

On a down-and-in the receiver usually feints the defensive cornerback assigned to cover him, races straight downfield and veers toward the center of the field beyond the defensive safetyman in that area.

On a down-and-out he makes the same preliminary moves but veers toward the sideline for the pass.

Shula was at his Miami Lakes home watching a videotape of the game at about 1:30 A.M., when the President phoned. They chatted for about 10 minutes.

"When the phone rang at that hour," Shula said, "I thought it might be some nut calling. But his aide said, 'Is this Mr. Shula?' Then he said, 'The President is calling.' Everybody in the house was asking, 'Who is it?' and I said, 'It's the President,' but I thought it might be a hoax. I was listening to make sure it was his voice. I appreciate his interest.

"He warned me that Tom Landry of the Cowboys is a real good coach," Shula said. "He wanted to talk technical football. He wanted to know about our tremendous blocking on Dick Anderson's interception return for a touchdown.

"He told me, 'Now you understand that I'm a Washington Redskin fan, but I'm a part-time resident of Miami and I've been following the Dolphins real close.'"

The President was an outspoken follower of the Redskins, who were eliminated by the San Francisco 49ers in the National Conference playoffs on Dec. 26. He even visited the Redskins' practice base to give an impromptu pep talk late in the season. But now he apparently has adopted the

Dolphins because of his home in nearby Key Biscayne. However, he told Shula that he doubted he could attend the Super Bowl.

In Washington on Dec. 27, Bill Brundige, a Redskin defensive lineman appeared on a television program and disclosed that the Redskin coach, George Allen, received a phone call from Mr. Nixon before the 24–20 loss to the 49ers.

"President Nixon told Allen, 'I'd like to see you run a flanker reverse with Roy Jefferson against the 49ers,' " Brundige said.

At San Francisco, it happened late in the second quarter. The situation: second down and 6 yards to go for the Redskins on the 49er 8-yard line. The play: a flanker reverse to Jefferson. The result: a 13-yard loss.

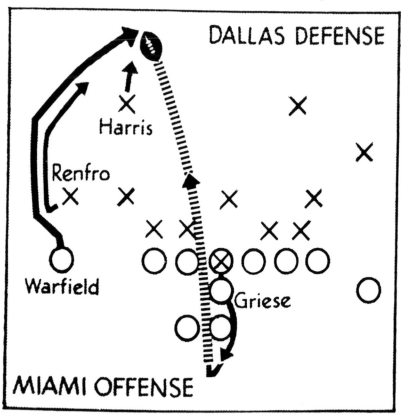

JAN. 4, 1972

Richard M. Nixon, known in his football playing days at Whittier College as "the most spirited bench warmer on the team," suggested to Miami coach Don Shula the play diagramed above. It indicates a pass from Bob Griese to Paul Warfield on a down-and-in pattern.

Shula is aware of the Cowboys' skill. The Dolphins never have played the National Conference champions. But Shula split two games with the Cowboys in his seven seasons as the Colts' coach before he came to Miami in 1970. His Colts also defeated the Cowboys in the 1966 Playoff Bowl between second-place teams.

"I've seen the Cowboys on TV lately," Shula said. "They're an all-around experienced, solid team. Ever since they've used Calvin Hill and Duane Thomas together as runners, they've been devastating. Roger Staubach is more disciplined now at quarterback than he was when I remember him. He really makes an effort to stay in there and throw the ball instead of running."

Shula, who was the Colts' coach when, as a 17-point favorite, they lost to the New York Jets in Super Bowl III following the 1968 season, ordered the Dolphins to re-assemble Wednesday. He and his coaching staff began to prepare at their Biscayne College base for the Cowboy game while reviewing films of yesterday's dramatic triumph.

He appeared to be most proud of the Dolphins' six spectacular blocks on Anderson's zigzagging 62-yard interception return.

"It was one of the great plays of all time, a classic," Shula said. "We measure how much a player wants to win by how close he is to the football. To see those blocks unfold was just tremendous. It was perfect reaction. Some teams practice yelling, 'Osky!' or 'Bingo!' at an interception to alert players to block. We don't use that. We just try to react."

In showing newsmen wide-angle game films of Anderson's run, Shula pointed out the blocks that turned six Colts upside-down.

"This is the first one, Jake Scott flipping Tom Mitchell," he said as Anderson began to run after snatching the ball, which had been deflected by Curtis Johnson, a cornerback. "Now watch Mike Kolen get Ray Perkins, then, as Anderson cuts across the field, Tim Foley gets John Williams; Doug Swift gets Dan Sullivan, Bill Stanfill gets Bill Curry and Bob Heinz gets John Unitas."

The film was stopped as Anderson eluded Bob Vogel, another Colt lineman, in a cutback into the end zone.

"Look at that," Shula said. "Six Colts on the ground are getting up. That's what football is all about."

L.B.J. Exhorts Cowboys, But Has No Play for Them

By DAVE ANDERSON

NEW ORLEANS, *Jan. 10*—Despite his loyalty to the Dallas Cowboys in the Super Bowl game, Lyndon B. Johnson will refrain from suggesting any plays to their coach, Tom Landry, for use Sunday against the Miami Dolphins.

In a telegram disclosed today by Landry, the former President said:

"My prayers and my presence will be with you in New Orleans although I don't plan to send in any plays."

Mr. Johnson and Lady Bird are scheduled to arrive here later in the week.

His reference to sending in plays was prompted by President Nixon's suggestion last week to Don Shula, the Dolphin coach, that Paul Warfield, the star wide receiver, be used on a down-and-in pattern for a pass from Bob Griese, the quarterback.

The emphasis on Mr. Nixon's suggestion appealed to Shula as a convenient ruse.

"It should help us set up our down-and-out pattern," he said today with a smile.

On a down-and-out Warfield would cut toward the sideline. On a down-and-in he would cut toward the center of the field. But no matter where Warfield goes, he will be scrutinized because of the notoriety surrounding him resulting from the President's suggestion.

"It doesn't necessarily mean that we'll go to the down-and-in," Warfield said, "and it doesn't necessarily mean that we'll stay away from it. We'll simply look for whatever weaknesses are in the Cowboy pass defense."

Before the Dolphin workout at Tulane Stadium today, Griese minimized the President's suggestion. However, he said, "the most important thing is that the President is interested in pro football."

Mel Renfro and Cliff Harris, the Cowboy defensive backs with the primary responsibility for covering Warfield, praised the wide receiver's ability. Renfro, at cornerback, will line up against Warfield, with Harris, a safetyman, assisting on coverage on deep patterns.

"Warfield weaves as he comes off the line, that's his basic approach," Renfro said. "It's hard to backpedal and weave with him at the same time. He likes to run 7 or 8 yards and then bend it in."

On pass defense the Cowboys prefer man-to-man coverage most of the time, with an occasional shift to zone coverage. In man-to-man coverage Renfro would be responsible for staying with Warfield, but in a zone Harris would take over the coverage when Warfield ran beyond the area for which Renfro was responsible.

"You can't sit in the man-to-man all the time," Harris said. "But the big danger with Warfield is his ability to run with the ball after catching it."

"I enjoyed the President getting interested in the Super Bowl game, no matter what way he went," Coach Landry said. "In the down-and-in with Warfield he selected a play that has a real possibility of happening. If it's completed, he ought to get a thrill out of it. And if it's intercepted, I'll get a thrill out of it."

Sports of The Times
The Silent Halfback

By ARTHUR DALEY

NEW ORLEANS, *Jan. 10*—When the sun finally burst through the clouds to flood the practice field of the Dallas Cowboys this morning, everything was warm and pleasant—except Duane Thomas. But at least the rebellious ball-carrying marvel condescended to make a personal appearance in the Super Bowl scene, and all the Cowboy rooters sighed with relief because this was a definite plus.

Amateur psychologists, including his teammates, have stopped trying to understand the gifted Duane. He rebelled against the Cowboys in July, was traded to the New England Patriots, rebelled against them, was returned to Dallas, where he reported after the season started, and has since been his sensational self. But last week he failed to show for practice and rumors flashed that Duane's vendetta against the world would cause him to boycott the Super Bowl. But he was back the next day, was fined for his absence by Coach Tom Landry and was reinstated. Now he is here, quick with everything but the conversation. He is a loner and doesn't appear to be especially civil, even when he exchanges words with teammates.

This first day of Super Bowl week was a no-work talkathon for the press and photographers and the space cadets with their electronic gadgets, the Cowboys in the morning and the Miami Dolphins at noon. As the Dallas players drifted out from the clubhouse in full uniform, they were shunted into the five rows of a jury box of a grandstand where they could be plucked forth for interviews. The press corps kept waiting and waiting. No one said why but everyone knew. Would Thomas, the uncommunicative recluse, show up? If so, would he break his long silence?

Virtually all the Cowboys were on the field or in the stands when Duane emerged and climbed alone to the next-to-last row in the stands at the far end from where the other Dallas players were clustered. He sprawled out and glowered. One reporter eased alongside of him. Then another joined them. A couple of questions were tossed up gently into the soft Louisiana air and Thomas let them float past.

"You were great last year, Duane," I said to him. "You were bright, lively, funny and talkative."

"I don't feel like being bothered now," he said with a note of grim finality.

"Did someone misquote you?" he was asked. "Has that caused you to clam up?"

"What time is it?" said Duane.

Obviously it was time to leave. So Duane Thomas, the loner, was left to sprawl in solitary majesty. No one else came near him and eventually he slipped away into the clubhouse, his task of winning friends and influencing people completed for the day.

While Duane smoldered silently in the little grandstand, his companion as a running back in the Dallas attacking platoon was chatting away with a group. He was Calvin Hill, a Yale man and house intellectual.

"I think it would be unfair to analyze Duane," said the cheerful Calvin, giving the impression that he had tried but wasn't too sure of his findings. "I never considered him unusual or untalkative. I found him cordial and warm. We've even discussed history and philosophy. That's more than you normally get during a discussion with a football player, most of whom prefer to discuss the game or girls. I have not considered him a loner but close to a lot of the guys.

"What does closeness mean to a football team? I've read in the New Orleans papers that the Saint players are closely knit. But they lose a lot. The Cowboys are considered close and much stress is placed on the importance of how well we mesh. But when you win, even the water boy is great.

"When you come right down to it, you can't take a group of men from every corner and section of the country, from all political beliefs, from differing economic backgrounds and have them weld into instant togetherness. If a conservative Republican throws the block that springs me loose for a touchdown, I like him immensely. And I'm not a conservative Republican. Hey, how did I ever get into discussing politics?

"I'm not in politics because I think it needs a special breed of animal and I just don't have the proper qualifications. When a man gets older, he realizes his limitations. I never can forget the time in the third or fourth grade when my teacher asked what I wanted to be when I grew up. 'The President of the United States,' I said. 'Impossible,' she said, explaining that a black had no chance. It was the first time I ever realized there was a difference and it was the low point of my life."

Yepremian and Clark Back on Beam

By DAVE ANDERSON

NEW ORLEANS, *Jan. 11*—As a rookie five seasons ago, Garo Yepremian slapped his cheek to stop it from twitching. In his ninth season two months ago, Mike Clark let the pressure "defeat me" in a duel for his job.

Such has been the strain of competition on the rival field-goal kickers of the Super Bowl game. But now, when Yepremian lines up for the Miami Dolphins, his cheek no longer twitches. And now, Clark of the Dallas Cowboys contends that Toni Fritsch, an Austrian soccer-stylist who replaced him briefly at midseason, "no longer exists" in his mind.

Yepremian, whose 37-yard field goal won football's longest game in the 27–24 playoff victory over the Kansas City Chiefs, has emerged as the National Football League's most compelling specialist.

"In that overtime," Yepremian was saying today, "I had been around football enough that I knew how much money is involved. I knew that this was the time to come through to let them know they are justified in paying me. And when I kicked the ball, I was making history. That ball going through the goal posts is a picture I'll never take out of my mind."

As recently as two seasons ago, Yepremian was unemployed in pro football. He was unwanted by the Detroit Lions, whom he had joined in 1966 after settling with his brother, Krikor, in Indianapolis.

"I am an Armenian," he recalled, "but my family moved to England because of the civil war in Cyprus and I attended an American school there. I played sandlot soccer. Then my brother invited me to Indianapolis for a visit and I fell in love with America right away. It was so clean. London had been so dirty, the soot."

His brother wrote to many teams, but only the Atlanta Falcons and the Lions granted the left-footed soccer-stylist a tryout.

"The Falcons liked me but the Lions offered more money. In my first game, against Green Bay, on the kickoff Herb Adderley ran it back and he had Ray Nitschke blocking. I didn't know who Ray Nitschke was then. I had no face mask on. Ray Nitschke hit me a forearm across the face but somehow he made Adderley fumble the ball."

After the 1968 season, which he spent with the minor league Michigan Arrows, he was released.

The next year he had a six-month Army hitch.

"By then, the Lions had Errol Mann but their general manager, Edwin Anderson, told me I should be kicking. He asked me, 'Do you mind if I write letters.' I was honored. Coach Don Shula of the Dolphins was the only one who replied with a positive answer. By the second game in 1970, I was activated. I have been ever since."

Clark, cut earlier by Philadelphia and Pittsburgh, thought he was a fixture with the Cowboys until they imported Fritsch last summer after a European scouting tour.

"I guess I let the pressure defeat me," Clark explained. "I kept my job during the preseason but rather than stopping then, Toni and I had to compete every day in practice. I couldn't relax because I knew I'd be competing the next day. It was a competitive situation that the coaches created. Mentally, I just wore out."

When he missed field goals of 25, 30 and 42 yards in a 23–19 loss to the Chicago Bears, he was replaced on the roster by Fritsch.

"Then two weeks later, I got lucky," Clark said. "Toni pulled a hamstring muscle. I knew I had my job back for at least two weeks. I relaxed. I went fishing, I flew. I fly a small plane. I forgot about him. Now he no longer exists in my mind."

The 31-year-old Clark, at 6 feet 1 inch and 205 pounds, resembles the fullback he was at Texas A. and M., while Yepremian resembles the men's tie-designer he is.

"I am 176 pounds," the baldish, 27-year-old Yepremian said with a smile. "And I am 5 feet 7½ inches. But if I comb my hair straight up, I'm 5-8."

Sports of The Times

Relentless Man in the Middle

By ARTHUR DALEY

NEW ORLEANS—Whenever any of the Dallas Cowboys begins to assay victory chances in Sunday's Super Bowl game, they all reach the same inevitable conclusion. Those victory chances will depend to a considerable extent on how skillful they are in bottling up the explosive charges of Nick Buoniconti, the Miami middle linebacker with the low center of gravity and the high percentage of smearing enemy ball-carriers. "We have to make certain on every play," said Tom Landry, the ranch foreman of the Cowboys, "that we block out Buoniconti. Otherwise our running game just won't work. He isn't big but he's quick, a hard-nosed guy who takes off running and begins piling up plays. He sets the tempo for the Miami defenses and it doesn't seem to me that he even is guessing where the play is going. It's as if he already knows. But it's his great pursuit that makes him such a great linebacker."

The object of this admiring appraisal is a mild-mannered, soft-spoken New Englander who ordinarily wouldn't scare anyone. But he has been such a ferocious middle linebacker that he won all-league honors for six of his first eight years as a professional. Yet he stands a mere 5 feet 11 inches tall and weighs in at 220 pounds, making him the smallest middle linebacker in the business. Some rueful ball-carriers, however, have compared colliding with Buoniconti to running into a fire hydrant. They get their fenders crumpled and the fire hydrant escapes undamaged.

When Nick first joined the Boston Patriots in 1962, Mike Holovak marveled at him. Said the Patriot coach:

"Nick not only can jam up the middle but he also can cover the sweeps to the outside."

Everyone may be high now on this linebacking terror, but he once was something of a low man on the totem pole. As an undergraduate at Notre Dame, he played as an undersized guard and tackle during the one-platoon era, with occasional assignments as a linebacker. He still was named to many all-American teams and waited confidently for the pro draft. The National Football League was still in a bidding war with the American Football League and it was cutthroat competition for talent. Nick expected to be a reasonably high pick by the N.F.L.

"It was embarrassing," he said today, his brown eyes dancing. "The N.F.L. went through the entire draft without any team being interested enough in me to draft me. But then I thought of something Joe Kuharich, my Notre Dame coach, had told me. I liked Joe and I liked his honesty.

" 'Nick,' he said to me in my senior year, 'I can't recommend you to any N.F.L. scouts. You're just too small for that league. But I think you might do well in the A.F.L.' "

That's the way it worked out, too. The Americans were a young and struggling league. They couldn't be as fussy as the Nationals at that particular time, although they were to change later. And Buoniconti was to become a tremendous player. Could he have achieved as much with the Nationals? He probably would have.

"Buoniconti's size and style," said Walt Garrison, the slashing Cowboy ball-carrier, "remind me of our middle linebacker, Lee Roy Jordan. I guess Lee Roy is a couple of inches taller but they both depend on quickness. They move a lot and they move fast. I would say, though, that Lee Roy is more disciplined than Buoniconti. He's a real free-wheeler." Nick, however, denies the description.

"Before Don Shula took over the Dolphins," he said, "I was a real free-wheeler. This is particularly true for most of my years with Boston. There would be a third down and six to go situation. Everyone knew what I'd say in the huddle. 'Now's the time to go, boys,' I'd say, and we'd all blast in with the blitz."

Buoniconti had become something of a folk hero in the Boston area. He also had passed the Massachusetts bar examination and appeared set for life. Then he was traded to Miami in 1969.

"It seemed like the end of the world for me," said Nick. "I hated to leave Boston but now I expect to spend the rest of my days happily in the Miami area. I passed the Florida bar exam and the future is bright for me.

"The future also is bright for the Miami Dolphins. When Don Shula signed as coach, he flew the entire squad in for a get-together meeting in April. That's when I first realized what a perfectionist he is. Don is the most complete coach I ever played for. He lays it out exactly, first as a generalization and then pinpointing everything. His rapport with the players is tremendous.

"If you wonder when we first thought we might land in the Super Bowl, my guess would be that it came in midseason when we upset the favored Los Angeles Rams. Our younger players looked at each other and suddenly said, 'Hey, maybe we can go all the way.' And we did."

COWBOYS FIVE-POINT FAVORITES
OVER DOLPHINS TODAY

Worthy Matchup

65 Million Expected to See It—Dallas Has Won Nine Straight

By WILLIAM N. WALLACE

NEW ORLEANS, *Jan. 15*—The Dallas Cowboys are favorites, by 5 points in wagering circles, to win the sixth Super Bowl game tomorrow from the Miami Dolphins before 81,023 people in Tulane Stadium.

There will be 800 times as many people watching the game on television—or an estimated audience of 65 million. The kickoff will be at 2:35 P.M., New York time, over Channel 2 in New York City with Ray Scott and Pat Summerall the broadcasters.

The Cowboy role of the slight favorite—less than a touchdown—accurately reflects the caution and the anticipation that surrounds this contest, which matches teams that have never played each other before. It's a good match.

The Cowboys have the experience of being in the big game—they lost last year's Super Bowl to Baltimore in the final five seconds. They have the confidence, nine victories in a row, including two in the playoffs over Minnesota and San Francisco. They have the players, with eight of them selected on the National Conference All-Star team for the Pro Bowl game.

But the youthful Dolphins have demonstrated tremendous enthusiasm; great leadership from Bob Griese, the quarterback voted by many of the players as the best in the National Football League this past season; and the affection of the President of the United States.

President Nixon's thought, which he expressed to Coach Don Shula, that Miami's down-and-in pass route for Paul Warfield would work well against Mel Renfro and Cliff Harris of Dallas, caused a furor around the country. It roused the former President, Lyndon B. Johnson, who is a Cowboy fan, and he will attend the game here today while President Nixon will not.

Coach Tom Landry of Dallas, when asked if the Cowboys would be ready for the Presidential play, said, "Sure. We expect to see a lot of Warfield. Obviously Warfield and Renfro is the classic matchup. We will double-cover him but not all the time. Renfro will do all right."

Warfield and Dallas's Bob Hayes, the dangerous wide receivers, represent the scoring potential of the big play. But the big plays come less frequently in pro football, especially in the playoff games, because the prevalent zone defenses shut them out. Most of the six playoff games this season turned into defensive battles with each side awaiting the other's mistakes and that could be true tomorrow.

"The running game will be the key to the ball game," said Landry, "assuming the turnovers [fumbles and interceptions] are even. They want to run on us. We want to run on them."

The Dallas runners will be Duane Thomas, the alienated young black who fumbled on the Colts' goal line in last year's Super Bowl game, and Walt Garrison, the little Cowboy who replaced Calvin Hill because of the latter's knee problems.

The Dolphins have Larry Csonka and Jim Kiick, the inseparable buddies who have been nicknamed Butch Cassidy and The Sundance Kid after the popular movie. Csonka, in the opinion of many, was the best running back in the game this season.

Score 2 for Dolphins

In assessing the teams the Dolphins would appear to have a slight edge in skills at running back and quarterback, Griese compared with Roger Staubach, but nowhere else. Both Griese and Staubach led their conferences in passing and their interception frequency was amazingly low, only four interceptions against Staubach in 211 pass attempts and nine for Griese in 203.

The young Dolphin defense, built around an old middle linebacker named Nick Buoniconti finishing his 10th season, is the questionable quality. This defense may try to rattle Staubach by shifting and moving on the line of scrimmage because the Dallas quarterback does not call his own plays and is still inexperienced in changing them verbally at the scrimmage line.

Such a maneuver would be looking for an edge and the Dolphins need every little edge they can find to overcome the Cowboy confidence and cannon power.

The economics of the game are $4-million expected in gross receipts from tickets, television, radio and films. The money will be divided among the players (the winning ones each receiving $15,000 and losers $7,500), the player pension fund and the commissioner's office to pay Pete Rozelle's $100,000 plus salary and staff expenses.

Herb Adderley is a seasoned Super Bowl man. The Dallas cornerback, who began his career with the Green Bay Packers, will be playing in his fourth Super Bowl game tomorrow and the only ones he has missed were Baltimore-New York Jets in 1969 and Minnesota-Kansas City in 1970. Adderley has been on the winning side twice and his monetary rewards for Super Bowl play have come to $91,000.

The Men Who Make Decisions Today

The Head Coaches

NEW ORLEANS, *Jan. 15*—The rival coaches in the Super Bowl, Tom Landry of the Dallas Cowboys and Don Shula of the Miami Dolphins, are also capitalists with that rare quality of their vocation, security. Both have stock interests in the teams they coach and it would be difficult to imagine them ever being discharged for failure to win.

Shula's teams have won three-fourths of their games in pro football. Landry's winning percentage is not as good because the Cowboys were an expansion team just getting started in the early nineteen-sixties against tough opposition. But in the last six seasons the Cowboys have won 69 of 96 games and have been in the postseason playoffs every year.

Dolphins Flipped for Shula

Shula and Landry were both defensive backs in the National Football League in the nineteen-fifties. Landry was an assistant coach with the New York Giants before taking charge of the Cowboys in 1960.

The same year Shula joined the staff of the Detroit Lions. He was hired as the head coach at Baltimore in 1963, succeeding Weeb Ewbank, and had the team in a league championship game the next season.

Shula moved to Miami early in 1970 despite the protests of Carroll Rosenbloom, the Colts' owner, who accused the Dolphins of tampering with his man in contractual discussions. Commissioner Pete Rozelle seemed to agree because the Dolphins had to give Baltimore a first draft choice as reparations.

Shula effected an immediate turnaround at Miami and his first club won 10 games compared with three the year before. Although it is an extremely youthful squad, Shula has held the team together with his organization and leadership.

In Baltimore he was known as a man with a short temper, quick to blame players for setbacks. He is said to have moderated considerably in Miami and his players speak most respectfully of him.

A Bomber Pilot in the War

Landry has been called "a plastic man" by one of his players, Duane Thomas, but that would be an exaggeration. Extremely forthright, Landry said this week that he thought he had improved; he hoped he learned something new about football and he believed he understood the players better.

Landry is a native Texan born 48 years ago at Mission. He flew 30 missions as a bomber pilot in World War II and attended the University of Texas. He and his wife, Alicia, have three children, Tom, Jr., 22, a law student; Kitty, 19, and Lisa, 13.

He is an admirer of President Nixon and they share a common friend, Billy Graham, the evangelist.

Landry was asked if he would welcome a suggested play from Graham, similar to the President's play selection for Shula. "I'd rather take Billy's prayers," replied Landry. "I know they will be better than any play he has."

Shula, 42 years old, is a native of Painesville, Ohio, and went to John Carroll University in Cleveland. He was one halfback at John Carroll in the late nineteen-forties and Carl Taseff another. Both went into professional football and Taseff is now on the Dolphin staff as a coaching assistant.

Watching the game tomorrow in Tulane Stadium will be Mrs. Dorothy Shula, the five Shula children and a host of Shula relations, including Don's triplet sisters and brother.

The Quarterbacks

NEW ORLEANS, *Jan. 15*—The quarterbacks in the Super Bowl, Bob Griese of the Miami Dolphins and Roger Staubach of the Dallas Cowboys, have much in common. Their wives are former nurses; they work in real estate apart from pro football; they are Catholics; they grew up in Ohio River cities not far apart, Staubach in Cincinnati and Griese in Evansville, Ind.; their uniform number is 12, and they both can throw a football with astounding accuracy and force.

Griese's route to pro football was direct and obvious while Staubach's was not. Griese was an all-America player at Purdue, famous for a great game against Notre Dame in 1966, runner-up for the Heisman Trophy and the Dolphins' first draft choice.

He became a regular his first season and a top star in the American Conference. He is 26 years old.

An Officer to the Rescue

Staubach was a hero of even greater dimension at the college level, the Heisman Trophy winner following his junior year at the Naval Academy in 1962. But he then served four years in the regular Navy, seeing service as a supply officer in Vietnam and playing almost no football.

He was the 10th round draft choice of the Cowboys, who were not very serious and hardly expected that he would ever become a pro football player. But Staubach reported to the Dallas training camp for a couple of weeks while on leave in 1968 and looked surprisingly good. He made the team following his discharge in 1969.

He saw little action the first two seasons as a replacement for Craig Morton. Halfway through this past season the Cowboys had lost three of seven games and looked sluggish.

Coach Tom Landry decided to make Staubach, who had been alternating with Morton, his regular at the position and the Cowboys have yet to lose, currently carrying a nine-game winning streak.

Both Griese and Staubach do more than throw the football. Each has potential as a runner and defenses must always be alert for this threat.

"Roger runs when he cannot find open receivers," says Landry. "But I wish he would not."

Although three years older, Staubach is not yet established in pro football like Griese, who is in complete command of his offense and a decision-maker. Landry calls all the plays for Staubach from the sidelines with Mike Ditka and Bill Truax, the tight ends, acting as messengers.

"Naturally I want to call the plays," says Staubach, "to be the complete quarterback. But I'm not ready yet."

"Maybe next year," says Landry.

Griese, trying to ease the Super Bowl pressure, calls tomorrow's event "just another game, but one that happens to be the only game in the world. Pressure builds if you allow it to."

He was coolly professional and curt in the massive press interviews prior to the game while Staubach was patient and expansive.

Don Shula, the Miami coach, says of Griese, "Bob has a magnificent football brain. He is second to none in a huddle or at the line of scrimmage."

Griese has a philosophy about playing in a game. "You never allow yourself to panic. You can't quarterback a team with the idea that you're going to score 20 points in one march. It's 7 at a time at the best. You must stick with the game plan."

How the Super Bowl Rivals Match Up, 1972

DALLAS ON OFFENSE

No.	Player	Ht.	Wt.	Pos.
22	Bob Hayes	5-11	185	WR
31	Gloster Richardson	6-0	200	WR
89	Mike Ditka	6-3	213	TE
70	Rayfield Wright	6-6	255	RT
61	Blaine Nye	6-4	251	RG
51	Dave Manders	6-2	250	C
76	John Niland	6-3	245	LG
64	Tony Liscio	6-5	255	LT
12	Roger Staubach	6-3	197	QB
33	Duane Thomas	6-1	205	HB
35	Calvin Hill	6-4	235	FB

MIAMI ON DEFENSE

No.	Player	Ht.	Wt.	Pos.
45	Curtis Johnson	6-1	196	RCB
25	Tim Foley	6-0	194	LCB
13	Jake Scott	6-0	188	SS
70	Jim Riley	6-4	250	LE
75	Manny Fernandez	6-2	248	LT
85	Nick Buoniconti	5-11	220	MLB
72	Bob Heinz	6-6	280	RT
84	Bill Stanfill	6-5	250	RE
40	Dick Anderson	6-2	196	FS
59	Doug Swift	6-3	228	LLB
57	Mike Kolen	6-2	220	RLB

DALLAS ON DEFENSE

No.	Player	Ht.	Wt.	Pos.
20	Mel Renfro	6-0	190	RCB
26	Herb Adderley	6-0	200	LCB
34	Cornell Green	6-3	208	SS
63	Larry Cole	6-4	255	LE
75	Jethro Pugh	6-6	260	LT
55	Lee Roy Jordan	6-1	221	MLB
74	Bob Lilly	6-5	260	RT
66	George Andrie	6-6	250	RE
43	Cliff Harris	6-1	180	FS
52	Dave Edwards	6-1	225	LLB
54	Chuck Howley	6-2	225	RLB

MIAMI ON OFFENSE

No.	Player	Ht.	Wt.	Pos.
42	Paul Warfield	6-0	185	WR
81	Howard Twilley	5-10	185	WR
80	Marv Fleming	6-4	235	TE
73	Norm Evans	6-5	252	RT
66	Larry Little	6-1	265	RG
61	Bob DeMarco	6-2	250	C
67	Bob Kuechenberg	6-2	247	LG
77	Doug Crusan	6-4	250	LT
12	Bob Griese	6-1	190	QB
21	Jim Kiick	5-11	215	HB
39	Larry Csonka	6-2	237	FB

DALLAS SUBSTITUTES

No.	Player	Ht.	Wt.	Pos.
10	Ron Widby	6-4	210	P
14	Craig Morton	6-4	214	QB
15	Toni Fritsch	5-7	185	K
19	Lance Alworth	6-0	180	WR
23	Maggene Adkins	5-10	183	WR
30	Dan Reeves	6-1	200	RB
32	Walt Garrison	6-0	205	RN
36	Joe Williams	6-0	195	RB
37	Isaac Thomas	6-2	193	CB
41	Charlie Waters	6-1	193	S
42	Claxton Welch	5-11	203	RB
46	Mark Washington	5-10	188	CB
50	D. D. Lewis	6-1	225	LB
56	Tom Stincic	6-4	230	LB
60	Lee Roy Caffey	6-3	240	LB
62	John Fitzgerald	6-5	250	C
67	Pat Toomay	6-5	244	DE
71	Rodney Wallace	6-5	255	G
72	Don Talbert	6-5	255	T
77	Bill Gregory	6-5	255	DT
79	Forrest Gregg	6-4	250	T
83	Mike Clark	6-1	205	K
85	Tody Smith	6-5	245	DE
87	Billy Truax	6-5	235	TE

MIAMI SUBSTITUTES

No.	Player	Ht.	Wt.	Pos.
1	Garo Yepremian	5-8	172	K
10	George Mira	5-11	192	QB
11	Jim Del Gaizo	6-1	198	QB
15	Charles Leigh	5-11	205	RB
20	Larry Seiple	6-0	215	TE-P
22	Mercury Morris	5-10	190	RB
24	Jack Clancy	6-1	195	WR
26	Lloyd Mumphord	5-10	180	CB
31	Terry Cole	6-1	220	RB
32	Hubert Ginn	5-10	188	RB
48	Bob Petrella	5-11	190	S
53	Bob Matheson	6-4	240	LB
56	Jesse Powell	6-2	215	LB
58	Dale Farley	6-3	235	LB
62	Jim Langer	6-2	250	G
64	Bill Griffin	6-5	255	T
65	Maulty Moore	6-5	265	DT
71	Frank Cornish	6-4	250	DT
74	John Richardson	6-2	248	DT
78	Wayne Mass	6-4	255	T
82	Otto Stowe	6-2	188	WR
86	Vern Den Herder	6-6	250	DE
89	Karl Noonan	6-2	198	WR

Facts on Super Bowl Contest, 1972

Title at Stake—World professional football championship.

Participants—Miami Dolphins, champion of the American Football Conference, and Dallas Cowboys, champion of the National Football Conference.

Site—Tulane Stadium, New Orleans.

Date—Today.

Starting Time—Kickoff 2:30 P.M. (New York time).

Seating Capacity—81,023.

Television—Nationwide by the Columbia Broadcasting System (New Orleans area blacked out). Air time 2:30 P.M., preceded by pregame show at 2 P.M.

Radio—Nationwide by Columbia Broadcasting System. Air time 2:20 P.M.

Players' Shares—$15,000 to each member of the winning team; $7,500 to each member of the losing team. Approximately $1.25-million total for the personnel of the competing clubs.

Division of Game Net Receipts—After deduction of taxes, expenses and players' shares, remainder will be distributed to the competing clubs and the player pension fund.

Uniforms—Miami will be the home team, will wear colored jerseys, and will use the West bench. Dallas will be the visiting team, will wear white jerseys, and will use the East bench.

Game Ball—The standard N.F.L. ball, adopted before the 1970 season and in use in all games this past season, will be used.

Sudden Death—If the game is tied at the end of regulation 60 minutes, it will continue in sudden-death overtime. The team scoring first by safety, field goal or touchdown, will win.

Officials—There will be six officials and two alternates appointed by the Commissioner's office.

Official Time—The scoreboard clock will be official.

Trophy—The winning team receives permanent possession of the Vince Lombardi Trophy, a sterling-silver football mounted on a three-sided base.

Regular-Season Figures

PASSING Dallas	Att.	Comp.	Pct.	Total Yds.	TDs	Int.
Staubach	211	126	59.7	1,882	15	4
Morton	143	78	54.5	1,131	7	8
Miami						
Griese	263	145	55.1	2,089	19	9
Mira	30	11	36.7	159	1	1

RUSHING Dallas	Att.	Total Yds.	Avg. Gain	Long Gain	TDs
D. Thomas	175	793	4.5	56	11
Hill	106	468	4.4	17	8
Garrison	127	429	3.4	34	1
Staubach	41	343	8.4	31	2
Miami					
Csonka	195	1,051	5.4	28	7
Kiick	162	738	4.6	34	3
Morris	57	315	5.5	51	1
Griese	26	82	3.2	21	0

RECEIVING Dallas	No. Caught	Total Yds.	Avg. Gain	Long Gain	TDs
Garrison	40	396	9.9	36	1
Hayes	35	840	24.0	85	8
Alworth	34	487	14.3	26	2
Ditka	30	360	12.0	29	1
Hill	19	244	12.8	27	3
Truax	15	232	15.5	25	1
D. Thomas	13	153	11.8	34	2
Miami					
Warfield	43	996	23.2	86	11
Kiick	40	338	8.5	27	0
Twilley	23	349	15.2	41	4
Fleming	13	137	10.5	23	2
Csonka	13	113	8.7	25	1
Noonan	10	180	18.0	43	0

| INTERCEPTIONS | | Total | Long | |
Dallas	No.	Yds.	Gain	TDs
Adderley	6	182	46	0
Howley	5	122	53	0
Renfro	4	11	7	0
Miami				
Scott	7	34	21	0
Foley	4	14	18	0
Johnson	2	34	34	0
Anderson	2	33	33	0

PUNTING	No.	Total Yds.	Avg. Punt	Long Punt	Had Blkd.
Widby, Dall.	56	2,329	41.6	59	1
Seiple, Mia.	52	2,087	40.1	73	1

Records of the Teams

DALLAS		MIAMI	
49—Buffalo	37	10—Denver	10
42—Philadelphia	7	29—Buffalo	14
16—Washington	20	10—N.Y. Jets	14
20—N.Y. Giants	13	23—Cincinnati	13
14—New Orleans	24	41—New England	3
44—New England	21	30—N.Y. Jets	14
19—Chicago	23	20—Los Angeles	14
16—St. Louis	13	34—Buffalo	0
20—Philadelphia	7	24—Pittsburgh	21
13—Washington	0	17—Baltimore	14
28—Los Angeles	21	34—Chicago	3
52—N.Y. Jets	10	13—New England	34
42—N.Y. Giants	14	3—Baltimore	14
31—St. Louis	12	27—Green Bay	6
20—Minnesota	12	27—Kansas City	24
14—San Francisco	3	21—Baltimore	0
440	237	363	198

Dallas Routs Miami in Super Bowl, 24–3

By WILLIAM N. WALLACE

NEW ORLEANS, *Jan. 16*—The Dallas Cowboys completed the trip to a Super Bowl championship today, a voyage they had begun but never finished five straight times before. The Cowboys were methodical and merciless as they turned back the Miami Dolphins, 24–3, in what amounted to a rout.

The margin of victory, 21 points, was 4 points fewer than in Green Bay's 35–10 triumph over the Kansas City Chiefs in the first Super Bowl game five years ago. But the manner in which the result was achieved today proved more decisive than any of the previous Super Bowl contests, the National Football League's championship event.

Dallas missed a fourth touchdown by a yard with two minutes to play when Calvin Hill fumbled on the Miami 1-yard line. It was the only mistake of the game for the winners.

The Dolphins, meanwhile, were guilty of two fumbles and one interception, which helped the Cowboys to score 10 points.

Dallas had qualified for the N.F.L. playoffs every year since 1966 but never before had won a championship, coming close a year ago when the Cowboys lost the Super Bowl in Miami to the Baltimore Colts in the last five seconds, 16–13.

They looked like winners all the way on this cold afternoon (39 degrees) in Tulane Stadium before a crowd of 81,023. The Cowboys established and maintained a crushing ground-gaining game, which the coaches, Tom Landry of Dallas and Don Shula of Miami, had said would be the key to the contest. Both were right.

But the Cowboys had the running game and the Dolphins did not. Duane Thomas gained 95 yards, with one touchdown, and Walt Garrison 74 as Dallas ran for 252 yards, a Super Bowl record. Miami managed only 80 yards, 40 each for Jim Kiick and Larry Csonka.

Said Landry afterward: "I can't describe how we feel. We fought so hard, came so close so many times. It's great for players like Bob Lilly and Chuck Howley who have been with the team for so long."

Lilly and Howley were stalwarts on defense, Howley intercepting Bob Griese's pass in the fourth quarter. The 35-year-old linebacker, who joined the Cowboys with Lilly in 1961, ran the ball back 40 yards to the Miami 10 and three plays later Mike Ditka scored from the 7 on a pass from Roger Staubach. That was the final score of the game.

Staubach, who became a regular only last October, was singled out by Sport magazine as the outstanding player and he will receive a new automobile as a prize. It was a reasonable choice but Sport might easily have given away 40 cars to all 40 Cowboys.

Staubach, the 29-year-old one-time Naval Academy hero and Navy lieutenant, was confused in the early going. But he settled down and threw two touchdown passes that were impeccable.

The first came 75 seconds before the half-time intermission with the ball on the Miami 7, first down. Lance Alworth, the wide receiver, went down into the corner where there was almost no room. He was also guarded by Curtis Johnson, the Dolphin cornerback.

Staubach drilled his pass to Alworth, who made a quick grab at chest-level and stepped into the end zone for a touchdown. Johnson had no chance to bat the ball away. That touchdown gave Dallas a 10–0 lead because Mike Clark had kicked a 9-yard field goal in the first quarter.

Miami came back and Garo Yepremian, the little Cypriot soccer-style kicker, booted a 31-yard field goal 4 seconds before the half ended for the Dolphins' only points.

As the second half began with Miami behind by a touchdown, there was still a chance for an exciting game worth the huge Super Bowl promotion. The Cowboys were not interested in excitement.

They received the kickoff and smashed 71 yards in eight plays for a decisive touchdown. Hill, in relief of Thomas, caught a swing pass for 12 yards but all the other plays were blasting runs: Thomas for 7, Thomas for 23, Bob Hayes for 15 on an end-round play and finally Thomas for 3 and into the end zone. The lead became 17–3.

The Cowboy offensive line, led by John Niland and Blaine Nye, the guards, blocked decisively. Seldom seen was Nick Buoniconti, the Dolphin middle linebacker, the key man of their defense and a particular Cowboy target.

"The drive that started the second half killed us," said Bill Stanfill, the Miami defensive end.

Also in trouble was Griese, the Dolphin quarterback who won so many honors this season. Griese could never get anything going and wound up with 12 pass completions in 23 attempts for only a net of 104 yards. He tried to scramble once in the first quarter and went back and back, finally tackled by Lilly and Larry Cole for a 29-yard loss at his 11.

Staubach, by contrast, completed 12 of 19 passes for 119 yards but said: "When the Cowboys run, everything else opens up. I guess I gave Coach Landry a few gray hairs at the beginning when I didn't see open receivers."

Shula may have had the last word. He said: "We played poorly. Dallas played a near-perfect game."

Super Bowl Scoring

Dallas Cowboys	3	7	7	7—	24
Miami Dolphins	0	3	0	0—	3

Dal.—FG, Clark, 9.
Dal.—Alworth, 7, pass from Staubach (Clark, kick).
Mia.—FG, Yepremian, 31.
Dal.—Thomas, 3, run (Clark, kick).
Dal.—Ditka, 7, pass from Staubach (Clark, kick).

Individual Statistics

RUSHES—Dal.: D. Thomas, 19 for 95 yards; Garrison, 14 for 74; Hill, 7 for 25; Staubach, 5 for 18; Hayes, 1 for 16; Reeves, 1 for 7; Ditka, 1 for 17. Mia.: Csonka, 9 for 40; Kiick, 7 for 40; Griese, 1 for 0.

PASSES—Dal.: Staubach, 12 of 19 for 119 yards. Mia.: Griese, 12 of 23 for 134.

RECEPTIONS—Dal.: D. Thomas, 3 for 17; Alworth, 2 for 28; Ditka, 2 for 28; Hayes, 2 for 23; Garrison, 2 for 11; Hill, 1 for 12. Mia.: Warfield, 4 for 39; Kiick, 3 for 21; Csonka, 2 for 18; Fleming, 1 for 27; Twilley, 1 for 20; Mandich, 1 for 9. Attendance—81,023.

Statistics of the Game

	Cowboys	Dolph.		Cowboys	Dolph.
First downs	23	10	Interceptions by	1	0
Rushing yardage	48-252	20-80	Punts	5-37	5-40
Passing yardage	119	134	Fumbles lost	1	2
Passes	12-19	12-23	Yards penalized	15	0

Sports of The Times

What Do They Do Now, Mr. President?

By RED SMITH

NEW ORLEANS, *Jan. 16*—On the Miami Dolphins' eighth play from scrimmage, Paul Dryden Warfield ran a down-and-in pattern from his wide flanker position, and history quivered in the throes of creation. Lee Roy Jordan, the Dallas Cowboys' middle linebacker, was helping Mel Renfro cover Miami's gifted receiver as Bob Griese cocked his throwing arm. The pass was high. Warfield leapt, but could only wave at the ball.

At least one fan, sitting in statesman-like comfort far from the bitter chill of Tulane Stadium, must have regarded the television screen with a disappointed frown.

"I think you can hit Warfield on a down-and-in pattern," the fan named Richard M. Nixon had told Don Shula, the Miami coach, after the Dolphins qualified to represent the American Conference in the playoff for the professional football championship of this mercenary world. Now it turned out that the fan could be mistaken like anybody else.

Indeed, it turned out that the fan had erred in more than one respect. He had not told Shula what to do about Roger Staubach, the Cowboy with the squirrel-rifle arm. He had set up no adequate defense against the rushes of Duane Thomas, Walt Garrison and Calvin Hill, who operated like infuriated beer trucks. He had prescribed no antidote for the violence of the Dallas offensive linemen, who charged like wounded water buffalo all afternoon, blasting avenues through the Miami defenses.

Due in part to these errors of omission, Super Bowl VI was a sorry letdown for at least half of the 81,023 witnesses present. Most of them—sharing the mistaken notion of Pete Rozelle, pro football's supreme being, that New Orleans was in the "warm weather"—had come poorly prepared for this day's windy 39 degrees. Physically miserable, they were not warmed spiritually by the competition, for as the game progressed it became almost as unhappy a mismatch as the Joe Frazier-Terry Daniels fist fight here last night.

Coming through at last after making a five-year career of failure in the big games, the Cowboys led all the way in this 24–3 romp, setting Super Bowl records with rushing gains of 252 yards and 23 first downs.

Not only did they muffle Coach Nixon's big weapon; they turned another of his favorite tactics to their own use.

During the regular season, the White House strategist urged George Allen, coach of the Washington Redskins, to use Roy Jefferson on a flanker reverse, sometimes described as the end-around play. Allen did, and Jefferson lost 13 yards. Today with the Cowboys leading, 10–3, Staubach used his wide receiver, Bob Hayes, on precisely that play, then Hayes swept 15 yards to the Miami 6-yard line. Two plays later Thomas raced on a stuttering slant into the end zone, and the game was out of the Dolphins' reach.

In the Dolphins' nomenclature, there is no such thing as a down-and-in pattern, but they do have two passes answering that description. On one, which they call simply a "slant," the receiver runs straight downfield 8 or 10 yards, then breaks toward the middle. On the other, called a "post pattern," the receiver goes deep and angles toward the goalposts.

Presumably it was the latter which the Machiavelli of Pennsylvania Avenue had in mind. The Dolphins never did make it work with Warfield.

That incomplete pass for Miami's eighth play was on the short slant pattern from Warfield's usual position far out on the left flank. The next time Griese threw his way, Warfield had started downfield and veered out toward the sideline. That pass was too high also, which was just as well politically. Herb Klein, of the White House staff, observed in a speech in Hot Springs, Ark., yesterday that no politician sensitive to economic issues would ever call a down-and-out.

Warfield went back to the short slant toward the middle, and for the third time the pass was too high for him. Not until his fourth attempt did he catch the ball, and that was in the flat zone for a 5-yard gain.

Late in the second quarter Warfield lined up in "slot left" formation (5 yards inside the wide receiver). He raced downfield, threw in a little sidestep, and clutched a pass on the Dallas 24. The gain put the Dolphins in position for their only score, on Garo Yepremian's field goal.

Minutes after the game ended, the telephone rang in the winners' dressing room. It was Washington calling. "He commented on every phase of the game," said Tom Landry, the Dallas coach. "He singled out our offensive line for praise. He said we played almost a perfect game."

How about the down-and-in pattern?

"He didn't mention it," Landry said.

Warfield Says Cowboys Closed Off
Nixon's Down-and-In Pass

Foe 'Made Sure' Play Would Be Checked by
Shifting Defense

NEW ORLEANS, *Jan. 16*—In his stoical manner Paul Warfield contended today that the Dallas Cowboys' pass defense had been committed to stopping the down-and-in pattern that President Nixon suggested to Coach Don Shula of the Dolphins nearly two weeks ago.

"They had two weeks to prepare," the Dolphins' star wide receiver said. "And they made sure that under any circumstances we wouldn't be able to catch that pass."

Warfield recognized the Cowboys' emphasis on that pattern in the early moments of the Super Bowl game. As he lined up against Mel Renfro, the Cowboy cornerback covering him, he noticed that Cornell Green, the Cowboys' strongside safetyman, had remained deep.

"In the films we'd seen," Warfield explained, "that safetyman normally moved up to shut off the run, leaving an open area downfield. Not so for us. When he saw me split out to the left, he backed up and turned in toward me, closing off that area to me."

If the game had been closer, he said, the Dolphins might have been able to exploit that type of Cowboy defense.

"But we were so far behind," he explained, "we couldn't do much. But next time they'll get a chance to see it.

"We made more errors, that's all," he said. "But we're capable of coming back next year and being in this game because we've been here and we have a good young club."

Warfield nearly scored when a deflected pass bounced off him near the goal line with the Cowboys leading, 10–0, late in the first half. Moments later the Dolphins settled for a 31-yard field goal.

"I couldn't do anything with that ball," he explained. "Sometimes a tipped ball will flutter up, but that one turned quickly and took off into my face. I'd need hands like Brooks Robinson to catch that one."

Among the Dolphin mistakes was Larry Csonka's first fumble after 248 plays in which he had handled the ball flawlessly—235 rushing attempts, 13 pass receptions.

"It was a bad exchange between Bob [Griese] and myself," Csonka said.

"They shut off our running backs," Griese said. "We worked hard all year. This is a disappointment, but we can come back."

Shula, now the only coach to have lost two Super Bowl games, was depressed.

"I'm very disappointed," said the coach who was with the Baltimore

Colts when they were upset by the New York Jets, 16–7, in Super Bowl III. "The Cowboys tore us apart defensively. They made one mistake, a fumble, but after the game was over.

"The only way we can make up for it is to win the Super Bowl another time. Winning 'x' number of games won't make up for this."

For Landry, Frustration Runs Out After 12 Years

NEW ORLEANS, *Jan. 16*—For the Dallas Cowboys, all their seasons of frustration appeared today to make their Super Bowl triumph more worth while.

"This," said Clint Murchison, their millionaire owner, "is the successful end to our 12-year plan."

Born in 1960, the Cowboys lost the Super Bowl game to the Baltimore Colts last year, lost to the Cleveland Browns in National Football League playoff games in both 1969 and 1968, and lost N.F.L. championship games to the Green Bay Packers in 1967 and 1966. But now, next year's champions, as they've been branded, are this year's champions.

"I feel like I lost two years off my age," said Bob Lilly, their all-N.F.L. defensive tackle. "I feel 29 again."

Three key members of the Dallas Super Bowl VI winners, Bob Hayes (22), Rayfield Wright (70) and Mel Renfro (20) run in front of jubilant coach Tom Landry as he is carried from the field.
WIDE WORLD PHOTOS

Landry Salutes Pair

Tom Landry, the coach of the Cowboys throughout their 12 seasons, mentioned Lilly and Chuck Howley, the aging linebacker, among the players for whom he was delighted after so much toil.

Landry, who often relies on clichés, credited "over-all determination" for the Cowboys' 24–3 triumph.

"We were all so determined, no one could stop us," Landry said. "We ran extremely well, and I've always felt that if you can run on a team, you can beat that team. This is especially true when you have the great defense we have, which we proved again today."

Roger Staubach, the quarterback, ignored bruised ribs.

Time Heals Wounds

"I've got a long time to heal," Staubach said. "Winning the Super Bowl is everything an athlete wants. The Dolphins played a zone and double-teamed our wide receivers."

Staubach, as usual, had the plays called by Landry, who shuttled tight ends with his selections.

"I'm going to study films more than ever," Staubach said, "but it will probably be hard to convince Coach Landry to let me call the plays after we won 10 in a row with him calling them."

As Mates Roar, Thomas Stings and Floats

By DAVE ANDERSON

NEW ORLEANS, *Jan. 16*—After so many years of frustration, the Dallas Cowboys were celebrating. One of their players yanked Gil Brandt, the personnel director, by the collar and tossed him, along with the silver Super Bowl trophy, under one of the shower sprays.

But nearby, Duane Thomas watched in silence as he sprinkled himself with Johnson's Baby Powder.

Thomas, the Cowboys' leading runner with 95 yards in 19 attempts, has resembled a Trappist monk in his relations with newsmen and even with some teammates throughout the season. And now, the first Cowboy out of the shower, he remained in the character he has formed.

"Got something to say?" he was asked.

Thomas looked up and smiled, but that was all.

"You've got a shot at the car."

He appeared bewildered at the reference to Sport magazine's annual award of a Dodge Charger to the game's outstanding player.

"I don't know what you're talking about," he said.

When it was explained to him, he stared silently. Suddenly, he said,

"Pardon me," and, half-dressed, he hurried through the shower room. Moments later, Roger Staubach was announced as the winner of the auto. And soon Thomas returned to resume dressing.

"You're like a guy landing on the moon," somebody said.

Thomas looked up quickly and said, "You been there?"

"Are you going to play in the Pro Bowl game next week?"

"Yeah," he replied softly. "Excuse me, I have to go up front a moment."

He disappeared through the steam in the shower room again.

Thomas later reappeared atop an equipment trunk where Tom Brookshier, the TV announcer, was interviewing players. With the Cowboy running back was Jim Brown, the Hall of Fame runner for the Cleveland Browns, who is now a motion-picture actor. He also has been Thomas's adviser this season. During the interview, Brookshier mentioned that Thomas must be faster than he appears to be.

"Evidently," the bearded Thomas replied.

Moments later, Thomas and Brown sat together for several minutes in a quiet area of the trainer's room. Their conversation over, another newsman cornered the Cowboy star.

"Are you happy?" the newsman asked him.

"I never said I was sad," Thomas said.

Brown has predicted that sometime soon, Thomas "will open up and talk" but for now, Thomas preferred virtual silence.

"Duane's his own man," Brown said. "He's one of the greatest backs who ever lived. He should get more money."

If he does, his teammates won't resent it.

"If I can be so forward to say it, I love Duane Thomas," said John Niland, the Cowboy guard from Amityville, L. I. "I love him as a football player and I loved him as a human being. In this life you don't find many men who give 110 per cent of themselves on the football field, or in any other field.

"I like to communicate with him. Of course, the answers he gives me are two, three words but I can see something in his eyes when he responds.

"You don't make all-pro with blocks in the line. You make all-pro leading a guy like Duane Thomas on the field. Whether you make the block or not, he makes the play for you with his running. The music was out there today. You execute because the blockers and the running backs hear the music together."

And with the music, there is blood sometimes. Niland's neck was bloodied from a bruise. Thomas had bloody scratches on his hands and arms. Walt Garrison, another running back, was spitting blood.

"Our line was leading us," Garrison said. "Our line was making their defensive linemen take a side. That's all you want them to do, and then you go to the daylight. You get a feeling in the first part of the game that you can run. No reason to quit something that's going good for you. You keep doing it."

He excused himself and moved toward the trainer's room.

"Let me go get this blood out of my mouth," he said. "I been swallowing a bunch of it."

Sports of The Times
Hot Off the Bench

By ARTHUR DALEY

NEW ORLEANS, *Jan. 17*—For the last half-dozen years there was a strong belief in many areas that the Dallas Cowboys were the best team in football. But no one could prove it because the bottom kept falling out of every argument since the team from Texas lost each convincer. On at least two occasions the frustration struck in closing seconds and Dallas was labeled a choke-up club that folded under pressure. It now is obvious that the reason for Dallas failure in the past was that it didn't have a quarterback with the total skills to direct it to the big one. But the Cowboys have one now in Roger Staubach. He is a dandy, a rather extraordinary individual who overcame huge odds even to gain his first-string job and then wound up as the most valuable player in the game. In the Super Bowl a year ago, Staubach didn't see action for even one play. Tom Landry, the Cowboy coach, was not ready to trust the destinies of his team to a man of such limited experience. So he went with Craig Morton, who made it close and that doesn't count. It was so close that Dallas was beaten by Baltimore, 16–13, on a field goal in the final seconds.

Staubach did so slick a quarterbacking job in yesterday's Super Bowl, however, that he left the Miami Dolphins gasping for air. He completed 12 of 19 passes for 119 yards and two touchdowns. He manipulated a running game that rolled up a record 252 yards. He was the main architect in the convincing 24–3 Cowboy success. That's not bad for last year's bench-warmer.

Differing Opinions

What kind of game was the production billed in fancy Roman numerals as Super Bowl VI? Miami fans thought it was a dull game. Dallas followers thought it was a great one. It was neither. I thought it was a highly interesting affair that held a strange fascination because there was so much flawless play by the Cowboy team.

I've never been able to resist perfection in sports, anyway. The greatest football game I ever saw was the 73–0 massacre of the Washington Redskins by the Chicago Bears in their unforgettable championship some three decades ago. These were such evenly matched teams that they had played a 7–3 game a fortnight earlier. But this time the Bears knocked out the hyphen and the Redskins in an exquisite display of absolute perfection.

The Cowboys were nowhere nearly that perfect against the Dolphins but they had many moments when they brushed against perfection and most teams will settle for that. Both Landry and his opposite number, Don Shula, had been repeating the same observation all week: the team that establishes its running game will win.

That's what Dallas did. And the Cowboy defenders, using zone blocking to shut off Miami slants into the line, clamped down heavily on Larry Csonka and Jim Kiick, the bulldozing pair with the ground-gaining leadership of their conference. They were contained to 40 yards each.

But Duane Thomas, the fast-moving sphinx from Dallas, carried messages with his twinkling feet. He gained more than both of them combined and was the ideal foil for Walt Garrison's slashes up the middle and Staubach's accurate passing. The on-the-target connections came later, after Roger had settled down. Staubach has most football observers baffled anyway, somewhat beyond the comprehension of most of them. Few believed that he could overcome the insuperable handicaps that faced him.

He was graduated from the Naval Academy at Annapolis, won the Heisman Trophy and signed with the Cowboys—for future delivery. Then he served four years in the service.

"Whenever possible," he said, "I ran and kept in training every day while I was in the Navy. This is what I was looking forward to. This is what I wanted to prove to myself."

Like Bill Bradley of the New York Knicks, he didn't have to engage in professional sports. But each loved the game and each went for the challenge. Each succeeded and each is a straight arrow, the tag Princetonians hung on Bradley to signify he was a pillar of rectitude and dedication.

Unfortunately, Roger the Dodger is approaching his 30th birthday, even though he has barely left the rookie category. But he thinks that he can go for another eight or nine years. If so, the Cowboys are in good shape, although only an overenthusiast would describe the situation as the start of a dynasty.

There were 81,023 customers at Super Bowl VI and except for the local gentry all others had to think how much better off they would have been in Miami where the temperature was in the 70's. Here it was a miserable 39 degrees and the facilities are wretched. But there is hope for the future. A domed stadium soon will be built and so will a huge new hotel. New Orleans has not been "a warm-weather site" in either of its Super Bowl offerings. Under the dome it won't matter.

At last the football season is virtually over and another Super Bowl game drops unostentatiously into a collection that has had few of the spectacular. The first truly great game of Super Bowl history has yet to be played.

Chapter 7

Super Bowl VII—1973

Super Bowl VII had something—going in—that none of its prede-cessors had and that none of its successors might have: an undefeated team.

The Miami Dolphins, losers of Super Bowl VI, had not lost since. This simple competitive fact brought a dimension to the game that no amount of artificial ballyhoo could ever match.

But there were other fascinating features, as well. The party of the other part, the Washington Redskins, had an exceptionally colorful history and cast. The site was again Los Angeles, where it had all began, in the Coliseum on the University of Southern California cam-pus, and the issue of sellout-vs.-television blackout was still unresolved. And the President of the United States, a football fan of unparalleled knowledge and intensity among White House occupants, had strong personal interest in both teams: the Redskins were his "home" team and the Dolphins were his "Florida home" team.

And for the first time since Vince Lombardi, the personalities of the coaches overshadowed the players. In the last four years the spot-light had been on Namath, Dawson, Morrall and Unitas, on Staubach and Thomas and the Dallas line, on Minnesota's defense. Now no player matched the status of Don Shula, who had built up the Dolphins so quickly but who was still the only coach ever to lose two Super Bowls; and certainly no player's public image matched that of George Allen, whose avowed dedication to victory at any price made Lombardi seem unmotivated by comparison.

As a super-production, in the show-business sense surrounding the game itself, Super Bowl VII surpassed the rest. It was approaching that fate of all super-productions, parody of itself. As a struggle for a championship, it would have been perfectly respectable but hardly stirring if Miami had arrived with even one defeat on its record. But the Dolphins were shooting for that mark of perfection that only football teams can dream about (since baseball and basketball and hockey teams play too many games to ever go undefeated), and that gave Super Bowl VII competitive purity (or at least an extra dimen-sion) that no previous game had.

Nixon Pledges Allegiance to Redskins

By DAVE ANDERSON

Jan. 1, 1973—President Nixon pledged allegiance yesterday to the Washington Redskins in the Super Bowl game against the Miami Dolphins, his choice a year ago.

George Allen, the Redskins' coach, and his family visited the White House to receive the President's personal congratulations. The invitation was extended during Mr. Nixon's congratulatory telephone call to Allen Sunday night after the Redskins had defeated the Dallas Cowboys, 26–3, thereby qualifying to oppose the Dolphins for the National Football League title at Los Angeles Jan. 14.

"I always root for the home team," the President told Allen. "And my home now is in Washington."

He also said, according to Allen, that "I'm a part-time resident of Florida and have a great deal of respect for the Dolphins," a reference to his Key Biscayne home. He did not phone Don Shula, the Dolphins' coach, as he did a year ago, when the Miami team qualified.

"I guess the President has changed sides," Shula said by phone from Miami. A year ago, Shula recalled, "he told me, 'Now, you understand that I'm a Washington Redskin fan, but I'm a part-time resident of Miami and I've been following the Dolphins real close.' "

In that call the President suggested a play for the Dolphins—a pass to Paul Warfield, the wide receiver, on a "down and in" pattern. The play never worked when the Dolphins lost to the Cowboys, 24–3, in the Super Bowl at New Orleans.

No mention was made yesterday of the President's having suggested any plays to Allen.

Mr. Nixon gave Allen a pin with the Presidential seal, and a letter to Billy Kilmer, the Redskins' quarterback. Both the pin and letter were for Kilmer's 13-year-old daughter, Kathy, who has cerebral palsy. She is a resident of Azusa, Calif.

Virtually all of the President's conversation with Allen was confidential. Newsmen were not permitted to ask questions.

Perhaps because of a common background, Mr. Nixon's interest in the Redskins has been intense since Allen took over the team in 1971. The President is a graduate of Whittier College in California, where Allen coached for six years (1951–1956).

When Allen quickly created a controversy with several major trades, dealing Redskin draft choices for experienced players, the President commented:

"I am betting on the Redskins for the championship in 1971 or 1972."

During the 1971 season, the President once visited the Redskins' practice complex in Virginia. In the club office is a color photo of the President and Allen on the practice field that day, with this inscription:

"To George Allen—with respect and admiration for his leadership, and with personal wishes. Richard Nixon."

The President suggested a play to Allen before the Redskins' 24–20 loss to the San Francisco 49ers in the 1971 National Conference playoffs. His choice was a reverse, with Roy Jefferson, a wide receiver, used as a ball carrier. The play lost 13 yards.

A week ago Mr. Nixon phoned Allen after the Redskins' 16–3 victory over the Green Bay Packers in their playoff opener.

"No, he didn't mention any plays," Allen said, smiling, in answer to a question about that phone call.

Accompanying the coach to the White House yesterday were his wife, Etty; their children, George, 20; Gregg, 20; Bruce, 16, and Jennifer, 11, and Mrs. Allen's parents, Mr. and Mrs. Felix Lumbrosso of Paris.

After the visit Allen returned to his suburban home to view films of the victory in the National Conference championship game and to watch the college bowl games on television.

He granted his staff of nine assistants a day off, their first since the Redskins opened training camp at Carlisle, Pa., nearly six months ago.

Preparations for the Super Bowl will begin today when the Redskins will know more about the condition of Terry Hermeling, the offensive tackle with a damaged left knee. He had to be helped off the field Sunday.

Allen's Gang Is Not So Over the Hill

By WILLIAM N. WALLACE

Jan. 2, 1973—Every pro football fan knows that after George Allen became head coach of the Washington Redskins early in 1971 he traded away his future draft choices for older players and in two seasons took the team, which he named "The Over The Hill Gang," to the Super Bowl. That is the myth. But of the players who will start at the 22 positions (plus two kickers for 24) for Washington in the Super Bowl on Jan. 14 against Miami, 16 of them joined the Redskins before Allen arrived. Fifteen had been regulars at one time or another during the 1969 and 1970 seasons when Vince Lombardi and Bill Austin were in charge.

Furthermore, the Redskins are not that old. The average age of the regulars is 28.8 years or only 1.2 over the average for the entire National Football League.

Therefore, Allen deserves credit not so much for his trades of draft choices but for taking the inherited talent and making winners out of them, big winners.

•

Of the George Allen Redskins, some like Billy Kilmer, are especially significant. Kilmer, the 32-year-old quarterback, was the first player Allen obtained by trade, from New Orleans for a fourth and eighth round draft choice plus Tom Roussel, a reserve linebacker. But Kilmer became the regular again this season only after Sonny Jurgensen ruptured his Achilles tendon.

The only other Allen acquisitions on offense are Roy Jefferson, the wide receiver, and John Wilbur, the guard. Following a 1971 contract dispute the Colts traded Jefferson for a first-round draft choice and a wide receiver, Cotton Speyrer. Wilbur came from the Rams in the famous deal involving seven players and eight draft choices on Jan. 28, 1971.

All the other offensive regulars were holdovers from the 1970 teams, including Terry Hermeling, the young tackle who became a regular for the first time this season. Hermeling tore a ligament in his left knee during the National Convention playoff victory over Dallas and is a questionable starter for the Super Bowl.

The defensive unit was the inspiration for "The Over The Hill Gang" label because Allen did trade for such highly visible players as Ron McDole, 32 years old; Jack Pardee, 36, and Roosevelt Taylor, 34. But two other Allen imports, Verlon Biggs and Diron Talbert, are still under 30 and two more, Myron Pottios, 33, and Richie Petitbon, 34, were displaced as regulars this season.

The accompanying Washington depth charts for the past four seasons, with the ages of the present team in parentheses, show that seven of the 12 defensive regulars are longtime Redskins and of those only one, Chris Hanburger, is past 30.

Over the hill?

Redskin Depth Chart, Last 4 Years

1969 W-7 L-5 T-2		1970 W-6 L-8 T-0	
Coach—Vince Lombardi		Coach—Bill Austin	
Offensive Alignments	**Defensive Alignments**	**Offensive Alignments**	**Defensive Alignments**
WR—Taylor	DE—Hoffman	WR—Taylor	DE—Carroll
Long	Kammerer	Roberts	Anderson
TE—J. Smith	DT—Peters	TE—J. Smith	DT—Brundige
OT—Snowden	Putgens	OT—Snowden	Bosch
Rock	LB—Roussell	Rock	LB—McLinton
G—Schoenke	Huff	G—Schoenke	McKeever
Promuto	Hanburger	Laaveg	Hanburger
C—Hauss	CB—Fischer	C—Hauss	CB—Fischer
QB—Jurgensen	Bass	QB—Jurgensen	Bass
RB—L. Brown	S—Harris	RB—L. Brown	S—Harris
Harraway	Owens	Harraway	Owens
K—Knight	P—Bragg	K—Knight	P—Bragg

Redskin Depth Chart, Last 4 Years (*continued*)

1971 W-9 L-4 T-1
Coach—George Allen

1972 W-11 L-3 T-0
Coach—George Allen

Offensive Alignments	Defensive Alignments	Offensive Alignments *(Ages in parentheses)*	Defensive Alignments
WR—Taylor*	DE—McDole	WR—C. Taylor (30)	DE—McDole (32)
McNeil	Biggs	Jefferson (28)	Biggs (29)
Jefferson	DT—Sistrunk	TE—J. Smith (29)	DT—Brundige (24)
TE—J. Smith	Talbert	OT—Hermel'g (26)	Talbert (28)
OT—Snowden	LB—Pardee	Rock (30)	LB—Pardee (36)
Rock	Pottios	G—Laaveg (24)	McLinton (25)
G—Schoenke	Hanburger	Wilbur (29)	Hanburger (31)
Wilbur	CB—Fischer	C—Hauss (30)	CB—Fischer (32)
C—Hauss	Bass	QB—Kilmer (32)	Bass (27)
QB—Kilmer	S—Petitbon	Jurg'sen (38)	S—R. Taylor (34)
Jurgensen*	Owens	RB—L. Brown (25)	Owens (29)
RB—L. Brown	P—Bragg	Harraway (27)	P—Bragg (25)
Harraway		K—Knight (29)	
K—Knight			

*Injured.

Sports of The Times

Case of the Regenerated Quarterback

By ARTHUR DALEY

Jan. 3, 1973—The natives were restless in the early part of the season. They were grumbling because George Allen, their genius coach, persisted in starting Billy Kilmer at quarterback over their long-time pet, Sonny Jurgensen. Although the Redskin fans conceded that this had been proper enough during the previous year when Jurgy was injured, they vehemently insisted that Jurgy's return to health had robbed this concept of all validity. With bumper stickers and other evidences of displeasure, they demanded the return of Christian Adolph Jurgensen 3d. Allen made the switch from Kilmer to Jurgy when he thought the time was right for it, not because of any public pressures. That he scorns. It almost seemed that Sonny hardly had had time to unlimber his throwing arm when he ripped an Achilles tendon, finishing him not only for the season but also perhaps for keeps.

Back into action again moved Kilmer, the not-too-stylish quarterback. Some of his passes follow the wobbly pattern of a loaf of bread thrown by your maiden aunt at the church strawberry festival. But he still does the job so well that he ranks as the No. 1 passer in his conference. More important still, he has guided the Redskins into the Super Bowl date with the Miami Dolphins a week from Sunday.

A Giant Gift

Although New York Giant fans would be unlikely to remember a somewhat ancient sequence of events, they should make grateful bows in Kilmer's direction for having nudged Y. A. Tittle all the way from San Francisco to New York. Three divisional championships and playoff berths came to the Giants with Tittle. In slightly left-handed fashion Kilmer was responsible for such benisons.

When William Lorland Kilmer, now 33 years old, was a shiny-eyed triple-threat halfback at U.C.L.A. in 1960, he led the nation in total offense as a runner and passer. At about the same time Red Hickey, coach of the San Francisco 49ers, was either experimenting or about to experiment with a radical new strategic concept.

It was known as the shotgun offense and was spun from the spread formation with the deep back taking a direct pass from center. Then he ran or passed. It was not used all the time, but as an alternate formation to the regular T. It drove the other teams crazy. At least it did in the beginning.

The 49ers then had three quarterbacks. Kilmer was the new eager-beaver and No. 1 draft choice. John Brodie had been around four or five years. Tittle had lasted for 10. The ideal man for the shotgun was Kilmer, an excellent ball carrier and an adequate passer. Brodie was so-so. He ran reluctantly and not well, but he passed beautifully. Tittle was hopeless. He couldn't outrun his own grandmother, but was a marvel at guiding a team from the pure T formation.

If the shotgun tossed enemy coaches into total confusion when it was first used, the condition was not permanent. They are too smart. Once they had studied the mechanics of it and figured out what made it tick, they destroyed it. Have you seen any shotgun offenses lately?

But while San Francisco's shotgun was glistening like a new toy, the board of strategy assayed the collection of quarterbacks. Kilmer, the ideal man, had to stay. So did the solid Brodie. But Tittle was 35 years old and expendable. He went to the Giants, took a plunge into the fountain of youth and finished his career with such a magnificent flourish that he didn't stop until he was in the pro football Hall of Fame at Canton, Ohio. He can write a thank-you note to Billy Kilmer for that one.

Now it is Kilmer who is the old pro, and no more professional job could have been done than the one he turned in last Sunday during the elimination from the Super Bowl of the Dallas Cowboys, the defending champions. He just whipsawed the Cowboys into their 26–3 defeat just as he had demolished the Green Bay Packers the week before.

Kilmer has been something of an itinerant quarterback whose luck has not always been the best. Early in his career he was in an automobile accident that almost cost him a leg. He missed one entire season, played sporadically in the next and not at all in the one after that. It was when he was with New Orleans later that he caught Allen's eye.

"He was just tough and never quit," said Allen, making Kilmer the first man picked in his multifarious trades that were swung in the rebuilding of the Redskins. It was to be a key selection. When Washington achieved the Super Bowl assignment, that proved it.

Super Bowl Rivals Emphasize Spiritual Values; Prayer Is Given Much Credit for Their Success

MIAMI, *Jan. 4*—Washington had just trounced Dallas for the National Football Conference championship and the victors were clomping into the dressing room. Television viewers across the nation braced for the postgame melée, but that's not what they saw.

Instead, at the whispered-tone bidding of Coach George Allen and following shouts of "Let's pray, let's pray," the Redskins got down on their knees and said thanks to God for the victory. They were led by a black evangelist, Tom Skinner, identified by Allen as the "team chaplain."

The television scene last Sunday was a startling contrast to the champagne celebration of most other championship locker rooms, but it was indicative of a spiritual element that figures to be a big part of this year's Super Bowl.

Battle of Families

"I think the game this year is unique in that you've got the two teams that most simulate the family relationship," said Loren Young, national director for special programs of the Fellowship of Christian Athletes, who has many personal friends on both teams.

Jack Pardee, Redskin linebacker, alluded to his team's thinking in a postgame interview when he said, "We don't care who scores—the offense or the defense—just so we score. We're a community."

The Dolphins have a similar feeling about each other, although they haven't voiced it on television.

Rabbi Solomon Schiff, one of the several Miami clergymen who alternately travel with the Dolphins, says many players have confided in him a feeling of "something beyond themselves," generated by a togetherness they share.

"Maybe it's because I'm a rabbi, but invariably the conversation turns to what is making them as good as they are, and they say that when they get down on that field and line up some sort of an outside force seems to be there and give them the edge."

Prayers Before Games

Not every Dolphin or Redskin goes to church, but a good many do. The Dolphin managing general partner, Joe Robbie, an active Catholic layman, says a majority of players attend services instituted for players before every game.

"People in intense competition look outside themselves for the maximum effort," says Robbie. "I saw this in World War II. You know the saying, 'There are no atheists in foxholes.' These players are competing for enormous stakes. They're up against the very best."

Skinner, a former ghetto gang leader who now heads a large evangelistic association in New York City, says 85 percent of the Redskins attend the voluntary services before games. "I think that's about the highest attendance of any club," he added.

Team members and observers alike say the most important factor contributing to the spirit on both teams has been the head coaches.

'Singleness of Purpose'

"Shula and Allen are different types," says Young, who knows each well. "But both exude this singleness of purpose—an intensity that they're all for their players. It enables them to somehow pull the best out of their men.

"I think it was Lombardi who said the X and O boys are a dime a dozen but the spiritual motivators are hard to find. When they come along, grab on."

Shula and Allen are Catholics and Shula attends mass almost every morning.

The Dolphins are the only National Football League team that has a public prayer as part of its pregame activities, according to an N.F.L. information director, Harold Rosenthal. Although the team has a high number of outspoken Christian players, everything is not somber with the team.

Robbie explains that one of the reasons the Dolphins took Archbishop Coleman F. Carroll to Pittsburgh last week was to "pull rank" on Art Rooney's brother, a priest, who usually always is on the Steelers' sideline during the games. Archibishop Carroll is the head of the Miami Archdiocese.

Norm Evans, a Dolphin tackle, recently wrote an autobiography entitled "On God's Squad," which among other things includes the story of his Christian conversion during the Dolphin training camp. Charlie Harraway, a Redskin running back, has written a chapter in "Super Goal," a new book of Christian testaments.

"One of the prerequisites of success is that the players play as a unit," says Robbie, "and the Dolphins are as close as a family. I wouldn't think to say religion is the reason we're in the Super Bowl, but it certainly helps in building a winning attitude."

Sports of The Times
The Star and the Stand-In

By DAVE ANDERSON

Jan. 6, 1973—On the scoreboard at Three Rivers Stadium last Sunday, the Miami Dolphins were leading the Pittsburgh Steelers, 21–17, in the final minutes of the American Conference championship game. In the excitement of their offensive huddle, several Dolphins were babbling suggestions.

"Watch the offside now," one of them was saying.

"Ram the ball down their throats," another said.

Suddenly, above the babble, the firm voice of Bob Griese snapped, "Shut up." With his teammates startled into silence, the quarterback ordered, "Let's get this drive going."

"That's the mark of a leader," Eugene (Mercury) Morris, the running back, said later. "That was his way of telling us to be cool."

"Guys were talking all at once," Larry Csonka, the other running back, explained. "He just said it once, that's all he had to."

And as Bob Griese had commanded, the Dolphins organized a ball-control drive that assured their trip to Los Angeles today for Super Bowl VII there next Sunday against the Washington Redskins. When they go into their first huddle, Bob Griese, although not fully recovered from an ankle injury, will be at quarterback, not Earl Morrall, the 38-year-old savior of their unbeaten record. Behind that decision, and also behind the timing of Griese's insertion last Sunday, is a history lesson from other Super Bowl games, as well as an insight into the coach and the two quarterbacks.

'One More Series'

Deep inside Shula is the memory of Super Bowl III, when his Baltimore Colts lost to the New York Jets, 16–7.

At half-time, the Jets were ahead, 7–0, because Morrall had thrown three interceptions. Despite a sore passing elbow, Johnny Unitas was available, but Shula decided to open the second half with Morrall.

"I wanted to give him one more series," Shula said later.

But on the first play of that series, Tom Matte fumbled, the Jets recovered and quickly added a field goal. Because the fumble had not been Morrall's fault, Shula decided to extend his opportunity, but Morrall couldn't produce a first down. Soon the Jets had another field goal. Unitas took over on the Colts' next series, but too late. When the Jets completed their historic upset, Shula wished he had changed quarterbacks at the half.

In a simlar situation last Sunday, he did.

With the score 7–7 at half-time in the A.F.C. championship game, Shula wasn't about to be trapped into granting Morrall "one more series." Somebody might fumble.

"Are you ready?" the coach asked Griese.

"I'm ready," the quarterback said coolly.

By the time the Dolphins' offensive unit got on the field, the Steelers were ahead, 10–7, but Griese generated two touchdown drives for the victory. The real Dolphin quarterback had returned, the quarterback around whom Shula had sculptured his offense, the quarterback his teammates considered their true leader. With the real Dolphin quarterback available, Shula was committed to naming him as the Super Bowl starter.

It's not the same situation that Tom Landry, the coach of the Dallas Cowboys, was confronted with a week ago when he chose Roger Staubach over Craig Morton as his starter against the Redskins.

By their natures, Staubach and Morton each is a starting quarterback. In the Dolphins' situation, Griese, by his nature, is a starter, a star, but Morrall is a stand-in. Morrall guided the Colts into Super Bowl III as a stand-in for Unitas, the real Colt quarterback. And when Unitas had to be removed from Super Bowl V with battered ribs, the stand-in emerged as the winning quarterback.

'At Our Strongest'

As a starter, Morrall was a losing Super Bowl quarterback. As a stand-in, he was a winning Super Bowl quarterback. And that, surely, is another bit of Super Bowl history that Shula has studied.

By his nature, Morrall is at his best as a stand-in, whether it is over several games or in one game. When it became obvious that Shula had to decide between Griese and Morrall as his Super Bowl starter, the coach didn't dawdle. He named Griese quickly and decisively.

"We're at our strongest going into the game," Shula said, "with Bob Griese as the starter and with Earl Morrall ready if he's needed."

The wisdom of Shula's decision will be determined by the outcome of the game. If the Dolphins win, he can't be wrong. If they lose, he can't be correct. But the logic of his decision, based on history and psychology, is flawless.

Super Bowl Back at Original Site

By BILL BECKER

LOS ANGELES, *Jan. 6*—The Super Bowl returns to its original home, the Los Angeles Memorial Coliseum, next Sunday. The six-year absence seemingly has made a lot of hearts fonder.

The hiatus also points up the expertise and organization the National Football League commissioner's office has built up since Super Bowl I.

That historic game on Jan. 15, 1967, saw Green Bay of the old N.F.L. defeat Kansas City, 35–10, to consummate the first season of marriage between the two pro circuits. However, it was hardly a public relations success hereabouts.

Confronted with the first championship television blackout locally, thousands of fans spent their first Super Sunday watching the game in San Diego, Las Vegas and even Bakersfield. Others just went to the mountains or to the beach. Instead of a sellout, the Coliseum was barely two-thirds full. Attendance was only 61,946.

Now after five years of shuttling between Miami and New Orleans, pro football's super extravaganza has bounced westward with happy results. The Coliseum is a 90,182 sellout for the title match between Washington and Miami—and Super Bowl VII will be seen on local TV as well as across the nation.

Scalpers reportedly are offering end zone seats for $50 apiece and better seats for $75 and $100. The official price for all tickets is $15.

The brisk interest can be attributed largely to the homecoming of sorts, of George Allen and his Redskins. The former Los Angeles coach and a half dozen ex-Rams assure Washington a sizable rooting section here.

Other southern Californians who may be in the stands include President Nixon and Governor Reagan. Both have been invited by Commissioner Pete Rozelle, and probably will accept.

Besides the 90,182 seats at $15 each, space will be provided for 1,100 bandsmen, 150 wheelchair viewers, 2,500 media personnel and 2,000 workers. Bleachers seating 2,640 will be installed at the peristyle (open) end of the Coliseum.

To make those seats worthwhile, the playing field is being shifted 20 yards eastward, Bill Nicholas, the Coliseum manager, says. Eight rows below the press box are being converted for the extra load of sports writers. Four more radio booths are being added on the press box roof.

Television and radio revenues will bring in $2,750,000 plus to N.F.L. coffers; gross ticket sales another $1,350,000.

The participating clubs and players will get at least a fourth of the $4.1 million pot. Each winning share is $15,000; each losing player gets $7,500. All 26 N.F.L. clubs split whatever is left after expenses.

Attention to detail may cement Super Bowl VII as the most successful in the series. Jim Kenzil, assistant to the commissioner, heads the staff of 10, which has been on the scene almost two weeks early. Rozelle will arrive next mid-week.

With the Los Angeles area added, Bob Cochran, N.F.L. broadcast coordinator, predicts TV of Super Bowl VII will be seen by more than 75 million persons. This is based on a record Nielsen rating of nearly 50 per cent of all TV sets in the nation forecast by industry spokesmen.

5,000 Autograph Hunters Force Redskins to Retreat

LOS ANGELES, *Jan. 8*—The Super Bowl hullabaloo began in not-so-blasé Los Angeles with a mob scene today that broke up the Washington Redskins' workout and their availability for 100 photographers and reporters at the photo-media session. Some 5,000 people, the majority males 6 to 16 years old, poured out of the stands at nearby Anaheim Stadium causing the 47 players to retreat and frightening the coach, George Allen.

Once surrounded by pushing youths seeking autographs the players broke off the interviews and ran for their locker room under the stands of this baseball stadium.

In letting the Redskins use the stadium this week to practice for Sunday's game against the Miami Dolphins, the City of Anaheim asked that the public be allowed to attend one session free. But only a handful of guards were provided to control the unruly crowd.

"We need an army for security," said Allen, the cautious coach who so dislikes the unexpected. "I was frightened that they might step on the players and break their legs. It was scary the way they were jumping over the fences. I've lost three hats in the last three weeks."

Earlier in the day, the Dolphins got through their photo-media session without incident, although 200 fans mingled with the press and players at Blair Field in Long Beach.

Scalpers' Prices

The point seemed to be that the Super Bowl game, to be played before a capacity crowd of 90,182 in the Los Angeles Coliseum, has excited this city, which barely responded to the first Super Bowl played here six years ago. There were 16,000 unsold seats and nobody bothered the teams, the Green Bay Packers and Kansas City Chiefs, before the game.

The Redskins are more of an attraction because Allen was the coach of the Los Angeles Rams for five years and eight of the players are former Rams. Allen has set up tight security for his athletes at the Saddleback Inn in Santa Ana, and visitors are being constantly challenged.

There were 30,000 tickets made available to the holders of Ram season tickets and all were snapped up. Some are available but for more than the $15 charge. The prices suggested by scalpers are $300 for a pair on the 50-yard line, $50 for a single seat in the end zone.

By the time the Super Bowl returned to Los Angeles in 1973 after having originated there in 1967, a ticket such as this one was probably the most coveted in professional sports.
THE NEW YORK TIMES

The capacity of the Coliseum was enlarged from 78,000, the total for the Rams' home games, to 90,182 by moving back the temporary stand that closes off one end of the field in this huge facility that has seated as many as 102,000 for football games. The new number was arbitrarily selected by Pete Rozelle, the commissioner of the National Football League, who runs this game.

Rozelle, a one-time general manager of the Rams and a native of this city, guessed correctly that the Super Bowl would sell out easily last October when he promised a Senate subcommittee that the local television blackout would be lifted in that event. He announced the lifting of the blackout last week.

The two squads will practice in seclusion behind closed gates for the rest of the week as the coaches, Allen and Don Shula of Miami, attempt to minimize distractions. Most of the heavy preparation work was completed last week back at their home practice sites in Virginia and Florida.

Super Bowl Grows Yearly

The Dolphins have made an arrangement whereby daily practice reports and taped interviews with players can be heard by calling a local telephone number. This is for the benefit of the press.

The N.F.L. expects to issue credentials for over 700 reporters, photographers, radio and television representatives and the figure could go higher, to 1,000. This will be a record in keeping with the growth of the Super Bowl, which each year generates more clamor, more ticket demands, more anticipation.

It is ironic that the Super Bowl will be played on the West Coast between teams from the East Coast. But the enthusiasm of the cities involved was such for their teams that the 24,000 tickets allotted to Dolphin and Redskin fans were immediately sold out, even though the cost of a round-trip over almost 6,000 miles for one football game would come to a minimum of $500 a person.

Allen Rates Miami 'Best Foe Ever'

Redskins' Coach Also Ranks His Team Highly

By WILLIAM N. WALLACE

ANAHEIM, CALIF., *Jan. 9*—George Allen went into the business of ranking football teams today and the coach of the Washington Redskins declared Sunday's opponent in the Super Bowl, the Miami Dolphins, to be "the best pro football team we've ever faced, better than the 1966 Packers."

Allen is one of those people who prefer "we" to "I." The players who faced the Green Bay Packers back in 1966 were the Los Angeles Rams coached by Allen. Thus, the justification for the comparison. Vince Lombardi's Packers of that year won the first Super Bowl game from Kansas City and are regarded as one of the more formidable professional teams in the annals of the National Football League.

Allen went on. "There isn't a weakness on the ball club," he said with regard to the Dolphins.

How did he feel about the Redskins being favored to beat Miami by 2 points in most areas? "I never can figure out how those people decide who's the favorite. We certainly don't deserve to be. Why gosh, Miami has set so many records I can't keep track of them."

Allen's Best Team

The Redskin coach, however, likes his team. "Washington this year is the best team I've ever had," he said, and he used "I," not "we."

He said these Redskins were better than his 1967 Ram team that "lost only two games out of 20" and the 1969 squad that "won 11 straight."

The trouble with those two Allen machines was that neither got to the Super Bowl. He was ready to explain why. "We went to Green Bay and it was zero cold and we lost." Actually, it was in Milwaukee, the temperature was in the 20's and the last Lombardi squad won easily, 28–7. In 1969 the Rams again played in cold weather, at Bloomington, Minn., against the Vikings and as Allen recalled it, "Joe Kapp got away with a couple of scrambles and they beat us, 23–20."

The coach added: "If both of those games had been played in the Los Angeles Coliseum, we would have won. In playoff games the home field is a tremendous advantage."

Tribute to Morris

Teams coached by Allen have lost three playoff games, all on the road, and won two at home. The victories came this season over Green Bay and Dallas.

Sunday's game in the Los Angeles Coliseum is a neutral court for both sides. But Allen likes it.

"If the game can't be played in RFK," he said with reference to the Robert F. Kennedy Stadium in Washington, "there's no place I'd rather have it than in the Coliseum. I certainly wouldn't want to have it in Miami."

Allen, like many others, believes the Dolphins this season are better than last because of the addition of Mercury Morris, the swift running back, to the club's offense. In working out his defensive unit in Anaheim Stadium here, Allen has a facsimile offense run the Dolphin plays. "We have a man who wears Morris's number," said Allen, "but he's about 20 pounds lighter and several seconds slower."

The actor is Herb Mul-Key, the reserve running back and returner of kickoffs whom Allen signed out of a tryout camp attended by 500 candidates.

Morris was angry that he played very little for Miami in the 1971 season and just before the Dolphins lost to Dallas in the last Super Bowl game, Mercury complained publicly. It was widely believed that his coach, Don Shula, might trade him because of this outburst. Allen, ever eager to trade, admitted that yes, he had talked to Shula last winter about a deal for Morris.

"But all I had to offer," he said, "was future draft choices. And Don didn't want to wait until 1977."

Shula and Allen know each other well. Over the years their teams have played one another eight times and the won-lost-tied record is 4-3-1 in favor of Shula. Their teams this time are remarkably similar.

"Both teams live by the run," said Allen. "Both pass sparingly. Their defense gave up the fewest points in their conference and ours the fewest in our conference. The teams are almost exactly alike."

Sports of The Times

Quarterback for the Redskin Defense

By ARTHUR DALEY

ANAHEIM, CALIF., *Jan. 10*—The oldest surviving member of George Allen's collection of elderly citizens on the Washington Redskins is Jack Pardee. The trail blazer for the famed Over the Hill Gang had been Sonny Jurgensen, aged 38. As if he were really an old crock, however, Sonny cracked up during the season and left it up to Pardee to use his seniority in leading the Skins in their inexorable advance toward Medicare and the Super Bowl.

Pardee is crowding 37 and is the most extraordinary old gaffer any football expert ever would want to see. He quarterbacks the defensive platoon that gave up the fewest points of any team in the conference, capping it by smothering Green Bay and Dallas to such an extent in playoffs that each emerged with one lone field goal and no touchdowns. Jack was an all-pro as far back as 1963 and he was all-pro in 1971. Some observers think he had his best season ever last year.

A thumping defender with savvy, Pardee manipulates that left linebacker spot as if he invented it. Maybe he did. He has size at 6 feet 2 inches and 225 pounds. He has sufficient speed to chop down the swifties on outside sweeps and he has the raw power to meet a Larry Csonka headon and jolt him to an abrupt stop. Since this is Jack's 15th year, it's inevitable that he should be asked how much longer he plans to continue.

Not Very Definite

"At least one more game," he says and the blue eyes twinkle.

The one more game, naturally enough, is the Super Bowl collision between the Redskins and the Miami Dolphins in the Los Angeles Coliseum on Sunday. That's virtually home territory for Pardee, because he played most of his career with the Rams.

"I can't even remember the first eight years," he said and the blue eyes clouded. "We didn't win and that's no fun. But I had the next seven years under the coaching of George Allen. He made winners of us, first here as Ram coach, and the past two years in Washington as Redskin coach. Winning is fun."

Although not many people in football have too high an opinion of George Allen, his players are his most enthusiastic supporters and the head cheerleader probably is Pardee. This is no dumb jock, either. He was on the dean's list at Texas A. and M., an academic as well as an athletic all-American. There are a couple of other items that set him apart from the herd. His original thought was to play pro ball for perhaps four years.

"When the Rams picked me as their second draft choice in 1957," he now says, "pro ball wasn't much of a profession. Salaries were still low and most of us regarded it as a stepping stone to something else."

If success trapped him into extending his tenure, this situation came to an almost frightening interruption after the 1963 season.

"I had just come off an all-pro year," he said. "I'd bought a new house and I had a growing family. I also had a black mole on my upper right arm. I paid no attention to it because it neither hurt nor bothered me. But my wife kept urging me to have a doctor examine it. I was busy and didn't. But then I read about Jim Umbricht, the Houston ballplayer, having the same kind of a mole on his leg. It was cancerous and in a short while he died. I stopped stalling. I went to the doctor.

"He discovered a malignancy and a week later I was in the hospital for an operation that took 11½ hours. I lost the use of my arm for a month and I lost much of my strength. I tried to play football in 1964, but I was bad and so were the Rams. I quit in 1965 and coached at Texas A. and M. It was almost like a sabbatical."

But in 1966 Allen assumed command of the Rams and the one player he wanted back most was Pardee. He pestered him daily over the phone, getting lyrical in his insistence that 28 was not too old for the resumption of a football career. After persuading the linebacker to pay him a visit, Allen gave Pardee's arm the right twist and Jack was back in action again. He has never regretted it.

As soon as Allen shifted from Los Angeles to Washington, he began raiding his old team so thoroughly that cynics were calling the Redskins the Ramskins. Pardee was part of one gigantic deal that brought Rams to the Redskins in gross lots. But Washington had its best record in 29 years. A prime contributor was John Perry Pardee, a man who still gets butterflies on the day of the game.

"I'm awake at 6 and the butterflies are churning within me," he says. "I drink coffee and that's all. I can't eat. I'm at the stadium so early that I almost beat the equipment men there. And when the game ends, I'm in such an emotional jumble that I can't eat until midnight."

But he enjoys it—as long as the Redskins win. If they add to his enjoyment by winning in Sunday's Super Bowl, it will be his competency as a defensive crasher that will help make it possible.

Sports of The Times
The Super Psyche of Superland

By DAVE ANDERSON

LOS ANGELES, *Jan. 12*—The game will occur Sunday after the two Super Bowl teams debark from separate caravans of buses outside the Coliseum as if they were movie extras imported for a battle scene. All week, they have been rehearsing their choreography in the Superland suburbs. The Miami Dolphins have been lodged in Long Beach, near oil fields where the pumps resemble big-beaked birds dipping rhythmically into the ground for worms. The Washington Redskins have been camped a few freeways over in Anaheim, not far from Disneyland, apparently the ideal atmosphere for a team whose coach, George Allen, thrives on vanilla ice cream. But some of his players prefer other flavors. "I was out with a few of them Monday night," says an acquaintance of several Redskin players. "Triple tequilas."

For both teams, Monday night was the last evening in which the players were permitted to act their age. Ever since, they have been under orders to be in their motel rooms for the 11 o'clock news.

"I'm glad there's a curfew tonight," one of the Dolphins said as he awaited Tuesday's roomcheck. "I need the rest."

Obviously, men will be men, especially when they're being paid for playing a boys' game. Which is why the coaches impose a curfew—to save the players from themselves. But the psychology of the curfew is only a small portion of the Super Psyche that has existed this week, as delivered by George Allen of the Redskins and minimized by Don Shula of the Dolphins. Virtually everything proclaimed by Allen, with his reputation for deviousness, appears to contain an ulterior motive, either to increase the pressure on the Dolphins or to lighten it on the Redskins.

A Funeral Oration

"Since we can't play in Washington," Allen said, "I can't think of a place I would rather play than in Los Angeles."

Freely translated, Allen was attempting to create a homefield advantage at a neutral site. Many of the Redskins performed for him when he coached the Rams here until he was discharged two years ago for ignoring the late Dan Reeves, then the owner.

"And the Dolphins," he said, "are the soundest team we have faced in my coaching career."

Since his coaching career included the 1966 Green Bay Packers, perhaps the strongest team in National Football League history, Allen had thrust upon the Dolphins the burden of justifying such monumental praise. But, like Mark Antony, he was hoping to bury his subject, not praise it. Shula understood.

"Suppose you get a muddy field?" the Dolphin coach was asked one day.

"Allen has made the statement that he has never lost in the rain," Shula replied drily. "So if it rains Sunday, we're going to forfeit."

Allen prefers a rah-rah approach; Shula is more businesslike.

"I can't imagine," Shula said grinning, "my leading Larry Csonka into 'Hail to the Dolphins.' C'mon, Larry, let's sing."

Allen's answers sound as if they're programmed by a computer.

"Give me a question," one of the Washington sports columnists has been asking other newsmen, "and I'll give you George Allen's answer."

Allen's reputation for spying is part of the psychology, too.

"During our practices in Miami before we came out here," Shula said, smiling, "there was a little old lady walking around the fence watching everything we did. She was just about the size of Charlie Winner."

Shula was referring to one of Allen's assistant coaches. But for many players, all the psychology is meaningless.

"It's overrated," said Manny Fernandez, a tackle on the Dolphins' defensive unit. "All coaches tell their players not to say anything that's going to rile up the other team. But hell, out here, I haven't read a newspaper all week. I only listen to FM radio. I read newspapers at home because it's delivered. But if it's not dropped off on my porch, I don't go out and buy 'em."

Looking ahead to Sunday's battle scene, Manny Fernandez shrugged.

"As far as the football game is concerned," he said, "you go out and play and it's over in three hours. Whatever happens, happens."

Redskins 2-Point Choice In Football's Showdown

By WILLIAM N. WALLACE

LOS ANGELES, *Jan. 13*—Mercury Morris and Larry Brown, two running backs whose skill and style set the pace for their teams, will largely determine the outcome of tomorrow's Super Bowl game between the Miami Dolphins and the Washington Redskins.

The squads are so evenly matched as to records, statistics and other less tangible strengths that it comes down to Morris, the swift outside runner for Miami, and Brown, the slasher keying the Washington attack.

The Redskins have been favorites in the semi-official world of betting odds. But the betting line, 2 points in favor of Washington, is so small that one assumes it was set merely to provoke wagering by both sides rather than to provide an objective view. The alleged experts, the football writers here on the scene, are torn. In a poll 51 preferred the Dolphins, 46 the Redskins.

The game in the Los Angeles Coliseum before a sellout crowd of 90,182 will begin at 3:40 P.M., New York time, with television over Channel 4. The nationwide television audience has been estimated by the National Broadcasting Company at 75-million.

Brown, 25 years old, and Morris, 26, both grew up in Pittsburgh but both have long since fled that city. Brown played for Schenley High School in the inner-city and came to the Redskins four seasons ago as an unknown from Kansas State. He blossomed to become the best runner in the game, the league's most valuable player this season.

Morris came from a more affluent area and was a star at Pittsburgh's Avonworth High before college at West Texas State.

Their paths had never crossed and they never knew of one another until they both came into the N.F.L. in 1969.

It is simple but true to say that the team with the best defense wins the big games. This one may turn out to be the best of the seven Super Bowl contests because of the evenness of the competitiors and their similarity as to strengths, coaching, training and attitude.

The Washington defense must hold the Morris excursions in check and the Miami defense must blunt the Brown blasts. Two linebackers this week put the tasks into perspective.

Nick Buoniconti, the middle linebacker for the Dolphins, said, "Brown running out of their I-formation is a problem. He can make his cuts anywhere he wants into the seams. The game will be decided in those two yards of the scrimmage line. If we get pushed back, we're in trouble. We'll beat them some of the time and they'll beat us some of the time."

The I-formation with Brown lining up behind Charlie Harraway, his blocking back, disguises Larry's intent. By seams, Buoniconti was talking about the little spaces left when the two lines hit into one another.

The common observation has been that Morris, running to the outside, made the Dolphins a much more formidable team than a year ago when they meekly lost the last Super Bowl to the Dallas Cowboys, 24–3. Mercury's contribution to the team's 16-game undefeated streak this season was considerable.

Chris Hanburger, the Redskin outside linebacker and all-pro candidate, said of Morris, "We've got to get to him early before he turns upfield, before he can cut and run against the grain. You don't want a fellow like that running loose beyond the pursuit."

Don't Forget Csonka

Pro football defenses are designed to flow toward the ball carrier with everyone pursuing. A fellow like Mercury can change direction quickly and run through the spaces in the pursuit or "against the grain."

Both sides have other attacking weapons like Larry Csonka, the muscled Miami fullback with the mustache who gained 1,117 yards in the regular season to 1,000 for Morris and 1,216 for Brown. The Redskins figure they can cope with a Csonka as they coped with MacArthur Lane and John Brockington of Green Bay, similar power runners. It is the spectre of speed, Mercury's, which frightens them. As for the Dolphins, their respect for the indefatigable Brown carrying at least 20 times is huge. No one really stops Larry Brown.

"Both sides live by the run and are sparing of the pass," says George Allen, the Redskin coach.

There will be passers and receivers on the field, however. Bob Griese, out for eight games of the season with a broken leg, is the Miami passer and quarterback. He will be choosey with his passes and will not throw many unless Miami inexplicably falls behind.

Bill Kilmer, the 32-year-old Washington quarterback, has the same approach. His policy in calling plays is "to mix it up," and he is a master at that. But he regards the Miami efficient zone defense as all but impenetrable when it comes to the long pass.

Kilmer will certainly test what may or may not be a Miami weakness by sending Charlie Taylor, his wide receiver, against Lloyd Mumphord, the Dolphin cornerback. Mumphord has replaced the regular, Tim Foley, out with a shoulder separation.

"You always go at a team's weakness," said Kilmer. Mumphord, a four-year pro and a one-time regular, said he was ready. "I've been around," he said. "I have confidence in my abilities."

This will be the largest crowd, by 10,000, to watch a Super Bowl game. The gross receipts will reach $4.2-million with television fees contributing $2.5-million. The winning players will each receive $15,000 plus a diamond ring, the losers $7,500 and no ring.

Something has been made of the fact that teams playing in the Super Bowl for a second time, having been honed to the hoopla generated by mass media, have always won. These would be the Green Bay Packers in 1968 over Oakland although the Packers also won the first Super Bowl in 1967; the Kansas City Chiefs of 1970 over Minnesota after losing to Green Bay in 1967; the Baltimore Colts of 1971 after losing to the New York Jets in 1969, and the Dallas Cowboys of 1972 after losing to Baltimore in 1971.

Coaches' Styles Contrasted

That may be only as good as all football statistics, often blown out of the stadium following the initial kickoff.

However, if coaches set the tone and style for their team's play, supposedly a large reason for coaches, then Don Shula of Miami had it all over Washington's Allen in the days leading up to tomorrow's game.

Shula, a losing coach in two prior Super Bowls with Baltimore in 1969 and Miami last year, accepted the extraordinary media demands and a wet practice field with unexpected, never failing good humor. He did not complain about having to bus his players to other sites for practice for three days because the field assigned, Blair Field in Long Beach, was too wet.

He imparted a smiling, easy confidence to his players and everyone else. "I'm 0–2 in Super Bowls," he said. "I intend to be 1–2 after Sunday."

For Allen the week has been a trial. A coach who prefers to cloister himself and his players so all can "concentrate," Allen hated the usual rules of exposure to press, television and radio set down by Commissioner Pete Rozelle to whom this show-case game belongs.

Allen's exhaustion and frustration over an unnatural environment to him were showing more and more. The tenseness he presented to his players may have little effect, however, because most of the key ones have been around a long time although only two were in prior Super Bowls. Those are Roy Jefferson, the wide receiver, a figure in the Baltimore victory of 1971, and Verlon Biggs, the defensive end who so enjoyed beating the Colts when he was a Jet in 1969.

Perhaps this was an Allen act. When told that his favorite Over the Hill Gang, the defensive unit, lacked comparable physical qualities of other leading N.F.L. teams, Allen showed his typical, cracked, quizzical smile and said, "Yes, but they always know where to be, and they play together better than any I've ever had."

Shula has stayed with humor. When told that the thorough Allen had appointed a "sun" coach, someone to go to the Coliseum and check on how the sun hits into the stadium, Shula said, "Oh, you mean the fellow who went blind."

The Super Bowl? What Super Bowl?

By STEVE CADY

Jan. 13, 1973—Irene Lopez plans to skip Super Bowl VII today so she can go sky-diving at the Ripcord Para-Center in Medford, N.J.

"It's my second jump and I'm really excited," said Miss Lopez, one of the millions of Americans who won't be watching pro football's annual television extravaganza.

Jens Nygaard, a concert pianist, and Gil Gordian, a lionkeeper at the Bronx Zoo, also won't be watching the Super Bowl, an unauthorized adding-machine survey discovered. Neither will Irving Caesar, the songwriter, or Anthony Cipriano, a Transit Authority motorman, or Mrs. Pat Kracht, a suburban homemaker, or Irving Levitz, a psychologist, or . . .

Promoters for Super Bowl VII say 75 million of America's 210 million residents will be tuned to the Redskins-Dolphins showdown. According to A. C. Nielsen, 64 million watched last year's Super Bowl game. The television-rating company anticipates a larger audience this time around.

Yet the unauthorized survey, made from an unscientifically selected sampling by a rank amateur, came up with a startlingly different projection: upwards of 172.3-million Americans not watching Super Bowl VII, leaving a viewing audience of 37.7-million.

Take your pick.

"Nielsen doesn't guess," said a spokesman for the New York company, whose estimates are based on "quasi-permanent" monitors and diary samples in 1,200 of the nation's 60-million TV-equipped homes.

Nevertheless, as today's classic approached, the survey of non-viewers continued to find large areas of indifference.

"You have to understand which groups can identify with the Super Bowl and which groups can't," said Levitz, a counselor for New York City's Bureau of Child Guidance. "The aggression and violence of pro football involves identifying with maleness, the virility syndrome. A lot of people don't need or want this kind of identifying."

But let's get out the adding machine. Sizable groups that won't be watching the National Broadcasting Company's spectacular include the following:

24.9-million children under the age of 7, virtually none of whom has the patience or interest to pay attention to the Super Bowl.

64.3-million women over the age of 7, representing 70 per cent of that group.

22-million persons in cars, trucks, buses, campers, taxis and other vehicles, assuming that nine of every 10 of the nation's 96-million cars and 21-million trucks are in the garage at the time of the Super Bowl; an assumption that 10 per cent of the fleet would be in motion (with two passengers per vehicle) was called "not unreasonable" by a spokesman for the Federal Highway Administration.

6.7-million persons over the age of 75, a majority of whom would not identify with the Super Bowl.

25-million people, or a fourth of videoland's projected over-all audience today, watching such other competing fare as "Suicide Commandos" and "Journey to the Center of the Earth."

Those are the big blocs. Smaller categories of non-viewers would have to include: 1.5-million businessmen, students, missionaries, diplomats and other Americans living abroad, not counting military personnel and dependents; 500,000 skiers, a sixth of the nation's 3-million hard-core skiers, out on the slopes at 1,000 ski resorts; 991,000 persons in mental institutions; 7 million people living in the 4 per cent of households that don't have a television set.

Below that level lies an endless variety of smaller groups the rating calculators may have neglected, ranging from the 34,260 patients on critical lists at American hospitals to the 9,750 women who will commit the faux pas of giving birth on Super Sunday.

Millions of non-viewers will be working, leaving the country by sea or air (16,000), taking a walk, reading a book, vacationing abroad, playing

cards, building snowmen, shopping for Sunday bargains, going to the movies, skating, studying for exams or even making love. Some of the would-be
viewers may even be stuck with out-of-order TV sets.

While the Redskins and Dolphins are knocking heads, Nygaard will
be playing Mozart concertos and conducting a 23-piece orchestra for an
audience of about 200 at the Young Men's Hebrew Association in the
Washington Heights section of Manhattan. "People love Mozart concertos," he said.

Three symphony orchestras, two ballet companies (one of which will
perform a work called "Who Cares?"), several modern-dance and operatic
groups, and assorted recitals are also on the cultural calendar here today.

At the Bronx Zoo, where 50 employees and several thousand visitors
are expected, Gordian will be feeding and caring for 27 lions, tigers, snow
leopards and jaguars.

Cipriano, one of 3,500 Transit Authority workers who won't see the
game, will be operating an M Line shuttle between Brooklyn and Queens
on the B.M.T. Subway. Six-thousand New York City policemen also will
be on duty during the game, many of them regretfully.

Mrs. Kracht, a mother of two small sons, said she'd be weaving belts
of Swedish rya rug-yarn on the loom she purchased recently. She said her
husband and two small sons wouldn't be watching the Super Bowl, either.
"It's idiotic, just another example of the commercialism of big business."

Levitz plans to spend the day with his children—not watching Super
Bowl VII. "A good portion of your academic community wouldn't be that
tuned in to pro football. Go down to the New School Library today, you'll
find it packed."

So it went, with one non-viewer after another cutting into the 75-
million audience projection.

"This is pollution," said Caesar, the "No, No, Nanette" lyricist who
wrote the words for such songs as "Swanee," "Tea For Two," "I Want to
Be Happy" and "Crazy Rhythm." They call the Super Bowl a free show,
but it's costing the economy millions. All those people sitting like zombies
in front of a TV screen all afternoon.

Caesar said his own Super Sunday would consist of some sweating at
a Turkish bath, followed by some Jack Daniels and a good cigar.

As for the surveyor's plans, the battle line has already been drawn. Let
the women in the family leave the room. Let them make snide remarks like
"Oh, gross." But don't touch that knob. Go you Redskins.

Shula: Tough, Practical And a Low-Key Coach

LOS ANGELES, *Jan. 13*—When he was a teen-ager, Don Shula finished
another football game on the playgrounds of Painesville, Ohio, and
snatched his jacket off a ledge where he had secured it with a brick. Shula
forgot about the brick, which broke his nose.

"As a kid I was the one who organized the games," Shula has said. "In grade school I chose the line-ups. In high school I knew what everyone was supposed to do and I corrected their mistakes. The coaches didn't always like that. That's my background."

Out of this mold emerged one of pro football's most successful coaches, a man who expects tomorrow to win his first Super Bowl game following two losses. Shula's Miami Dolphins have won 16 games in a row and they believe they will make the Washington Redskins No. 17.

The 42-year old coach has his team fully prepared and this week he faced up to the promotional rigors of Super Bowl week with considerably more ease than his counterpart, George Allen of the Redskins.

Stops the Press

In the daily press conferences, Allen said on Tuesday that the Miami Dolphins were the finest team of all time, a familiar coaching ploy. Shula began his Wednesday conference by saying, "I think they [the Redskins] are the finest team we've ever . . ." He left it there and laughed.

When asked about the gung-ho Allen who leads the three cheers for the Redskins in the locker room, Shula said, "Can you imagine me leading Larry Csonka in singing 'Three Cheers For the Dolphins'?" No one could.

Shula is tough and practical. He has his players' respect and he listens to them. He works them hard and repetition may be the key to his success if there is one. "At practice he'll tell us exactly what he wants," says Nick Buoniconti, the middle linebacker and defensive leader. "You think, oh my God, do we have to do that again for the 500th time? We do it."

Repetitive drills make his players more letter-perfect and Shula teams are never renowned for the mistakes, fumbles, sloppy kicking teams, missed plays, interceptions that decide so many games.

One Game Short

Shula, the son of an immigrant Hungarian nurseryman and dock worker, went to college to Cleveland at John Carroll University on a football scholarship. He played pro football with Cleveland, Baltimore and Washington for seven seasons. Then he went into coaching, first at the college level and next with the professionals. He was named head coach of the Baltimore Colts in 1963 and had immediate success.

But his teams never could win the ultimate game. The Colts lost the league title game to Cleveland in 1964 and the Super Bowl to the Jets in 1969 when heavily favored. That outcome soured the Baltimore owner, Carroll Rosenbloom, on Shula, who felt the change and decided to accept an offer to go to Miami.

Joe Robbie, the Dolphin owner who promised Shula 10 per cent ownership in the team, was accused of tampering by Rosenbloom and the league awarded a Miami first draft choice to Baltimore as a result. Shula thought this was terrible. The Dolphins, an expansion team that first played in 1966, had never had a winning team. Shula's first one there made the playoffs. His

second reached the Super Bowl and lost to Dallas. His third is in the Super
Bowl again.

"I don't care about winning the press conferences," said a relaxed
Shula the other day, making small jokes with reporters. "I want to win the
game."

To Allen, Winning Is Living

LOS ANGELES, *Jan. 13*—George Allen received his master's degree in physical education from the University of Michigan in 1948 and the title of his
thesis was "A study of outstanding football coaches' attitudes and practices
in scouting." The document had 176 pages of appendices.

Allen works at football all day, every day. He makes some of his trades
on the telephone from home. His wife, Etty, says: "He's in bed next to me
and I hear him on the phone at 3 A.M. making those calls to the West
Coast."

Winning games is all that matters to the 50-year-old Allen. He trims
from life all extraneous matter and withdraws himself and his team so that
they can concentrate on the matter at hand, the winning of the next contest.

That is why this week, leading to tomorrow's Super Bowl game matching Allen's Washington Redskins and the Miami Dolphins, has been such
a trying one for Allen.

The National Football League, which regards the Super Bowl as its
showcase, demands that the coaches make themselves and their players
available on a daily basis to 500 reporters to answer all kinds of questions.

Like the Redskins' No. 1 fan, President Nixon, Allen resists press
conferences. The coach regards them as a waste of time that could be better
spent watching football films. He is not testy, but uncomfortable and unin-
formative, during the conferences.

There were a number of pressures on Allen, to whom the Super Bowl
is a new experience. He was back in Los Angeles, where he had coached
the local team, the Rams, for five years, and his old critics could be heard.

Because the stakes were so high, Allen drove himself even more than
usual trying to squeeze out an edge over Miami by even more thorough
preparation and attention to detail. The coach appeared to be an exhausted
man, one hanging on by his fingernails.

Allen and his counterpart, Don Shula of Miami, believe in detailed,
thorough coaching with nothing left to chance. Their teams are virtually
identical in offensive and defensive concepts and formations. Since 1966,
when Allen first became head coach of the Rams, his teams have met Shula
teams eight times and Shula has won four, lost three, tied one.

Allen is a native of Detroit, where he was a 148-pound high school
basketball star. Following graduation from Michigan, he went right into
college coaching at such small institutions as Morningside in Iowa and
Whittier in California, President Nixon's school.

He joined the Chicago Bears' staff in 1958 and did such a good job as a defensive specialist that the owner, George Halas, instituted a lawsuit when the Rams hired him away. But Allen, who will do anything to assure victory, cut corners on player contracts and generally acted unethically in the opinion of the late Dan Reeves, the Los Angeles owner.

Reeves discharged him, but the players said they would not play unless he was rehired. Allen survived one more year with the Rams—his teams were always winners there—and then Reeves got him out.

There were plenty of employment opportunities with less sensitive owners and when Allen went to Washington in 1971, the president, Edward Bennett Williams, gave him full powers and a $125,000 salary.

Later Williams said: "George Allen was given an unlimited expense account and he has already exceeded it." One item was a $500,000 secluded practice site near Dulles Airport, where the players could "concentrate" without interruptions.

He spoils his players and meets almost all their demands. But once they are in the fold he can be indifferent to them. As a coach he is still dedicated to defense and the team's offensive star, Larry Brown, says he has very little contact with the boss.

By trading away future draft choices he no longer owned, Allen earned the ire of his competitors and was fined by the commissioner, Pete Rozelle.

"That's all over," says Allen. "It's in the past."

No Day for the Tube to Conk Out

By LEONARD KOPPETT

LOS ANGELES, *Jan. 13*—It will take 180 National Broadcasting Company employees and $200,000 in one-day expenses to bring the Super Bowl game into America's living rooms, but only five of these people will be seen or heard in public.

On the other hand, a sponsor who hasn't been part of a season-long package with the National Football League will have to pay $200,000 for one minute of commercial time during the game.

If the forecasts of N.B.C.'s analysts are borne out, the television audience tomorrow may be the largest for a single program. The record is 33,960,000 homes (as determined by Neilsen ratings) for the movie "Love Story," shown last year. According to N.B.C.'s predictions, this one will do 34,150,000.

In the television industry, an audience expressed in number of homes is considered a better yardstick than "viewers," because such a figure is obtained by multiplying the homes by an estimate of viewers-per-home. Last year's television audience was estimated at 74 million and the prediction now is for 75 million plus.

To reach all these people, a network of 500 television stations will be in operation. Of these, 225 are in the continental United States. There are stations in Alaska, Hawaii, Puerto Rico, the Virgin Islands and 20 in Mexico. The rest are in Canada, where in many cases a French commentator will be added to the N.B.C. picture.

In addition, the game will be televised to various points around the globe, on tape delay, by the American Forces Network, which will also carry the radio broadcasts. This service, aimed primarily at servicemen and other Americans abroad, picks up the N.B.C. picture and commentary.

And even in Britain, where interest in American football is not known to be intense, there will be a tape-delay telecast.

On your home screen, you will see and hear Curt Gowdy do most of the play-by-play, with Al DeRogatis breaking in with instant analysis. Bill Enis, of Houston will be the third member of the team, working at field level before, after, and during the game. For the postgame dressing-room show, Enis and Kyle Rote will do the interviewing.

Rote and Jim Simpson will do the radio broadcast—presumably for those 140 million or so Americans out of range of a television set and driving around in cars. Their description will be carried by 700 stations throughout the United States.

But these five couldn't do anything without the other 175 N.B.C. people: cameramen, engineers, directors, technical experts, electricians, producers, publicity people, statisticians and other television business people on a bewildering number of levels.

Most of them were brought here from New York and nearby Burbank, where N.B.C.'s West Coast base is, and a few from Chicago.

To the National Football League, the income from radio-television rights is $2.75-million, a sum stipulated in the general $32-million contract for season-long rights with N.B.C. and the Columbia Broadcasting System (the Monday night games on the American Broadcasting Company are a separate deal). This year, N.B.C. pays the $2.75-million, which is distributed equally among the 26 clubs; last year, and in the alternate years when it carried the game, C.B.S. paid.

Since there are approximately 20 commercial spots available during the game, the network would collect $4-million if it sold each for $200,000 —and since the outlay to the clubs plus working expenses is only $2.8-million, there would be a profit of $1.2-million on the day.

But it doesn't work that way.

Some national sponsors who have been season-long regulars, like Chrysler Motors or Goodyear or Gillette or Xerox, have their Super Bowl commercial time staked out as part of their year-long arrangement. It's hard to compute exactly what portion of their full-season payments goes to Super Bowl time, and it's an arbitrary division. Actual sales at the $200,000-a-minute figure probably account for less than half the spots.

The actual number of spots can't be firmly fixed, because events in the game may introduce unexpected delays and opportunities for an extra commercial or two.

There is also a pregame show, sponsored by American Motors, and the postgame show (from the dressing rooms), sponsored by Sperry Rand.

Considering the N.B.C. crew, the 1,500 or so other media people here covering the game, the 2,000 or so members of the National Football League (players and officials), the dozen or so huge business corporations involved in sponsorship with their own advertising and other executives—and their ad agencies and the 90,000 paying customers at the Coliseum and their families and close friends—the Super Bowl game will touch directly the lives of an astonishing number of people, aside from passive (or not so passive) home viewers.

Facts on Super Bowl Contest, 1973

Title at Stake—World professional football championship.

Participants—Miami Dolphins, champion of the American Football Conference, and Washington Redskins, champion of the National Football Conference.

Site—Los Angeles Memorial Coliseum, Los Angeles.

Date—Today.

Starting Time—Kickoff 3:30 P.M. (New York time).

Seating Capacity—90,182.

Television—Nationwide by the National Broadcasting Company (Channel 4 in New York). Air Time—3:30 P.M., preceded by pregame show at 3 P.M.

Radio—Nationwide by the National Broadcasting Company (WNBC, 660 on the radio dial in New York). Air Time—3:15 P.M. (New York time).

Players' Shares—$15,000 to each member of the winning team; $7,500 to each member of the losing team. Approximately $1.35-million total for the personnel of the competing clubs.

Division of Game Net Receipts—After deduction of taxes, expenses and players' shares, remainder will be distributed to the competing clubs and the player pension fund.

Uniforms—Miami will be the visiting team, will wear white jerseys, and will use the North bench. Washington will be the home team, will wear colored jerseys, and will use the South bench.

Game Ball—The standard N.F.L. ball, adopted before the 1970 season and used in all games this past season, will be used.

Sudden Death—If the game is tied at the end of regulation 60 minutes, it will continue in sudden-death overtime. The team scoring first by safety, field goal or touchdown, will win.

Officials—There will be six officials and two alternates appointed by the Commissioner's office.

Official Time—The scoreboard clock will be official.

Trophy—The winning team receives permanent possession of the Vince Lombardi Trophy, a sterling-silver football mounted on a three-sided base.

Regular-Season Figure Comparisons

PASSING

Miami	Att.	Comp.	Pct.	Total Yds.	TDs	Int.
Morrall	150	83	55.3	1,360	11	7
Griese	97	53	54.6	638	4	4
Washington						
Kilmer	225	120	53.3	1,648	19	11
Jurgensen	59	39	66.1	633	2	4

RUSHING

Miami	Att.	Total Yds.	Avg. Gain	Long Gain	TDs
Csonka	213	1,117	5.2	45	6
Morris	190	1,000	5.3	33	12
Kiick	137	521	3.8	26	5
Ginn	27	142	5.3	22	1
Leigh	21	79	3.8	10	0
Washington					
Brown	285	1,216	4.3	38	8
Harraway	148	567	3.8	24	6
Mul-Key	33	155	4.7	35	1
Brunet	30	82	2.7	18	2

RECEIVING

Miami	No. Caught	Total Yds.	Avg. Gain	Long Gain	TDs
Warfield	29	606	20.9	47	3
Kiick	21	147	7.0	15	1
Twilley	20	364	18.2	44	3
Briscoe	16	279	17.4	51	4
Morris	15	168	11.2	34	0
Stowe	13	276	21.2	49	2
Fleming	13	156	12.0	31	1
Mandich	11	168	15.3	39	3
Csonka	5	48	9.6	14	0
Washington					
C. Taylor	49	673	13.7	70	7
Jefferson	35	550	15.7	45	3
L. Brown	32	473	14.8	89	4
J. Smith	21	353	16.8	34	7
Harraway	15	105	7.0	24	0
Mul-Key	4	66	16.5	28	0
Alston	2	53	26.5	36	0
Brunet	1	8	8.0	8	0

INTERCEPTIONS

Miami	No.	Total Yds.	Long Gain	TDs
Scott	5	73	31	0
Mumphord	4	50	28	1
Anderson	3	34	22	0
Johnson	3	20	13	0
Swift	3	5	4	0
Washington				
Hanburger	4	98	41	1
Fischer	4	61	35	0
Bass	3	53	29	0
McLinton	2	22	19	0

PUNTING	No.	Total Yds.	Avg. Punt	Long Punt	Had Blkd.
Seiple, Mia.	36	1,437	39.9	54	0
Lothridge, Mia.	4	150	37.5	42	0
Anderson, Mia.	4	147	36.8	45	0
Bragg, Wash.	59	2,273	38.5	62	0

How the Super Bowl Rivals Match Up, 1973

MIAMI ON OFFENSE

No.	Player	Ht.	Wt.	Pos.
42	Paul Warfield	6-0	188	WR
81	Howard Twilley	5-10	185	WR
80	Marv Fleming	6-4	232	TE
73	Norm Evans	6-5	250	RT
66	Larry Little	6-1	265	RG
62	Jim Langer	6-2	250	C
67	Bob Kuechenberg	6-2	248	LG
77	Doug Crusan	6-4	250	LT
12	Bob Griese	6-1	190	QB
22	Mercury Morris	5-10	190	HB
39	Larry Csonka	6-2	237	FB

WASHINGTON ON DEFENSE

No.	Player	Ht.	Wt.	Pos.
41	Mike Bass	6-0	190	RCB
37	Pat Fischer	5-9	170	LCB
23	Brig Owens	5-11	190	SS
79	Ron McDole	6-4	265	LE
77	Bill Brundige	6-5	270	LT
53	Harold McLinton	6-2	235	MLB
72	Diron Talbert	6-5	255	RT
89	Verlon Biggs	6-4	275	RE
22	Roosevelt Taylor	5-11	186	FS
32	Jack Pardee	6-2	225	LLB
55	Chris Hanburger	6-2	218	RLB

MIAMI ON DEFENSE

No.	Player	Ht.	Wt.	Pos.
45	Curtis Johnson	6-1	196	RCB
26	Lloyd Mumphord	5-10	176	LCB
13	Jake Scott	6-0	188	SS
83	Vern Den Herder	6-6	250	LE
75	Manny Fernandez	6-2	250	LT
85	Nick Buoniconti	5-11	220	MLB
72	Bob Heinz	6-6	265	RT
84	Bill Stanfill	6-5	250	RE
40	Dick Anderson	6-2	196	FS
59	Doug Swift	6-3	226	LLB
57	Mike Kolen	6-2	220	RLB

WASHINGTON ON OFFENSE

No.	Player	Ht.	Wt.	Pos.
42	Charlie Taylor	6-2	210	WR
85	Clifton McNeil	6-2	187	WR
87	Jerry Smith	6-3	208	TE
76	Walter Rock	6-5	255	RT
60	John Wilbur	6-3	251	RG
56	Len Hauss	6-2	235	C
73	Paul Laaveg	6-4	250	LG
75	Terry Hermeling	6-5	255	LT
17	Billy Kilmer	6-0	204	QB
43	Larry Brown	5-11	195	HB
31	Charlie Harraway	6-2	215	FB

MIAMI SUBSTITUTES

No.	Player	Ht.	Wt.	Pos.
1	Garo Yepremian	5-8	175	K
15	Earl Morrall	6-2	210	QB
29	Larry Seiple	6-0	214	TE-P
23	Charles Leigh	5-11	206	RB
32	Hubert Ginn	5-10	185	RB
47	Henry Stuckey	6-0	180	DB
49	Charles Babb	6-0	190	S
51	Larry Ball	6-6	225	LB
53	Bob Matheson	6-4	235	LB
54	Howard Kindig	6-6	260	T-C
56	Jesse Powell	6-2	220	LB
60	Al Jenkins	6-2	245	G-T
65	Maulty Moore	6-5	265	DT
79	Wayne Moore	6-6	265	T
82	Otto Stowe	6-2	188	WR
86	Marlin Briscoe	5-11	178	WR
88	Jim Mandich	6-2	224	TE

WASHINGTON SUBSTITUTES

No.	Player	Ht.	Wt.	Pos.
4	Mike Bragg	5-11	186	P
5	Curt Knight	6-2	190	K
13	Alvin Haymond	6-0	194	S
18	Sam Wyche	6-4	218	QB
25	Mike Hull	6-3	220	RB
26	Bob Brunet	6-1	205	RB
28	Herb Mul-Key	6-0	190	RB
29	Ted Vactor	6-0	185	CB
44	Jeff Severson	6-1	180	DB
58	George Burman	6-3	255	C-G
62	Ray Schoenke	6-4	250	T
64	Manuel Sistrunk	6-5	265	DT
66	Myron Pottios	6-2	230	LB
67	Rusty Tillman	6-2	230	LB
68	Mike Fanucci	6-4	225	DE
80	Roy Jefferson	6-2	195	WR
81	Mack Alston	6-2	230	TE
82	Jimmie Jones	6-5	215	DE

Records of the Teams

MIAMI			WASHINGTON		
20—Kansas City	10		24—Minnesota	21	
34—Houston	13		24—St. Louis	10	
16—Minnesota	14		23—New England	24	
27—N.Y. Jets	17		14—Philadelphia	0	
24—San Diego	10		33—St. Louis	3	
24—Buffalo	23		24—Dallas	20	
23—Baltimore	0		23—N.Y. Giants	16	
30—Buffalo	16		35—N.Y. Jets	17	
52—New England	0		27—N.Y. Giants	13	
28—N.Y. Jets	24		24—Atlanta	13	
31—St. Louis	10		21—Green Bay	16	
37—New England	21		23—Philadelphia	7	
23—N.Y. Giants	13		24—Dallas	34	
16—Baltimore	0		17—Buffalo	24	
20—Cleveland	14		16—Green Bay	3	
21—Pittsburgh	17		26—Dallas	3	
426	202		378	224	

Miami Wins in Bowl for Perfect Season

By WILLIAM N. WALLACE

LOS ANGELES, *Jan. 14*—The big scoreboard in the Coliseum flashed a message over and over, "The Dolphins Are Super," at the end of the Super Bowl contest today, and indeed the Miami team had played an almost perfect game in defeating the Washington Redskins, 14–7, for a perfect season and the championship.

The game was watched by millions on national television. [Many television sets in the metropolitan New York area were affected by atmospheric disturbances that interrupted the program.]

The score of the undefeated Dolphins' 17th victory could easily have been a more decisive 21–0 or 17–0 except for a single botched Miami play near the end of the game. That play featured little Garo Yepremian, the soccer-kicking specialist from Cyprus, attempting the skills of the big fellows, passing and tackling. Yepremian tried futilely to throw a pass after his 42-yard field-goal attempt had been blocked.

This pass was intercepted by Mike Bass, the cornerback who ran 49 yards for the Redskins' only touchdown with 2 minutes 7 seconds left to play. The 155-pound Yepremian missed the tackle. This score put some suspense into a game that otherwise had generated little excitement because Miami was the dominant team from the start.

The Redskins had the ball one more time with 74 seconds remaining, but the Dolphin defense harassed Bill Kilmer, the Washington quarterback, and the final play was symbolic. Kilmer was dropped by Bill Stanfill and Vern Den Herder for a 9-yard loss on his 17-yard line.

Larry Csonka ran for 112 yards for Miami, 9 short of the Super Bowl record set by Matt Snell of the New York Jets in 1969, while Larry Brown, the Redskins' No. 1 carrier, scratched out 72 in 22 carries. His average was 3.3 yards, a yard below his standard during the regular season. Brown's longest run was for 11 yards while Csonka had one of 49 yards, the most yards the Redskins' defense had given up on a single ground play all season.

Csonka's running mate, Jim Kiick, scored the second Miami touchdown on a 1-yard run in the second period and Howard Twilley, the wide receiver, made the first on a dazzling play in the opening quarter. Twilley, cutting inside and then outside, caught a pass from Bob Griese on the 5 and scored to complete a 28-yard play. Twilley turned the defending back, Pat Fischer, all the way around on his fake.

Jake Scott, the Miami free safety, won the automobile when he was voted the game's outstanding player by a panel on the basis of his two interceptions. The choice of Scott was hardly a clear-cut one because all 11 players on the Dolphin defense were outstanding.

George Allen, the Redskin coach, had anticipated his defense giving Miami 14 or even 17 points, but his hope for victory expired because his offense was shut out rather than scoring the expected 21 or 24 points.

Allen said: "We felt we had to get on the board early against them because when they get ahead they have the talent to hold the ball and ground it out." That is what happened before the crowd of 81,706.

Allen added: "There was great pressure on Kilmer because we were unable to run as we would have liked to. It was a difficult day for him. But he brought us where we are today. They stopped our running better than I thought they would."

This attack, with Brown held in check, never moved into Miami territory until the third quarter began. That drive failed when Curt Knight's 33-yard field-goal try went wide.

The Redskins' only other drive, in the final period, ended when Kilmer's pass on third down to Charlie Taylor was intercepted by Scott in his end zone.

Kilmer had little luck when attempting to pass into the middle of the Miami zone defense. His first effort in the second quarter was intercepted by Scott and his second, in the same period, was picked off by Nick Buoniconti.

Washington had four turnover errors, the three interceptions and a lost fumble, to just one, an interception, for Miami. This interception, of a Griese pass by Brig Owens in his own end zone, prevented a Miami touchdown late in the third quarter that would have put the game out of Washington's sights with a 21–0 score.

The early Miami touchdowns came after a six-play, 63-yard drive, which ended with the Twilley score, and a 27-yard drive following Buoniconti's interception and 32-yard return. Kiick slammed over the goal from the 1 behind a block by Csonka to make it 14–0 at half-time.

So Miami became the first team in the 53-year history of the National Football League to go through a season undefeated and untied. For the coach, Don Shula, a Super Bowl victory had been some time in coming. His two earlier qualifiers, the 1969 Baltimore Colts and last year's Dolphins, had lost, to the Jets and to the Dallas Cowboys.

"I'm 0–2," said Shula last week, "and on Sunday night I intend to be 1–2." He made it.

For Allen and the Redskins, there was disappointment at the end of a glorious season that had carried the coach and the Washington entry to the Super Bowl for the first time.

Form held up. The Dolphins were the fourth team to win the Super Bowl on the second try after losing on the first. The others were Kansas City in 1970, Baltimore in 1971 and Dallas last year.

In the locker room, Shula said: "There is no empty feeling this year. This is the ultimate."

Griese added: "I'm really happy for Don Shula. This year we won it for him."

Each of the 40 Dolphins also won for themselves $15,000, the Super Bowl prize money. The Redskins will receive half as much.

A downcast Allen commented: "It doesn't do any good to play in the Super Bowl if you don't win. We just lost to a team that played a better game."

Allen said the Redskin kicking game "was not up to par," a reference to Mike Bragg's weak 31-yard punting average and Knight's missed field-goal attempt.

Then Allen said: "I can't get out of here [Los Angeles] fast enough. There will be a lot of hours of agony tonight." George will start working on next season tomorrow.

Shula will linger to savor the victory. "This team," he said of the Dolphins, "is the greatest I have been associated with. It went undefeated and won at the end and they have to be given credit for their achievement."

Miami Dolphins . . . . 7 7 0 0—14
Washington Redskins . . . . 0 0 0 7— 7

    Mia.—Twilley, 28, pass from Griese (Yepremian, kick).
    Mia.—Kiick, 1, run (Yepremian, kick).
    Wash.—Bass, 49, fumble recovery return (Knight, kick).
    Attendance—81,706.

Individual Statistics

RUSHES—Mia.: Csonka, 15 for 112 yards; Kiick, 12 for 38; Morris, 10 for 34.
    Wash.: Brown, 22 for 72; Harraway, 10 for 37; Kilmer, 2 for 18.
PASSES—Mia.: Griese, 8 of 11 for 88 yards. Wash.: Kilmer, 14 of 28 for 104.
RECEPTIONS—Mia.: Warfield, 3 for 36 yards; Kiick, 2 for 6; Twilley, 1 for 28;
    Mandich, 1 for 19; Csonka, 1 for minus 1. Wash.: Jefferson, 5 for 50; Brown,
    5 for 26; C. Taylor, 2 for 20; J. Smith, 1 for 11; Harraway, 1 for minus 3.

Statistics of the Game

	Dolphins	Reds.		Dolphins	Reds.
First downs	12	16	Interceptions by	3	0
Rushing yardage	37-184	36-141	Punts	7-43	5-31
Passing yardage	69	87	Fumbles lost	1	0
Passes	8-11	14-28	Yards penalized	35	25

Sports of The Times

Success on the Second Time Around

By ARTHUR DALEY

LOS ANGELES, *Jan. 14*—It's cause and effect rather than coincidence, but one inescapable Super Bowl fact remains: Every team making a return visit to the Super Bowl made good on the second chance by winning. If anyone so desires, he even can count Vince Lombardi's Green Bay Packers, who started the series with two thumping victories. By taking their second game as easily as they had their first, they proved the point. It was a return visit, wasn't it?

Kansas City lost the first, but came back to win the fourth. Baltimore dropped the historic third Super Bowl game to the Jets, but took the fifth from Dallas, which knocked off Miami in the sixth. Today the Dolphins completed the sequence by crushing the Washington Redskins, 14 to 7.

Don't let that score fool you. It wasn't that close a game. The Dolphins dominated all the way, yielded a freakish touchdown late in the action and practically yawned their way through to complete a perfect season of 17 and 0. For Coach Don Shula it was particularly precious because he had been on the wrong end twice, once with Baltimore and last year with Miami. He's finally on the alkaline side.

A Fluke From the Past

That second time around may even be worthy of a psychological study. When a team makes its debut in the Super Bowl, everyone says, "Wow, we made it." An objective has been attained, blurring the essential objective, a Super victory. But the losers readjust their sights and shoot for the moon, the stars and victory. Thus far, everyone of them has achieved it.

Once the Dolphins entered the swim with a slick touchdown late in the first quarter and tacked on another late in the second quarter, the Redskins were barely able to get out of the glub. They made not one penetration of any consequence in the entire first half, had one abortive attempt in the third quarter and had to believe that nothing ever would work for them.

Here's a sample: In the final period the Redskins engineered their most noble effort of the game, driving down to the Dolphins' 10. Then a strange thing happened, something that had historians blinking their eyes in amazement. Jerry Smith broke clear in the end zone and Bill Kilmer fired a pass right at him. But the ball hit the upright. It was no dice. On the next play the Dolphins intercepted to avert the threat.

But what made trusty historians do a mental flip-flop was a recollection of a costly similar play in the 1945 championship playoff, the last one in which the Redskins were involved. Backed into his end zone, the incomparable Sammy Baugh threw an escape pass. It also hit the upright and bounced back through the end zone. According to the rules then in effect, it was a safety. It also meant the difference between victory and defeat because the 'Skins lost, 15 to 14.

Kicker Violates Precept

However, nothing much would have saved the Redskins today. When they scored, they did it on a freakish play that is even a little fuzzy to eye-witnesses and may not be clear in everyone's mind until the official movies are premiered. Garo Yepremian, the left-footed Cypriot who manufactures ties and field goals, attempted a 42-yarder. Bill Brundige blocked it and the ball bounced off crazily to Yepremian's right.

In hot pursuit was the baldish little kicker who is supposed to shun all active combat. He violated all union rules. Instead of following the precepts found in the kickers' handbook, he went for the ball. Since he is far more used to touching it with his foot than with his hands, he juggled that hot potato while fire-eating Redskin monsters bore down on him. It looked as if he were trying to throw a forward pass—of all things. Whatever it was, it was ruled a fumble.

Mike Bass plunked the ball out of the air and raced downfield for the goal line. Miami defenders were totally out of position. The only one in the neighborhood was Yepremian, the non-combatant. He violated the union code again. He tried to make a tackle. He missed, and the Redskins' cornerback streaked down the sideline for a touchdown.

Thus did the Redskins finally get into the swim, far too late for it to help them much. By the time the researchers had completed all their chores, they were able to offer the observation that the touchdowns were scored by two Dolphins and one Bass. It could be from a script plucked out of an old Lloyd Bridges underwater series.

The crowd in the cavernous Coliseum, a mere 81,706 for a record, was unashamedly in favor of the Redskins because Coach George Allen and so many of his elderly Over the Hill Gang had once been Los Angeles Rams. Seated in the stands, however, were most of the owners and coaches of the National Football League. They definitely were not rooting for Allen, the low man in their hit parade.

When it all was over, Allen was saying something that most first-time coaches in the Super Bowl said in the past. It was:

"We all probably learned something."

Scalpers Take a Beating, Tickets Go at Face Value

LOS ANGELES, *Jan. 14 (AP)*—Scalpers apparently took a beating on the Super Bowl game today.

An hour before gametime, operatives were selling $15 tickets at face value outside Memorial Coliseum. A broker across the street was asking $100 apiece for 50-yard line tickets, a third of the pre-blackout price.

No. 1 Fan Dismayed By Defeat

KEY BISCAYNE, FLA., *Jan. 14 (AP)*—President Nixon watched with dismay today as his favorite team, the Washington Redskins, lost to Miami, 14–7, in what he called "One of the best Super Bowl games ever."

"That was a fine game," the President said, in comments relayed by a deputy press secretary, Neal Ball, ". . . because there was suspense right up to the end.

"The people of Washington and the people of Miami can both be proud of their teams," he added. "They played well."

Scores of motorists drove past the Nixon compound after the game blowing their horns to "show their resentment at Nixon's support for the Redskins," one motorist explained.

In Los Angeles the coaches waited, but the nation's No. 1 fan failed to put in his traditional postgame call.

"The President phoned before the game," said George Allen, coach of the Redskins. "He said he wouldn't call until Monday."

In the Miami dressing room, a neatly-dressed man pushed his way in front of Don Shula, Miami's coach.

"Who are you?" Shula asked.

"I am with the President," replied the man, Herb Klein, White House Director of Communications. Then he was caught up in the confusion.

Nixon Sends Wires to Shula and Allen

KEY BISCAYNE, FLA., *Jan. 14 (UPI)*—President Nixon sent telegrams tonight to both Super Bowl coaches offering congratulations to Don Shula and his Dolphins and condolences to George Allen and the Redskins.

The telegram to Shula read: "Today's victory was a smashing climax to a truly perfect season. You and all the Dolphins have my heartiest congratulations. It was a great victory for all of your players, for all of your devoted followers throughout the country, and especially for you, Don—the man who brought the Vince Lombardi Trophy to Miami. Once again my congratulations and warmest personal regards to you and all the Dolphins."

He wired Allen that the loss was "a keen disappointment for all Red-skins fans but it certainly has done nothing to diminish our admiration and love for the team that you have coached so masterfully this season.

"The Redskins played gallantly from the opening kickoff this fall through the final seconds in the Coliseum, bringing a new sense of pride to the entire Washington community. You will never be 'over the hill' in our book and we'll all be in there rooting for you next season, fully confident you can go all the way."

'Thought I Gave Game Away,' Says Miami's Yepremian

Kickers 'Mind Went Blank' as Miscue Let Foe Score

By DAVE ANDERSON

LOS ANGELES, *Jan. 14*—In his relief over the Miami victory today, Garo Yepremian sighed.

"I never prayed so much," the Cyprus-born place-kicker acknowledged, "And God came through for me."

Yepremian was discussing the aborted field-goal attempt from the Washington Redskins' 42-yard line with about two minutes remaining that resulted in Mike Bass's 49-yard run for a touchdown. Another Redskin touchdown and extra point would have produced overtime.

"I thought I gave the game away," Yepremian said. "I picked up the blocked kick, but my mind went blank. I tried to throw a pass. I just saw some of our uniforms downfield, I don't know who they were. But the ball slipped out of my hand."

Scolded by Coach

As the baldish, 5-foot-8-inch kicker trotted to the sideline after having been outrun by Bass for the touchdown, he was scolded by Coach Don Shula.

Following the Redskin kick after the touchdown, the Dolphin offense went on the field with 1:57 remaining and first down on the Miami 16.

"In the huddle I said that we knew that this was what we'd been working for since July," said Larry Csonka, the big running back. "We knew we had to get a couple of first downs to kill the clock and keep the ball away from them. And then Norm Evans said: 'We don't have to say it. We all know what we have to do now. So let's just do it.' "

The brief passing career of Garo Yepremian (1) led to Washington's only score in Super Bowl VII as an aborted field goal attempt and a bizarre lob led to an interception by Mike Bass (41).

WIDE WORLD PHOTOS

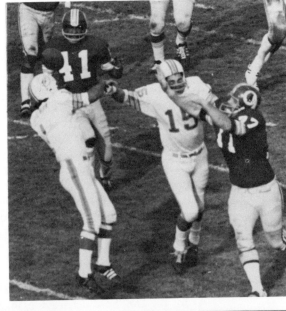

In a second-and-7 situation, Bob Griese threw a sideline pass to Paul Warfield for a first down at the Dolphin 30.

"That was a big play," Shula said. "Mike Bass, the cornerback, was lined up way inside Warfield. Bob and I talked about it. Bob had the confidence to do it, and I had the confidence to let him do it. When it worked, it gave us two extra plays to help kill the clock with."

Back to Yepremian.

"Shula told me I should've fallen on the fall," he said. "I knew that, but I didn't think fast enough to do it. But the guys on the sideline came up to me and told me not to worry about it—Norm Evans, Larry Ball, Tim Foley, Larry Seiple."

Snap Was Low

On the field-goal attempt, Howard Kindig's snap was low, forcing Earl Morrall, the holder, to position it quickly.

"Garo hit it good," Morrall said, "but the ball didn't get up in the air fast enough; they penetrated to block it."

Yepremian recalled a similar situation during a victory over the St. Louis Cardinals.

"I picked the ball up and fumbled it," the 28-year-old soccer-style kicker said. "I'm not used to throwing. I kick with my left foot, but I throw with my right hand, like I tried to. The ball just slipped. The only time I throw the ball is in practice when I throw to the guys just for fun. This wasn't fun."

Shula said the game plan was to exploit the Redskin pass defense in various situations.

"Like the pass to Warfield for the touchdown that was nullified," the coach said. "In that situation we thought the Redskins wouldn't be looking for that. And the pass to Jim Mandich that set up the second touchdown. On the first touchdown, Howard Twilley got away from Pat Fischer on the bump and run. Howard likes that."

3 Standouts in Line

As for the Dolphins' defensive plan, as designed by Bill Arnsparger, an assistant coach, Shula mentioned the line led by Manny Fernandez, Bill Stanfill and Vern Den Herder.

"We felt that if we could whip'em up front and stay in our pursuit lanes, we'd have somebody there when Larry Brown looked to cut back," he said. "And that's what we did. We wanted to contain their running game to short gains and make'em pass more than they wanted to."

After two Super Bowl losses as coach of the Baltimore Colts four years ago and the Dolphins last year, Shula was delighted.

"It's the greatest moment of my coaching career," he said. "All along I've had an empty feeling of not having accomplished the ultimate.

"With a 17–0 record, I don't know what we can do for an encore. But right now I'm just going to sit back and relish this for a while. This team gets better every season. I don't know what I'm going to tell 'em when training camp opens."

Man in the News: The Coach Who Has the Last Laugh

Donald Shula

By MICHAEL KATZ

Jan. 14, 1973—In the often overdramatic world of professional football, where coaches exhort their teams each week "to win one for the Gipper," and where locker-room truisms like "Winning Is Everything" are hailed as philosophy, Don Shula usually cooled it.

All week long, the coach of the Miami Dolphins had reacted to the pressures of Super Bowl week with a loose, graceful humor, a refreshing contrast to the gung-ho George Allen, his counterpart with the Washington Redskins.

And the joking, relaxed Shula set the tone for his team, which defeated the tense Redskins, 14–7, yesterday in Super Bowl VII and capped a season in which it won everything—all 14 regular-season games, two playoff contests and the Super Bowl.

For the 42-year-old Shula, yesterday's triumph was the "ultimate" one after he twice before coached losing teams in the Super Bowl.

Filling a Void

"All along I've had an empty feeling," admitted Shula afterwards in the winners' locker room, "of not having accomplished the ultimate.

"And this right here," he said tapping the Vince Lombardi Trophy for the National Football League championship, which had been presented to him moments before by Commissioner Pete Rozelle, "is the ultimate."

This was the third time around for Shula, whose Baltimore Colts lost the 1969 Super Bowl to the New York Jets and whose Dolphins were defeated last season by the Dallas Cowboys.

Even Then, He Knew

"I hadn't done too well in my first two [Super Bowl games], as a lot of people kept reminding me," he said.

Shula doesn't have to remind anyone about his professional coaching record—five times he has been voted somebody's coach of the year and he is the first coach to win 100 games in only 10 N.F.L. seasons. In his 10 seasons, his won-lost-tied record, including playoffs, is 109-33-5.

He did it mainly with a tough, practical, professional approach. In a way, Donald Shula, the son of an immigrant Hungarian nurseryman and dock worker, had been preparing himself to be a professional football coach as early as childhood.

"As a kid, I was the one who organized the games," he has said of the sandlot football he played in the lots around Painesville, Ohio, a Cleveland suburb. "In grade school I chose the line-ups. In high school I knew what everyone was supposed to do and I corrected their mistakes. That's my background."

That background included the ubiquitous "will to win."

"He hates to lose," said his mother, Mary, who accompanied his father, Dan, to the Los Angeles Coliseum yesterday. "When he was 8 years old, he would play cards with his grandmother. If he lost, he would tear up the cards and run and hide under the porch. You couldn't pry him out for supper."

Shula didn't tear up his playbook when the Dolphins lost last year's Super Bowl. "You set a goal to be the best and then work hard every hour, every day striving to reach that goal," he has said.

He worked the Dolphins hard, too. It has been said that the key to Shula's success as a coach is repetition—he makes his players practice the same thing over and over until he finally is satisfied. His teams seldom make mistakes.

Shula, who played halfback at John Carroll University in Cleveland and had an undistinguished seven-year N.F.L. career as a defensive back with the Cleveland Browns, Baltimore Colts and Washington Redskins, began his coaching career in 1958 as an assistant at the University of Virginia. He also was an assistant at the University of Kentucky and with the Detroit Lions before becoming the Colts' head coach in 1963.

He took over the Dolphins in 1970 after a falling out with Carroll Rosenbloom, the Colts' owner, and built the expansion club into a contender in his first season at Miami.

Thinking Unbeaten

The Dolphins followed their relaxed leader loyally all season and were able to resist the growing pressures of their winning streak.

"We weren't thinking about being 13–0, 14–0, 15–0 or 16–0," Shula said yesterday. "We were only thinking about being 17–0, like right now."

Next week, the Dolphins won't have to worry about being 18–0. "Next," said Shula, "is relaxation and enjoyment."

Shula will relax with his wife Dorothy and their five children—David, Donna, Sharon Lee, Ann Marie and Michael. Winning isn't everything.

New Auto Right Make for Scott

LOS ANGELES, *Jan. 14*—Jake Scott, whose two interceptions sparked the defensive unit in the Miami Dolphins' 14–7 victory, was awarded a Dodge Charger by Sport magazine today as the most valuable player of the Super Bowl game.

"That's great," the free safetyman said, grinning. "I work for a Dodge dealer in Miami."

Scott performed spectacularly despite a sore right shoulder that required a pregame injection of Xylocaine as a pain-killer and despite bone chips in his right wrist that will require surgery.

"I didn't practice for two weeks," he said. "But my shoulder only hurt me once, when I landed on it covering a pass."

Scott's first interception occurred early in the second quarter at midfield, halting a Redskin drive when the Dolphins had a 7–0 lead. In the fourth quarter, he ran his second interception out of the end zone to the Redskins' 48-yard line.

One Season in Canada

"I was lucky on the first one," he said. "I batted the ball in the air and caught it. On the second, Lloyd Mumphord and I were covering Charlie Taylor, with Lloyd outside and me inside, but Bill Kilmer didn't see me cut over and the ball came to me."

Scott was drafted by the Dolphins in 1970 after he had played in the Canadian Football League for one season.

"I wasn't eligible for the N.F.L. draft, and I had a year of eligibility left at Georgia, but all my buddies had graduated," he recalled. "And when Vancouver of the Canadian League made me an offer I couldn't refuse, I took it."

Oddly, the 27-year-old native of Athens, Ga., was a wide receiver in the C.F.L., not a defensive back.

$5,000 Salary Cut

"Then they traded me to Montreal, but several N.F.L. teams were interested in drafting me. The Dallas Cowboys talked to me, but then nobody took me until the Dolphins did on the seventh round. I had to take a $5,000 pay cut to join them."

Scott's reasoning was that he preferred to compete in the N.F.L. rather than remain in Canada.

In the rise of the Dolphins, Scott has been one of their most consistent performers, earning all-N.F.L. recognition despite the reputation of the Dolphins for having a "no-name" defensive unit. Asked if people will know his name now, he grinned.

"I hope so," he said.

Blackout Ammunition: 8,476 Unused Tickets

LOS ANGELES, *Jan. 14*—Although the Super Bowl crowd today was recorded as 90,182, the National Football League announced that 8,476 ticket-holders did not watch the game at the Coliseum. "There were 8,476 no-shows," an N.F.L. spokesman said.

Although the N.F.L. did not mention the absence of a local TV blackout, the number of "no-shows" surely will be used as ammunition in its campaign to maintain the blackout policy. The blackout for this Super Bowl game was lifted 10 days ago when the game was a sellout, as promised by Commissioner Pete Rozelle.

The actual Coliseum attendance today was 81,706, although 90,182 tickets were sold. The actual crowd still set a Super Bowl record, breaking the 80,591 mark in Miami last year.

Redskins Rejected Use of Onside Kick In Hope of Break

LOS ANGELES, *Jan. 14*—With 2 minutes 7 seconds left in the Super Bowl game today and behind by 7 points why did the Washington Redskins forgo an onside kickoff to try to get the ball back from the Miami Dolphins after scoring their touchdown?

That was the big second guess left over from Miami's 14–7 victory, a second guess directed towards George Allen, the losing coach.

Allen explained that there was too much time rather than too little left in his opinion. He said, "There was too much time left to try an onside kick. In that situation you just try to kick deep, hold them and maybe block the punt." It was a strange reply subject to challenge.

The Redskins did kickoff deep to the Miami end zone but they did not achieve their other two aims.

3 Time Outs Left

The risk of an onside kick seemed worthwhile because the Redskins had all three of their time-outs left with another to come at the television commercial pause with two minutes left. If the kick had been successful and the Redskins had gained possession around midfield they would have been in a controlling position. What they needed was a touchdown to tie the game and send it into sudden-death overtime.

Instead the ball went over to the Dolphins and Washington's defense had to call all three time outs to try to stop the clock as Miami moved to one first down.

Nixon's Call to Shula Is Blacked Out

LOS ANGELES, *Jan. 15*—Don Shula, the coach of the Super Bowl champion Miami Dolphins, was congratulated by President Nixon today.

"He is in Florida," Shula said. "He just called to congratulate me. He knew how important the victory was for the football team and for me personally." Shula had coached two Super Bowl losers.

The President had telephoned Shula at the Super Bowl headquarters in nearby Newport Beach. When advised that the press was gathered to overhear the conversation, however, Mr. Nixon requested that Shula call back in private.

Two weeks ago, the President pledged his allegiance to the Washington Redskins for yesterday's game, which the Dolphins won, 14–7. He backed Miami in 1972, when Dallas won.

"He said that he watched the game yesterday with a great deal of interest," Shula said. "He mentioned that our young offensive line is about the same age as the Redskins' offensive line. To me, it's remarkable that he's as involved and interested as he is in football.

"He wanted me to know he understood how I felt—that he had experienced losing, then had experienced the other side," Shula said.

An aide said that the President also had telephoned George Allen, the losing coach.

Super Bowl Marks
RECORDS SET

Highest Passing Efficiency—72.7 per cent, Bob Griese, Miami, 8 completions in 11 attempts.

Most Yards on Interceptions—63, Jake Scott, Miami, 2 Interceptions.

Fewest Points, Both Teams—21.

Fewest Points Winning Team—14, Miami.

Most Rushing Attempts, Both Teams—73: Miami 37, Washington 36.

Fewest Passing Attempts, Both Teams—39: Miami 11, Washington 28.

Fewest Passes Completed, Both Teams—22: Miami 8, Washington 14.

Fewest Yards Passing, Both Teams—156: Miami 69, Washington 87.

Most Yards on Interceptions—Miami 95.

Lowest Punting Average—Washington, 31.2

Fewest Yards on Punt Returns, Both Teams—13: Miami 4, Washington 9.

Fewest Kickoff Returns, Both Teams—5: Miami 2, Washington 3.

Fewest Yards on Kickoff Returns, Both Teams—78: Miami 33, Washington 45.

RECORDS TIED

Most Games Played—Marv Fleming, Miami, 4. Also played with Green Bay in 1967 and 1968, and with Miami in 1972.

Most interceptions—Jake Scott, Miami, 2.

Chapter 8

Super Bowl VIII—1974

And it came to pass, in January of 1974, that the Super Bowl Phenomenon came full cycle to its predictable station: universal complaints of boredom, overexposure, overemphasis, lack of drama and anything else that could express jaded taste.

It was, truly, inevitable. If an event is hailed as the occurrence of the century, its eighth repetition in eight years can hardly retain cosmic significance. If the original Super Bowl was overplayed, we all shared guilt in going along with it and were embarrassed now to admit it; if it had really been that unique, obviously it couldn't be unique forever. So the natural reaction, arrived at from either direction, was ho-hum, that old thing again.

This was, of course, unfair and unrealistic. As a football game, Super Bowl VIII was no better or worse than hundreds of other fine, professional football games. As a test of championship mettle, it was admirably decisive in that there were no flukes and no lucky breaks, just proof of who was the better team that day. As a commercial venture, it was as successful as ever. As a match-up to be anticipated, it was certainly first-rate, with the champion Dolphins on hand to defend their title and a challenger, Minnesota, with as interesting a figure as Fran Tarkenton on hand.

Yet, the cries of dullness went up, so long and so loud, that they added important impetus to pressures already building for actual changes in playing rules to make the N.F.L. game "more attractive again." The bogeymen were "conservative coaches" and the "zone defense" which discouraged long passes, but the true culprit was seldom identified: familiarty.

And the football world was learning what only a few profound philosophers had ever bothered to articulate: the price of success is . . . success, with all its problems.

Sports of The Times

The Super Bowl Plot

By DAVE ANDERSON

Jan. 5, 1974—Fran Tarkenton once threw a football as far as he could. Sixty-one and one-half yards. "I thought that was my limit on distance," he says, "but I know now that it's really not." He knows because last Sunday, when the Minnesota Vikings were playing the Dallas Cowboys for the National Conference championship, he threw a pass to John Gilliam that traveled nearly 65 yards. He had seen Gilliam sprinting into the clear beyond what Tarkenton thought was his limit, but in that moment, he recalls, "All my 20 years of football told me, 'Throw it.'" Gilliam caught the pass for the touchdown that assured the 27–10 victory that put the Vikings into the Super Bowl game next Sunday against the Miami Dolphins in Houston. Tarkenton credits the "intensity" of the National Football League playoffs for creating the adrenalin that propelled a football farther than he thought he could.

"The intensity is unreal," says Tarkenton, experiencing it for the first time in 13 seasons. "There are three seasons in one in this league—the exhibitions, the regular season and the playoffs. Each is played on a different level. There's no way we could play 14 weeks like we play in the playoffs. The intensity is awesome."

Not that he's awed. Instead, he's thriving on it. When the notebooks, the cameras and the tape-recorders begin to surround him in Houston tomorrow, his presence in the Super Bowl for the first time will provide the primary plot for next Sunday's game. It's the best Super Bowl plot since Len Dawson of the Kansas City Chiefs performed almost perfectly in the shadow of a doubt created by an alleged subpoena in a Detroit gambling investigation. The subpoena never materialized. The year before that, Joe Namath "guaranteed" the New York Jets' upset. Before that, the mystique of Vince Lombardi dominated the first two Super Bowl plots. Now, on center stage, is Fran Tarkenton, the "scrambler," the "loser."

"For years I heard a scrambler couldn't win," he says. "And then Roger Staubach and Bob Griese were quarterbacks on Super Bowl winners. I haven't heard anybody say it lately. It was the greatest lie ever perpetrated on the pro football public."

He still hears himself described as a "loser," but it's unfair. He isn't a boxer or a golfer or a tennis player. He's on a team that wins or loses. Any quarterback on a Super Bowl team deserves to be considered a winner, even if his team loses the game.

"In the 50's," he says, "the quarterback was built up as the man who won the championship. The quarterbacks seemed to be saying, 'Let's have our own exclusive club.' And they built the aura. The old guards and tackles heard it so much, they believed it. But it's ridiculous. You can't forget the other players. On our team, you can't forget Alan Page and Carl Eller, Bobby Bryant and Ron Yary. It's unfair to them to credit the quarterback so much. Getting to the Super Bowl isn't an ego trip for me."

Nor is Tarkenton awed by the Dolphins, in the Super Bowl for an unprecedented third time, winners of 31 of their last 33 games.

"Their 53-defense is a little bit different," he says, meaning the insertion of a linebacker for a defensive tackle. "But all that means to me is that you have to approach it a little bit different. Some teams defy it. They think they can run their own stuff against it, but that doesn't seem to work. I think you've got to prepare for the 53-defense, you've got to make it so the Dolphins don't know what to expect. I'm sure we'll prepare a little bit different."

During the 1972 season, the Vikings probed the 53-defense for a 14–6 lead in the final quarter.

"But they beat us with a 51-yard field goal, Yepremian's longest, and two fourth-down plays."

Not being in the Super Bowl before has haunted him. He attended only one, Super Bowl IV, when the Vikings lost to the Chiefs, 23–7.

"I went to that one because my people, the Vikings I'd played with years ago, were in it. But it was so frustrating to sit there."

He watched the others on TV at home, even though last year he spent the Saturday before the game in the Los Angeles area.

"I took a 1 A.M. flight home to Atlanta that night," he says. "I just didn't want to be there unless I was in the game myself."

Now that he is in it, he'll predict only that, "I think it will be the best Super Bowl we've ever had." He makes no guarantee.

"I think it was wonderful that Joe Namath guaranteed it for the Jets," he says, "but that didn't have anything to do with the winning of the game. And it wouldn't have had anything to do with the losing of the game if the Jets had lost."

By next Sunday, the plot will be even thicker.

Sports of The Times

Dolphins Better Than the Packers

By DAVE ANDERSON

HOUSTON, *Jan. 7*—When the Miami Dolphins won the Super Bowl a year ago, they still had their skeptics. It was almost as if, by streaking through 17 games, they had been too perfect to be accepted for what they were— the best team in National Football League history. But this season they've convinced the skeptics. They've even convinced the oddsmakers.

For the first time in eight Super Bowl games, the team from the American Conference, the other league, is the betting favorite over the team from the National Conference, the establishment. The Dolphins are listed as a 7-point choice. If they defeat the Minnesota Vikings on Sunday, they will join the Green Bay Packers as the only teams to win two consecutive Super Bowl games. More important, they will earn a stature comparable to the Packer teams that Vince Lombardi left as his legacy.

But the Dolphins aren't awed by their opportunity. In their clinical, almost detached manner, they believe they're better than those Packer teams were. And in a few seasons, they agree, another team will be better than they are.

"I think we're better than the Packers, but I'm prejudiced," Larry Csonka said, smiling. "I think we're a little deeper and I think we have a better passing attack than the Packers had."

When the Packers were winning the first two Super Bowl games, most of the current Dolphins, such as Csonka, were in college. Now the Dolphins are competing in their third consecutive Super Bowl. When they appeared today in their aqua jerseys, they acted as though the Super Bowl had been part of their schedule all along. That attitude is typical of the approach Don Shula creates as their coach.

"Lombardi and Shula are the same type of coach," said Marv Fleming, the tight end who was on those two Packer teams and has been on the three Dolphin teams. "Each is a disciplinarian. Each demands a lot. The difference is that Shula is more personable. You can walk up to him after practice and say, 'Coach, can I see you a minute?' and he'll stop and talk to you. With Lombardi, you had to make an appointment."

Fleming has earned approximately $140,000 in post-season money with the Packers and Dolphins. "When it came down to the money part, it was like grabs on the Packers, they were a lot more money-oriented," he said. "The guys on the Dolphins are a lot more friendly."

On offense, the Packers never had a running back with the breakaway talent of Mercury Morris. "That might be the difference right there," Morris said with a wink. "To me, comparing us to the Packers is like comparing Muhammad Ali to Rocky Marciano, two different styles. We're a little more wide open. I never played under Lombardi so I don't know about him, but I know about our mentor. Don Shula is basically a realistic coach. No rah-rah stuff. That rah-rah stuff is false. In a crisis, it turns on you."

The Packers also didn't have a wide receiver in a class with Paul Warfield as a deep threat. "They had good, solid receivers," Warfield agreed, thinking of Boyd Dowler, Max McGee and Carroll Dale, who is now on the Vikings. "But nobody that could hurt you with the bomb."

But the Dolphin quarterback, Bob Griese, is almost a replica of Bart Starr as a strategist. "I knew all about Starr but I never tried to copy him," Griese said. "I look at the way he played and I see a similarity. We're each the same part of the machine. It makes you wonder if that's the way you have to be as a quarterback to have a good club."

On defense, the Dolphins use the zone pass defense that is popular now, whereas the Packers usually employed man-to-man coverage. "We've got more wrinkles in our coverages," Dick Anderson, the Dolphin strong safety, said. "They played tough and beat everybody that way. Other than that I can't compare the defenses, but I remember watching Jim Taylor run. He was a thrashing-type runner. Csonka is a much bigger man. Zonk draws a bead on a guy and runs over him. Taylor followed his blockers more and was a little faster."

Evolution and Romance

The evolution of the athletes is another reason the Dolphins believe they're superior to the Packer teams. "Athletes get better," Jim Kiick said. "Look at Gale Sayers. He ran 9.8 and everybody thought he was fast. But now O. J. Simpson runs at 9.3 with the same ability. O. J.'s better. I think our team's better for the same reason. Athletes keep getting bigger, faster, quicker, stronger. In a few seasons, there'll be another team better than we are."

But the romance of comparison with the Packers doesn't appeal to all the Dolphin players. "That's just so much bull," said Manny Fernandez, the defensive tackle. "I just play football. I don't worry about whether we're better than the Packers were. The important thing to me is that we're better than the Vikings in next Sunday's game. I never read much about Lombardi. Coaches don't mean that much to me."

The romance of a game with those Packers appeals only to one Dolphin—the former Packer, Fleming. "Whenever anybody asks me which team would win," he says, "I always tell them, 'Whichever one I'm on.'"

Vikings Say Camp Is Not Very Super

By WILLIAM N. WALLACE

HOUSTON, *Jan. 7*—Super Bowl week began today with Fran Tarkenton and Bud Grant of the Minnesota Vikings and Jim Mandich of the Miami Dolphins in the spotlight for different reasons.

Of the 97 players available to play in Sunday's Super Bowl game at Rice Stadium, Tarkenton was the most sought in the two one-hour media sessions at the practice sites today. Mandich raised a line-up problem, the only one for the 48 playing positions in pro football's championship game.

Coach Grant was grim and complained about the dressing room facilities, cramped and crude, made available by the league to the Vikings at the high school field where they will practice. Grant claimed that the Dolphins were better off, which was true.

"This is shabby treatment," the usually placid Minnesota coach said.

"This is a Super Bowl game, not a pick-up game. The league is responsible and Pete Rozelle runs the league.

"I don't think our players have seen something like this since junior high school. It's something their kids would play in on a Saturday afternoon.

"Miami can walk from its hotel to its field, but we have a 20-minute bus ride. And we don't have any blocking sleds and the Dolphins do."

As the designated "home" team, the Dolphins of the American Conference were assigned the best facility, namely the practice field and dressing quarters of the local pro team, the Houston Oilers.

In California a year ago, the Redskins of the National Conference were the home team and had the preferred practice site, the Anaheim Stadium.

Mandich played tight end in Miami's impressive playoff victories over Cincinnati and Oakland in spite of a broken left hand, and he wants to keep on playing. But he fears that Don Shula, his coach, will go back to the seasoned Marv Fleming, a stronger blocker, against Minnesota.

"If that happens I'll be disappointed and very upset," said Mandich, a 25-year-old fourth-year pro.

There is more to it. Mandich, a Michigan alumnus who received academic citations in college, refused to sign a contract this season in a hassle with Shula over $1,500 in salary and has exercised the option clause. As of May 1, he will become a free agent, the first Dolphin to play out his option in the Shula reign, which stresses a homogenous all's-well spirit.

"It's simple," said Mandich. "I want to play and I know I'm good enough to play in the Super Bowl or any place. I caught 27 balls this season."

When asked about the tight end position for Sunday, Shula said, "We'll see." Which one he picks, Mandich or Fleming, may indicate how the Dolphins intend to attack the formidable Minnesota defense.

If it is Fleming, Shula will hope to continue the remarkable Miami running game, featuring Larry Csonka and Mercury Morris, and control the ball. Fleming, about to play in his fifth Super Bowl, would be in there to block the defensive ends, Carl Eller and Jim Marshall, which he does so well single-handedly. Few passes are thrown his way and he caught only three in the last season.

If Mandich perseveres, Shula may be adding finesse to his offense and expect to pass more. In the last Miami game, against Oakland, Bob Griese threw only six passes as the Dolphins ran 53 rushing plays for 266 yards.

When the Vikings last met Miami in a regular-season contest, Oct. 1, 1972, it was Mandich who caught the winning touchdown pass from the 3-yard line late in the game as the Dolphins won, 16–14.

Minnesota has no such line-up questions, especially at quarterback. Stepping into his first Super Bowl week with obvious relish, Tarkenton was bouncy and talkative as more than 100 reporters, photographers and broadcasters descended upon him at Delmar High School field.

One of the onlookers was Fred Dryer, a former New York Giant teammate of Tarkenton's and now a Los Angeles Ram. "Freddy, my man," said Tarkenton as they embraced.

The offensive unit lined up for an old-fashioned team picture, the seven offensive linemen, who happen to be white, down in their stance with Tarkenton standing right behind the center, Mick Tingelhoff. Behind them were the three backs, Oscar Reed, Chuck Foreman and John Gilliam, who happen to be black.

Tarkenton turned back and said: "That's discrimination. You guys way back there and us guys up here in the pit."

A photographer shouted, "How about an ugly look, Tarkenton?"

His reply, "Try Yary," the reference being to try Ron Yary, the offensive tackle.

The offense ran one simulated play for film. It was out of a shotgun formation with Tarkenton six yards behind center.

"We're showing all our new stuff," he said illogically.

Except for interviews in their hotels, the players were on view for the last time because future practices will be closed. The weather is expected to remain the same—damp, overcast and cold. Csonka, for example, said of the Vikings:

"They have no weaknesses. They deserve to be here. For the first time the Super Bowl will match two strong teams that came right through their schedules without a hitch. I foresee a close, physical game."

Grady Alderman, the Minnesota tackle, added, "We're prepared to play our best."

Dolphins' Scott, Vikings' Tarkenton: A 2-Man Mutual Admiration Society

By WILLIAM N. WALLACE

HOUSTON, *Jan. 8*—The most significant matchup in Sunday's Super Bowl game here will be Jake Scott, the free safety for the Miami Dolphins, and Fran Tarkenton, the Minnesota Vikings' quarterback. Scott will be deep in the Miami zone defense attempting to think right along with Tarkenton in the latter's play selection. He will try to pick the brains of the hero of his boyhood back in Athens, Ga., in the late nineteen-fifties.

Each spoke of the other today, fondly and respectfully. "When I was in seventh and eighth grade, Fran was the big hero on the Athens High School football team," said Scott. "In high school he was just like he is in the pros, a real leader. I knew his two brothers, the whole family. We played together. Years later he recruited me to go to the University of Georgia in Athens."

Said Tarkenton, five years the senior: "His mother taught me a course in college at Georgia, educational psychology. A brilliant woman. Athens was a small town. I remembered Jake from those kid football programs the 'Y' ran."

The Scott family moved to Washington in 1962 and Jake went to school at Bullis Prep in Silver Spring, Md., where he caught the attention of the Georgia scouts.

"I was with the Vikings by then," said Tarkenton. "I stopped by and saw him and got him to come to Georgia. He's the only player I ever recruited. After he signed, I remember the Georgia coach I was with said, 'Gee, I wonder if he can make our team.' "

Scott, on the scrawny side, was an all-Southeastern conference defensive back as a sophomore, an all-American as a junior and then quit, playing one season (1969) for Vancouver in the Canadian League before becoming eligible for the National League the following season.

The Dolphins drafted him on the seventh round and he arrived in Miami along with Don Shula, the new coach. Shula immediately made him a regular and now he is an all-pro performer, voted the most valuable player in last year's Super Bowl.

"I always have said," Tarkenton continued, "that when it comes to how to play the free safety position, Willie Wood of the Green Bay Packers was the best. He set the tone, the standard. Now I consider Jake Scott to be the absolute equal of Willie. I know of no higher praise."

Wood retired two seasons ago and is now a coach at San Diego.

Scott in turn said, "Fran makes all the plays. He's a helluva man. He can turn a bad play into a good play just like that. You can't predict what he will do. That will make it tough on me. He has so many wrinkles. He is so tough to defense."

They have played against each other twice, last summer when the Vikings stopped the Dolphins' long victory streak by winning an exhibition game and in the 1972 season when Miami came from behind to edge Minnesota, 18–14.

The first score in the latter contest was a 56-yard touchdown pass, Tarkenton to John Gilliam. "We never give up plays like that," said Scott. "Our coverage broke down."

Who's fault was it? "The cornerback," said Scott, failing to specify which cornerback—Tim Foley or Curtis Johnson. "We're not going to give him a play like that on Sunday."

Tarkenton is inclined to agree. "However," he added, "I don't belong to this school which says a zone defense like theirs cannot be attacked deep. The defense always has to give the offense something: It's up to me to find out what it is. We'll go from there."

Warfield Pulls Leg Muscle at Practice;
May Be Sidelined For Super Bowl Game

By WILLIAM N. WALLACE

HOUSTON, *Jan. 10*—Paul Warfield was listed today as a doubtful performer in Sunday's Super Bowl game here. Since Warfield, probably pro football's most effective pass receiver, is the leading single-play offensive threat of the Miami Dolphins, the responses to his possible absence were many.

Warfield pulled the hamstring muscle in his right thigh while the team worked out yesterday on the artificial turf of Rice Stadium. He immediately walked off the field and will not run again until just before game time on Sunday.

"Then I'll know if I can play," he said, "but not until then."

But Larry Gardner, the Miami trainer, said, "there is an excellent shot that Warfield will play Sunday. We are being ultra-conservative. Actually, we are not all that concerned about the injury."

It was the opinion of the opposing coach, Bud Grant of the Minnesota Vikings, and several others that Warfield's inability to play would not necessarily lessen Miami's chances, but would change the fashion in which the game is played.

The reason concerns his replacement, Howard Twilley, a much different type of receiver who relies almost entirely on moves—sharp cuts outside or inside at short and medium range—while the swift Warfield can take a pass deep over the middle 30 to 40 yards downfield better than anyone.

Said Grant of Warfield: "His loss would hurt them because he is a big-play guy. But it won't change anything that much. Miami is primarily a running team and they are going to try to run on us like we're going to try to run on them. That's how to control the game."

Don Shula, the Dolphin coach, said "anytime you lose a receiver of that magnitude it's got to hurt you. Paul's worth is not only as a receiver but what he does as a threat to pass coverages and what he adds as a blocker."

Bobby Bryant, the Minnesota cornerback primarily responsible for the coverage of Warfield or Twilley, said he did not think his job would be any easier with Warfield on the bench. "Twilley can do things to you, too," he said.

"Playing cornerback in a championship game is a high-risk business. If you make one mistake, an awful lot of people are watching. But I look forward to it. I can hardly wait for the game."

Twilley, who caught a touchdown pass in the Super Bowl a year ago against Washington, said, "You can't replace a guy like Warfield, no matter who you replace him with. But I think I can make a contribution."

Marlin Briscoe, Miami's wide receiver on the other side, said that if Warfield did not play he expected the defensive coverage on him would be more intense. "I don't mind," he added.

Warfield said he had only one leg muscle pull in the past and that was 10 years ago. "Yes, it affected my mobility, but I played," he recalled. "All runners—sprinters—worry about muscle pulls. There are not many precautions you can take. They happen and you don't know why or when. For a receiver, anything that goes wrong with his legs has got to be worrisome."

Because the speed of Twilley is limited—"slow to the left, slow to the right," as he puts it—the problems of the Minnesota free safety, Paul Krause, may be lessened in the deep coverage of passes.

The Viking had a smile but no comment when told it would take Twilley a week to get down to Krause; that Paul should give back the $15,000 he would receive if Minnesota wins and Warfield does not play.

The conjecture over Warfield's muscle pull was the major point of the day here, another gray one with humidity. A cold front is due. "We'll welcome it," said Grant.

The coach continued to carp mildly about the supposed advantages the Dolphins had in practice times and sites. Since this is so unlike the mild Grant, there was suspicion that the Viking mentor was attempting to stir his players or to psychologically combat Shula, who has been a vaudevillian with continuing quips, easy-going repartee, oozing confidence all the while.

Sports of The Times
The Super Rookie of the Vikings
By DAVE ANDERSON

HOUSTON, *Jan. 11*—Shortly before Thanksgiving, one of the older players on the Minnesota Vikings approached Chuck Foreman.

"Rookie," he said, "be sure to get your free turkey."

"What free turkey?" the rookie running back asked.

The older player told him about a supermarket where it was traditional for members of the Vikings to receive a free turkey. Other rookies also were told about it. After practice that day, a few of them stopped by the supermarket and asked for the manager.

"We're here for our turkeys," Foreman said.

"What turkeys?" the manager wanted to know.

"We're with the Vikings," said Foreman, "and we were told you give free turkeys at Thanksgiving to all the players."

"You must have the wrong store," the manager said.

The free turkeys, of course, had been a playful hoax perpetrated by the older Vikings on their rookies. Not even their super rookie had been exempt.

"That's all right," Chuck Foreman says now. "I don't want to be a veteran too soon. I want to enjoy being a rookie."

He has enjoyed it as few rookies have. "He doesn't know," says Fran Tarkenton, the Viking quarterback in the National Football League playoffs for the first time in his 13 seasons, "what it is to have to wait to get into a Super Bowl game." But without him, Tarkenton might still be waiting. When the Vikings challenge the Miami Dolphins here Sunday, the 6-foot-2-inch, 215-pound rookie could be Tarkenton's most important weapon, both as a running back and as a pass receiver.

"He creates problems either way," acknowledges Bill Arnsparger, the Dolphins' defensive coach. "On offense, he's the difference in the Vikings this season as compared to last season."

Although he missed three games with a leg injury during the regular season, he ran for 801 yards and caught 37 passes for 362 yards. In the two National Conference playoff games he ran for 116 yards and caught seven passes for 51 yards. In the matchup with Mercury Morris, the Dolphin halfback, he is "bigger, a better blocker and a better pass receiver," according to Bud Grant, the Viking coach. But the irony of his presence here is that several Dolphins, including Morris, befriended him when he was a University of Miami senior.

"I was rooting for the Dolphins in the Super Bowl a year ago," he says, "and now I'm playing against them."

At this time last year, the Vikings, who needed a running back, were hoping to draft Sam Cunningham, who had scored four touchdowns for the University of Southern California in the Rose Bowl game. But the New England Patriots selected Cunningham.

"After that," says Jim Finks, the Viking general manager, "we decided to take Chuck."

As a college junior Foreman had been a running back, but he was shifted to wide receiver as a senior. In the North-South game, he was used as a running back, but his most memorable moment occurred when he fumbled on the 1-yard line. When he arrived to play in the Senior Bowl game, Weeb Ewbank, then the New York Jets' coach, who was guiding one squad, talked to him.

"Forget that fumble, it's water over the dam," Ewbank said. "You're a fine running back."

With that encouragement, Foreman ran for 167 yards, was voted the Senior Bowl's most valuable player and impressed the N.F.L. scouts. After the Vikings selected him in the first round, several Dolphins provided additional advice.

"They kept telling me about the mental part, that there would be so much to learn," he says. "I knew I had to know the plays, but my attitude was, if I hustled and did things right, I'd get a chance to play."

He also accepted the initiation that Viking rookies endure. At meal-time during training camp, he had to sing his college song. In the evening he was sent to bring back hamburgers and pizzas to the older players. But on the field, the older Vikings quickly realized he might bring them to the Super Bowl game.

"In training camp, I'd hear the older guys saying, 'Keep running like that,' and it gave me confidence."

His confidence is still somewhat diluted by his tendency to fumble. Although the Vikings defeated the Dallas Cowboys, 27–10, two weeks ago for the National Conference title, he fumbled twice, once on the Vikings' 5-yard line. Fortunately for the Vikings, the Cowboys also fumbled immediately.

"I still hear that talk about me being a fumbler," he was saying. "Bobby Mitchell had that reputation, too, but he wasn't."

As a youngster in Frederick, Md., he had followed the Washington Redskins, for whom Mitchell was a runner and receiver.

"Some guys are stronger than others, like Larry Csonka. He's so strong, when he holds the ball, he hardly ever fumbles. But nobody tries to fumble. Hey, let's not talk about fumbling. I don't want to talk about it. I don't even want to think about it."

Not with Super Bowl VIII only hours away.

Dolphins Choice Over Vikings In Today's Super Showdown

By WILLIAM N. WALLACE

HOUSTON, *Jan. 12*—Tomorrow will be Super Bowl day at last. After two weeks of impatient waiting, the Miami Dolphins and Minnesota Vikings will settle the championship of the National Football League on the synthetic turf of Rice Stadium before a crowd of 71,882, with 80 million expected to watch on television in the United States, Canada, Venezuela and Mexico.

The telecast of the game will begin at 3:30 P.M., Eastern daylight time, with Channel 2 the New York outlet.

The weather forecast is for cloudy skies, temperatures in the sixties and winds up to 18 miles an hour. If the wind forecast is true, it will add a tactical dimension to the contest in terms of passing and kicking and which goal to defend, the windward or leeward one, in which quarter. Neither team and few of the players have ever played in this big open stadium before.

The Dolphins, who won the Super Bowl game last year from Washington and lost it the year before to Dallas, are favored by 6 points. However, the Vikings conducted themselves so well and with so much confidence through this last week of hoopla preceding the game that they gained supporters.

The teams are alike in that they try to do the same things, run the ball, thereby controlling the game offensively by eating up big chunks of playing time and playing without error in fast-reacting zone defenses. They are unalike in that they have some of the most distinctive players in the game.

The Vikings have Fran Tarkenton, a quarterback totally unpredictable, while Miami's Bob Griese is totally conventional. The Dolphins have little Garo Yepremian, a native of Cyprus who makes neckties and is the best long-distance field-goal kicker in the game.

They have Manny Fernandez, a defensive tackle hired as a free agent because his Latin name might sell tickets. He disappointed management by confessing he couldn't speak a word of Spanish. They have Nick Buoniconti, a Notre Dame lawyer of Italian extraction, playing middle linebacker in an effective style all his own.

The Vikings have a seasoned and sensitive defensive end, Jim Marshall, who characterized the Super Bowl promotion as "a ripoff matching ripoffers and ripoffees," two ruthless linebackers, one of whom, Roy Winston, gave the Miami running star, Larry Csonka, "the hardest hit I've ever had," in a game 15 months ago, and a smart coach, Bud Grant, whose players adore him because he hardly ever speaks to them.

In 'Wright' Place

Minnesota also has the Wright "brothers, Orville and Wilbur," as Carl Eller, the defensive end, introduced them at training camp last August. They are not brothers and Jeff Wright, the one whose pigmentation is white, opposed to Nate's, which is black, said later, "No one has told Nate or I just who is Orville and who is Wilbur."

Both filled large gaps in the Viking defensive backfield this season and filled them well, Nate at cornerback, which had long been a Minnesota Achilles heel, and Jeff at strong safety, replacing Karl Kassulke, crippled in a motorcycle accident.

It would be simple to say that the whole darn game comes down to Tarkenton; that the distribution of the prize monies—$15,000 to each winner and $7,500 to each loser—will be determined by what he can accomplish. And by what mistakes he may make.

Simple but true.

Tarkenton, in his 13th pro season, is playing on his first championship team. He has played in dozens of games, most of them losing efforts, and was always a factor, although not a determinant one as to victory or defeat. He has been a high-risk quarterback, meaning one whose judgment sometimes could go awry.

It was written once that his epitaph might read, "Here lies Francis Tarkenton, 7 and 7." The later reference is to a team's won-and-lost record in the N.F.L. When reminded of that excessive stroke this week, Tarkenton was given the option of substituting another epitaph.

"Gee, I'll have to think about that," he said. "You know, quarterbacks are not that big a deal. It's the other guys who make or break quarterbacks."

In this case the other guys rate out about even. Grady Alderman, the offensive tackle who with Tarkenton helped establish the Vikings in their natal season of 1961, is not going to shut out the efforts of Bill Stanfill, the all-pro Miami defensive end opposite him. Nor is Stanfill going to run over Alderman.

The outcome will be determined by what Tarkenton can or cannot do. The flow of the game can be easily guessed if Don Shula's powers apply. The Dolphins would win the flip of the coin, choose to receive the kickoff, then drive about 77 yards to a touchdown in 16 small-gaining plays, almost all on the ground, featuring Larry Csonka's muscle and consuming nine minutes of playing time.

Master of Surprises

To keep the ball and not let Tarkenton play with it would be the purpose. Francis does need time. He probes and sets up. Like a mime, he requires time to get into the gut of those sharing the scene, the Dolphins in this case.

Once there, he can be a virtuoso, carving out great strokes by throwing passes when passes are the least expected—first down or third down and short yardage—or initiating simple plunges into the line by the quick and speedy neophyte, Chuck Foreman, against the most heavily stacked and expectant defense.

There have been some excessive statements made about this game, which in fact is merely No. 189 on the 1973 schedule of the National Football League in its 54th season. "It should be the best Super Bowl game of all because the teams are so good and so evenly matched," said Grant, who must have meant it, because he never makes excessive statements.

He brought another team to the Super Bowl, the 1969 Vikings, who lost to Kansas City in New Orleans four years ago, and since then has changed exactly half their starting personnel, all for the better.

But the Dolphins are so smooth, so efficient, albeit so dull to some, as they go about their business—which is winning the important decisive and final games. The 13 days of speculation about such values and happenings end at midnight tonight.

Thank heaven the athletes can take over tomorrow and have the opportunity to decide which will win and which will lose.

Sports of The Times

Super Happening

By DAVE ANDERSON

HOUSTON, *Jan. 12*—Surrounded by a red curtain, a dozen prize beef cattle were standing in straw, their rumps resembling an offensive line poised for a play. On the sawdust floor of the Astrodome, 25 bartenders were pouring drinks. Smoke drifted from two fires where a dressed beef and a whole pig were being barbecued. At the buffet tables, beef, pork, baked beans and Mexican delicacies were available. Soothing the heart, as well as the heartburn, was the voice of Charlie Pride, the country singer. Just a little "Texas hoedown," as the invitation read, tossed by Pete Rozelle and his bride, Carolyn, as a prelude to tomorrow's Super Bowl game. Exactly 2,836 guests materialized for the National Football League's annual bash last night for its club executives, dignitaries, media and other assorted visitors to the first Super Bowl in the alleged great state of Texas. Just about everybody showed except the competing players. Confined by their team curfews, they might as well have been in Huntsville State Prison up the road a piece.

"There are more people at this party," said Billy Sullivan, the president of the New England Patriots, "than we used to have at our games."

The Oilers' Shortages

But the Super Bowl isn't merely a game. It's a week-long happening, a pro football convention, a chunk of Americana to go with the Kentucky Derby, the Indianapolis 500 and the Masters golf tournament. The attraction of those three events is that each is in the same location each year. The site of the Super Bowl changes but, unlike the World Series, the site is known two years ahead. People can plan for it.

Of the 72,000 spectators at tomorrow's game, about 50,000 will be visitors who arranged to arrive long before the Miami Dolphins and the Minnesota Vikings did.

The people here don't seem too excited. But that's understandable. Their team, the Oilers, had an energy crisis long before the nation did. The Oilers have won two games in two seasons. The other day a woman with a Texas twang turned to her son, perhaps 12 years old.

"You wanna go to the game?" she asked.

"Nah," the boy said. "I like baseball."

Richard Nixon isn't interested either. After having supported two losing Super Bowl teams, the Washington Redskins last year and the Dolphins the previous year, he hasn't supported either of the qualifiers this time. Operation Candor apparently couldn't risk the candor of being a three-time loser. It's just as well. If the President had another loser, 18 minutes of the game might be erased by mistake.

But for three hours tomorrow, the Super Bowl game will be more important to most of the nation than, say, the energy crisis or the space program. That's the nature of the American mentality.

The gas shortage isn't obvious here, which confirms the suspicion of some visitors that Texas isn't really part of the United States, anyway. Here you simply drive in and fill it up. No lines. No gouging. The price has remained under 40 cents a gallon.

"Super Bowl's more important to me than gas," a taxi driver was saying. "Super Bowl means money to me this weekend. I can always get gas."

While millions will be watching tomorrow's game on TV, three Skylab astronauts will be whirling in space. They've been up there for several weeks and they'll be up there for a few more. But only a relatively few Americans know their names. Ask almost anybody to name three Dolphins or three Vikings and it's easy. Csonka, Griese, and Buoniconti. Tarkenton, Page and Eller. Not nearly as many people know the names of the three Skylab astronauts.

"Sure the Super Bowl is more important to most people than the space program," agrees Alan Shepard, the astronaut. "People can relate to the Super Bowl easier. It's difficult for people to relate to technology and research that won't affect them for several years. Even the satellite weather maps they seen on TV, they don't think of that as a product of the space program. It's just part of the TV show. The space program is a continual selling job."

Purchasing Power

For three hours tomorrow, the Apollo 14 astronaut will be like most people. He will be more concerned with the Super Bowl than anything else.

"I've got four season tickets to the Oilers' games here," he said. "That gave me the right to buy two Super Bowl tickets. I'll be sitting in the end zone." There's also no point spread on the energy crisis or the Skylab mission. This week "the spread" here didn't mean how many acres you had.

"What's with Warfield?" people were saying with more concern than they have for the stock market when it was announced that the Dolphins' wide receiver had pulled up with an ailing thigh muscle in Wednesday's practice. "Has the spread changed? If he doesn't play, I don't know if the Dolphins can win. What's the spread now?"

With or without Paul Warfield, the Dolphins should win big, say 27–10. They're the best team ever to play football. With or on anybody's spread.

Records of the Teams

MIAMI		MINNESOTA	
21—San Francisco	13	24—Oakland	16
7—Oakland	12	22—Chicago	13
44—New England	23	11—Green Bay	3
31—N.Y. Jets	3	23—Detroit	9
17—Cleveland	9	17—San Francisco	13
27—Buffalo	6	28—Philadelphia	21
30—New England	14	10—Los Angeles	9
24—N.Y. Jets	14	26—Cleveland	3
44—Baltimore	0	28—Detroit	7
17—Buffalo	0	14—Atlanta	20
14—Dallas	7	31—Chicago	13
30—Pittsburgh	26	0—Cincinnati	27
3—Baltimore	16	31—Green Bay	7
34—Detroit	7	31—N.Y. Giants	7
34—Cincinnati	16	27—Washington	20
27—Oakland	10	27—Dallas	10
404	176	350	198

1973 Season Statistics

PASSING				Total		
Miami	Att.	Comp.	Pct.	Yds.	TDs	Int.
Griese	218	116	53.2	1,422	17	8
Morrall	38	17	44.7	253	0	4
Minnesota						
Tarkenton	274	169	61.7	2,113	15	7
Berry	24	10	41.7	121	1	2

RUSHING		Total	Avg.	Long	
Miami	Att.	Yds.	Gain	Gain	TDs
Csonka	219	1,003	4.6	25	5
Morris	149	954	6.4	70	10
Kiick	76	257	3.4	32	0
Nottingham	24	134	5.6	30	0
Minnesota					
Foreman	182	801	4.4	50	4
Reed	100	401	4.0	30	3
Marinaro	95	302	3.2	27	2
Osborn	48	216	4.5	14	0
B. Brown	47	206	4.4	21	3
Tarkenton	41	202	4.9	16	1

RECEIVING	No.	Total	Avg.	Long	
Miami	Caught	Yds.	Gain	Gain	TDs
Briscoe.....................	30	447	14.9	53	2
Warfield	29	514	17.7	45	11
Kiick	27	208	7.7	22	0
Mandich.....................	24	302	12.6	28	4
Minnesota					
Gilliam.....................	42	907	21.6	54	8
Foreman	37	362	9.8	35	2
Marinaro	26	196	7.5	17	2
Voigt.......................	23	318	13.8	43	2
Reed	19	122	6.4	13	0
Dale	14	192	13.7	40	0

INTERCEPTIONS		Total	Long	
Miami	No.	Yds.	Gain	TDs
Anderson	8	163	38	2
Scott........................	4	71	29	0
Kolen	2	54	29	0
Foley	2	22	15	0
Johnson......................	2	19	17	0
Minnesota				
Bryant.......................	7	105	46	1
Krause.......................	4	28	24	0
J. Wright	3	31	25	0
N. Wright	3	6	6	0
Siemon	2	24	21	0

PUNTING	No.	Total Yds.	Avg. Punt	Long Punt	Had Blkd.
Seiple, Mia.	48	2,031	42.3	57	0
Eischeid, Minn.	66	2,628	39.8	57	0

How Super Bowl Rivals Match Up, 1974

MIAMI ON OFFENSE

No.	Player	Ht.	Wt.	Pos.
42	Paul Warfield	6-0	188	WR
86	Marlin Briscoe	5-11	175	WR
88	Jim Mandich.	6-2	224	TE
73	Norm Evans	6-5	250	RT
66	Larry Little	6-1	265	RG
62	Jim Langer.	6-2	253	C
67	Bob Kuechenberg. .	6-5	262	LG
79	Wayne Moore	6-6	265	LT
12	Bob Griese	6-1	190	QB
22	Mercury Morris . . .	5-10	192	HB
39	Larry Csonka	6-2	237	FB

MINNESOTA ON DEFENSE

No.	Player	Ht.	Wt.	Pos.
20	Bob Bryant.	6-1	170	RCB
43	Nate Wright.	5-11	180	LCB
22	Paul Krause.	6-3	200	SS
81	Carl Eller	6-6	247	LE
77	Gary Larsen	6-5	255	LT
50	Jeff Siemon.	6-2	230	MLB
88	Alan Page	6-4	245	RT
70	Jim Marshall	6-4	240	RE
23	Jeff Wright	5-11	190	FS
60	Roy Winston	5-11	222	LLB
58	Wally Hilgenberg. .	6-3	229	RLB

MIAMI ON DEFENSE

No.	P Player	Ht.	Wt.	Pos.
45	Curtis Johnson. . . .	6-1	195	RCB
26	Lloyd Mumphord. .	5-10	176	LCB
13	Jake Scott	6-0	188	SS
83	Vern Den Herder . .	6-6	252	LE
75	Manny Fernandez. .	6-2	250	LT
85	Nick Buoniconti. . .	5-11	220	MLB
72	Bob Heinz	6-6	265	RT
84	Bill Stanfill.	6-5	252	RE
40	Dick Anderson. . . .	6-2	196	FS
59	Doug Swift.	6-3	226	LLB
57	Mike Kolen.	6-2	222	RLB

MINNESOTA ON OFFENSE

No.	Player	Ht.	Wt.	Pos.
42	John Gilliam	6-1	195	WR
84	Carroll Dale.	6-2	200	WR
83	Stu Voigt	6-1	225	TE
73	Ron Yary	6-5	255	RT
64	Milt Sunde	6-2	250	RG
53	Mick Tingelhoff . .	6-2	237	C
62	Ed White	6-2	262	LG
67	Grady Alderman . .	6-2	247	LT
10	Fran Tarkenton . .	6-0	190	QB
44	Chuck Foreman . .	6-2	216	HB
32	Oscar Reed	6-0	222	FB

MIAMI SUBSTITUTES

No	Player	Ht.	Wt.	Pos.
1	Garo Yepremian. . .	5-8	175	K
15	Earl Morrall	6-2	210	QB
20	Larry Seiple	6-0	214	P-TE
21	Jim Kiick.	6-1	214	RB
25	Tim Foley	6-0	194	CB
34	Ron Sellers	6-4	204	WR
36	Don Nottingham . .	5-10	210	RB
48	Henry Stuckey. . .	5-10	185	CB
49	Charles Babb. . . .	6-0	190	S
51	Larry Ball	6-6	235	LB
53	Bob Matheson . . .	6-4	235	LB
55	Irv Goode	6-2	252	G
58	Bruce Bannon . . .	6-3	225	LB
64	Ed Newman	6-2	245	G
65	Maulty Moore . . .	6-5	265	T
77	Doug Crusan. . . .	6-4	250	T
80	Marv Fleming . . .	6-4	230	TE
81	Howard Twilley . .	6-1	180	WR

MINNESOTA SUBSTITUTES

No.	Player	Ht.	Wt.	Pos.
11	Mike Eischeid. . . .	6-0	190	P
14	Fred Cox	5-10	200	K
17	Bob Berry.	5-11	185	QB
24	Terry Brown	6-2	205	S
30	Bill Brown	5-11	222	RB
34	Al Randolph	6-2	205	S
40	Charlie West	6-1	197	CB
41	Dave Osborn	6-0	208	RB
49	Ed Marinaro	6-2	212	RB
51	G. Zaunbrecher . .	6-2	240	C
52	Ron Porter	6-3	232	LB
55	Amos Martin	6-3	228	LB
68	Charles Goodrum .	6-3	256	T-G
69	Doug Sutherland. .	6-3	250	DT
75	Bob Lurtsema . . .	6-6	250	DT-DE
82	Jim Lash	6-2	199	WR
85	Gary Ballman. . . .	6-1	215	TE
89	Doug Kingsriter . .	6-2	222	TE

Facts on Super Bowl, 1974

Title at Stake—World professional football championship.

Participants—Miami Dolphins, champion of the American Football Conference, and Minnesota Vikings, champion of the National Football Conference.

Site—Rice Stadium, Houston.

Seating Capacity—71,882.

Date—Today.

Starting Time—3:30 P.M., New York time.

Television—Nationwide by the Columbia Broadcasting System (Channel 2 in New York). Air time 3:30 P.M., pregame show 3 P.M.

Radio—Nationwide by the Columbia Broadcasting System (WCBS, 880 on the dial in New York). Air time 3:35 P.M.

Players' Shares—$15,000 to each member of the winning team, $7,500 to each member of the losing team.

Division of Game Net Receipts—After deduction of taxes, expenses and players' shares, remainder will be distributed to the competing clubs and the player pension fund.

Uniforms—Minnesota, the visiting team, will wear white jerseys and will use the East bench. Miami, the home team, will wear colored jerseys and will use the West bench.

Game Ball—The standard N.F.L. ball, adopted before the 1970 season and used in all games the past season, will be used.

Sudden Death—If the game is tied at the end of the regulation 60 minutes, it will continue in sudden-death overtime. The team scoring first —by safety, field goal or touchdown—will win.

Officials—There will be six officials and two alternates appointed by the Commissioner's office.

Official Time—The scoreboard clock will be official.

Trophy—The winning team will receive permanent possession of the Vince Lombardi Trophy, a sterling-silver football mounted on a three-sided base.

Miami Takes Super Bowl Again, 24–7

By GERALD ESKENAZI

Jan. 13, 1974—Football's Super Sunday brought to an end yesterday the National League's championship season amid the sounds of jingling cash registers and the happy wails of football widows who reclaimed their husbands.

Thanks to the burly Larry Csonka, who rushed for a Super Bowl record of 145 yards and got two touchdowns, the Miami Dolphins enriched themselves by $15,000 a man with a 24–7 victory over the Minnesota Vikings.

A crowd of 68,142 at Rice Stadium in Houston saw the Miamians take the big prize for the second year. Only the Green Bay Packers had done that in seven previous games.

The Super Bowl game did more than decide a title—it changed a nation's traditional day of rest. Restaurants had to wait until the game was over before the crowds came in. Airline captains announced the score to passengers. Hospital patients created a bull market in rented television sets.

New sponsors who wanted their products seen over the Columbia Broadcasting System TV network had to spend $210,000 for a 60-second commercial. The price was $10,000 more than for last year's game.

The biggest football spendthrift is the Ford Motor Company, which spends more than $4-million a year. In return, it receives three one-minute commercials each Sunday—including Super Sunday.

The N.F.L. proclaims that more than a quarter of the United States' population—about 60 million people—watches the Super Bowl game. However, the actual number probably is half that amount since TV ratings count every person in the home or apartment where a television set is on.

But the show was seen on 500 stations around the world. It brought perhaps $8-million worth of business to Houston, including the landing fees for the 20 privately chartered jets that landed at Hobby Airport. The squadron included the Playboy jet.

Not everyone was ecstatic. An official of Restaurant Associates, which owns Mamma Leone's and the Brasserie here, said there would be a "tail-off in terms of a masculine audience. Normally, our places are filled at 4 P.M. on a Sunday." But he added, hopefully:

"Afterwards they go out—even more than normal. And I think it's because they feel they owe the wife something. You know, 'Football's over. Let's kiss and make up, darling.'"

There was no drop-off in attendance at a "live" sex show in Times Square. A topless dancer fought a losing battle trying to correlate her hip movements with the drumbeat, while a full house of men applauded and whistled.

"It's a funny business," said the doorman, who works as a Good Humor ice cream salesman in warmer weather. "I guess the Super Bowl can't compete with eight beautiful girls in a two-hour show."

A sidewalk spieler on Eighth Avenue near 42d Street interrupted his pleas to passers-by to explain what the game had done to his business—16-millimeter pornographic films.

"These people must be more interested in watching the television than what we've got—sex movies, real hardcore pornography. Maybe after the game. . . . "

If New York is an indication, there was a remarkable upsurge in demand for television rentals. An operator at Lin Communications, which rents sets to patients at several hospitals in the city, said she had received more than 200 calls yesterday for sets to be delivered by 3:30 P.M.—game time in the East.

"Usually we get 25 or 30 calls on the weekend," she said.

Were there enough to go around?

"I hope so," she answered.

But in several police stations round the city, Super Sunday had little effect on crime. There just isn't much on a cold Sunday in January.

"It's our slowest day of the week anyway," said a sergeant at the 48th Precinct in the Bronx. "People are home and the burglars know that. No, we haven't had any complaints about people kicking their television sets. You'd have to wait until the game is at least half over before that happens."

Earlier in the week, airlines were flooded with calls by people who realized they would be airborne during game-time. They wanted earlier flights.

"I know that I was booked on an afternoon flight from Pittsburgh," said one Trans World Airlines official. "I changed it to a flight leaving at 7 A.M."

An American Airlines spokesman said that requests for different flying times began last Monday and continued through yesterday morning.

Much of what happened had to do with money. These were some of the ways smart people made the Super Bowl pay:

¶Vikings' and Dolphins' knit caps were hawked for $10 apiece at Rice Stadium. Normally, they're a $2 item. In downtown Houston they were fetching $6 each.

¶To lure people aboard the queen of the National Boat Show at the Coliseum, the Hatteras company put a television set on the deck of its 46-footer. The boat costs $162,000.

¶C.B.S. will pay its 140-man crew between $250,000 to $500,000 for the mammoth job of producing the spectacle. More than 6,000 man hours went into the production, and the hardware included 84 TV monitors, 15 cameras (and a Goodyear blimp) and a few miles of cable. Sixteen announcers found employment.

Among those who covered the game, which was played over freshly painted artificial turf, were newsmen from the Ivory Coast, Singapore, Rumania, Egypt, Hong Kong and Peru. In all, 1,698 newsmen were accredited—a record, eclipsing last year's 1,500.

It is likely that many people who were lucky enough to get to the game slept not at all. The Houston Visitors Bureau reported that by Saturday night it still had a waiting list of several hundred attempting to find rooms.

For millions of Americans, perhaps, there would be a return to normal. When Mrs. Marilyn Brown, a Roslyn, L. I., housewife, was asked what the end of the season meant to her, she exclaimed, "Thank God!"

But for Mr. Brown, Sundays are more than afternoon football.

"There's always hockey at night," he said.

Dolphins Rout Vikings, 24–7, to Win 2d Super Bowl in Row

M.V.P. Car Given to Csonka

Miami Hero Rushes for 145 Yards

By WILLIAM N. WALLACE

HOUSTON, *Jan. 13*—On the scoreboard it was not the most one-sided Super Bowl victory of all, the Green Bay Packers retaining that distinction for their 25-point triumph over the Kansas City Chiefs in the first of pro football's extravaganzas seven years ago. But the flow of the play on the artificial turf of Rice Stadium today was the most decisive in Super Bowl annals as the Miami Dolphins annihilated the Minnesota Vikings, 24–7, to win the championship of the National Football League for the second year in a row.

The Dolphins followed exactly the formula for success devised by their coach, Don Shula, who has walked off the field a winner 32 times in the last 34 games, including successive Super Bowls.

The Miami offense ground out the yards, led by that astounding 238-pound former farmboy, Larry Csonka, who set a Super Bowl record by rushing for 145 yards. Bob Griese, the quarterback, threw only seven no-risk passes, completing six, and the Minnesota attackers were left standing on the sideline waiting for a chance to try their stuff.

By the time Francis Tarkenton, the Minnesota magician, had some room in which to maneuver, the Dolphins were ahead, 17–0, and smug. That was midway through the second quarter.

Csonka won a car, a football and universal plaudits. The car was for being the most valuable performer of the 75 players in action, and he received one of two game balls, the symbols of victory, given out by the Dolphins. The other went to Bill Arnsparger, the defensive coach, as a farewell gesture. Shula said, "The Giants are getting a great coach," confirming the hiring of Arnsparger, whose appointment will be announced officially in New York on Wednesday.

Following the Shula formula further, the Dolphins made no mistakes —no lost fumbles, no intercepted passes and only one penalty for a loss of 4 unimportant yards. They tackled in teams of twos and threes. They covered receivers in group fashion and left Tarkenton with only one type of play that worked at all. That was the pass to the tight end, of which there were four completions.

Stu Voigt caught three of them for 46 yards and he was the leading gainer for the Vikings, which said a lot.

Following the opening kickoff, the grinding process began. Mercury

Morris gained 4 yards on the first play, Csonka 2 on the second and Griese hit Jim Mandich for 13 on the third. That achieved the first of Miami's 21 first downs and the drive went on for five more minutes.

Csonka carried on five of the 10 plays for 36 of the 62 yards. He scored the touchdown from the 5 with a full bore blast up the middle, Paul Krause and Jeff Siemon of the Vikings bouncing off him like handballs off the wall.

The second drive, starting the next time Miami got the ball, came out of the same cutter—56 yards, 10 plays, 5:46 of playing time, Csonka carrying three times for 28 yards. His buddy, Jim Kiick, scored from the 1 on an inside blast, the first touchdown of the season for him in the final game.

So Miami was ahead, 14–0, with the first period not yet completed. Another drive of 44 yards set up a 28-yard field goal by Garo Yepremian for a 17–0 lead and the Vikings, the National Conference champions who had won 12 of 14 regular-season games as the Dolphins of the American Conference had, were comatose.

Tarkenton kicked some life into them but the first of a series of small disasters befell Minnesota. The Vikings drove 74 yards to the Miami 6. On fourth down Coach Bud Grant waived a field-goal attempt and Oscar Reed was sent into the line in search of a yard and a first down. He never got it.

Nick Buoniconti hit Reed so hard he fumbled a yard short and Jake Scott recovered for Miami. That would have been a good place for the Vikings to score and keep the television audience of 60 million interested for the second half.

The last 30 minutes began inauspiciously for the Vikes. John Gilliam returned the kickoff 65 yards to the Miami 34 but Voigt was penalized for clipping and Minnesota was on its 10 rather than in Miami's backyard.

Miami took over next at its 43 and there was more of the same, an eight-play touchdown drive with Griese passing 27 yards to Paul Warfield for the big play. Csonka made the victors' last touchdown from the 2.

The Vikings, behind, 24–0, then scored early in the final period as Tarkenton ran round right end from the 4, culminating a 57-yard drive. Tarkenton completed five of seven pass attempts in the 10 plays. The pass was all he had left. For the game he tried 28 and completed 18, the latter figure setting a Super Bowl record.

Said Grant: "Tarkenton faced many difficult situations and under the circumstances did well. When you fall 14 points behind it's pretty hard to overcome that against a good team."

The Vikings' last shot was also wiped out by a penalty. Fred Cox artfully achieved a short kickoff covered by Terry Brown, his teammate, on Miami's 48, which would have kept the ball in Minnesota's hands and out of Csonka's. But Ron Porter was offside and Cox had to kick over, this time deep.

The game concluded on a dull note. Tarkenton's last pass was intercepted under the Miami goal post by Curtis Johnson when Jim Lash, the receiver, slowed up on the pattern. Then the Dolphins, again in their fashion, took over and killed the last 6 minutes 24 seconds of playing time. It was dull but decisive football.

Are the Dolphins the best team of all time? Shula said, "It's not my job to say, although I feel that way."

Fran Tarkenton, being thrown for a loss here by a swarm of Miami Dolphins, couldn't move the Vikings as his long-awaited chance for a championship became a lost opportunity.
WIDE WORLD PHOTOS

Super Bowl at a Glance

Mia.	Minn.	
7	0	**First Quarter** Csonka 5-yard run at 5:27. 62-yard drive in 10 plays. Key gains: Mandich 13-yard pass from Griese; Csonka 16 and 8 yard runs. Yepremian kick.
14	0	Kiick 1-yard run at 13:38. 56-yard drive in 10 plays. Key gains: Csonka 12 and 8 yard runs. Yepremian kick.
17	0	**Second Quarter** Yepremian 28-yard field goal at 8:58. 44-yard drive in 7 plays. Key gains: Morris 10-yard run, Csonka 9-yard run. Key play: 15-yard penalty against Minnesota's Hilgenberg, unsportsmanlike conduct.
24	0	**Third Quarter** Csonka 2-yard run at 6:16. 43-yard drive in 8 plays. Key gain: Warfield 27-yard pass from Griese. Yepremian kick.
24	7	**Fourth Quarter** Tarkenton 4-yard run at 3:09. 57-yard drive in 10 plays. Key gains: Voigt 15- and Lash 9-yard passes from Tarkenton. Cox kick.

Miami Dolphins...................................... 14 3 7 0—24
Minnesota Vikings.................................... 0 0 0 7— 7

Mia.—Csonka, 5, run (Yepremian, kick).
Mia.—Kiick, 1, run (Yepremian, kick).
Mia.—FG, Yepremian, 28.
Mia.—Csonka, 2, run (Yepremian, kick).
Minn.—Tarkenton, 4, run (Cox, kick).
Attendance—68,142.

Individual Statistics

RUSHES—Mia.: Csonka, 33 for 145 yards; Morris, 11 for 34; Kiick, 7 for 10; Griese, 2 for 7. Minn.: Reed, 11 for 32; Foreman, 7 for 18; Tarkenton, 4 for 17; Marinaro, 1 for 3; Brown, 1 for 2.

PASSES—Mia.: Griese, 6 completions of 7 attempts for 73 yards. Minn.: Tarkenton, 18 of 28 for 182.

RECEPTIONS—Mia.: Warfield, 2 for 33 yards; Mandich, 2 for 21; Briscoe, 2 for 19. Minn.: Foreman, 5 for 27; Gilliam, 4 for 44; Voigt, 3 for 46; Marinaro, 2 for 39; Kingsriter, 1 for 9; Lash, 1 for 9; B. Brown, 1 for 9; Reed, 1 for minus 1.

Statistics of the Game

	Dolphins	Vikings		Dolphins	Vikings
First Downs	26	14	Interceptions by	1	0
Rushing yardage	196	72	Punts	3-40	5-42
Passing yardage	63	166	Fumbles lost	0	1
Passes	6-7	18-28	Yards penalized	4	65

Vikings Now Believe Tales About Dolphins

By NEIL AMDUR

HOUSTON, *Jan. 13*—"It's the most well-coordinated offensive team I've ever seen," Jack Patera said today in a tribute to the Miami Dolphins and their 24–7 Super Bowl victory.

Patera, the defensive line coach of the Minnesota Vikings, had prepared for the Dolphins' offense on the premise that the Vikings could muster enough muscle to contain the strong Miami running game.

"We looked at them on film, and they were the most impressive offensive team we'd seen," Patera said. "But we thought maybe some of those other teams like Cincinnati or Oakland didn't prepare for them properly. We took great pains to prepare for this game, but they went out and did the same thing to us."

The Dolphins' overwhelming dominance was reflected by the air of resignation in the Minnesota dressing room, almost as if the Vikings were relieved to be free of further embarrassment.

Viking players offered few explanations for the countless mistakes and penalties that continually nullified their bright moments.

Fran Tarkenton defended the decision to run on fourth down from the Miami 6-yard line late in the second quarter. The Vikings, trailing 17–0, needed "three inches" for the first down, according to Tarkenton.

"We had the first down made," said the Minnesota quarterback, who was forced to pass more than he had anticipated because of the early deficit and the inability of the Vikings to mount a serious running game. "We (Oscar Reed) just fumbled the ball."

A defensive holding penalty against Wally Hilgenberg, a linebacker, also gave the Dolphins the impetus for their final touchdown, after the Vikings had seemingly trapped Mercury Morris for an 8-yard loss on third-and-4 at the Viking 5-yard line.

"They called Wally for holding their pulling guard on the play, (Bob) Kuechenberg," Patera said. "It's inconceivable that a linebacker would want to hold an offensive guard. I've never seen one called like that."

Coach Bud Grant ruled out the possibility that the week off he had given the Vikings before coming here (Miami took no break) had stripped some of the sharpness from the Minnesota attack or contributed to the clipping and holding penalties.

"There's no magic to what they do," Tarkenton said of the Dolphins' meticulous efficiency. "We never did establish much of a running game even when they were laying back for the pass. They just played well."

"They're just a great team, and they execute well," said Jeff Siemon, the Vikings' middle linebacker, who was neutralized most of the game by effective blocking from the interior Dolphin offensive line.

Patera said he thought the Dolphins hurt the Vikings with quick-hitters involving Larry Csonka, the 238-pound fullback, particularly when Alan Page, and other defensive linemen, came off the line too aggressively and were cross-blocked before they could fill the open hole.

"I don't know there's anything we could have done," Page, the defensive tackle, said on how the Vikings might have stopped Csonka and company.

Patera, who had been mentioned as a possible head coach of the Giants before Bill Arnsparger, the Dolphins' defensive coach, settled that issue, said the Miami blocking patterns were "well-conceived."

"We made a few adjustments, like throwing in odd-man fronts instead of our normal four-three," Patera said. "We thought it might give us an edge, but they picked that up."

Another disappointed player was Ron Porter, a special team member, who had been ruled offside on an onside kick that the Vikings recovered in the fourth quarter following their only touchdown.

"I didn't even realize I was offside," Porter said, in what seemed to mirror Minnesota's confused mood.

Tarkenton seemed more stoic than frustrated by the failure to leave a winner.

"You play the game at great risk," he said. "We went out and gave it a shot and weren't good enough."

Tarkenton praised Csonka as the "strongest fullback I've ever seen. I don't think I ever saw a fullback play any better," he added. "They are an excellent football team and played as near to perfect as you can play."

Page defended his tactics in flattening Bob Griese, the Miami quarterback, during a fourth-quarter handoff.

"When the quarterback has his back to you you have a split second to determine if he has the ball," the all-pro defensive lineman said afterward. "When in doubt, you hit him. That's what I did."

Page was asked when it became obvious that the Vikings, National Conference champions, might be facing a long afternoon.

"After the first few plays," he said.

Sports of The Times
Super Is a Prefix for Superficial
By RED SMITH

HOUSTON, *Jan. 13*—In the bright archaic lexicon of Noah Webster, "super" means "higher, greater, more than, above." Employing this prefix, we get "superfluous," "superficial," "supernumerary" and "supersede," which Webster defined as "replace with something better." Here in Rice Stadium, where the professional football championship of all known planets has just been decided in Super Bowl VIII, the question is: What is Pete Rozelle waiting for?

For the first time in eight confrontations between the champions of the National and American Conferences, the title was decided in a sudden-death period—the first period. In the opening 13 minutes and 38 seconds, the Miami Dolphins ran or passed the ball 20 times, gained 120 yards and scored 14 points. The offensive unit did, that is. In the same space, the Miami defensive forces permitted the Minnesota Vikings to run the ball twice and pass it once for 9 yards and nothing else.

Not until the very last play of the quarter did Minnesota make a first down, on a 9-yard pass by Francis Tarkenton that advanced the ball to the Vikings' 27-yard line. By then, a sellout crowd was remembering with longing the thrills that had preceded the kickoff, when marching musicians, baton twirlers and other entertainers with talent put on a 41-minute show for television.

Considering that the Dolphins had swept everything before them in a 17-game rush to the championship a year ago and had won 14 of 16 games in the campaign that brought them here today, their superiority astonished nobody. Even the hawkers of souvenirs must have suspected what was coming. On the streets and in hotel lobbies, orange buttons the size of dinner plates emblazoned with a dolphin sold at $4 each; purple ones bearing the horned helmet of a Norseman were $3.

Those odds of 4-to-3 reflected the difference between the teams more accurately than the official betting line that favored Miami by only 7 points.

The difference was glaring, even in the murky Texas climate which reduced visibility to a minimum. The weather was almost as glum, but not quite, as the Minnesota coach, Bud Grant, who stood on the sideline muttering into a headset while his purple windbreaker and purple slacks turned pale.

As is their custom in postseason games, the Dolphins won the coin toss, elected to receive and smashed methodically ahead to score the first two times they had the ball. They had done this against Cincinnati when they won the first half of the American Conference championship, and against Oakland when they took the remaining half.

Not until the second period, after 18 minutes and 29 seconds of play, did they have to give up position on a punt.

Disgorging the ball like that seemed to embarrass them, and they set about quickly to show that it hadn't really been necessary. On the very next time they had possession, they went gamboling down to the Minnesota 21-yard line, where it was fourth down with about 14 inches to go. They were leading by only 14 points at the time, and a team less sure of itself than Miami might have gone for a first down and tried to add a third touchdown.

The Dolphins, however, just trotted in little Garo Yepremian, who sideswiped the ball 28 yards for a lead of 17–0. At this point Miami had gained 153 yards, Minnesota 27.

"At $15 a ticket," a man said, "this show is a disaster. They ought to hire Abe Burrows to write in some laughs."

Mr. Burrows wasn't available, but the Vikings contributed some low comedy on their own. About two-thirds of the way through the third period, their defense flattened Mercury Morris for an 8-yard loss on a third-down play that started only 5 yards from the goal line. It looked as though they might actually be blunting a scoring threat, but Wally Hilgenberg, the Minnesota linebacker, was tagged for defensive holding on the play, the Dolphins got the first down, and moments later the score was 24–0.

At long last, the Vikings scored, but swiftly reverted to type and took another pratfall. They tried a short kickoff, recovered the bounding ball near midfield, and had to give it up because somebody had been offside on the kick. It was comical, but it wasn't funny.

By the way, the final score was 24–7.

Man in The News: A Tough, Sensitive Athlete

Larry Richard Csonka

By DAVE ANDERSON

HOUSTON, *Jan. 13*—Slowly, the teen-age girl approached Larry Csonka for an autograph. Noticing her cautious manner, the 238-pound fullback of the Miami Dolphins smiled. "I won't bite you," he said, signing her photo of him. On the fields of the National Football League, the 27-year-old Csonka (pronounced Zonka) is the essence of the Super Bowl champions, as he was today in smashing for 145 yards in the Dolphins' 24–7 victory. As such, he is thought of as a "battering ram" or an "animal," images that contradict the true personality in repose of this thoughtful, intelligent, sensitive athlete.

"Just because I'm a fullback doesn't mean people have to be afraid of me," he explains. "Like that girl who wanted the autograph. I could tell that she was a little wary of me. Little kids do that, too. It really makes me wonder about what football is doing to people in this country."

But his image is a product of his skill. Not since Bronko Nagurski of the Chicago Bears nearly four decades ago has there been a fullback quite like him. He succeeds with brute force rather than finesse. He usually runs through the middle of the line, where opposing linemen and linebackers wait for him.

"It's nice," he says, "to know that you're punishing these guys as much as they're punishing you."

Once he described what it's like to run with a football through these tacklers who surround him.

"You can hear the noise of the clack of equipment and you can see their eyes peering at you through their facemasks and their hands clawing for

The great Larry Csonka (39) set a Super Bowl rushing record of 145 yards
as Miami moved to its second consecutive championship.

you. With good blocking, you know you're getting away from them and
even for a few yards, that's a great feeling."

It's a feeling he first experienced as a youngster in Stow, near Akron,
Ohio, where his father still works in the Goodyear tire plant.

"To be a running back," Larry says, "you've got to be the kind of a
kid who liked to be chased. Even if you got caught, the chase was the big
thing. I've had everybody chase me—farmers, cops, older kids. We used to
throw snowballs at the cops' car just so they'd stop and chase us through
the woods."

Born on Christmas Day 1946 of parents of Hungarian ancestry, he was
baptized Larry (not Lawrence) Richard Csonka. He was the second of three
sons in a family of six children who lived in a small farmhouse.

As a $70,000-a-year fullback, he lives now with his wife, Pam, and two
sons, Doug, 7, and Paul, 5, in Plantation, Fla.

The potential he displayed at Stow High School resulted in his going to Syracuse University, where the coach, Ben Schwartzwalder, used him at linebacker as a sophomore.

"They thought I was too big to be a running back," he says, "but then somebody got hurt and when I asked to be moved over to offense, Ben agreed. Ben told me later that it would have been the worst mistake he ever made if he had kept me at linebacker. And once I got a chance to run, they never thought about moving me back to defense."

At Syracuse, he still holds the career rushing record, surpassing the totals of Jim Brown, the late Ernie Davis, Jim Nance and Floyd Little. He was the Dolphins' first-round draft choice in 1968. Two years later, when Don Shula took over as the Dolphins' coach, the team began to win and he began to emerge as the N.F.L.'s premier fullback.

In each of the last three seasons, he has run for more than 1,000 yards, only the fifth to accomplish that. In the Dolphins' victory in the Super Bowl a year ago, he ran for 112 yards. His 145 yards today contributed to his winning a Dodge Charger by Sport Magazine as the Super Bowl's most valuable player.

Dolphins' Offensive Line in Superb Form Despite Injuries

HOUSTON, *Jan. 13*—Bob Kuechenberg of the Miami Dolphins summed up today the basic ingredient in their Super Bowl victory.

"Man for man," said the left guard, whose primary assignment was to block Alan Page of the Minnesota Vikings, "I thought we whipped 'em."

But the Dolphins' offensive line did it with blocking specifically designed for the Vikings by Monte Clark, an assistant coach.

"We thought it would be tough to get outside their defensive ends because they're so wide-conscious," Clark said. "So we wanted to run inside more, but to do that we had to fool them into thinking we might be going wide, or trapping them so that there'd be a hole. The linemen had to adjust, and the backs had to adjust to the linemen."

Kuechenberg occasionally was helped by Jim Langer, the Dolphin center, in blocking Page, the Vikings' all-pro defensive tackle.

"We ran at Page sometimes," Clark acknowledged, "but we figured that was better than running away from him because he's everywhere."

Near the end of the Dolphins' 24–7 triumph, Page almost boiled over with frustration at the Vikings' inability to stop them.

"He was a little annoyed," Kuechenberg said, smiling. "He was saying a lot of things out there. We talked a little bit, but all we talked about was the Sugar Bowl game."

Kuechenberg and Page had been teammates at Notre Dame, whose current team won the recent Sugar Bowl game.

"Alan made a couple big plays, too," Kuechenberg said. "You can't stop a player like Alan Page on every play."

Kuechenberg played with a cast on his left arm, broken several weeks ago. But he was only one of the walking wounded on the Dolphins' interior line who, despite their various ailments, blocked for 196 rushing yards. The others were Wayne Moore, the left tackle, Langer, Larry Little, the right guard, and Norm Evans, the right tackle.

"Moore's got a bad knee and a dislocated shoulder, he'll need surgery," Clark said. "Langer has a bruised calf muscle, Little has a bad knee and Evans has a bad ankle."

Another unusual aspect is that each interior lineman had been considered expendable by other teams. Moore was cut by the San Francisco 49ers, Kuechenberg by the Philadelphia Eagles, Langer by the Cleveland Browns. Little was obtained in a trade with the San Diego Chargers. Evans was selected from the Houston Oilers in the 1966 pool to stock the Dolphins.

Because of the success of the running game, Bob Griese threw only seven passes. He completed six, including two to Paul Warfield, the wide receiver who was slowed slightly by a leg ailment.

"I was only about 70 per cent," Warfield said. "I think the only time I extended myself was when I lunged for that pass near the goal line. I was annoyed at Bobby Bryant saying during the week that he hoped I'd be 100 per cent so that he could stop me at my 'best.' He didn't get me at 100 per cent, but I think he saw enough at 70 per cent. Justice was done."

On defense Bill Arnsparger, the assistant head coach, who is expected to be the New York Giants' new head coach, disclosed that no new strategy had been employed to confuse Fran Tarkenton, the Viking quarterback.

"It was very helpful to us to get ahead," Arnsparger said. "It meant they had to throw more. Tarkenton is a great passer, a great quarterback, but if you know a quarterback has to throw, it makes it easier to defend against him. We played well, but that interception by Curtis Johnson made me feel better."

With more than six minutes remaining, Johnson's interception at the goal line stopped a Viking drive.

Dolphins So Much in Charge Even Blunders Don't Matter

Confusion on Snap Count Fails to Thwart Score

By WILLIAM N. WALLACE

HOUSTON, *Jan. 14*—Don Shula, their coach, said today that the Miami Dolphins "played our best football of the season" in defeating the Minnesota Vikings, 24–7, in the Super Bowl game here yesterday. That assessment was understandable, but Shula added depth to the style of the victory by noting that the Dolphins on three occasions made basic blunders but survived them all beautifully.

Bob Griese, the quarterback, forgot the signal number on a play at the Minnesota 2-yard line, and when he asked Larry Csonka to prompt him he received bad information. The play went off one signal count earlier than Griese expected but Csonka still scored a touchdown.

On a second occasion the Dolphins had only 10 men on the field in a punting situation because Ed Newman, the designated 11th man, "forgot." Was the punt blocked? No, Larry Seiple got it away and it went 57 yards, downed on the Minnesota 3.

Another time Csonka ran into his own tackle, Wayne Moore, and almost tripped. What could have been a busted play wound up as a typical Csonka 8-yard gain.

Shula elaborated on the blunders at a news conference here. "Griese went up to the line of scrimmage with a lot on his mind," the coach said. "But he had forgotten what the snap count was."

The snap count is the verbal signal, shouted by the quarterback, which initiates the action, the center, Jim Langer, then snapping the football to Griese. The quarterback in the huddle had announced the snap count as "one" and then forgot.

At the scrimmage line he turned casually back to Csonka to ask him. Csonka replied, "two." So the ball came back to Griese one count sooner than he had expected. Fumbles can result from such situations.

Csonka is known to be casual about matters like practices, which he dislikes, and signal counts, but not about games or carrying the ball in them.

"Bob turned around and asked Larry. Csonka never knows," said Shula with a smile. Langer snapped the ball to Griese, who handed it off to Csonka, who stormed yards into the Viking end zone.

After the punting situation, Shula said with reference to Newman, "I grabbed him by the face mask." That was an exaggeration. "Newman is a rookie and he just forgot to go in. He's a good kid. Yes, he was told about it later."

Shula said that this season was "a greater accomplishment" than last season when Miami won all 17 of its games. "This year everybody was coming after us. We were down for a couple of games [defeats by Oakland and Baltimore] and a couple where we didn't play very well but managed to win. This team rises to the occasion."

Was he surprised by the decisiveness with which the Dolphins defeated the Vikings? "No," he said. "Any time a team executes you shouldn't be surprised. That's what you work for."

And the Dolphins worked for 152 yards in the first half—116 on the ground and 36 in the air. The Vikings totaled 103, with 31 rushing and 72 passing. Time of possession over all found Miami ahead, 33 minutes 47 seconds to Minnesota's 26:13, with the greater disparity in the first quarter when the Dolphins scored two touchdowns—11:13 to 3:47.

   Shula said he had not given any thought to retiring as a coach and that recently he had signed a new contract with Joe Robbie, the Dolphins' chief executive. "I enjoy what I'm doing," he said. "I'm only 44 years old."

   In the last two years Mercury Morris gradually supplanted Jim Kiick as the Dolphins's halfback, much to the expressed disgust of Kiick, Csonka's best friend on the team.

Leonard Koppett came to The New York Times in 1963 to cover baseball, basketball and football, having previously written sports for The New York Herald Tribune (which subsequently died) and The New York Post (which subsequently thrived). Most recently he has been established by The Times as its first full-time West Coast sports correspondent. A Russian-born New Yorker exposed to Yankee Stadium at the age of six, he is also the author of eight books on sports, including *The New York Times Guide to Spectator Sports* and *All About Baseball,* both published by Quadrangle/The New York Times Book Co.